Stand Out 2

Lesson Planner

Second Edition

Rob Jenkins

Staci Johnson

Australia • Brazil • Japan • Korea • Mexico • Singapore • Spain • United Kingdom • United States

Stand Out 2: Lesson Planner, Second Edition
Rob Jenkins and Staci Johnson

Publisher: Sherrise Roehr

Acquisitions Editor: Tom Jefferies

Development Editor: Michael Ryall

Director of Content and Media Production:
  Michael Burggren

Executive Marketing Manager, U.S.:
  Jim McDonough

Product Marketing Manager: Katie Kelley

Sr. Content Project Manager:
  Maryellen E. Killeen

Sr. Print Buyer: Mary Beth Hennebury

Development Editor: Kasia McNabb

Project Manager: Tunde A. Dewey

Cover / Text Designer: Studio Montage

Photo Researcher: Erika Hokanson

Illustrators: James Edwards, Scott McNeill,
  S.I. International

Compositor: PrePressPMG

ISBN-13: 978-1-4240-1934-2

ISBN-10: 1-4240-1934-6

National Geographic Learning
20 Channel Center Street
Boston, MA 02210
USA

Cengage Learning is a leading provider of customized learning solutions with office locations around the globe, including Singapore, the United Kingdom, Australia, Mexico, Brazil, and Japan.

Cengage Learning products are represented in Canada by Nelson Education, Ltd.

Visit National Geographic Learning online at **elt.heinle.com**

Visit our corporate website at **www.cengage.com**

Printed in China
3 4 5 6 7 17 16 15 14 13

ACKNOWLEDGMENTS

Elizabeth Aderman
New York City Board of Education, New York, NY

Sharon Baker
Roseville Adult School, Roseville, CA

Lillian Barredo
Stockton School for Adults, Stockton, CA

Linda Boice
Elk Grove Adult Education, Elk Grove, CA

Chan Bostwick
Los Angeles Unified School District, Los Angeles, CA

Debra Brooks
Manhattan BEGIN Program, New York, NY

Anne Byrnes
North Hollywood-Polytechnic Community Adult School, Sun Valley, CA

Rose Cantu
John Jay High School, San Antonio, TX

Toni Chapralis
Fremont School for Adults, Sacramento, CA

Melanie Chitwood
Miami-Dade College, Miami, FL

Geri Creamer
Stockton School for Adults, Stockton, CA

Stephanie Daubar
Harry W. Brewster Technical Center, Tampa, FL

Irene Dennis
San Antonio College, San Antonio, TX

Eileen Duffell
P.S. 64, New York, NY

Nancy Dunlap
Northside Independent School District, San Antonio, TX

Gloria Eriksson
Old Marshall Adult Education Center, Sacramento, CA

Marti Estrin
Santa Rosa Junior College, Santa Rosa, CA

Lawrence Fish
Shorefront YM-YWHA English Language Program, Brooklyn, NY

Victoria Florit
Miami-Dade College, Miami, FL

Rhoda Gilbert
New York City Board of Education, New York, NY

Kathleen Jimenez
Miami-Dade College, Miami, FL

Nancy Jordan
John Jay High School Adult Education, San Antonio, TX

Renee Klosz
Lindsey Hopkins Technical Education Center, Miami, FL

David Lauter
Stockton School for Adults, Stockton, CA

Patricia Long
Old Marshall Adult Education Center, Sacramento, CA

Daniel Loos
Seattle Community College, Seattle, WA

Maria Miranda
Lindsey Hopkins Technical Education Center, Miami, FL

Karen Moore
Stockton School for Adults, Stockton, CA

George Myskiw
Malcolm X College, Chicago, IL

Heidi Perez
Lawrence Public Schools Adult Learning Center, Lawrence, MA

Marta Pitt
Lindsey Hopkins Technical Education Center, Miami, FL

Sylvia Rambach
Stockton School for Adults, Stockton, CA

Eric Rosenbaum
BEGIN Managed Programs, New York, NY

Laura Rowley
Old Marshall Adult Education Center, Sacramento, CA

Stephanie Schmitter
Mercer County Community College, Trenton, NJ

Amy Schneider
Pacoima Skills Center, Pacoima, CA

Sr. M. B. Theresa Spittle
Stockton School for Adults, Stockton, CA

Andre Sutton
Belmont Adult School, Los Angeles, CA

Jennifer Swoyer
Northside Independent School District, San Antonio, TX

Claire Valier
Palm Beach County School District, West Palm Beach, FL

Rob Jenkins

Staci Johnson

I love teaching. I love to see the expressions on my students' faces when the light goes on and their eyes show such sincere joy of learning. I knew the first time I stepped into an ESL classroom that this was where I needed to be and I have never questioned that resolution. I have worked in business, sales, and publishing, and I've found challenge in all, but nothing can compare to the satisfaction of reaching people in such a personal way.

Ever since I can remember, I've been fascinated with other cultures and languages. I love to travel and every place I go, the first thing I want to do is meet the people, learn their language, and understand their culture. Becoming an ESL teacher was a perfect way to turn what I love to do into my profession. There's nothing more incredible than the exchange of teaching and learning from one another that goes on in an ESL classroom. And there's nothing more rewarding than helping a student succeed.

We are so happy that instructors and agencies have embraced the lesson planning and project-based activities that we introduced in the first edition and are so enthusiastically teaching with **Stand Out**. It is fantastic that so many of our colleagues are as excited to be in this profession as we are. After writing over 500 lesson plans and implementing them in our own classrooms and after personal discussions with thousands of instructors all over the United States and in different parts of the world, we have found ourselves in a position to improve upon our successful model. One of the most notable things in the new edition is that we have continued to stress integrating skills in each lesson and have made this integration more apparent and obvious. To accomplish any life skill, students need to incorporate a combination of reading, writing, listening, speaking, grammar, pronunciation, and academic skills while developing vocabulary and these skills should be taught together in a lesson! We have accomplished this by extending the presentation of lessons in the book, so each lesson is more fully developed. You will also notice an extended list of ancillaries and a tighter correlation of these ancillaries to each book. The ancillaries allow you to extend practice on particular skill areas beyond the lesson in the text. We are so excited about this curriculum and know that as you implement it, you and your students will ***stand out***.

Our goal is to give students challenging opportunities to be successful in their language-learning experience so they develop confidence and become independent, lifelong learners.

Rob Jenkins
Staci Johnson

ABOUT THE SERIES

The **Stand Out** series is designed to facilitate *active* learning while challenging students to build a nurturing and effective learning community.

The student books are divided into eight distinct units, mirroring competency areas most useful to newcomers. These areas are outlined in CASAS assessment programs and different state model standards for adults. Each unit in *Stand Out 2* is then divided into five lessons, a review, and a team project. Lessons are driven by performance objectives and are filled with challenging activities that progress from teacher-presented to student-centered tasks.

SUPPLEMENTAL MATERIALS

- The *Stand Out 2 Lesson Planner* is in full color with 60 complete lesson plans, taking the instructor through each stage of a lesson from warm-up and review through application.
- The *Stand Out 2 Activity Bank CD-ROM* has an abundance of customizable worksheets. Print or download and modify what you need for your particular class.
- The *Stand Out 2 Grammar Challenge* is a workbook that gives additional grammar explanation and practice in context.
- The *Reading and Writing Challenge* workbooks are designed to capture the principle ideas in the student book, and allow students to improve their vocabulary, academic, reading, and writing skills.
- The *Stand Out 2 Assessment CD-ROM with ExamView®* allows you to customize pre- and post-tests for each unit as well as a pre- and post-test for the book.
- Listening scripts are found in the back of the student book and in the Lesson Planner. CDs are available with focused listening activities described in the Lesson Planner.

STAND OUT 2 LESSON PLANNER

The *Stand Out 2 Lesson Planner* is a new and innovative approach. As many seasoned teachers know, good lesson planning can make a substantial difference in the classroom. Students continue coming to class, understanding, applying, and remembering more of what they learn. They are more confident in their learning when good lesson planning techniques are incorporated.

We have developed lesson plans that are designed to be used each day and to reduce preparation time. The planner includes:

- Standard lesson progression (Warm-up and Review, Introduction, Presentation, Practice, Evaluation, and Application)

- A creative and complete way to approach varied class lengths so that each lesson will work within a class period.
- 180 hours of classroom activities
- Time suggestions for each activity
- Pedagogical comments
- Space for teacher notes and future planning
- Identification of LCP standards in addition to SCANS and CASAS standards

USER QUESTIONS ABOUT *STAND OUT*

- **What are SCANS and EFF and how do they integrate into the book?**
  SCANS is the Secretary's Commission on Achieving Necessary Skills. SCANS was developed to encourage students to prepare for the workplace. The standards developed through SCANS have been incorporated throughout the **Stand Out** student books and components.

  Stand Out addresses SCANS a little differently than do other books. SCANS standards elicit effective teaching strategies by incorporating essential skills such as critical thinking and group work. We have incorporated SCANS standards in every lesson, not isolating these standards in the work unit. All new texts have followed our lead.

  EFF, or Equipped For the Future, is another set of standards established to address students' roles as parents, workers, and citizens, with a vision of student literacy and lifelong learning. **Stand Out** addresses these standards and integrates them into the materials in a similar way to SCANS.

- **What about CASAS?** The federal government has mandated that states show student outcomes as a prerequisite to receiving funding. Some states have incorporated the Comprehensive Adult Student Assessment System (CASAS) testing to standardize agency reporting. Unfortunately, many of our students are unfamiliar with standardized testing and therefore struggle with it. Adult schools need to develop lesson plans to address specific concerns. **Stand Out** was developed with careful attention to CASAS skill areas in most lessons and performance objectives.

- **Are the tasks too challenging for my students?**
  Students learn by doing and learn more when challenged. **Stand Out** provides tasks that encourage critical thinking in a variety of ways. The tasks in each lesson move from teacher-directed to student-centered so the learner clearly understands what's expected and is willing to "take a risk." The lessons are expected to be challenging.

In this way, students learn that when they work together as a learning community, anything becomes possible. The satisfaction of accomplishing something both as an individual and as a member of a team results in greater confidence and effective learning.

- **Do I need to understand lesson planning to teach from the student book?** If you don't understand lesson planning when you start, you will when you finish! Teaching from **Stand Out** is like a course on lesson planning, especially if you use the Lesson Planner on a daily basis.

  Stand Out does *stand out* because, when we developed this series, we first established performance objectives for each lesson. Then we designed lesson plans, followed by student book pages. The introduction to each lesson varies because different objectives demand different approaches. **Stand Out's** variety of tasks makes learning more interesting for the student.

- **What are team projects?** The final lesson of each unit is a **team project**. This is often a team simulation that incorporates the objectives of the unit and provides an additional opportunity for students to actively apply what they have learned. The project allows students to produce something that represents their progress in learning. These end-of-unit projects were created with a variety of learning styles and individual skills in mind. The team projects can be skipped or simplified, but we encourage instructors to implement them, enriching the overall student experience.

- **What do you mean by a customizable Activity Bank?** Every class, student, teacher, and approach is different. Since no one textbook can meet all these differences, the *Stand Out Activity Bank CD-ROM* allows you to customize **Stand Out** for your class. You can copy different activities and worksheets from the CD-ROM to your hard drive and then:

  - change items in supplemental vocabulary, grammar, and life skill activities;
  - personalize activities with student names and popular locations in your area;
  - extend every lesson with additional practice where you feel it is most needed.

  The Activity Bank also includes the following resources:

  - Multilevel worksheets – worksheets based on the standard worksheets described above, but at one level higher and one level lower.
  - Graphic organizer templates – templates that can be used to facilitate learning. They include graphs, charts, VENN diagrams, and so on.

- Computer worksheets – worksheets designed to supplement each unit and progress from simple to complex operations in word processing; and spreadsheets for labs and computer enhanced classrooms.

- Internet worksheets – worksheets designed to supplement each unit and provide application opportunities beyond the lessons in the book.

- **Is *Stand Out* grammar-based or competency-based?** **Stand Out** is a competency-based series; however, students are exposed to basic grammar structures. We believe that grammar instruction in context is extremely important. Grammar is a necessary component for achieving most competencies; therefore it is integrated into most lessons. Students are first provided with context that incorporates the grammar, followed by an explanation and practice. At this level, we expect students to learn basic structures, but we do not expect them to acquire them. It has been our experience that students are exposed several times within their learning experience to language structures before they actually acquire them. For teachers who want to enhance grammar instruction, the *Activity Bank CD-ROM* and/or the *Grammar Challenge* workbooks provide ample opportunities.

  The six competencies that drive **Stand Out** are basic communication, consumer economics, community resources, health, occupational knowledge, and lifelong learning (government and law replace lifelong learning in Books 3 and 4).

- **Are there enough activities so I don't have to supplement?** **Stand Out** stands alone in providing 180 hours of instruction and activities, even without the additional suggestions in the Lesson Planner. The Lesson Planner also shows you how to streamline lessons to provide 90 hours of classwork and still have thorough lessons if you meet less often. When supplementing with the *Stand Out Activity Bank CD-ROM*, the *Assessment CD-ROM with ExamView®* and the *Stand Out Grammar Challenge* workbook, you gain unlimited opportunities to extend class hours and provide activities related directly to each lesson objective. Calculate how many hours your class meets in a semester and look to **Stand Out** to address the full class experience.

  Stand Out is a comprehensive approach to adult language learning, meeting needs of students and instructors completely and effectively.

CONTENTS

• Grammar points that are new   △ Grammar points that are being recycled

Correlations to the latest state-specific standards are on our website.

	Numeracy/ Academic Skills	EFF	SCANS	CASAS
Pre-Unit	• Clarification strategies • Focused listening	• Speaking so others can understand • Listening actively • Cooperating with others • Taking responsibility for learning • Reflecting and evaluating	**Many SCAN skills are incorporated in this unit with an emphasis on:** • Acquiring and evaluating information • Listening • Speaking • Sociability	**1:** 0.1.4, 0.2.1 **2:** 0.1.2, 0.1.4, 0.2.1, 0.2.2, 4.8.1 **3:** 0.1.2, 0.1.5, 0.1.6, 7.5.6
Unit 1	• Making bar graphs • Classifying • Developing study skills • Evaluating • Focused listening • Paragraph writing • Peer-editing • Predicting • Reviewing	**Most EFF skills are incorporated into this unit with an emphasis on:** • Cooperating with others • Planning (Technology is optional.)	**Most SCANS are incorporated into this unit with an emphasis on:** • Understanding systems • Seeing things in the mind's eye • Self-management • Sociability (Technology is optional.)	**1:** 0.1.1, 0.1.4, 0.2.1, 7.5.6 **2:** 0.1.2, 0.2.1 **3:** 0.1.2, 1.1.4, 4.8.1, 4.8.6 **4:** 0.1.2, 0.2.1, 0.2.4, 2,3,1, 2.3.2, 7.4.7 **5:** 1.1.5, 2.3.3 **R:** 0.1.1, 0.1.2, 0.1.4, 0.2.1, 0.2.4, 1.1.4, 1.1.5, 2.3.1, 2.3.2, 2.3.3, **TP:** 0.1.1, 0.1.2, 0.1.4, 0.2.1, 0.2.4, 2.3.1, 2.3.2, 2.3.3, 4.8.1
Unit 2	• Classifying • Developing study skills • Evaluating • Focused listening • Peer-editing • Predicting • Reading charts and graphs • Reviewing	**Most EFF skills are incorporated into this unit with an emphasis on:** • Using mathematics in problem solving and communication (Technology is optional.)	**Many SCAN skills are incorporated in this unit with an emphasis on:** • Allocating money • Understanding systems • Arithmetic (Technology is optional.)	**1:** 1.3.9 **2:** 1.1.6, 1.2.1, 1.2.2, 1.2.4, 1.3.9 **3:** 1.1.9, 1.3.9 **4:** 0.1.2, 0.1.3, 1.2.1, 1.2.2, 1.2.4, 1.3.9, 4.8.1 **5:** 0.1.3, 1.3.3, 1.3.9 **R:** 0.1.2, 0.1.3, 1.1.6, 1.1.9, 1.2.1, 1.2.2, 1.2.4, 1.3.3, 1.3.9 **TP:** 0.1.2, 0.1.3, 1.1.6, 1.1.9, 1.2.1, 1.2.2, 1.2.4, 1.3.3, 1.3.9

CONTENTS

• Grammar points that are new △ Grammar points that are being recycled

	Numeracy/ Academic Skills	EFF	SCANS	CASAS
Unit 3	• Clarifying • Developing study skills • Evaluating • Focused listening • Note taking • Predicting • Reviewing • Scanning • VENN diagrams	**Most EFF skills are incorporated into this unit with an emphasis on:** • Solving problems and making decisions • Planning • Reflecting and evaluating (Technology is optional.)	**Many SCAN skills are incorporated in this unit with an emphasis on:** • Decision making • Problem solving • Self-management (Technology is optional.)	**1:** 1.3.8, 2.6.4 **2:** 1.1.7, 1.3.8 **3:** 1.1.7, 1.3.7, 1.3.8, 2.5.4 **4:** 1.3.8, 3.5.2, 3.5.9 **5:** 1.1.1, 1.1.7, 1.3.8 **R:** 1.1.1, 1.1.7, 1.3.7, 1.3.8, 2.5.4, 2.6.4, 3.5.2, 3.5.9 **TP:** 1.1.1, 1.1.7, 1.3.7, 1.3.8, 2.5.4, 2.6.4, 3.5.2, 3.5.9
Unit 4	• Academic reading • Developing study skills • Evaluating • Focused listening • Negotiating • Note taking • Making pie charts • Predicting • Reviewing • Scanning	**Most EFF skills are incorporated into this unit with an emphasis on:** • Using mathematics in problem solving and communication • Planning (Technology is optional.)	**Many SCAN skills are incorporated in this unit with an emphasis on:** • Allocating money • Arithmetic • Creative thinking • Self-management (Technology is optional.)	**1:** 1.1.3, 1.4.1, 1.4.2, 6.7.2 **2:** 1.4.2 **3:** 1.4.2, 1.4.3 **4:** 4.1.1, 6.1.1, 6.1.3 **5:** 1.5.1, 1.8.1, 6.1.1 **R:** 1.4.1, 1.4.2, 1.4.3, 1.5.1, 6.1.1, 6.1.3 **TP:** 1.4.1, 1.4.2, 1.4.3, 1.5.1, 6.1.1, 6.1.3, 4.8.1
Unit 5	• Brainstorming • Clarification strategies • Classifying • Focused listening • Listening to a lecture • Predicting • Scanning	**Most EFF skills are incorporated into this unit with an emphasis on:** • Conveying ideas in writing • Speaking so others can understand (Technology is optional.)	**Many SCAN skills are incorporated in this unit with an emphasis on:** • Acquiring and evaluating information • Writing • Speaking (Technology is optional.)	**1:** 1.1.3, 1.9.4, 2.2.4, 7.2.6 **2:** 2.1.1, 2.4.2 **3:** 1.1.3, 1.9.4, 2.2.1, 2.2.5 **4:** 0.2.3 **5:** 0.2.3 **R:** 0.2.3, 1.1.3, 1.9.4, 2.1.1, 2.2.1, 2.2.5 **TP:** 0.2.3, 1.1.3, 1.9.4, 2.1.1, 2.2.1, 2.2.5, 4.8.1

CONTENTS

• Grammar points that are new   △ Grammar points that are being recycled

	Numeracy/ Academic Skills	EFF	SCANS	CASAS
Unit 6	• Making bar graphs • Developing study skills • Evaluating • Focused listening • Making pie charts • Calculating percentages • Predicting • Reviewing	**Most EFF skills are incorporated into this unit with an emphasis on:** • Solving problems and making decisions • Reflecting and evaluating (Technology is optional.)	**Many SCAN skills are incorporated in this unit with an emphasis on:** • Understanding systems • Problem solving • Decision making • Self-management (Technology is optional.)	**1:** 3.5.8, 3.5.9 **2:** 3.1.1 **3:** 2.1.8, 3.1.1, 3.1.2, 3.1.3 **4:** 3.3.1, 3.3.2, 3.3.3, 3.4.1 **5:** 2.1.1, 2.1.8, 2.5.1, 3.1.1, 6.7.4 **R:** 3.1.1, 3.1.2, 3.1.3, 3.3.1, 3.3.2, 3.4.1, 3.5.8, 3.5.9 **TP:** 3.1.1, 3.1.2, 3.1.3, 3.3.1, 3.3.2, 3.4.1, 3.5.8, 3.5.9
Unit 7	• Brainstorming • Developing study skills • Evaluating • Focused listening • Reading for main idea • Reviewing	**Most EFF skills are incorporated into this unit with an emphasis on:** • Solving problems and making decisions • Reflecting and evaluating (Technology is optional.)	**Many SCAN skills are incorporated in this unit with an emphasis on:** • Organizing and maintaining information • Problem solving • Decision making • Self-management (Technology is optional.)	**1:** 4.4.2, 4.7.3 **2:** 4.1.2, 4.1.8, 4.5.1 **3:** 4.1.1, 4.1.2, 4.1.3, 4.1.6 **4:** 4.1.5, 4.1.7 **5:** 1.7.3, 4.6.1 **R:** 1.7.3, 4.1.1, 4.1.2, 4.1.3, 4.1.5, 4.1.6, 4.1.7, 4.1.8, 4.4.2, 4.5.1, 4.6.1, 4.7.3 **TP:** 1.7.3, 4.1.1, 4.1.2, 4.1.3, 4.1.5, 4.1.6, 4.1.7, 4.1.8, 4.4.2, 4.5.1, 4.6.1, 4.7.3
Unit 8	• Developing study skills • Evaluating • Focused listening • Listening for main idea • Note taking • Paragraph writing • Predicting • Reading a pie chart • Reviewing • Scanning • VENN diagrams	**Most EFF skills are incorporated into this unit with an emphasis on:** • Planning • Taking responsibility for learning • Reflecting and evaluating (Technology is optional.)	**Many SCAN skills are incorporated in this unit with an emphasis on:** • Understanding systems • Knowing how to learn • Responsibility • Self-management (Technology is optional.)	**1:** 4.4.5, 7.1.1, 7.5.1 **2:** 4.4.5, 7.1.1, 7.5.1 **3:** 4.4.5 **4:** 2.5.6, 7.2.7, 7.5.5 **5:** 4.4.5 **R:** 4.4.5, 7.1.1, 7.2.7, 7.5.1, 7.5.5 **TP:** 4.4.5, 7.1.1, 7.2.7, 7.5.1, 7.5.5

Welcome to Stand Out, Second Edition

Stand Out works.

And now it works even better!

Built from the standards necessary for adult English learners, the second edition of *Stand Out* gives students the foundation and tools they need to develop confidence and become independent, lifelong learners.

- Key **vocabulary** is introduced visually and orally.

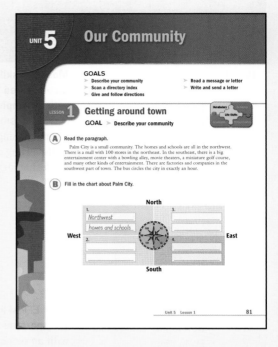

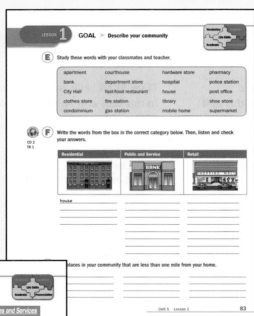

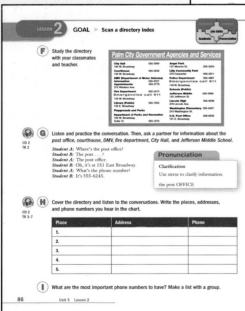

- Clearly defined **goals** provide a roadmap of learning for the student.
- State and federally required **life skills and competencies** are taught, helping students meet necessary benchmarks.

- Activities involving **academic skills** increase students' ability to navigate through the academic classroom.
- **Pronunciation** activities are integrated through the program.

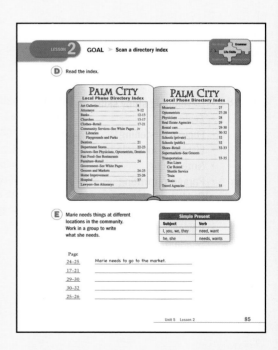

- A variety of **examples from real life**, like bank checks, newspaper ads, maps, etc. help students learn to access information and resources in their community.

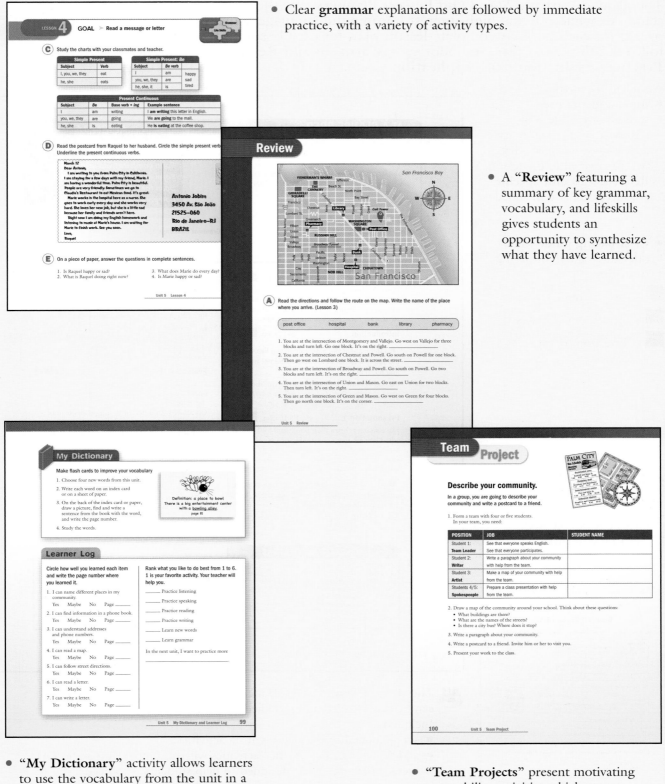

- Clear **grammar** explanations are followed by immediate practice, with a variety of activity types.

- A "**Review**" featuring a summary of key grammar, vocabulary, and lifeskills gives students an opportunity to synthesize what they have learned.

- "**My Dictionary**" activity allows learners to use the vocabulary from the unit in a new way, increasing the likelihood that they will acquire the words.
- "**Learner Log**" provides opportunities for learner self-assessment.

- "**Team Projects**" present motivating cross-ability activities which group learners of different levels together to complete a task that applies the unit objective.

The ground-breaking *Stand Out* **Lesson Planners** take the guesswork out of meeting the standards while offering high-interest, meaningful language activities, and three levels of pacing for each book. A complete **lesson plan** for each lesson in the student book is provided, following the *Stand Out* methodology – **Warm-up and Review, Introduction, Presentation, Practice, Evaluation, and Application** (see page xviii).

- An **at-a-glance prep** section for each lesson ensures that instructors have a clear knowledge of what will be covered in the lesson. References to **unit-specific resources** are also included

- Clear **pacing guide** icons offer three different pacing strategies.

  ▪ = for 1 ½ hour classes

  ▪ = for 2 ½ hour classes

  ▪ = for 3 hour or more classes

- **Standards Correlations** appear directly on the page, detailing how *Stand Out* meets CASAS, SCANS, and EFF standards.

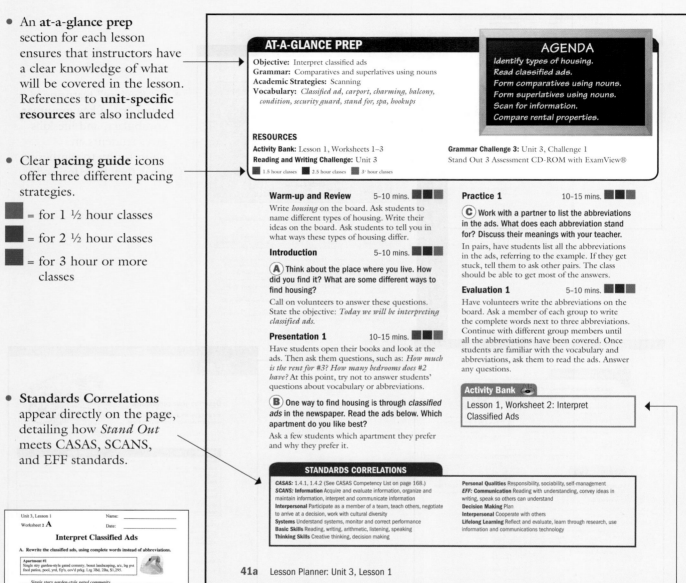

AT-A-GLANCE PREP

Objective: Interpret classified ads
Grammar: Comparatives and superlatives using nouns
Academic Strategies: Scanning
Vocabulary: *Classified ad, carport, charming, balcony, condition, security guard, stand for, spa, hookups*

AGENDA
Identify types of housing.
Read classified ads.
Form comparatives using nouns.
Form superlatives using nouns.
Scan for information.
Compare rental properties.

RESOURCES

Activity Bank: Lesson 1, Worksheets 1–3
Reading and Writing Challenge: Unit 3
▪ 1.5 hour classes ▪ 2.5 hour classes ▪ 3+ hour classes

Grammar Challenge 3: Unit 3, Challenge 1
Stand Out 3 Assessment CD-ROM with ExamView®

Warm-up and Review 5–10 mins. ▪▪▪
Write *housing* on the board. Ask students to name different types of housing. Write their ideas on the board. Ask students to tell you in what ways these types of housing differ.

Introduction 5–10 mins. ▪▪▪
(A) Think about the place where you live. How did you find it? What are some different ways to find housing?
Call on volunteers to answer these questions. State the objective: *Today we will be interpreting classified ads.*

Presentation 1 10–15 mins. ▪▪▪
Have students open their books and look at the ads. Then ask them questions, such as: *How much is the rent for #3? How many bedrooms does #2 have?* At this point, try not to answer students' questions about vocabulary or abbreviations.

(B) One way to find housing is through *classified ads* in the newspaper. Read the ads below. Which apartment do you like best?
Ask a few students which apartment they prefer and why they prefer it.

Practice 1 10–15 mins. ▪▪▪
(C) Work with a partner to list the abbreviations in the ads. What does each abbreviation stand for? Discuss their meanings with your teacher.
In pairs, have students list all the abbreviations in the ads, referring to the example. If they get stuck, tell them to ask other pairs. The class should be able to get most of the answers.

Evaluation 1 5–10 mins. ▪▪▪
Have volunteers write the abbreviations on the board. Ask a member of each group to write the complete words next to three abbreviations. Continue with different group members until all the abbreviations have been covered. Once students are familiar with the vocabulary and abbreviations, ask them to read the ads. Answer any questions.

Activity Bank 💿
Lesson 1, Worksheet 2: Interpret Classified Ads

STANDARDS CORRELATIONS

CASAS: 1.4.1, 1.4.2 (See CASAS Competency List on page 168.)
SCANS: Information Acquire and evaluate information, organize and maintain information, interpret and communicate information
Interpersonal Participate as a member of a team, teach others, negotiate to arrive at a decision, work with cultural diversity
Systems Understand systems, monitor and correct performance
Basic Skills Reading, writing, arithmetic, listening, speaking
Thinking Skills Creative thinking, decision making

Personal Qualities Responsibility, sociability, self-management
EFF: Communication Reading with understanding, convey ideas in writing, speak so others can understand
Decision Making Plan
Interpersonal Cooperate with others
Lifelong Learning Reflect and evaluate, learn through research, use information and communications technology

41a Lesson Planner: Unit 3, Lesson 1

Unit 3, Lesson 1   Name: _____
Worksheet **2 A**   Date: _____

Interpret Classified Ads

A. Rewrite the classified ads, using complete words instead of abbreviations.

Apartment #1
Single stry garden-style gated commty, beaut landscaping, a/c, lrg pvt fncd patios, pool, yrd, f/p's, cov'd prkg. Lrg 3Bd, 2Ba, $1,295.

Single story garden-style gated community,
_____

Apartment #2
Spacious, 2BD, 2BA, new crpt, a/c, frplc, w/d bkup, 1 level, lrg prvt encl 2-car gar w/storage cabinets, pool, quiet loc. No pets.

Spacious, two-bedroom,
_____

B. What do the two apartments above have in common? Make a list.

1. *Two bathrooms* _____
2. *Pool* _____
3. _____
4. _____
5. _____

C. Which apartment would you rather rent? Discuss your answer with a partner.

Copyright © Heinle
Stand Out 3 Activity Bank

💿 The *Activity Bank CD-ROM* includes the following worksheets that can be downloaded and modified to meet the needs of your class. Included are:
- supplemental reading and writing activities.
- additional listening practice activities with accompanying audio CD.
- literacy practice sheets designed to help students who need introductory-level written language tasks.
- **multilevel activity masters** for each lesson that can be printed or downloaded and modified for classroom needs.

Presentation 2   10-15 mins. ■■■

Ask students to imagine they are moving to a new home. Tell them they need to cancel the electricity in their current home and get it turned on at their new home. Ask them how they would do this. (Call the electric company.) Ask what sort of information they would need to give to the company's representative to make this happen.

Practice 2   5-10 mins. ■■■

Tell students they will be listening to Vu call the electric company to prepare for his family's move. Direct their attention to Exercise C and tell them they will be listening for four pieces of information.

Teaching Tip

Focused listening

The purpose of teaching focused listening is to help students learn how to understand the main ideas in a conversation even when they don't understand every word.

It's important to remind students that they will not understand every word each time they do a focused listening activity. Otherwise, they may become frustrated and stop listening all together. Preparing students for the listening activity will make them much more effective listeners.

1. Explain the context of the conversation.
2. Ask students what they think they might hear.
3. Show students specifically what they are listening for.

C Vu and his family are getting ready to move. Vu calls the electric company to speak to a customer service representative. Listen to the recording and write short answers for the following information.

Listening Script   CD 1, Track 8

Recording: *Thank you for calling Texas Electric. Your call is very important to us. Please choose from the following options. For new service or to cancel your existing service, press 1. To report a problem with your service, press 2. If you have questions about your bill, press 3. For all other questions, press 4. (Vu presses 1.) Thank you. Just one moment.*

Representative: *Hello, my name is Kristen. How may I help you?*
Vu: *Um, yes. My family is moving next week. We need to cancel our current service and get service in our new home.*
Representative: *What is your current address?*
Vu: *3324 Maple Road.*
Representative: *Are you Vu Nguyen?*
Vu: *Yes.*
Representative: *When would you like the service turned off?*
Vu: *Next Wednesday, please.*
Representative: *And what is your new address?*
Vu: *5829 Bay Road.*
Representative: *And when would you like the service turned on?*
Vu: *This Monday, please.*
Representative: *OK. Your current service will be turned off sometime between 8 and 12 on Wednesday the 11th. Your new service will be on before 9 on Monday morning the 9th. Is there anything else I can do for you?*
Vu: *No, that's it.*
Representative: *Thank you for calling Texas Electric. Have a nice day.*
Vu: *You, too.*

D Listen to the recording again and answer the questions.
Prepare students for the information they are to listen for. (CD 1, Track 8)

Evaluation 2   5 mins. ■■
Go over the answers with the class.

Pronunciation

Rising and Falling Intonation

Ask students a few information questions. Ask if your voice goes up or down at the end of each question. Students should be able to recognize the rising and falling intonation. Explain that this rising and falling intonation helps the listener know that you are asking a question that requires an answer.

Go over the examples in the box in the student book, emphasizing the intonation. Have students practice by repeating after you, first as a class and then individually.

Lesson Planner: Unit 3, Lesson 3   **48a**

- **Teaching Tips** and **Culture Tips** provide ideas and strategies for teaching diverse learners in the classroom.

- **Listening Scripts** from the *Audio CD* are included next to the student book page for ease-of-use.

- *Grammar Challenge* workbooks include supplemental activities for students who desire even more **contextual grammar** and **vocabulary practice.**

- *Reading & Writing Challenge* workbooks provide challenging materials and exercises for students who want even **more practice in reading, vocabulary development,** and **writing.**

- **Exam***View*® **Test Bank** allows you to create **customizable pre- and post-tests for every unit.** The questions are correlated to CASAS and state standards and include multiple choice, true/false, numeric response, and matching types. Listening questions are included along with an audio CD.

The *Stand Out* Lesson Planner methodology ensures success!

Stand Out ensures student success through good lesson planning and instruction. Each of the five Lessons in every Unit has a lesson plan. Unlike most textbooks, the Lesson Planner was written before the student book materials. A lot of learning occurs with the student books closed so by writing the lesson plans first, we could ensure that each objective was clearly achieved. Each lesson plan follows a systematic and proven format:

W Warm-up and/or review

I Introduction

P Presentation

P Practice

E Evaluation

A Application

WARM-UP AND/OR REVIEW
The warm-up activities establish a context and purpose for the lesson. Exercises use previously learned content and materials that are familiar to students from previous lessons.

INTRODUCTION
In the introduction step, exercises focus the students' attention on the goals of the lesson by asking questions, showing visuals, telling a story, etc. Instructors should state the objective of the lesson and tell students what they will be doing. The objective should address what students are expected to be able to do by the end of the lesson.

PRESENTATION
The presentation activities provide students with the building blocks and skills they need to achieve the objectives set in the introduction. The exercises introduce new information to the students through visuals, realia, description, listenings, explanation, or written text. This is the time to check students' comprehension.

PRACTICE
Practice activities provide meaningful tasks for students to practice what they have just learned through different activities. These activities can be done as a class, in small groups, pairs, or individually. All of these activities are student centered and involve cooperative learning. Instructors should model each activity, monitor progress, and provide feedback.

EVALUATION
Evaluation ensures that students are successful. Instructors should evaluate students on attainment of the objective set at the start of the lesson. This can be done by oral, written, or demonstrated performance. At this point, if students need more practice, instructors can go back and do additional practice activities before moving on to the application.

APPLICATION
Application activities help students apply new knowledge to their own lives or new situations. This is one of the most important steps of the lesson plan. If students can accomplish the application task, it will build their confidence to be able to use what they've learned out in the community. The Team Projects are an application of unit objectives that involves task-based activities with a product.

In addition to each lesson plan following the WIPPEA model, each Unit in *Stand Out* follows this same approach. The first lesson is always an Introduction to the Unit, introducing new vocabulary and the basic concepts that will be expanded upon in the unit. The following four lessons are the Presentations and Practices for the unit topic. Following the five lessons is a Review lesson, which allows students to do more practice with everything they already learned. The final lesson is an Application for everything they learned in the unit, a team project.

AT-A-GLANCE PREP

Objective: Greet your friends and describe feelings
Grammar: *Be*
Pronunciation: /m/
Academic Strategy: Focused listening
Vocabulary: Feelings: *fine, angry, nervous, sad, happy, hungry, tired*

RESOURCES

Activity Bank: Pre-Unit, Lesson 1, Worksheets 1–2
Grammar Challenge: Pre-Unit, Challenge 1

 1.5 hour classes   2.5 hour classes   3⁺ hour classes

Audio: CD 1, Tracks 1–5
Heinle Picture Dictionary: Wave, Greet, Smile, pages 40–41; Feelings, pages 38–39
Stand Out 2 Assessment CD-ROM with *ExamView®*

 Preassessment *(optional)*

Use the Stand Out 2 Assessment CD-ROM with *ExamView®* to create a pretest for the Pre-Unit.

Warm-up and Review   2-5 mins.

On the board, write: *Nice to meet you.* Shake hands with several students as you say the phrase. Ask students to repeat the phrase after you. Since this is the first class, getting to know students' names should be the instructor's main objective.

Introduction   2 mins.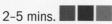

Point to the agenda on the board and state the objective: *Today we will greet one another and describe our feelings.*

Presentation 1   15-20 mins.

Before students open their books, do a few icebreaker activities that will allow you to learn students' names and that will help build a sense of community in the classroom. To learn more about building a community in the classroom, see the teaching tip on the next page.

The following activities can help you learn students' names.

1. Do a chain drill where you ask Student A his or her name. Student A answers and then asks Student B for his or her name. Student B must remember Student A's name before asking Student C, and so on.

2. Ask students to line up in the classroom in alphabetical order by first or last name.

3. Randomly pass around a ball or wad of paper and ask students to say their names and where they are from when they catch it.

4. Ask students to introduce themselves to a classmate and then introduce their partner to the class.

(A) Listen and practice.

Ask students to open their books and look at the picture. Ask students the questions in the box. Then, ask them to listen to and read the conversation.

 Listening Script   CD 1, Track 1

The listening script matches the conversation in Exercise A.

Prepare students for practice by asking questions about the conversation: *Who is the new student? How do you know?* Prepare students for focused listening.

Practice 1   5 mins.

(B) Listen to the conversations. Circle the new student.

Note: The listening script for Exercise B is on page P2a.

Evaluation 1   5-7 mins.

Go over the answers with students. Listen to the recording again, pausing to discuss what was said in each conversation.

STANDARDS CORRELATIONS

CASAS: 0.1.4, 0.2.1 (See CASAS Competency List on pages 169–175.)
SCANS: Information Acquire and evaluate information
Basic Skills Listening, speaking
Personal Qualities Sociability
EFF: Communication Speak so others can understand, listen actively

---

Welcome to Our Class

GOALS

➤ Greet your friends and describe feelings

➤ Complete a registration form

➤ Follow classroom instructions

LESSON 1

Nice to meet you!

GOAL ➤ Greet your friends and describe feelings

Where are the students?
Who is the new student?

CD 1
TR 1

A Listen and practice.

Mario: Hello, what's your name?
Lien: My name is Lien.
Mario: Nice to meet you, Lien. I'm Mario.
Lien: Hi, Mario. Nice to meet you, too.
Mario: Welcome to our class, Lien.

CD 1
TR 2-5

B Listen to the conversations. Circle the new student.

1. Mario   (Lien)

2. (Esteban)   Cecilia

3. (Alexi)   Jonathan

4. (Rick)   Nadia

GOAL ➤ **Greet your friends and describe feelings**

C Look at the pictures of feelings. Say the words.

nervous

sad

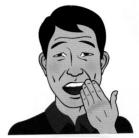

tired

happy

angry

hungry

Pronunciation

/m/
I'm

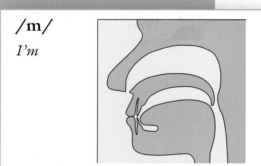

D Practice the conversations.

Mario: Hi, Lien!
Lien: Hello, Mario.
Mario: How are you today?
Lien: I'm <u>nervous</u>.
Mario: Me, too.

Jonathan: Hi, Alexi!
Alexi: Hello, Jonathan.
Jonathan: How are you today?
Alexi: I'm <u>sad</u>.
Jonathan: Not me. I'm <u>happy</u> today.

E Practice the conversations with a partner. Use different feelings.

Listening Script   CD 1, Tracks 2–5

1. **Mario:** *Hello, what's your name?*
   Lien: *My name is Lien.*
   Mario: *Nice to meet you, Lien. I'm Mario.*
   Lien: *Hi, Mario. Nice to meet you, too.*
   Mario: *Welcome to our class, Lien.*

2. **Cecilia:** *Hello. What's your name?*
   Esteban: *I'm Esteban. I'm new.*
   Cecilia: *Nice to meet you. Welcome.*
   Esteban: *Thanks. I am a little nervous.*

3. **Alexi:** *I'm Alexi. It's nice to meet you. This is my first day.*
   Jonathan: *I'm Jonathan. Welcome to the class. It's nice to meet you, too.*

4. **Rick:** *Hello, I'm Rick. What's your name?*
   Nadia: *I'm Nadia. Are you new?*
   Rick: *Yes, I am. I hope this is a good class.*
   Nadia: *It is. The teacher is great!*

Presentation 2   15–20 mins.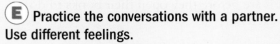

Continue to build community in the classroom by working on learning students' names. Write *nervous* on the board. Ask students what the word means. Tell them that sometimes everyone feels nervous, but that there is no reason to feel nervous in class because you are a family or a community. Pantomime a few feelings and see if students can call them out before opening their books. Model correct pronunciation.

C Look at the pictures of feelings. Say the words.

Go over the words with students and again model the pronunciation. This time, use complete sentences with *I'm*.

Pronunciation

/m/

Students may avoid touching their lips together when pronouncing the /m/ in *I'm*. Help students pronounce the /m/ first in isolation and then as part of the phrase they are practicing. Exaggerating the sound at first will help them to discern the target sound. Don't single any students out if they are having problems. After several students have made similar errors, go over the pronunciation of the target sound again. Again, be careful not to overcorrect.

For shorter classes, ask students to do Exercises D and E for homework.

D Practice the conversations.

Go over the conversations in Exercise D with students. Model good pronunciation.

Practice 2   7–10 mins.

E Practice the conversations with a partner. Use different feelings.

Show students how to substitute other feelings in the conversation. Add any feelings to the list that students might come up with.

Evaluation 2   7–10 mins.

Ask volunteers to demonstrate their conversations in front of the class.

Teaching Tip

Names and community

Both students and the instructor should feel that they are part of a community. *Stand Out* will provide many opportunities to create this atmosphere. To encourage community from the beginning, it is important to establish a good rapport between instructor and students. The following suggestions will enhance a community feeling:

- Learn students' names.
- Use students' names regularly (every student, every day).
- Share personal stories with the class.
- Establish early on that you care about the students and want them to be successful.

Presentation 3   7–15 mins. ■■■

In the Pre-Unit of *Stand Out*, you are reviewing things that students should already know. The *be* verb is essential to success at this level. Make sure that students already understand the *be* verb and its conjugations by asking them what the forms are before they open their books to do the exercise.

(F) Study the chart with your classmates and teacher.

As you go over the chart, model proper pronunciation. Ask students which questions the example sentences answer.

Practice 3   10–15 mins. ■

(G) Complete the sentences with the correct form of *be*.

Ask students to create conversations in pairs where they use the different forms of the verb. To ensure they use the different forms, count pairs off 1, 2, and 3. Ask all the pairs designated as "ones" to write and use any *be* verb, but they must use *am* at least twice. "Twos" must use *are*, and "threes" must use *is*.

Evaluation 3   7–10 mins. ■

Go over Exercise G and ask volunteers from each of the three groups to perform their conversation for the class.

Application   5–7 mins. ■■■

(H) Ask three classmates. Write their answers in the chart.

Students complete the chart. Encourage them to avoid reading the conversations in Exercise D. They should be able to do the activity without it, although it is OK to allow them to reference it when necessary.

(I) In a group, talk about your conversations.

Ask students to report to their group on the information they got from their classmates. Ask students to take turns reporting. To monitor student activity, you may choose to ask students who are reporting to stand so you can visually confirm students are on task. Monitor groups around the classroom.

 Refer students to *Stand Out 2 Grammar Challenge*, Pre-Unit, Challenge 1 for more practice with *be*.

Activity Bank

Pre-Unit, Lesson 1, Worksheet 1: Say *Hello!*
Pre-Unit, Lesson 1, Worksheet 2: *Be* Verb

Instructor's Notes

_____
_____
_____
_____
_____
_____
_____
_____
_____
_____
_____
_____
_____
_____
_____
_____
_____
_____
_____
_____
_____
_____

GOAL ➤ Greet your friends and describe feelings

F Study the chart with your classmates and teacher.

Be Verb to Express Feelings			
Subject	*Be*	**Feelings**	**Example sentence**
I	am	fine	I **am** fine. (I**'m** fine.)
you, we, they	are	nervous sad tired happy	You **are** tired. (You**'re** tired.) We **are** hungry. (We**'re** hungry) They **are** nervous. (They**'re** nervous.)
he, she, it	is	angry hungry	He **is** happy. (He**'s** happy.) She **is** angry. (She**'s** angry.)

G Complete the sentences with the correct form of *be*.

1. Mauricio _____is_____ tired today.

2. They _____are_____ hungry.

3. Antonio and I _____are_____ angry.

4. I _____am_____ fine, thank you.

5. Alice _____is_____ nervous.

6. You _____are_____ happy.

H Ask three classmates. Write their answers in the chart. (Answers will vary.)

Student name	Feelings
Mario	happy

I In a group, talk about your conversations.

EXAMPLE: Mario is one name in my chart. He's happy.

What's your name and number?

GOAL ➤ Complete a registration form

A Read Mario's school registration form.

Alton Adult School Registration Form

Date _September 3, 2009_

PERSONAL INFORMATION

Name: _Garcia_ _Mario_   Phone: _(714) 555-7564_
         Last   First

Birth Date: _July 12, 1977_

Street Address: _8237 Henderson Lane_

City: _Midland_   State: _CA_   Zip Code: _90631_

B Write the information.

1. Mario's last name is _Garcia_.
2. His phone number is _(714) 555-7564_.
3. His address is _8237 Henderson Lane, Midland, CA_.
4. His zip code is _90631_.
5. His birth date is _July 12, 1977_.

C Listen and write the information you hear.

CD 1
TR 6

1. My first name is _Esteban_.
2. My last name is _Garcia_.
3. I live on _Tremont_ Street.
4. I live in _Sausalito_.
5. I am from _Mexico_.
6. My teacher's last name is _Parelli_.

AT-A-GLANCE PREP

Objective: Complete a registration form
Grammar: Possessive adjectives
Pronunciation: /θ/
Academic Strategy: Focused listening
Vocabulary: Possessive adjectives, *birth date*

RESOURCES

Activity Bank: Pre-Unit, Lesson 2, Worksheet 1
Grammar Challenge: Pre-Unit, Challenge 2

Audio: CD 1, Tracks 6–11
Heinle Picture Dictionary: Documents, pages 42–43

■ 1.5 hour classes   ■ 2.5 hour classes   ■ 3⁺ hour classes

AGENDA

Discuss classmates' names.
Read a registration form.
Listen for important information.
Complete a registration form.

Warm-up and Review   10-12 mins.

Ask students to get into groups of three or four. Ask each group to make a list of all the students in the class. They will start with the names of the students in their groups. If no one in the group can identify people in other groups, they will send a representative to the other groups to ask for the names and report back to the group. To extend this activity, ask the groups to put their lists in alphabetical order.

Introduction   5 mins. ■■■

Point to the agenda. Go over the activities. Ask students if they had to register for the class. State the objective: *Today we will complete a registration form.*

Presentation 1   15 mins. ■■■

Before students open their books, ask them what information goes on a registration form. List the information elicited from students on the board.

(A) Read Mario's school registration form.

Look at the different parts of the form together. A few details might be interesting to discuss. For example, discuss the difference between *birthday* and *birth date*. Also go over the difference in pronunciation. Students from many countries have trouble pronouncing the final consonant of words in isolation or at the end of phrases. Help them to distinguish their words while speaking.

You might also discuss the comma when the last name is written before the first name. Discuss different ways to write phone numbers and area codes. Show students how the second word in two-word street names are uppercase, as in *Henderson Lane.*

(B) Write the information.

Do this activity as a class and then prepare for focused listening. To read more about focused listening, see the teaching tip on the next page.

Practice 1   5 mins. ■■■

(C) Listen and write the information you hear.

 Listening Script   *CD 1, Track 6*

Ms. Parelli: *Welcome to our class. It is great to have you here.*
Esteban: *Thanks. I'm a little nervous.*
Ms. Parelli: *No need to be. What's your name?*
Esteban: *It's Esteban—E-S-T-E-B-A-N—Garcia—G-A-R-C-I-A.*
Ms. Parelli: *OK, Esteban. Where do you live?*
Esteban: *I live on Tremont Street—T-R-E-M-O-N-T—in Sausalito—S-A-U-S-A-L-I-T-O.*
Ms. Parelli: *Thanks. You're from Mexico, right?*
Esteban: *Right. Excuse me, what is your name?*
Ms. Parelli: *It's Ms. Parelli.*
Esteban: *How do you spell that?*
Ms. Parelli: *It's P-A-R-E-L-L-I.*
Esteban: *It's nice to meet you, Ms. Parelli.*

Evaluation 1   5 mins. ■■■

Go over the listening activity and help students check their answers for accuracy.

STANDARDS CORRELATIONS

CASAS: : 0.1.2, 0.1.4, 0.2.1, 0.2.2, 4.8.1 (See CASAS Competency List on pages 169–175.)
SCANS: **Resources** Allocate human resources
Information Organize and maintain information
Interpersonal Participate as a member of a team
Basic Skills Reading, writing, listening, speaking
Personal Qualities Sociability
EFF: **Communication** Speak so others can understand, listen actively, observe critically
Interpersonal Cooperate with others

Presentation 2 · 10–15 mins.

This presentation will ensure that students are ready to write numbers for addresses and phone numbers. Most students should have no problem with these activities, but it is good to make sure you know the level of each student.

D Listen and practice saying the numbers.

> **🎧 Listening Script** · CD 1, Track 7
>
> *The listening script matches the activity in Exercise D.*

Pronunciation of numbers is often a challenge for students. Help them to pronounce the /th/ in *third*, *thirteen*, and *thirty*.

Exaggerate the sound by showing students how to bite down on the tongue and build pressure by pushing air. Then show them how to release the /th/ in an explosive manner.

E Listen and write the phone numbers you hear.

Note that this activity is not focused listening, but it prepares students to do the true focused listening in Exercise F.

> **🎧 Listening Script** · CD 1, Track 8
>
> 1. (619) 555-6391
> 2. (312) 555-5100
> 3. (786) 555-2852
> 4. (915) 555-5280
> 5. (323) 555-3967
> 6. (347) 555-1743

Teaching Tip

Focused listening

Focused listening is prevalent throughout the *Stand Out* series. The recordings are at an authentic speed and are filled with language students may not understand. The purpose of a focused-listening task is to help students develop the ability to pull meaning out of complex and natural conversations by identifying key words.

It's important to remind students to listen for overall meaning every time you do a focused-listening activity so they don't become frustrated and stop listening all together.

Practice 2 · 12–15 mins.

F Listen to the conversations. Write the missing information.

> **🎧 Listening Script** · CD 1, Tracks 9–11
>
> 1. **Marie speaks to her teacher.**
>   **Marie:** *I am new. Do I need to complete a registration form?*
>   **Teacher:** *Yes, but I will help you. First, what is your phone number?*
>   **Marie:** *It's 555-4769.*
>   **Teacher:** *OK, I have it. Where are you from?*
>   **Marie:** *I'm from Haiti*
>
> 2. **Kenji speaks to a taxi driver.**
>   **Taxi Driver:** *Where to?*
>   **Kenji:** *I live in Los Angeles.*
>   **Taxi Driver:** *Oh. That is a little far.*
>   **Kenji:** *I know, but I don't have time to take the bus.*
>   **Taxi Driver:** *OK, what is your address?*
>   **Kenji:** *It's 6789 Third Street.*
>
> 3. **Mario speaks to a new friend.**
>   **Mario:** *It is good to meet you. I hope we can talk again soon.*
>   **Friend:** *Of course. What's your phone number?*
>   **Mario:** *It's 555-7892, and my address is 3745 Hamilton Street.*

Play the recording two or three times to allow students time to record the information.

Evaluation 2 · 5 mins.

Ask students to peer-check their work. Be prepared to play the recording one more time if students have questions.

LESSON 2

GOAL ➤ **Complete a registration form**

CD 1
TR 7

D Listen and practice saying the numbers.

0	1	2	3	4	5	6	7	8	9
10	11	12	13	14	15	16	17	18	19
20	21	22	23	24	25	26	27	28	29
30	40	50	60	70	80	90	100		

CD 1
TR 8

E Listen and write the phone numbers you hear.

EXAMPLE: ___(617) 555-9264___

1. ___(619) 555-6391___   3. ___(786) 555-2852___   5. ___(323) 555-3967___

2. ___(312) 555-5100___   4. ___(915) 555-5280___   6. ___(347) 555-1743___

CD 1
TR 9-11

F Listen to the conversations. Write the missing information.

1. My name is Marie. I live in Palm City. I go to Adam's Adult School. My phone number is ___555-4769___. My last name is Collell.

2. My name is Kenji. I'm from Japan. My address is ___6789___ Third Street.

3. My name is Mario. It's nice to meet you. My phone number is ___555-7892___. My address is ___3745___ Hamilton Street.

LESSON **2** **GOAL** ➤ Complete a registration form

G Study the chart with your classmates and teacher.

Possessive Adjectives		
Pronoun	**Possessive adjective**	**Example sentence**
I	my	**My** address is 3356 Archer Blvd.
you	your	**Your** phone number is 555-5678.
he	his	**His** last name is Jones.
she	her	**Her** first name is Lien.
we	our	**Our** teacher is Mr. Kelley.
they	their	**Their** home is in Sausalito.

H Write the possessive adjective.

1. I live in San Francisco. _____My_____ address is 2354 Yerba Buena.

2. They live in Portland. _____Their_____ phone number is 555-6732.

3. We live in Dallas. _____Our_____ last name is Peters.

4. Maria is a happy woman. _____Her_____ school is in New York.

5. He is a good student. _____His_____ name is Esteban Garcia.

6. You live on Hilton Street. _____Your_____ home is in Rockledge. Is that right?

I Talk to a partner. Complete the form with your partner's information.
(Answers will vary.)

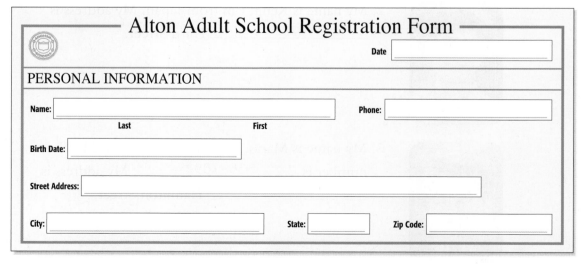

Presentation 3   8-10 mins. ■■■□

With books closed, write the first two columns of the chart from Exercise G on the board. Don't write in any possessive adjectives except *my*. Ask volunteers to come to the board and write in the correct words.

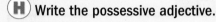 **Study the chart with your classmates and teacher.**

Ask students to open their books and go over the chart and the example sentences.

For shorter classes, ask students to do Exercise H for homework.

Practice 3   5-8 mins. ■

Ⓗ Write the possessive adjective.

Evaluation 3   2-5 mins. ■

Go over Exercise H with students. Consider giving a dictation of the statements to extend the practice and further check for understanding.

Application   7-10 mins. ■■■□

Help students with developing the questions they need to complete Exercise H. You may ask students to write in their partners' books so that one student's personal information is not written in another student's book.

 Talk to a partner. Complete the form with your partner's information.

Students report to a group of three or four students and give the information about their partners.

Note: If students are concerned about giving out personal information, let them know that it is OK to make up their answers.

Teaching Tip

Groups

There are many ways to form groups. It is a good idea to form groups in different ways throughout the course, both to provide variety and to maximize interaction between students. More will be said later about different ways to form groups.

It is also important to form small groups. Four in a group is optimum because more interaction is possible in groups of four than in groups of three. A group of more than four often results in some students not participating because other students are more vocal. Also, it is much harder to manage groups of more than four and focus on the task at hand.

Refer students to *Stand Out 2 Grammar Challenge*, Pre-Unit, Challenge 2 for more practice with possessive pronouns.

Activity Bank

Pre-Unit, Lesson 2, Worksheet 1: Personal Information

Instructor's Notes

_____

_____

_____

_____

_____

_____

_____

_____

_____

_____

AT-A-GLANCE PREP

Objective: Follow classroom instructions
Grammar: Questions with *can*
Pronunciation: *Yes/No* question intonation
Academic Strategies: Focused listening, clarification
Vocabulary: *help, answer, repeat, say, speak, spell*

RESOURCES

Activity Bank: Pre-Unit, Lesson 3, Worksheet 1
Grammar Challenge: Pre-Unit, Challenge 3

■ 1.5 hour classes ■ 2.5 hour classes ■ 3⁺ hour classes

Audio: CD 1, Tracks 12–14
Heinle Picture Dictionary: Classroom, pages 18–19; Listen, Read, Write, pages 20–21

AGENDA

Create a phone directory.
Understand classroom instructions.
Ask for clarification.
Practice asking for help.
Give instructions.

Warm-up and Review 15–20 mins. ■■■

Ask students to create a class phone directory. Students can take their lists of classmates that they created in the previous lesson warm-up and add phone numbers to them. Students will have to talk to each other to get this information. If students do not want to share their phone numbers, it is OK to write *unlisted*. Complete a class phone list from all the information and supply the list to the class.

Introduction 5 mins. ■■■

Go over the agenda for the day with students and state the objective: *Today we will learn to follow classroom directions.*

Presentation 1 15–20 mins. ■■■

With students' books closed, pantomime the actions in Exercise A: *listen to a CD, open a book, talk to a partner*, and *go to the board*. See if students can figure out what you are doing. An alternative to this presentation is to write the actions on 3-by-5 index cards and play charades. Students are each given a card and they must pantomime the action for their classmates to guess. Include additional actions as needed.

 Match the instructions with the pictures. Write the correct letter next to each sentence.

Practice 1 7–10 mins. ■■■

 Work with a partner. Circle the words that describe classroom activities.

Ask students to first do this activity in pairs and then for the pairs to meet with a second pair of students to compare answers.

Teaching Tip

Books closed

Our lesson plans often suggest that instructors first present material before students open their books. It would be easier and faster to open the books and ask students to merely look at the information, but allowing students to first discuss the concepts with books closed provides the following benefits:

1. In student-centered instruction, students are more involved in the presentation because the information is first elicited from them.
2. The instructor can better determine what students already know and evaluate their needs.
3. Students remember more because they are required to think and process information.
4. Often there is a tie to students' lives, which further empowers and helps students apply learning.

Evaluation 1 5–7 mins.

Go over the words as a class and make a sentence with each word. You might also continue with the charades game from the presentation stage using these additional words.

STANDARDS CORRELATIONS

CASAS: 0.1.2, 0.1.5, 0.1.6, 7.5.6 (See CASAS Competency List on pages 169–175)
SCANS: Basic Skills Listening, speaking
EFF: Communication Speak so others can understand, listen actively

---

Open your books!

GOAL ➤ Follow classroom instructions

A Match the instructions with the pictures. Write the correct letter next to each sentence.

a.

c.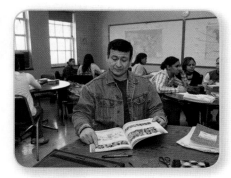

b.

d.

____b____ 1. Listen to the CD.

____c____ 2. Open the book.

____d____ 3. Talk to a partner.

____a____ 4. Go to the board.

B Work with a partner. Circle the words that describe classroom activities.

(answer)	ride	(take out)
eat	run	(talk)
(listen)	(sit down)	(watch)
(open)	sleep	(work)
(practice)	(stand up)	(write)

LESSON 3

GOAL ➤ **Follow classroom instructions**

  C **Read and listen to the conversation.**

CD 1
TR 12

Mr. Jones: Kenji, please write a sentence on the board.
Kenji: Excuse me?
Mr. Jones: Write a sentence on the board.
Kenji: I'm sorry, I don't understand.
Mr. Jones: I can help you. Please come to the board.
Kenji: OK.

D **Study the clarification phrases with your classmates and teacher.**

I'm sorry, I don't understand.	Excuse me?
Please speak slower.	Can you say that again, please?
Please speak louder.	Can you spell that?

 E **Listen and circle a clarification phrase. Sometimes there is more than one correct answer.**

CD 1
TR 13

1. Please speak slower.   (Can you spell that?)   Excuse me?

2. I'm sorry, I don't understand.   (Can you say that again?)   Can you spell that?

3. Please speak louder.   (Please speak slower.)   (Can you say that again?)

4. (I'm sorry, I don't understand.)   Please speak slower.   (Excuse me?)

Presentation 2   10-15 mins. ■■■

Give students a few instructions, but first say them too fast. If students ask you to slow down, speak slower, but so quietly that they can't hear you. Ask students to open their books and look at the picture at the top of the page. Ask them what they think is happening. Accept all answers. Some students will undoubtedly read the conversation below. This is expected.

(C) Read and listen to the conversation.

Ask the students to listen. Then, write the clarification phrases that are in the conversation on the board. Repeat what you did earlier and give instructions that are not clear. Allow students to ask for clarification using the phrases on the board

 Listening Script   CD 1, Track 12

The listening script matches the conversation in Exercise C.

(D) Study the clarification phrases with your classmates and teacher.

Go over each of the phrases and allow students to become comfortable with them by giving instructions that would prompt each one. You may choose to continue with the charades game by writing the phrases on 3-by-5 cards. Then, ask the students to do something to prompt the responses from their classmates.

Practice 2   5-7 mins. ■■

(E) Listen and circle a clarification phrase. Sometimes there is more than one correct answer.

 Listening Script   CD 1, Track 13

1. *Please write down my name. It's Stephanopoulos.*
2. *I need a few things right away. Can you please make a list?*
3. *Please, stand up, walk to the door, turn right, and talk to the first person you see.*
4. *Please give me the digits to your communication device.*

Evaluation 2   3-5 mins. ■■

Go over the correct answers after students have compared their answers. Make sure you accept most answers. Play the recording again.

Presentation 3   10–15 mins.

On the board, write: *Can you help me?* Ask students if they can think of similar questions a student might ask a teacher. Accept all questions that students may come up with, but be careful to write the questions correctly on the board.

F Study the chart with your classmates and teacher.

Go over the structure. Show students how to start the question with *can*.

Pronunciation

Intonation

When students are learning a language, they often have trouble in the midst of all the new linguistic matter to realize the context even when it is clearly presented like in *Stand Out*. Many languages have the same rising intonation for *yes/no* questions, but students may not transfer the intonation to English because they are distracted by the other linguistic elements.

Stress the rising intonation here by having students do different activities to demonstrate the intonation. For example, have them all stand or raise their hands as they complete the question.

Practice 3   7–10 mins.

G Complete the conversation with questions from the chart above. Then, practice the conversation with a partner.

At this point, students should be ready to write additional conversations with the new clarification phrases. Ask them to do so and be prepared to report them to the class.

Evaluation 3   5 mins.

Ask volunteers to perform their conversations for the class.

Application   5–7 mins.

H Listen and write the instructions. Then, give the instructions to a partner.

 Listening Script   CD 1, Track 14

1. *Stand up.*
2. *Sit down.*
3. *Open your book to page 33.*
4. *Say your address.*
5. *Repeat your address.*
6. *Close your book, look at the teacher, and say hello to the teacher.*

 Refer students to *Stand Out 2 Grammar Challenge*, Pre-Unit, Challenge 3 for more practice with questions with *can*.

Activity Bank

Pre-Unit, Lesson 3, Worksheet 1: Classroom

Instructor's Notes

_____
_____
_____
_____
_____
_____
_____
_____
_____
_____
_____
_____
_____
_____
_____
_____
_____

LESSON 3 **GOAL** ➤ **Follow classroom instructions**

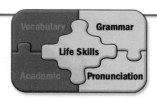

F Study the chart with your classmates and teacher.

Questions with *Can*			
Can	Pronoun	Verb	Example sentence
Can	you	help answer repeat say speak spell	Can you help me? Can you answer the question? Can you repeat that, please? Can you say it again, please? Can you speak slower? Can you spell it, please?

Pronunciation

Yes/No Questions

Yes/No questions have rising intonation.

➤ Can you help me?

➤ Can you speak slower?

G Complete the conversation with questions from the chart above. Then, practice the conversation with a partner.

Student A: I have a problem. <u>Can you help me?</u>
Student B: Sure.
Student A: Your name is difficult to write. <u>Can you spell it, please</u>?
Student B: Yes, it is R-O-X-A-N-N-A.
Student A: You speak very fast. <u>Can you speak slower</u>?
Student B: Yes, of course. It's R-O-X-A-N-N-A.
Student A: Thanks!

  H Listen and write the instructions. Then, give the instructions to a partner.

CD 1
TR 14

1. <u>Stand up.</u>

2. <u>Sit down.</u>

3. <u>Open your book to page 33.</u>

4. <u>Say your address.</u>

5. <u>Repeat your address.</u>

6. <u>Close your book, look at the teacher, and say hello to the teacher.</u>

My Dictionary

Make flash cards to improve your vocabulary.

1. Choose four new words from this unit.
2. Write each word on an index card or on a sheet of paper.
3. On the back of the index card or paper, draw a picture, find and write a sentence from the book with the word, and write the page number.
4. Study the words.

birth date

His birth date is July 2, 1977.   page P4

Learner Log

Circle how well you learned each item and write the page number where you learned it.

1. I can greet friends and describe feelings.

   Yes   Maybe   No   Page _____

2. I can complete a registration form.

   Yes   Maybe   No   Page _____

3. I can follow classroom instructions.

   Yes   Maybe   No   Page _____

Rank what you like to do best from 1 to 6. 1 is your favorite activity. Your teacher will help you.

_____ Practice listening

_____ Practice speaking

_____ Practice reading

_____ Practice writing

_____ Learn new words

_____ Learn grammar

In the next unit, I want to practice more

_____.

Presentation 1

My Dictionary

7-10 mins.

Go over the steps of My Dictionary as a class.

Practice 1

5-7 mins.

Do the dictionary activity as a class before students work on their own for at least the first few units of the book to ensure that students understand what to do.

Evaluation 1

5 mins.

Ask students to share their cards.

Presentation 2

5 mins.

Learner Log

Go over the concepts of the Learner Log. Make sure students understand the concepts and how to complete the log including circling the answers, finding page numbers where the concept is taught, and ranking favorite activities.

Teaching Tip

Learner Logs

Learner Logs function to help students in many different ways.

1. They serve as part of the review process.
2. They help students to gain confidence and to document what they have learned. Consequently, students see that they are progressing in their learning.
3. They provide students with a tool that they can use over and over to check and recheck their understanding of the target language. In this way, students become independent learners.

Practice 2

10-15 mins.

Ask students to complete the Learner Log.

Evaluation 2

2 mins.

Go over the Learner Log with students.

Application 2

5-7 mins.

Ask students to record their favorite lesson or page in the unit.

Assessment

Use the Stand Out 2 Assessment CD-ROM with Exam*View*® to create a posttest for the Pre-Unit.

Instructor's Notes

_____

_____

_____

_____

_____

_____

_____

_____

_____

_____

_____

_____

_____

_____

_____

_____

_____

_____

_____

_____

_____

_____

_____

_____

Objective: Ask for and give personal information
Grammar: Simple present: *live* and *be*
Pronunciation: /v/, final /s/, question intonation
Academic Strategies: Predicting, classifying, peer-editing
Vocabulary: Personal information words: *marital status, age, residence, nationality, old*

AGENDA

Practice greetings.
Ask: Where are you from?
Ask for more personal information.
Practice the simple present tense.
Talk in groups.

RESOURCES

Activity Bank: Unit 1, Lesson 1, Worksheets 1–2
Reading and Writing Challenge: Unit 1
Grammar Challenge: Unit 1, Challenge 1

■ 1.5 hour classes ■ 2.5 hour classes ■ 3⁺ hour classes

Audio: CD 1, Track 15
Heinle Picture Dictionary: Wave, Greet, Smile, pages 40–41

Stand Out 2 Assessment CD-ROM with Exam*View*®

 Preassessment (optional)

Use the Stand Out 2 Assessment CD-ROM with Exam*View*® to create a pretest for Unit 1.

Warm-up and Review   10-15 mins.

In the United States, we shake hands by firmly curling our fingers around the other person's hand and maintaining eye contact. It is important to teach this style of handshake by modeling it and explaining it verbally. Be aware that students may have a different concept of what is an appropriate handshake.

Ask students to walk around the room and greet other students as they shake hands. Review students' names by standing near or behind a student and asking: *What is his/her name?* Challenge individuals to try and say the names of all of the students in the class.

Introduction   2 mins. ■ ■ ■

Go over the agenda with students and state the objective: *Today we will ask for and give personal information.*

Presentation 1   10-15 mins. ■ ■ ■

On the board, write: *Where are you from?* Ask a few students where they are from. Expect one-word answers. Pointing to yourself, say: *I'm from [your country].* Continue to ask individual students where they are from. Reiterate students' responses by asking: *Where's he/she from?* Model: *He's from [student's country]* or *She's from [student's country].* Ask individuals to try to name the countries of each student who has responded.

Ⓐ **Look at the map. Draw a line from your country to where you live now.**

Ask students to open their books. Look at the map of the United States and label the location of the school together as a class. Identify some of the students' native countries. Ask them to draw a line from their countries to the school location.

Practice 1   3-5 mins.

Ⓑ **Write.**

Ask students to look at the map and complete the sentences with the information on the map.

Evaluation 1   3-5 mins.

Ask volunteers to write the complete sentences from Exercise B on the board.

Teaching Tip

Volunteers

The first time you invite students to the board, you may want to ask for volunteers. Once all the students understand the activity, call on some of the quieter students to respond. Getting students up in the front of the classroom is a great way to help prepare them for the classroom presentations that they will be giving at the end of each unit.

STANDARDS CORRELATIONS

CASAS: 0.1.1, 0.1.4, 0.2.1, 7.5.6 (See CASAS Competency List on pages 169–175.)
SCANS: Information Acquire and evaluate information
Basic Skills Writing, listening, speaking
Personal Qualities Sociability
EFF: Communication Speak so others can understand, listen actively

UNIT 1 Everyday Life

GOALS

➤ Ask for and give personal information
➤ Identify family relationships
➤ Describe people

➤ Interpret and write schedules
➤ Interpret information about weather

LESSON 1

Where are you from?

GOAL ➤ Ask for and give personal information

Vocabulary / Grammar
Life Skills
Academic / Pronunciation

A Look at the map. Draw a line from your country to where you live now.

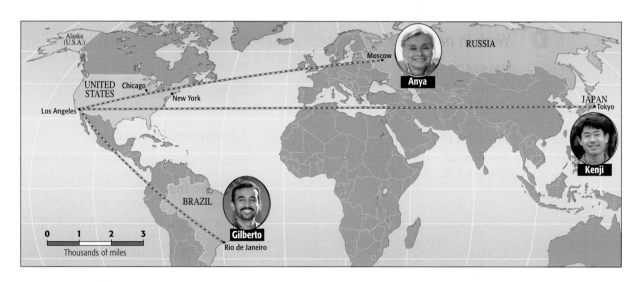

B Write.

1. Kenji is from _____Tokyo, Japan_____. He lives in _____Los Angeles_____.

2. Anya is from _____Moscow, Russia_____. _____She lives in Los Angeles._____

3. Gilberto _____is from Rio de Janeiro, Brazil_____. _____He lives in Los Angeles._____

4. I'm from _____. I live in _____.

GOAL ➤ **Ask for and give personal information**

Vocabulary · Grammar · Life Skills · Academic · Pronunciation

C Look at the words in the box. Then, complete the chart below with the words.

25 years old	divorced	single
city	married	state
~~country~~	old	young

Marital status	Age	Residence
divorced	25 years old	country
married	old	city
single	young	state

D Work in pairs. Ask and answer questions about the students below.

EXAMPLE:
Student A: Where is Kenji from?
Student B: He is from Japan.
Student A: How old is he?
Student B: He is 22 years old.
Student A: Is he married?
Student B: No, he is single.

Pronunciation

Question Intonation

Yes/No questions have rising intonation.

➤ Is he married?

Information questions have falling intonation.

➤ Where is Kenji from?

Kenji
Single
22 years old
Tokyo, Japan

Anya
Married
68 years old
Moscow, Russia

Gilberto
Single
30 years old
Rio de Janeiro, Brazil

Marie
Divorced
32 years old
Port-au-Prince, Haiti

Presentation 2
10–15 mins.

With students' books closed, write *Personal Information* on the board. Ask students what personal information is and ask for examples. Students may come up with information such as age, nationality, name, address, phone number, and so on. Write their ideas on the board.

C Look at the words in the box. Then, complete the chart below with the words.

Go over the words and phrases with students and confirm that they understand all of them. Help them with the headings in the chart. They may be unfamiliar with the terms *marital status* and *residence*. Complete the chart as a class. Since students are doing this activity with the instructor, it is considered part of the presentation stage.

Review the rising intonation used in *yes/no* questions. Contrast it with falling intonation used in information questions. Point out examples of these two types of questions by going over the conversation in Exercise D in preparation for the practice.

Ask students to briefly close their books. Write *name, age, marital status,* and *native country* on the board. Ask students to help you form questions about this information. They have just seen examples in the conversation, so they should be able to do this.

Practice 2
7–10 mins.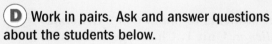

D Work in pairs. Ask and answer questions about the students below.

Ask students to do this activity with a partner. When you feel that students have had ample time to practice, ask them to cover the conversation and practice it again without looking.

Evaluation 2
7–10 mins.

Observe students doing the activity and then, invite students to demonstrate their questions and answers in front of the class.

Teaching Tip

Timing

All classes are multilevel in one aspect or another. It is probable that in every activity some students will finish early. There are several strategies to deal with this. In this particular activity, encourage students to continue practicing until you tell them to stop. They should just repeat the exercise again. Another thing you can do here is to ask them to change partners.

Here are more ideas for students who finish an activity early:

1. If students in pairs or in groups have answered a question that has one answer, don't confirm that they have the right answer. Instead, pose the question: *Are you sure?*
2. Have additional worksheets ready for students who finish early. There are worksheets on the Activity Bank CD-ROM that are available as an extension to many of the activities in the student book.
3. Help students who take longer to finish so they can wrap up the activity faster than they would without your help.
4. Ask the students who finish early questions about their learning and try to get at needs they may have that you are not aware of.

Presentation 3   10–15 mins.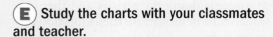

E Study the charts with your classmates and teacher.

Students may need help with the pronunciation of /v/. Many languages don't have this sound or have something similar but not written the same way. They may also have difficulties pronouncing the third-person singular /s/ definitively enough.

Pronunciation

/v/

There are many ways to teach /v/. First, remember that many languages don't have this sound. Some languages have a similar sound, but it is not written with the letter *v*, a difference that can cause confusion.

One approach to introducing /v/ is to teach the points of articulation. The top teeth are slightly over the bottom lip. This explanation alone is not sufficient, however, because the same articulation points are used to create /f/. Many students can already pronounce /f/ because their languages have the sound and, furthermore, Latin-based languages use the letter *f* to represent it. Ask students to pronounce an /f/ sound and attach a word to it, such as *Frank* or *farm*, or even *pharmacy*. Ask students to put two fingers on their voice boxes and make them vibrate as they do when they pronounce /m/.

Note: Many pronunciation books would recommend that you contrast /b/ with /v/. Both of these sounds are voiced so you would invert the previous explanation. Start with the voiced sounds and then show students the points of articulation.

Teaching Tip

Grammar principles

1. Remember that most students don't master grammar structures the first time they are exposed to them. Therefore, we recycle them and introduce them at various times in the *Stand Out* curriculum.
2. Not all students will be able to interpret a chart the first time they see one.
3. Drilling can be an effective tool; however, overusing it diminishes the effect of the context.

Practice 3   5–7 mins. ■

F Listen to the information about Mario and Lien. Complete the sentences.

Before playing the recording, show students how they should predict before listening. Have them go through the exercise first and try to guess at the answers. They should be able to do several of them. Then, play the recording.

 Listening Script   CD 1, Track 15

1. *Lien is from Ho Chi Minh City, Vietnam.*
2. *She is 28 years old.*
3. *She lives in Los Angeles.*
4. *Mario is 33 years old.*
5. *He also lives in Los Angeles.*
6. *He is from Mexico.*
7. *Mario and Lien are not married. They are friends.*

Evaluation 3   3–5 mins. ■

Ask students to peer-edit their work and then, go over the answers as a class.

Application   5–7 mins. ■ ■ ■

G In a group, ask classmates for personal information.

Ask students to try to ask questions without referring to the book whenever possible. Encourage groups to peer-correct. Also, have the person asking the questions stand so you can better monitor the activity in each group.

 Refer students to *Stand Out 2 Grammar Challenge*, Unit 1, Challenge 1 for more practice with the simple present.

Activity Bank

Unit 1, Lesson 1, Worksheet 1: Applications
Unit 1, Lesson 1, Worksheet 2: Simple Present: *Be* and *Live*

GOAL ➤ **Ask for and give personal information**

 E Study the charts with your classmates and teacher.

Simple Present: *Live*			
Subject	**Verb**	**Information**	**Example sentence**
I, we, you, they	live	in Los Angeles in California in the United States	I **live** in Los Angeles. You **live** in Los Angeles, California.
he, she	lives		He **lives** in the United States. She **lives** in Mexico.

Simple Present: *Be*			
Subject	**Verb**	**Information**	**Example sentence**
I	am	from Mexico single divorced 23 years old	I **am** from Mexico.
we, you, they	are		We **are** single. You **are** 23 years old.
he, she	is		He **is** divorced. She **is** from Vietnam.

CD 1
TR 15

F Listen to the information about Mario and Lien.
Complete the sentences.

Lien

1. Lien _____is_____ from Ho Chi Minh City, Vietnam.

2. She _____is_____ 28 years old.

3. She _____lives_____ in _____Los Angeles_____.

4. Mario is _____33_____ years old.

5. He also _____lives_____ in Los Angeles.

6. He _____is_____ from _____Mexico_____.

7. Mario and Lien are not married. They _____are friends_____.

Mario

 G In a group, ask classmates for personal information.

Kenji's family

GOAL ➤ Identify family relationships

  A Read and listen to Kenji's story.

CD 1
TR 16

My name is Kenji Nakamura. I have a wonderful family. We live in the United States. I have one sister and two brothers. I also have uncles and an aunt here. My father has two brothers and no sisters. My mother has one brother and one sister. My grandparents are in Japan. I'm sad because they are not here with my family.

How many people are in Kenji's family?

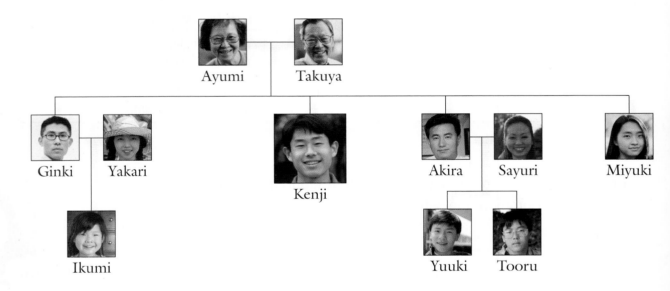

B Complete the sentences.

1. Kenji has _____one_____ sister.

2. Kenji has _____two_____ brothers.

3. Kenji's father has _____two_____ brothers and _____no_____ sisters.

4. Kenji's mother has _____one_____ sister and _____one_____ brother.

5. Kenji has _____one_____ aunt and _____three_____ uncles.

AT-A-GLANCE PREP

Objective: Identify family relationships
Grammar: Simple present: *have*
Pronunciation: /ð/
Academic Strategies: Focused listening, bar graphs, peer-editing
Vocabulary: Family relationship vocabulary

RESOURCES

Activity Bank: Unit 1, Lesson 2, Worksheets 1–3
Reading and Writing Challenge: Unit 1
Grammar Challenge: Unit 1, Challenge 2

Audio: CD 1, Tracks 16–17
Heinle Picture Dictionary: Family, pages 26–27

■ 1.5 hour classes ■ 2.5 hour classes ■ 3+ hour classes

AGENDA

Ask for personal information.
Read about families.
Learn new vocabulary.
Use have and has in the simple
  present tense.
Write sentences and make a graph.

Warm-up and Review   8–12 mins. ■■■

Ask individual students where they are from. With each response, ask the student if he or she has family in their native country or if all of their family members are in the U.S. For example: *Where is your family—in the U.S. or in your country?* Tell students that you have [number of] sisters and [number of] brothers and they are in [name of country or city]. Write these sentences about yourself on the board.

Introduction   5 mins. ■■■

Write *families* on the board. Ask students if they have big families or small families. Find out what students consider big families and small families by asking them questions. Refer students to the agenda and go over each step. State the objective: *Today we will identify family relationships.*

Presentation 1   15–20 mins. ■■■

Ask students to look at the pictures at the top of the page. Ask: *How many people are in Kenji's family?* Tell students they are going to listen to a story about Kenji's family. Write *sisters* and *brothers* on the board. Ask students to close their books and listen for how many brothers and sisters Kenji has by applying focused listening techniques.

Play the recording. After listening, ask how many sisters and brothers Kenji has again. Play the recording again to confirm students' responses.

Ask students to open their books and go over the family tree. Discuss briefly the family vocabulary. More of this discussion will continue in Presentation 2.

Practice 1   7–10 mins. ■■■

A **Read and listen to Kenji's story.**

Ask students to read the story individually and then, do Exercise B.

 Listening Script   CD 1, Track 16

The listening script matches the paragraph in Exercise A.

B **Complete the sentences.**

Students should read and complete this activity by themselves.

Teaching Tip

Independent learners

Part of the *Stand Out* Mission Statement indicates that we are striving for students to become independent learners. Although the series encourages a lot of partner and group work and the application of cooperative learning techniques, there are times when students should do activities alone to build confidence in their own abilities.

Evaluation 1   7–10 mins. ■■■

Ask students to peer-edit their work and then go over the answers as a class.

STANDARDS CORRELATIONS

CASAS: 0.1.2, 0.2.1 (See CASAS Competency List on pages 169–175.)
SCANS: **Information** Organize and maintain information
Basic Skills Reading, writing, listening, speaking
Personal Qualities Sociability
EFF: **Communication** Read with understanding, speak so others can understand, listen actively

Presentation 2   15–20 mins.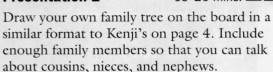

Draw your own family tree on the board in a similar format to Kenji's on page 4. Include enough family members so that you can talk about cousins, nieces, and nephews.

C **Study the new words with your classmates and teacher.**

Help students understand these words by referring to your family tree on the board. Use yours instead of Kenji's on page 4 so that students can practice with Kenji's later.

Review the sound /ð/.

Quiz students on your family tree as they will be quizzed in Exercise D. Point out two people and ask for their relationship to each other.

Practice 2   8–10 mins.

D **Look at the family tree on page 4. Write the correct words under each picture.**

Evaluation 2   5–7 mins.

Ask students questions like those in Exercise E.

E **Ask and answer questions about Kenji's family tree.**

Remind students to use *they are* or *they're*. Monitor students as they practice to determine if they understand and are ready for the next practice.

Teaching Tip

Evaluation

The evaluation step of the lesson is extremely important. Although we often don't elaborate in the Lesson Planner, remember that this step allows you to determine if students are ready to go on to the next activity or if additional practice is necessary. The evaluation ultimately determines if you can be confident to leave students to do the application on their own.

Instructor's Notes

_____
_____
_____
_____
_____
_____
_____
_____
_____
_____
_____
_____
_____
_____
_____
_____
_____
_____
_____
_____
_____
_____

GOAL ➤ **Identify family relationships**

C Study the new words with your classmates and teacher.

parents	daughter	aunt	grandfather
father	son	uncle	grandmother
mother	brother	niece	grandson
husband	sister	nephew	granddaughter
wife		cousin	

D Look at the family tree on page 4. Write the correct words under each picture.

1.

grandfather / _granddaughter_

2.

husband / _wife_

3.

mother / _daughter_

4.

grandmother / _grandson_

5.

aunt / _niece_

6.

uncle / _nephew_

E Ask and answer questions about Kenji's family tree.

EXAMPLE: *Student A:* Who are Takuya and Ikumi?
           Student B: They are grandfather and granddaughter.

F Study the chart with your classmates and teacher.

Present Simple: *Have*			
Subject	**Verb**	**Information**	**Example sentence**
I, you, we, they	have	three brothers two sisters	I **have** three brothers. You **have** two sisters.
he, she	has	no cousins three sons	He **has** no cousins. She **has** three sons.

CD 1
TR 17

G Write the correct form of *have*. Then, listen and write the missing information.

1. Thanh ___has___ ___three___ sisters.

2. I ___have___ ___three___ brothers.

3. Ricardo and Patty ___have___ ___three___ children.

4. Orlando, you ___have___ ___38___ cousins.

5. Maria ___has___ ___two___ sisters.

6. We ___have___ ___one___ child.

H Talk to four classmates and write sentences. Then, make a bar graph about your classmates. (Answers will vary.)

EXAMPLE:
You: How many brothers and sisters do you have?
Juan: I have three brothers and two sisters.

1. Juan has three brothers and two sisters.

2. _____

3. _____

4. _____

5. _____

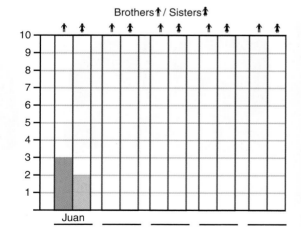

I Active Task. Design your own family tree and share it with the class.

Presentation 3   10–15 mins. ■■■

With students' books closed, write the following sentences on the board:

1. *Juan _____ three brothers and two sisters.*
2. *Natalie _____ two brothers and three sisters.*
3. *James _____ two brothers and no sisters.*
4. *Simon _____ one brother and one sister.*
5. *Natalie and James _____ _____ brothers each.*
6. *Simon and Natalie _____ _____ sisters each.*

Ask volunteers to complete the sentences. Then, make a bar graph like the one on the page and complete the graph as a class.

(F) **Study the chart with your classmates and teacher.**

Go over the graph based on what was learned in the presentation stage.

Practice 3   7–10 mins. ■

(G) **Write the correct form of *have*. Then, listen and write the missing information.**

 Listening Script   *CD 1, Track 17*

Thank you all for coming to the party. I want to see how much I know about each of you so I will start with Thanh and work my way around the room.

Thanh is a good friend. She lives in Seattle with her three sisters. I think my three brothers would be very interested in meeting them.

Ricardo and Patty, you have been married for four years and already have three children, right? Your children's names are Zack, Manny, and Courtney.

I think Orlando has the most cousins of any of us. I understand you have 38 cousins. Wow, I hope you know all their names.

Maria, you are a great niece to me. I appreciate how you and your two sisters worked so hard to make this party happen. Sophie and I are happy to be here with our only child so far, Colleen.

Teaching Tip

Repeat listening

It may be necessary with focused listening to replay the audio. You may ask students to compare answers before you play a recording a second and third time.

It is very difficult for students at this level to listen and write at the same time. Teach students the dictation strategy of listening to a recording completely before attempting to write anything. You may also wish to pause the recording when necessary to allow students plenty of time to write.

Evaluation 3   3–7 mins. ■

Go over the answers with students.

Application   10–15 mins. ■■■

(H) **Talk to four classmates and write sentences. Then, make a bar graph about your classmates.**

(I) **Active Task. Design your own family tree and share it with the class.**

 Refer students to *Stand Out 2 Grammar Challenge*, Unit 1, Challenge 2 for more practice with *have*.

Activity Bank

Unit 1, Lesson 2, Worksheet 1: Family Vocabulary
Unit 1, Lesson 2, Worksheet 2: *Have* and Family
Unit 1, Lesson 2, Worksheet 3: Family Tree

AT-A-GLANCE PREP

Objective: Describe people
Grammar: Comparative and superlative adjectives
Academic Strategies: Focused listening, paragraph writing, bar graphs
Vocabulary: Hair and eye color, height, weight

RESOURCES

Activity Bank: Unit 1, Lesson 3, Worksheets 1–2
Reading and Writing Challenge: Unit 1
Grammar Challenge: Unit 1, Challenge 3

■ 1.5 hour classes ■ 2.5 hour classes ■ 3⁺ hour classes

Audio: CD 1, Track 18
Heinle Picture Dictionary: Family, pages 26–27; Face and Hair, pages 32–33

Warm-up and Review   10-12 mins.

Ask students to make a family tree if they didn't do so in the previous lesson. If they did, ask them to share their family trees with a partner and talk about their families. There is a blank family tree on the Activity Bank CD-ROM (Unit 1, Lesson 2, Worksheet 3).

Introduction   15-20 mins. ■■■

Ask all the students in the class to stand. Then, ask all students with red hair to sit down. Some students may not understand at this point. If any students have red hair, point to their hair and ask them to sit down. Do the same with blond hair, brown hair, white hair, and black hair. Go over the agenda and state the objective: *Today we will describe people.*

Presentation 1   10-15 mins. ■■■

(A) Look at the picture and answer the questions in the box.

Discuss the picture of Kenji's class with your class. See how much vocabulary students already know related to physical descriptions. Review the vocabulary in the box and drill students. Identify

Teaching Tip

Questioning strategies

Research shows that some teachers are quick to answer their own questions if the answers don't come within a few seconds. Try to allow students to answer even if it takes them some time to respond. The silence in the room often prompts a student to answer. Encourage students by praising them for making the effort even when they don't answer as completely as you may like.

students in the class and in the picture who may meet the descriptions. Make special note of the verbs to use with each type of description.

Before students do the practice, you may wish to review the conjugation of *have.*

A common error students make is omitting the second verb when trying to combine descriptions. For example, they may write: *Dalva is short and green eyes.* Show students the correct way to make these sentences. You may take this opportunity to teach compound sentences with the conjunction *and.*

Practice 1   10-15 mins.

(B) Write sentences about the students in the picture. Describe their hair, eyes, height, and weight. Use the words from the boxes above.

Evaluation 1   10-15 mins.

Ask volunteers to write their sentences on the board. As a class, look at the descriptions on the board and see if all students agree. Some may not agree, for example, about eye color, or if someone is short or average height. These discrepancies of opinions are appropriate. Presentation 2 will give students concrete answers.

STANDARDS CORRELATIONS

CASAS: 0.1.2, 1.1.4, 4.8.1, 4.8.6 (See CASAS Competency List on pages 169–175.)
SCANS: Information Acquire and evaluate information, organize and maintain information, interpret and communicate information
Interpersonal Participate as a member of a team, teach others, negotiate to arrive at a decision
Basic Skills Reading, writing, listening, speaking
EFF: Communication Read with understanding, convey ideas in writing, speak so others can understand, listen actively, observe critically
Decision Making Solve problems and make decisions
Interpersonal Cooperate with others, resolve conflict and negotiate, guide others

Kenji's class

GOAL ➤ **Describe people**

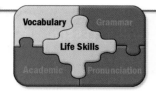

A Look at the picture and answer the questions in the box.

How many students are in Kenji's class?
Who is tall? Who has blond hair?

He *is* tall and average weight.

Height: tall, short, average height

Weight: thin, heavy, average weight

She *has* brown eyes and black hair.

Eyes: brown, blue, green, gray, hazel

Hair: black, brown, blond, red, gray, white

B Write sentences about the students in the picture. Describe their hair, eyes, height, and weight. Use the words from the boxes above. (Answers will vary. Sample answers are given.)

EXAMPLE: Dalva has green eyes and blond hair.

1. Mario is short and has black hair.

2. Anya has white hair and blue eyes.

3. Lien is tall and thin.

4. Steve is tall and has blue eyes.

LESSON **3**   **GOAL** ➤ **Describe people**

  C Listen and complete the bar graph about Kenji's class. Write sentences.

CD 1
TR 18

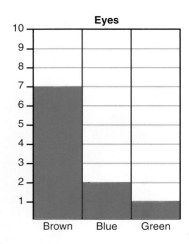

Eyes

1. Seven students have brown eyes.

2. Two students have blue eyes.

3. One student has green eyes.

D Look at the picture on page 7. In a group, fill in the bar graphs about Kenji's class.
(Answers will vary. Sample answers are given.)

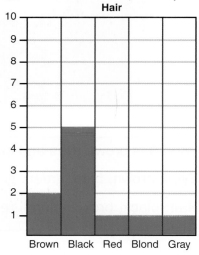

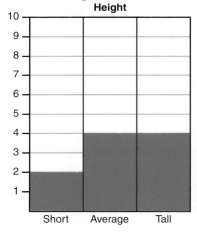

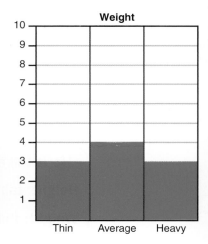

 E Look at the picture on page 7. Describe a student from Kenji's class to your partner. Your partner will guess who it is.

EXAMPLE: *Student A:* He is short and heavy. Guess who.
            Student B: Mario?

Presentation 2   10–15 mins.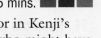

Read the bar graph about eye color in Kenji's class. See if students can identify who might have the different eye colors.

Prepare students for focused listening by going over the vocabulary again for hair color, height, and weight.

Teaching Tip

Presentation *vs.* practice

Here students are preparing to do the practice; however, it is completely teacher-directed. The teacher has control. The teacher asks the questions and students respond. The teacher describes the graph and helps students to complete it. The focused listening in this case is done more slowly and carefully because students are still in the presentation stage. In the practice stage, the teacher gives up some of the control to students. Practice can be individual work, pair work, or group work, but it is rarely the class working as a whole.

C Listen and complete the bar graph about Kenji's class. Write sentences.

 Listening Script   CD 1, Track 18

We have studied Kenji's class and come up with the following conclusions: There are seven students with brown eyes. Two students have a lighter complexion. They have blue eyes. There is even one student with green eyes. I think her name is Dalva.

Practice 2   7–10 mins.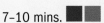

D Look at the picture on page 7. In a group, fill in the bar graphs about Kenji's class.

Evaluation 2   7–10 mins.

Ask groups to report to the class.

E Look at the picture on page 7. Describe a student from Kenji's class to your partner. Your partner will guess who it is.

Observe students doing the activity to confirm that they understand the task and are ready for the next task.

Presentation 3
10–15 mins. ■■■

Ask three students to come to the front of the room. Ask them to line up left to right by height. Write *height* on the board and allow students to figure out if they should go from the tallest to the shortest or vice versa.

Write *tall, taller, tallest* and *short, shorter, shortest* on the board. Avoid using students to describe *heavy*. You may wish to interject that the word *fat* is not used to describe people in social situations because it can be degrading.

F Read the chart with your classmates and teacher.

Provide example sentences for each of the adjectives given. Use the students in the picture on page 7 rather than students in the classroom. Write the examples on the board. Help students understand that the word *than* is necessary when using comparative adjectives. You may need to express here that your comparisons are opinions and they may not all agree.

Practice 3
7–10 mins. ■

G In a group, answer the questions about Kenji's class.

Because this activity relies on opinion, groups may disagree. Try to encourage members of each group to compromise as necessary so that they can prepare a report for the class.

Evaluation 3
7–10 mins. ■

Ask group representatives to report to the class.

For shorter classes, do Exercises H and I for homework.

Teaching Tip

Numbered heads

This is a technique where students in each group count off. Typically the members of the groups have different responsibilities. Student 1 might be the leader, Student 2 the timekeeper, Student 3 the secretary, and Student 4 the spokesperson.

Sometimes you might number heads and arbitrarily, as in this case, ask all students numbered *three* to report to the class. Next time, you might ask students numbered *two* to report. In this way, all students of a group will try to be prepared in case they are asked to report.

Application
5–7 mins. ■■■

H Read the paragraph.

Ask students to read the paragraph individually.

I Write a paragraph about your class. Use the paragraph above as a model.

Students will be expected to occasionally write paragraphs in *Stand Out 2*. There will usually be a model to guide them through it. By the end of the book, students will have been taught how to write clear, well-formatted paragraphs with less dependency on models. There are also additional opportunities in the *Stand Out Reading and Writing Challenge* to improve student writing.

📖 **Refer students to *Stand Out 2 Grammar Challenge*, Unit 1, Challenge 3 for more practice with comparative and superlative adjectives.**

Activity Bank 💿

Unit 1, Lesson 3, Worksheet 1: Describing People
Unit 1, Lesson 3, Worksheet 2: Describing People

Instructor's Notes

_____

_____

_____

_____

_____

_____

_____

_____

_____

_____

_____

_____

LESSON 3 **GOAL** ➤ **Describe people**

F Read the chart with your classmates and teacher.

Comparative and Superlative Adjectives		
Adjective	**Comparative adjective**	**Superlative adjective**
tall	taller	the tallest
short	shorter	the shortest
heavy	heavier	the heaviest
thin	thinner	the thinnest
old	older	the oldest
young	younger	the youngest

G In a group, answer the questions about Kenji's class.

1. Who is taller than Kenji? _____ Lien is taller than Kenji. _____

2. Who is the tallest in the class? _____ Lien is the tallest. _____

3. Who is shorter than Dalva? _____ Mario is shorter than Dalva. _____

4. Who is the thinnest in the class? _____ Lien is the thinnest. _____

5. Who is the youngest in the class? _____ Kenji is the youngest. _____

6. Who is older than the teacher? _____ Anya is older than the teacher. _____

H Read the paragraph.

   There are thirty students in my class. Twenty-five students have black hair. Five students have brown hair. The tallest student in the class is Francisco. The shortest is Eva. I think the youngest student is Nadia.

I Write a paragraph about your class. Use the paragraph above as a model.
(Answers will vary.)

_____

_____

_____

_____

My schedule

GOAL ➤ Interpret and write schedules

Who is Kenji talking to?
Where is she?

A Read and listen to the conversation.

CD 1
TR 19

Grandmother: What time is it there?
Kenji: It's 4:00 P.M.
Grandmother: What do you do at 4:00?
Kenji: I go to school.

September 22		September 22	
IN THE MORNING		2:00	
5:00 AM	wake up	2:30	
5:30		3:00	
6:00		3:30	
6:30	take Akiko to school	4:00	go to school
7:00		4:30	
7:30		5:00	
8:00		5:30	finish school
8:30			
9:00	go to work	**AT NIGHT**	
9:30		6:00 PM	
10:00		6:30	
10:30		7:00	
11:00		7:30	eat dinner
11:30		8:00	
		8:30	
IN THE AFTERNOON		9:00	
12:00 PM	take a lunch break	9:30	
12:30		10:00	
1:00		10:30	go to bed
1:30	take a 15-minute break		

B You are Kenji. Talk about your day with a partner.

EXAMPLE: *Grandmother:* What do you do at <u>4:00 P.M.</u>?
           Kenji: <u>I go to school.</u>

AT-A-GLANCE PREP

Objective: Interpret and write schedules
Grammar: Simple present, adverbs of frequency
Pronunciation: Final /s/, /z/
Academic Strategies: Focused listening, making graphs
Vocabulary: Days of the week, months, and time vocabulary

RESOURCES

Activity Bank: Unit 1, Lesson 4, Worksheets 1–4
Reading and Writing Challenge: Unit 1
Grammar Challenge: Unit 1, Challenge 4

Audio: CD 1, Tracks 19–20
Heinle Picture Dictionary: Daily Activities, pages 34–35

■ 1.5 hour classes ■ 2.5 hour classes ■ 3⁺ hour classes

AGENDA

Create bar graphs.
Read about Kenji's schedule.
Read about Gilberto's schedule.
Use the simple present tense.
Write a schedule.

Warm-up and Review 15-20 mins.

Provide students with bar graph templates from the template folder on the Activity Bank CD-ROM or have them create their own. Ask students to make graphs about the eye and hair color of the students in their class. Then, ask them to present the graphs to the class.

Introduction 5 mins.

If you have a personal planner, show the class your schedule for the day. Ask students what time they wake up in the morning and what time they go to bed. Share this information about yourself. Go over the agenda for the day and state the objective: *Today we will interpret and write schedules.*

Presentation 1 15-20 mins.

Ask students to open their books and look at the picture of Kenji and his grandmother. Ask the questions in the question box and any other questions you deem appropriate. Prepare students to listen.

A Read and listen to the conversation.

The conversation shown in the student book is embedded in a longer one. Ask students to listen for when the conversation that is written in the book starts.

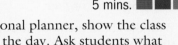 **Listening Script** CD 1, Track 19

Grandma: *Hello, Kenji. I miss you so much. It is lonely here in Japan without you.*
Kenji: *It is lonely here, too, Grandma. I miss you. How are you?*
Grandma: *I'm fine. I'm just tired. It is late here.*
Kenji: *Oh, I didn't know it was so late.*
Grandma: *What time is it there?*
Kenji: *It's 4:00 P.M.*
Grandma: *What do you do at 4:00?*
Kenji: *I go to school.*
Grandma: *Then you had better go. I will call you later. Bye.*
Kenji: *Bye, Grandma.*

Look over Kenji's planner as a class. Note where it says he goes to school at 4:00. Ask the question that is asked in Exercise B about different times.

Practice 1 15-20 mins.

B You are Kenji. Talk about your day with a partner.

Students pretend to be Kenji to avoid using the third person at this time.

Evaluation 1 5-7 mins.

Ask volunteers to demonstrate their conversation in front of the class.

STANDARDS CORRELATIONS

CASAS: 0.1.2, 0.2.1, 0.2.4, 2.3.1, 2.3.2, 7.4.7 (See CASAS Competency List on pages 169–175.)
SCANS: **Resources** Allocate time
Information Organize and maintain information, interpret and communicate information

Basic Skills Reading, writing, listening
Personal Qualities Self management
EFF: **Communication** Speak so others can understand, listen actively

Presentation 2   15–20 mins. ■■■

Review the days of the week with students. Since ordinal numbers have not been introduced in *Stand Out* up to now, this would be a good place to introduce them. Show students the shorthand way to write *first, second, third* (1st, 2nd, 3rd), and so on. The Activity Bank CD-ROM has additional practice with days of the week if a review is in order. The Activity Bank also contains practice with ordinal numbers (Unit 1, Lesson 4, Worksheets 3 and 4).

C Read the information on Gilberto's calendar. Then, listen and point to the day.

Ask students what activities Gilberto does for work, home, and school. Help students to understand the frequency adverbs by going over the calendar as a class. Write sentences on the board using *always, often, sometimes, rarely,* and *never* based on the calendar and the graphic about frequencies. Write the sentences in the third-person singular, such as: Gilberto *goes* to school *on Tuesday.* Underline the verbs in the third-person singular.

Show students how the third-person singular verb is different from the verb they used in the previous practice. Write *I* and transform the sentences that you have written on the board into first-person singular.

Listening Script   CD 1, Track 20

Gilberto is very busy every day. He has plenty to do. For example, tomorrow, on the ninth, he will help with the children early and still go to work. On Saturday the nineteenth, he will work overtime. This is good financially, but it is hard work. Gilberto plays soccer on Sundays and this gives him a break. Gilberto also studies English. He goes to school five days a week. He goes to school Monday, Tuesday, Wednesday, Thursday, and Friday. I don't know when he sleeps!

For shorter classes, ask students to do Exercises D and E for homework.

Practice 2   5–7 mins. ■■■

D Circle the answers to the questions about the calendar.

Ask students to complete this activity and Exercise E individually, not in pairs. You might present it to them as a test if you would like to discourage them from working together.

E Circle *True* or *False* for each sentence.

Evaluation 2   7–10 mins. ■■

Go over the answers to Exercises D and E and then ask the class *true* and *false* questions about Gilberto's calendar. Ask students to show one finger for *true* and two fingers for *false* instead of responding orally.

Teaching Tip

Monitoring student responses

An obvious way to monitor responses is to have students simply respond verbally with a word. Say: *true* or *false*.

With the above method, however, the stronger students sometimes overwhelm the students who need more time to think when asked for a verbal response. You may choose other ways for students to respond where students are less likely to "go along with the crowd." One such response method could be to use 3-by-5 index cards where students hold up the card with the correct answer facing you. Each card could read *true* on one side and *false* on the other. Or you can have students keep two cards that are different colors with them throughout the course where one color represents *true* and the other represents *false*. Students can use them again and again.

Another way is described in this lesson. Students will respond by showing the number of fingers that correspond to *true* or *false*.

GOAL ➤ **Interpret and write schedules**

  C Read the information on Gilberto's calendar. Then, listen and point to the day.

CD 1
TR 20

		Gilberto's Calendar				
SUNDAY	**MONDAY**	**TUESDAY**	**WEDNESDAY**	**THURSDAY**	**FRIDAY**	**SATURDAY**
		1 wake up at 5:00 A.M. go to school work	**2** wake up at 5:00 A.M. go to school help with children work	**3** wake up at 5:00 A.M. go to school work	**4** wake up at 5:00 A.M. go to school work	**5** wake up at 5:00 A.M. work overtime
6 wake up at 6:00 A.M. play soccer	**7** wake up at 5:00 A.M. go to school help with children work	**8** wake up at 5:00 A.M. go to school work	**9** wake up at 5:00 A.M. go to school help with children work	**10** wake up at 5:00 A.M. go to school work	**11** wake up at 5:00 A.M. go to school work	**12** wake up at 5:00 A.M. go to school take bus to the beach
13 wake up at 6:00 A.M. play soccer	**14** wake up at 5:00 A.M. go to school help with children work	**15** wake up at 5:00 A.M. go to school work	**16** wake up at 5:00 A.M. go to school help with children work	**17** wake up at 5:00 A.M. go to school work	**18** wake up at 5:00 A.M. go to school work	**19** wake up at 5:00 A.M. work overtime

never — 0%
rarely
sometimes — 50%
often
always — 100%

D Circle the answers to the questions about the calendar.

1. What does Gilberto do from Monday to Friday?
   a. He goes to the beach.
   b. *He works and goes to school.*
   c. He plays soccer.

2. What does he do every Monday and Wednesday?
   a. *He helps with the children.*
   b. He works overtime.
   c. He wakes up at 7:00 A.M.

E Circle *True* or *False* for each sentence.

1. Gilberto sometimes goes to work on Saturday.   *True*   False

2. He never plays soccer on Sunday.   True   *False*

3. He always gets up at 5:00 A.M.   True   *False*

4. He often helps with the children.   *True*   False

F Study the chart with your classmates and teacher.

Simple Present			
Subject	**Verb**	**Information**	**Example sentence**
I, you, we, they	eat	lunch	I **eat** lunch at 4:00 P.M.
	go	to school	You **go** to school at 8:00 A.M.
	help	with the children	We sometimes **help** with the children.
	play	soccer	They **play** soccer on Saturday.
he, she	eat**s***	lunch	He **eats** lunch at 12:00 P.M.
	goe**s****	to school	Nadia **goes** to school at 10:00 A.M.
	help**s***	with the children	Gilberto **helps** with the children.
	play**s****	soccer	She **plays** soccer on Friday.
Pronunciation: */s/ **/z/			

G Ask your partner questions about what Gilberto does.

EXAMPLE: *Student A:* What does Gilberto do on Monday?
Student B: He works and goes to school on Monday.

H Work with a partner. Ask: "What do you do in the morning?" Write your partner's schedule for the morning. Then, report to a group.

(Answers will vary.)

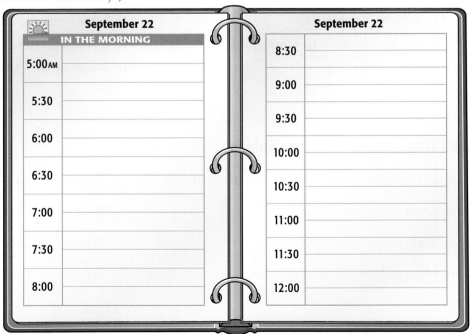

Presentation 3   15–20 mins.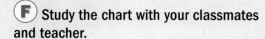

F **Study the chart with your classmates and teacher.**

Go over the chart with students. Also, help them with the correct pronunciation of the third-person singular *s*.

Review the difference between the subjects *he/she* and *I* carefully. Drill students on the verb forms in various ways. Use the example sentences in your drills.

Teaching Tip

Drills

Drills can be a good way to help students become familiar with vocabulary, grammar structures, and proper pronunciation. They also help students to gain confidence, especially when performing together with their classmates. However, drills should not be the sole practice or method used to help students memorize something or acquire a grammar structure. There are several ways to drill (choral repetition, substitution, build up, backward build up, etc.) If particular drills are overused, there is a risk of losing meaning for structure.

On the board, write the question using *does* that will be used in Exercise G. Ask students to help you create questions about the calendar on the previous page.

Practice 3   8–12 mins.

G **Ask your partner questions about what Gilberto does.**

It is intentional that students have to turn the page to see the calendar and to see the example of the conversation. Encourage students to do this activity without flipping to the model conversation, but by looking only at the calendar. When they can do this, they will have more confidence and not feel dependent on the book.

Evaluation 3   7–10 mins.

Monitor students' performance and confirm that they are using the third-person singular *s* and pronouncing it correctly. Ask a few volunteers to demonstrate their questions and answers in front of the class. Try to encourage students who haven't performed in front of the class in the past to try it this time.

Application   10–12 mins.

H **Work with a partner. Ask: "What do you do in the morning?" Write your partner's schedule for the morning. Then, report to a group.**

Ask students to complete the schedule and practice before they report to the group. There is also a blank planner page available on the Activity Bank CD-ROM (Unit 1, Lesson 4, Worksheet 1).

Refer students to *Stand Out 2 Grammar Challenge*, Unit 1, Challenge 4 for more practice with the simple present and frequency words.

Activity Bank

Templates: Bar graph
Unit 1, Lesson 4, Worksheet 1: Daily Planner
Unit 1, Lesson 4, Worksheet 2: Simple Present
Unit 1, Lesson 4, Worksheet 3: Review Calendars
Unit 1, Lesson 4, Worksheet 4: Ordinal Numbers

Instructor's Notes

_____

_____

_____

_____

_____

_____

_____

_____

_____

_____

_____

_____

Objective: Interpret information about weather
Grammar: Short *yes/no* answers
Pronunciation: Accented syllables
Academic Strategies: Focused listening, prediction
Vocabulary: Weather vocabulary

RESOURCES

Activity Bank: Unit 1, Lesson 5, Worksheets 1–2
Reading and Writing Challenge: Unit 1
Grammar Challenge: Unit 1, Challenge 5

■ 1.5 hour classes ■ 2.5 hour classes ■ 3⁺ hour classes

Audio: CD 1, Track 21
Heinle Picture Dictionary: Weather, pages 166–167; The World, pages 174–175

AGENDA

Write your schedule.
Discuss weather vocabulary.
Listen to a weather report.
Ask about the weather.

Warm-up and Review   15-20 mins. ■■■

Ask students to write out their own planner page and share it with a partner. There is a blank planner page available on the Activity Bank CD-ROM (Unit 1, Lesson 4, Worksheet 1).

Introduction   5-7 mins. ■■■

Ask the class: *How's the weather today?* Ask if it's *hot* or *cold* and demonstrate these words with body language. Ask students about their own countries while pointing to them on a world map. Ask: *Is it hot or cold in your country today?* State the objective: *Today we are going to interpret information about weather.* Read through the agenda with the students.

Presentation 1   15-20 mins. ■■■

Go over the vocabulary with students from the box in Exercise A. Make sure they understand each word and can pronounce it correctly. Make gestures that represent each type of weather and quiz students on the different types.

 A **Write the correct word below each picture.**

Each picture is numbered. This will give you an opportunity to quiz students and help them use focused listening. Ask students to show the number of fingers that represent the number of the picture when you say the words.

Go over the grammar box as a review.

Practice 1   8-12 mins. ■■■

 B **Ask your partner questions about the weather.**

Go over the example with students before they attempt this exercise.

Teaching Tip

Building focused-listening skills

Every lesson in this level has an activity that requires students to use focused-listening skills. Generally, we supply a conversation or denser text than students can probably understand completely to allow them to practice listening for important target vocabulary and information. In fact, we will do this later in the lesson. However, here we are providing an opportunity to help students learn gradually and develop this skill at a pace you set.

Follow these steps:

1. Say the word in isolation and ask students to respond by showing the number of fingers that corresponds to the number of the picture. Do this until you are confident that most students are able to do it without relying on their classmates.
2. Say words in the context of sentences and encourage students to repeat.
3. Say words in discourse slowly at first and then speed up, allowing students to respond appropriately at a faster pace.

Evaluation 1   ■■■

Check that students understand by observing them as they do the practice.

STANDARDS CORRELATIONS

CASAS: 1.1.5, 2.3.3 (See CASAS Competency List on pages 169-175.)
SCANS: **Information** Acquire and evaluate information, interpret and communicate information
Basic Skills Listening, speaking
EFF: **Communication** Speak so others can understand, listen actively

---

How is the weather today?

GOAL ➤ Interpret information about weather

A Write the correct word below each picture.

| sunny | rainy | cloudy | snowy | windy | foggy |

1.
    rainy

2.
    sunny

3.
    windy

4.
    snowy

5.
    cloudy

6.
    foggy

B Ask your partner questions about the weather.

EXAMPLE:
Student A points to the sunny picture.

Student A: How's the weather today?
Student B: It's sunny.

Student B points to the snowy picture.

Student B: Is it cold today?
Student A: Yes, it is.

Short Answers
Yes, it is.
No, it isn't.

GOAL ➤ **Interpret information about weather**

  C Listen to the world weather report and write the correct temperatures on the map.

CD 1
TR 21

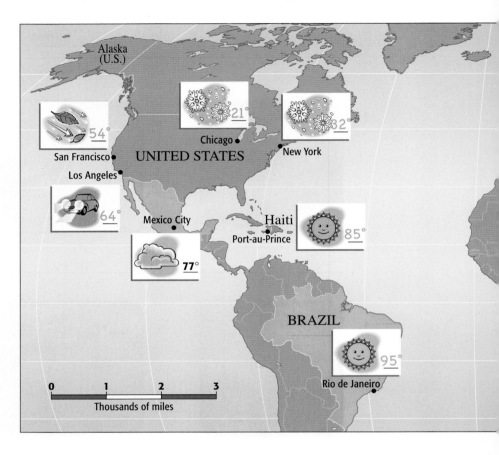

D Work in pairs. Ask your partner questions about the map to fill in your chart. Then, switch roles.

EXAMPLE: *Student A:* How's the weather in Tokyo?
          Student B: It's rainy and 46 degrees.

Student A

City	Weather	Degrees
Tokyo	rainy	46°
Moscow	cold	15°
Ho Chi Minh City	cloudy	90°
Rio de Janeiro	sunny	95°

Presentation 2   15–20 mins.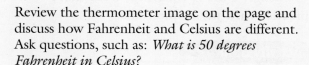

Review the thermometer image on the page and discuss how Fahrenheit and Celsius are different. Ask questions, such as: *What is 50 degrees Fahrenheit in Celsius?*

Look at the map with students. Help them see what information is already provided. Ask them to predict the weather in a few places. Help them to say the phrase as it is in Exercise D: *It's rainy and 46 degrees.*

Practice 2   8–12 mins.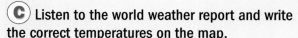

C Listen to the world weather report and write the correct temperatures on the map.

This is a difficult activity. Consider having students listen in groups. Play the recording once and allow students to discuss and compare answers. Then, play it a second and possibly a third time. Another more complicated approach, but better for team building, might be to have different people in the group listen only for specific places.

Listening Script   CD 1, Track 21

Hello, everyone! Today's international weather map shows that Mexico City is cloudy with temperatures around 77 degrees. A beautiful day in the city of Port-au-Prince! Port-au-Prince is sunny with a warm temperature of 85 degrees. To the south, Rio de Janeiro is a sunny 95 degrees. We see that Ho Chi Minh City is cloudy with a temperature of 90 degrees, and the weather in Tokyo is rainy with a daytime temperature of 46 degrees. Wear a warm coat if you're in Moscow! Moscow is cloudy and very cold at a temperature of 15 degrees. Today's national weather report shows that New York City is snowy with a temperature of 32 degrees. Chicago is also snowy today with a cold temperature of 21 degrees. Los Angeles is foggy today with temperatures around 64 degrees, and San Francisco is windy with daytime temperatures of around 54 degrees. That's all for now. We'll be back with international weather updates in one hour.

Evaluation 2   5–7 mins.

Go over each answer and be prepared to play the recording again. Be aware that it is possible that students will hear *50 degrees* instead of *15 degrees*. Take this opportunity to help them hear the difference and briefly drill them on the two numbers.

Pronunciation

15 and 50

There are significant differences between *15* and *50* in pronunciation. To simplify the explanation, however, it is productive to concentrate on only one difference. In this case try focusing on the accented syllables—FIFty and fifTEEN. Write *50* in the top right-hand corner of the board and *15* in the opposite one. Say the words first in isolation and ask students to point to the one you are saying, Then, use them in sentences and finally in discourse.

D Work in pairs. Ask your partner questions about the map to fill in your chart. Then, switch roles.

See Presentation and Practice 3 on page 15a.

Instructor's Notes

_____
_____
_____
_____
_____
_____
_____
_____
_____
_____
_____
_____
_____
_____
_____
_____
_____

Presentation 3

7-10 mins. ■■■ Refer students to *Stand Out 2 Grammar Challenge*, Unit 1, Challenge 5 for more practice with *yes/no* questions.

The practice (Exercise D) is an information-gap activity. This activity works best if students cover the information their partner will give them. Carefully walk students through the procedure and use a few students as models.

Activity Bank 💿

Unit 1, Lesson 5, Worksheet 1: Weather Report
Unit 1, Lesson 5, Worksheet 2: Simple Present

Teaching Tip

Facilitating information-gap activities

Information-gap activities are activities that allow one student to give new information to another. In the *Stand Out* approach, there are many opportunities to do these types of activities.

Sometimes the procedure of this activity is difficult to understand for students. There are several things to do to help students understand.

1. Model the activity several times with several different students.
2. Make sure students know who is Student A and who is Student B. To do this, ask all Student As to stand up.
3. Monitor the practice. If a pair of students is having trouble, do the exercise with them.
4. Do the activity in groups of four with at least one student who can direct the others. In groups of four, one pair goes first and the other listens. Then, the other pair performs.

Practice 3

10-15 mins. ■

D Work in pairs. Ask your partner questions about the map to fill in your chart. Then, switch roles.

Evaluation 3

5-7 mins. ■

Draw the charts on the board and ask students to come up and write their answers.

As each student fills in the information, have him or her say the statement as the example given in Exercise D.

Application

5-7 mins. ■■■

E Ask about your partner's native country.

Have students do this activity and report to a group.

Instructor's Notes

_____
_____
_____
_____
_____
_____
_____
_____
_____
_____
_____
_____
_____
_____
_____
_____
_____
_____
_____
_____
_____
_____

GOAL ➤ Interpret information about weather

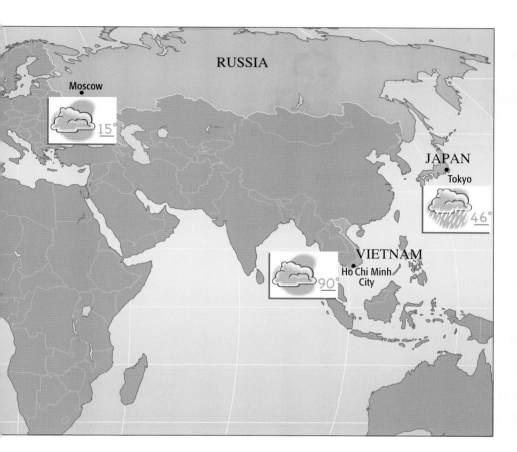

RUSSIA

Moscow

15°

JAPAN

Tokyo

46°

VIETNAM

Ho Chi Minh City

90°

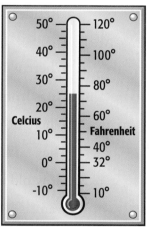

50°	120°
40°	100°
30°	80°
20°	60°
Celcius	
10°	Fahrenheit
	40°
0°	32°
-10°	10°

Student B

City	Weather	Degrees
Mexico City	cloudy	77°
Los Angeles	foggy	64°
New York	snowy	32°
Port-au-Prince	warm	85°

 E Ask about your partner's native country.

Country: _____

Weather	Degrees

Review

A Look at the information about Ivan and Anya. Answer the questions in complete sentences. (Lesson 1)

 **Ivan**

 **Anya**

Married
70 years old
Moscow, Russia
Residence: California

Married
68 years old
Moscow, Russia
Residence: California

1. Where is Ivan from?

   He is from __Moscow, Russia__.

2. Where do Anya and Ivan live?

   They __live in California__.

3. How old is Ivan?

   Ivan __is 70 years old__.

4. Who is older, Ivan or Anya?

   __Ivan is older than Anya.__

5. Are Ivan and Anya married?

   __They are married.__

B Write *live* or *lives*. (Lesson 1)

1. Gilberto and Lien __live__ in Los Angeles.

2. We __live__ with our mother and father.

3. I __live__ in California.

4. Mario __lives__ in a house.

5. Lien __lives__ in Vietnam in the summer and Los Angeles in the winter.

6. You __live__ in the United States.

Objective: All unit objectives
Grammar: All unit grammar
Academic Strategies: Reviewing, evaluating, developing study skills
Vocabulary: All unit vocabulary

■ 1.5 hour classes   ■ 2.5 hour classes   ■ 3⁺ hour classes

AGENDA

Discuss unit objectives.
Complete the review.
Do My Dictionary.
Evaluate and reflect on progress.

Warm-up and Review   10–15 mins.

Ask students to write their schedule on a 3-by-5 index card without their names. Collect the cards and pass them out to different people. Ask students to find the author of their cards by asking questions. Write example questions on the board and show them how to do this activity by practicing with a few students. The questions would be based on the card, such as: *When do you eat breakfast? What time do you eat breakfast?*

Introduction   2 mins.

Write all the objectives on the board from Unit 1. Show students the first page of the unit and say the five objectives. Explain that today they will review the whole unit.

Note: Depending on the length of the term, you may decide to have students do Presentation 1 and Practice 1 for homework and then review student work as either the warm-up or another class activity.

Presentation 1   10–15 mins.

This presentation will cover the first three pages of the review. Quickly go to the first page of each lesson. Discuss the objective of each. Ask simple questions to remind students of what they have learned.

Practice 1   15–20 mins.

(A) Look at the information about Ivan and Anya. Answer the questions in complete sentences. (Lesson 1)

(B) Write *live* or *lives*. (Lesson 1)

Teaching Tip

Recycling/Review

The review and the project that follows are part of the recycling/review process. Students at this level often need to be reintroduced to concepts to solidify what they have learned. Many concepts are learned and forgotten while learning other new concepts. This is because students learn but are not necessarily ready to acquire language concepts.

Therefore, it becomes very important to review and to show students how to review on their own. It is also important to recycle the new concepts in different contexts.

STANDARDS CORRELATIONS

CASAS: 0.1.1, 0.1.2, 0.1.4, 0.2.1, 0.2.4, 1.1.4, 1.1.5, 2.3.1, 2.3.2, 2.3.3 (See CASAS Competency List on pages 169–175.)
SCANS: **Information** Acquire and evaluate information, organize and maintain information

Basic Skills Reading, writing, speaking
Personal Qualities Responsibility, self-management
EFF: **Communication** Speak so others can understand
Lifelong Learning Take responsibility for learning, reflect and evaluate

Practice 1 (continued)

C Look at Anya's family tree and write the relationships. (Lesson 2)

D Describe Mario on page 7. Describe his height, weight, age, hair, and eyes. (Lesson 3)

C Look at Anya's family tree and write the relationships. (Lesson 2)

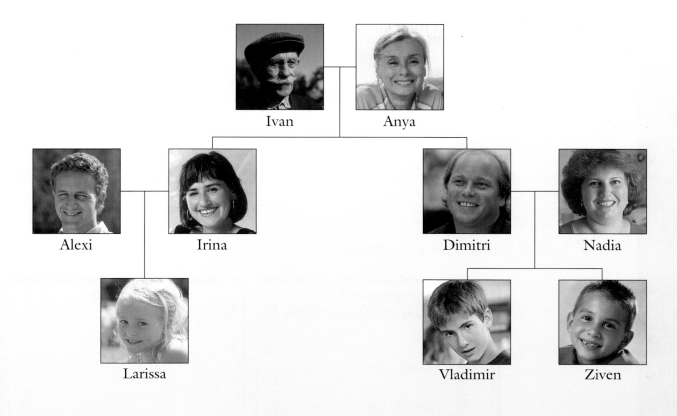

Ivan   Anya

Alexi   Irina   Dimitri   Nadia

Larissa   Vladimir   Ziven

1. Dimitri and Nadia are _____husband_____ and _____wife_____.
2. Dimitri and Vladimir are _____father_____ and _____son_____.
3. Nadia and Larissa are _____aunt_____ and _____niece_____.
4. Irina and Larissa are _____mother_____ and _____daughter_____.
5. Ivan and Vladimir are _____grandfather_____ and _____grandson_____.

D Describe Mario on page 7. Describe his height, weight, age, hair, and eyes. (Lesson 3)

Mario is short and heavy. He has black hair and brown eyes.

He is young.

_____

_____

_____

_____

Review

E Write the weather word under the picture. (Lesson 5)

1. ___windy___ 2. ___cloudy___ 3. ___foggy___ 4. ___snowy___

F Read Larissa's planner. (Lesson 4)

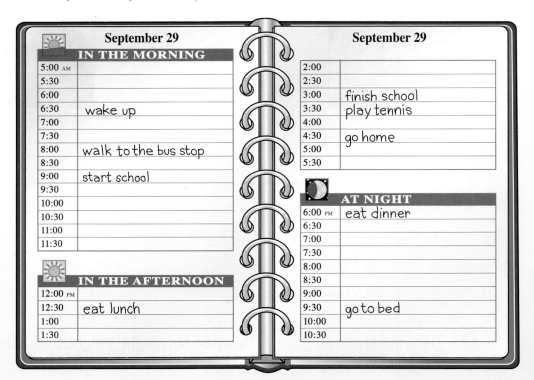

September 29		September 29	
IN THE MORNING			
5:00 AM		2:00	
5:30		2:30	
6:00		3:00	finish school
6:30	wake up	3:30	play tennis
7:00		4:00	
7:30		4:30	go home
8:00	walk to the bus stop	5:00	
8:30		5:30	
9:00	start school		
9:30			
10:00		**AT NIGHT**	
10:30		6:00 PM	eat dinner
11:00		6:30	
11:30		7:00	
IN THE AFTERNOON		7:30	
12:00 PM		8:00	
12:30	eat lunch	8:30	
1:00		9:00	
1:30		9:30	go to bed
		10:00	
		10:30	

G Describe Larissa's day. Write four complete sentences. (Lesson 4)
(Answers will vary. Sample answers are given.)

1. Larissa wakes up at 6:30.

2. Larissa eats lunch at 12:30.

3. Larissa finishes school at 3:00.

4. Larissa goes to bed at 9:30.

Practice 1 *(continued)*

E Write the weather word under the picture. (Lesson 5)

F Read Larissa's planner. (Lesson 4)

G Describe Larissa's day. Write four complete sentences. (Lesson 4)

Evaluation 1   10 mins. ■ ■ ■

Go around the room and check on students' progress. Help individuals when needed. If you see consistent errors among several students, interrupt the class and give a mini lesson or review to help students feel comfortable with the concept.

Activity Bank

Unit 1: Computer Worksheets
Unit 1: Internet Worksheets

Presentation 2
7-10 mins. ■■□ **Assessment** ■■□

My Dictionary

Go over the steps of My Dictionary as a class.

Practice 2
5-7 mins. ■■

Do the dictionary activity as a class before students work on their own for at least the first few units of the book to ensure that students understand what to do.

Evaluation 2
5 mins. ■■□

Ask students to share their cards.

Presentation 3
5 mins. ■■■

Learner Log

Review the concepts of the Learner Log. Make sure students understand the concepts and how to complete the log including circling the answers, finding page numbers where the concept is taught, and ranking favorite activities.

> ## Teaching Tip
>
> ### Learner Logs
>
> Learner Logs function to help students in many different ways.
>
> 1. They serve as part of the review process.
> 2. They help students to gain confidence and to document what they have learned. Consequently, students see that they are progressing in their learning.
> 3. They provide students with a tool that they can use over and over to check and recheck their understanding of the target language. In this way, students become independent learners.

Practice 3
10-15 mins. ■

Ask students to complete the Learner Log.

Evaluation 3
2 mins. ■

Go over the Learner Log with students.

Application
5-7 mins. ■■■

Ask students to record their favorite lesson or page in the unit.

Use the Stand Out 2 Assessment CD-ROM with Exam *View*® to create a posttest for Unit 1.

Refer students to *Stand Out 2 Grammar Challenge*, Unit 1, Extension Challenge 1 for more practice with negative statements with *be* and Extension Challenge 2 for more practice with *yes/no* questions with *be*.

Instructor's Notes

_____

_____

_____

_____

_____

_____

_____

_____

_____

_____

_____

_____

_____

_____

_____

_____

_____

_____

_____

_____

_____

_____

My Dictionary

Make flash cards to improve your vocabulary.

1. Choose four new words from this unit.

2. Write each word on an index card or on a sheet of paper.

3. On the back of the index card or paper, draw a picture, find and write a sentence from the book with the word, and write the page number.

4. Study the words.

tallest

The <u>tallest</u> student in the class is Francisco.   page 9

Learner Log

Circle how well you learned each item and write the page number where you learned it.

1. I can ask for and give personal information.

   Yes   Maybe   No   Page _____

2. I can identify family relationships.

   Yes   Maybe   No   Page _____

3. I can describe people.

   Yes   Maybe   No   Page _____

4. I can interpret information about weather.

   Yes   Maybe   No   Page _____

5. I can interpret and write schedules.

   Yes   Maybe   No   Page _____

Rank what you like to do best from 1 to 6. 1 is your favorite activity. Your teacher will help you.

_____ Practice listening

_____ Practice speaking

_____ Practice reading

_____ Practice writing

_____ Learn new words

_____ Learn grammar

In the next unit, I want to practice more

_____.

Team Project

Describe a student.

In this project, you are going to describe a student on your team or a student from the picture on page 7. You will include a family tree, a one-day planner and a one-month calendar for the student.

1. Form a team of four or five students. In your team, you need:

POSITION	JOB	STUDENT NAME
Student 1: **Team Leader**	See that everyone speaks English. See that everyone participates.	
Student 2: **Writer**	Write a paragraph with help from the team.	
Student 3: **Artist**	Make a family tree with help from the team.	
Students 4/5: **Planners**	Make a one-day planner and a one-month calendar with help from the team.	

2. Choose a student from your team or a student from page 7 (not Kenji or Anya).

3. Write a paragraph about the student and his or her family. Answer these questions in your paragraph:

   Where is the student from?

   Where does he or she live now?

   How many brothers and sisters does he or she have?

4. Make a family tree for the student.

5. Make a one-day planner for the student.

6. Make a one-month calendar for the student.

7. Report to the class.

Introduction   5 mins.

Team Project

Describe a student.

In this project, students will work together to create a portfolio of information about an imaginary student from the student book or one of the students in their group.

Students will then present this information to the other groups as an oral and written report. Among the items in the "portfolio" will be a descriptive paragraph about the student and his or her family, a family tree, and a monthly calendar with a daily planner page. The following lesson plan is a one-to-two day simulation, depending on the length and needs of the class.

Stage 1   10-15 mins.

Form a team with four or five students.

Help students form groups and assign positions in their groups. On the spot, students will have to choose who will be the leader of their group. Review the responsibility of the leader and ask students to write the name of their leader in their books. Do the same with the remaining positions: writer, artist, and planner(s). Every member of each group should have a responsibility.

Stage 2   5 mins.

Choose a student from your team or a student from page 7 (not Kenji or Anya).

Each group should choose a student to create the portfolio for. It is OK for groups to choose an imaginary student from page 7 if no one on the team feels comfortable giving out personal information.

Stage 3   25-30 mins.

Write a paragraph about the student and his or her family.

Have group members interview the student and write a paragraph. If you like, you can give students the interview worksheet from the Activity Bank CD-ROM (Unit 1, Project, Worksheet 1). Tell students that one team member should ask the questions and another member should record the answers. The other team members should assist or provide answers in the case of an imaginary student.

Stage 4   25-30 mins.

Make a family tree for the student.

The team should work together to create the family tree. If you like, provide students with the family tree template from the Activity Bank CD-ROM (Unit 1, Project, Worksheet 2).

Stages 5 and 6   35-40 mins.

Make a one-day planner for the student.
Make a one-month calendar for the student.

If you like, provide teams with the daily planner and calendar templates from the Activity Bank CD-ROM (Unit 1, Project, Worksheets 3 and 4). Ask teams to list what the student does in his or her routine, including things he or she does every day, always, often, sometimes, and rarely. Have group members fill in both the calendar and planner pages.

Stage 7   20-40 mins.

Report to the class.

Have students practice with their teams and report the information to the class as a team.

Activity Bank 👁

Unit 1, Project, Worksheet 1: Student Profile
Unit 1, Project, Worksheet 2: Family Chart
Unit 1, Project, Worksheet 3: Daily Planner
Unit 1, Project, Worksheet 4: Calendar
Unit 1, Extension 1: Height and Weight

STANDARDS CORRELATIONS

CASAS: 0.1.1, 0.1.2, 0.1.4, 0.2.1, 0.2.4, 2.3.1, 2.3.2, 2.3.3, 4.8.1 (See CASAS Competency List on pages 169–175.)
SCANS: **Resources** Allocate time, allocate materials and facility resources, allocate human resources
Information Acquire and evaluate information, organize and maintain information, interpret and communicate information
Interpersonal Participate as a member of a team, teach others, exercise leadership, negotiate to arrive at a decision, work with cultural diversity
Systems Understand systems, monitor and correct performance
Basic Skills Reading, writing, listening, speaking

Thinking Skills Think creatively, make decisions, solve problems, see things in the mind's eye
Personal Qualities Responsibility, sociability, self-management
EFF: **Communication** Read with understanding, convey ideas in writing, speak so others can understand, listen actively, observe critically
Decision Making Solve problems and make decisions, plan
Interpersonal Cooperate with others, advocate and influence, resolve conflict and negotiate, guide others
Lifelong Learning Take responsibility for learning, reflect and evaluate

Objective: Identify clothing
Grammar: Simple present
Academic Strategies: Focused listening, predicting
Vocabulary: Clothing vocabulary

RESOURCES

Activity Bank: Unit 2, Lesson 1, Worksheets 1–2
Reading and Writing Challenge: Unit 2
Grammar Challenge: Unit 2, Challenge 1

■ 1.5 hour ■ 2.5 hour ■ 3⁺ hour

AGENDA

Talk about seasons.
Talk about the Hernandez family.
Learn new clothing words.
Review the simple present tense.
Talk about what we wear to school.

Audio: CD 1, Track 22
Heinle Picture Dictionary: Calendar, pages 6–7; Weather, pages 166–167; Clothing, pages 104–117
Stand Out 2 Assessment CD-ROM with Exam*View*®

 Preassessment *(optional)*

Use the Stand Out 2 Assessment CD-ROM with Exam*View*® to create a pretest for Unit 2.

Warm-up and Review   5-7 mins.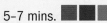

Write the four seasons on the board. Say what season you like the best. Ask students which season they like. Take a class poll.

Teaching Tip

Teach the logic of the book

Take opportunities throughout the term to help students understand the logic of the book. As students understand why they are doing different activities and how activities relate to one another, they will have more confidence in the process.

Near the beginning of using the book, show students how the objectives relate to the different lessons and that each lesson is a one-day activity. Soon students will be anticipating the next lesson and understand the purpose of the objective. At the end of each lesson, ask students if they feel they have accomplished the objective and can do what is asked of them even outside of the classroom.

Introduction   5-7 mins.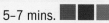

Continuing with the seasons still listed on the board, ask students what they might wear during each season. Explain that in this unit they will study clothing and making clothing purchases. Ask students to look at the goals for the unit in the book. Next, go over the agenda for the

---

day's work and state the objective: *Today we will identify different kinds of clothing.*

Presentation 1   10-15 mins.

Ask students to give examples of clothing for the winter and summer. Write their responses on the board in two columns. Write *do not* on the board and circle *not*. Help students see that *not* indicates that the negative is being used. As an example, write the sentence: *I do not wear shorts in the winter.* Point to *shorts* on the summer list from the board.

(A) **Look at the picture and answer the questions. Then, read about the Hernandez family.**

Ask students to cover the paragraph. Then, ask them questions about the picture, such as: *How many people are in their family? Where do you think they are from?*

Ask students to uncover the paragraph and do Exercise A. Read the paragraph about Mario's family with the class.

Practice 1   8-12 mins.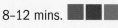

(B) **Answer questions about the Hernandez family. Then, listen and add to your answers.**

Note: The listening script for Exercise B is on page 22a.

STANDARDS CORRELATIONS

CASAS: 1.3.9 (See CASAS Competency List on pages 169–175.)
SCANS: **Basic Skills** Reading, writing, listening, speaking
EFF: **Communication** Read with understanding, convey ideas in writing, speak so others can understand, listen actively

---

UNIT 2

Let's go shopping!

GOALS

➤ Identify clothing
➤ Ask about prices
➤ Describe clothing

➤ Read advertisements and receipts
➤ Ask for assistance

LESSON 1

Shopping for clothes

GOAL ➤ Identify clothing

A Look at the picture and answer the questions.
Then, read about the Hernandez family.

This is the Hernandez family.
Mario is the husband. Teresa is the
wife. They have a beautiful
11-month-old baby daughter. Her
name is Graciela. They don't have
any sons. They moved from Mexico
to Chicago in the summer. Now it's
winter and it's hot in Mexico, but it's
cold in Chicago. Mario and his family
wear warm clothes in Chicago in the
winter. They don't wear shorts or
sandals in the winter. The Hernandez
family likes Chicago, but they don't
like the winter.

Where does the
Hernandez family live?
What season is it?

CD 1
TR 22

B Answer the questions about the Hernandez family. Then, listen
and add to your answers.

1. What clothes do they wear in the winter?

   They wear coats, gloves, scarves, and long pants in the winter.

2. What clothes do you think they wear in the summer?

   They wear shorts, sandals, sunglasses and t-shirts in the summer.

C Look at the picture.

D Write the letter from the picture above next to each word.

_h_ blouses   _b_ shirts   _c_ ties   _g_ pants   _i_ skirts

_f_ coats   _e_ sweaters   _d_ jackets   _a_ socks   _j_ dresses

E In a group, list the clothes you wear in the summer and in the winter.
(Answers will vary. Sample answers are given.)

Summer	Winter
shorts	coats
sandals	gloves
t-shirts	boots
bathing suits	sweaters
hats	pants

Listening Script   *CD 1, Track 22*

This is the Hernandez family. They are from Mexico and they need to wear warm clothing in the winter. For example, Mario always wears a coat in the winter. He also wears gloves. Teresa, his wife, also wears a coat and gloves. She also wears a scarf for those very cold mornings when she takes her walk. They both wear long pants and no shorts. Shorts, sandals, sunglasses, and t-shirts are the only things they wear in the summer. It is much more like their native city in Mexico in the summer.

Evaluation 1   3-5 mins.

Make a list on the board of the students' answers to Exercise B. Discuss them and make sure you emphasize the use of the negative.

Presentation 2   15-20 mins.

Ask: *Where do you shop for clothes?* Write a list of stores on the board.

C Look at the picture.

Ask students to open their books. Then, ask: *What is the name of this store?* Ask if the store is for men, women, or both. Don't spend too much time identifying the individual items.

For shorter classes, have students do Exercise D for homework.

Practice 2   5-7 mins.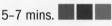

D Write the letter from the picture above next to each word.

Ask students to work in pairs to complete this activity. Then, ask them to write the words in alphabetical order. This is a mechanical practice that will give students an opportunity to write the words and think a little about spelling.

Evaluation 2   10-12 mins.

E In a group, list the clothes you wear in the summer and in the winter.

Ask groups to report to the class to confirm that they understood the previous practice.

Instructor's Notes

_____
_____
_____
_____
_____
_____
_____
_____
_____
_____
_____
_____
_____
_____
_____
_____
_____
_____
_____
_____

Presentation 3

10-15 mins.

(F) Study the charts with your classmates and teacher.

Explain the chart of the negative simple present to students. Drill students on the form. Extend the chart to include other verbs in the simple present having to do with clothing. Work with students to make negative and affirmative statements about things they buy, wear, and have. (Review *have* with the students as necessary.) Write a few correct sentences elicited from students on the board.

Review the pronunciation of the final *s* in the third-person singular form of the verb. Here it is productive to elongate the *s* to emphasize it. Often, students will write how they speak and may leave the *s* off of words because they don't clearly pronounce it.

For shorter classes, have students do Exercise G for homework.

Practice 3

10-15 mins. ■

(G) Answer the questions about Mario.

Ask students to complete this activity either individually or in pairs.

(H) Talk in a group about what Mario wears to work and to the beach.

Go over the example as a class. Again, it is effective to manage the group work by asking the person who is speaking to stand. If you see a group of students where no one is standing, you know that they are off task.

Then, write on the board: *What do you wear to work?* and *What do you wear to the beach?*

Teaching Tip

Step-by-step

At this level, it is important that when there are several tasks to perform, you only ask students to do one at a time. Carefully model the target activity for students. Let students know how much time they have to complete each task you give to them, but monitor them to make sure they don't complete early and lose interest before the allotted time.

Evaluation 3

5-7 mins. ■

Go over Exercises G and H with students and ask volunteers to say the phrases they came up with in Exercise H.

Application

10-12 mins. ■■■

(I) Write sentences about what you and your classmates wear to school.

Write on the board: *What do you wear to school?* Ask volunteers to write their sentences on the board. For further practice, have them write their sentences in their notebooks.

 Refer students to *Stand Out 2 Grammar Challenge*, Unit 2, Challenge 1 for more practice with the simple present affirmative and negative.

Activity Bank

Unit 2, Lesson 1, Worksheet 1: Clothing

Unit 2, Lesson 1, Worksheet 2: Affirmative and Negative Simple Present

GOAL ➤ Identify clothing

 F Study the charts with your classmates and teacher.

Simple Present		
Subject	**Verb**	
I, you, we, they	wear	shoes
he, she	wears*	
Pronunciation: */z/		

Negative Simple Present			
Subject	**Negative**	**Base verb**	
I, you, we, they	don't	wear	sandals
he, she	doesn't		

G Answer the questions about Mario. (Answers will vary. Sample answers are given.)

1. What does Mario wear to work?

   <u>Mario wears a hat, gloves, a belt,</u>

   <u>boots, and pants.</u>

   _____

2. What does Mario wear to the beach?

   <u>Mario wears shorts, sandals,</u>

   <u>and a t-shirt.</u>

   _____

 H Talk in a group about what Mario wears to work and to the beach.

EXAMPLE: Mario wears boots to work. He wears sandals to the beach.

I Write sentences about what you and your classmates wear to school.
(Answers will vary.)

1. The student next to me wears _____ to school. He/She doesn't wear

   _____.

2. I wear _____ to school. _____.

3. My classmates _____ to school. They _____.

How much is it?

GOAL ➤ Ask about prices

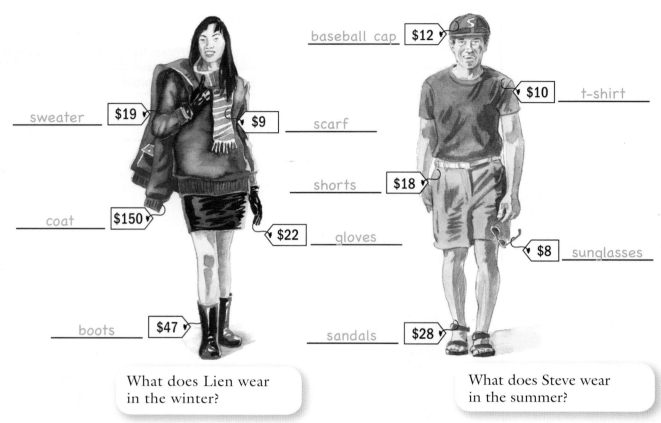

baseball cap | $12

sweater | $19

$9 | scarf

$10 | t-shirt

shorts | $18

coat | $150

$22 | gloves

$8 | sunglasses

boots | $47

sandals | $28

What does Lien wear in the winter?

What does Steve wear in the summer?

A Write the words from the box next to the clothing above.

t-shirt	gloves	sunglasses	sweater	shorts
coat	scarf	boots	sandals	baseball cap

B Work in pairs. Ask and answer questions about the pictures.

EXAMPLE:
Student A: How much is Lien's scarf?   *Student B:* How much are the sunglasses?
Student B: It's $9.00.   *Student A:* They're $8.00.

C What is the total cost of each person's clothing?

1. How much are Lien's winter clothes? ___$247___

2. How much are Steve's summer clothes? ___$76___

AT-A-GLANCE PREP

Objective: Ask about prices
Grammar: Comparative and superlative adjectives
Pronunciation: *dollar*
Academic Strategy: Focused listening, classifying
Vocabulary: Clothing, *cheaper, more expensive, tax, receipt, total*

RESOURCES

Activity Bank: Unit 2, Lesson 2, Worksheets 1–2
Reading and Writing Challenge: Unit 2
Grammar Challenge: Unit 2, Challenge 2

■ 1.5 hour ■ 2.5 hour ■ 3⁺ hour

AGENDA

Talk about clothing stores.
Talk about prices and ask questions.
Compare prices.
Read receipts and answer questions.
Make a list.

Audio: CD 1, Tracks 23–25
Heinle Picture Dictionary: Clothing, pages 104–117; Money and Shopping, pages 8–9

Warm-up and Review   8-10 mins.

Ask students about department stores and clothing stores in your area. Discuss which stores are the cheapest.

Introduction   2 mins.

Ask students which type of clothing is more expensive—summer or winter clothing. Walk students through the day's agenda and then state the objective: *Today we will learn how to ask about prices.*

Presentation 1   15-20 mins.

Discuss any new vocabulary on the page by asking what Lien wears in the winter and what Steve wears in the summer. Repeat the words with students and help them with pronunciation as needed. Ask individuals if they own any of the items in the pictures.

Write the following items on the board to remind students of the rules for saying numbers and money amounts:

> *Ten dollars and twenty-five cents (good)*
> *Ten, twenty-five (good)*
> ~~*Ten dollars and twenty-five*~~ *(not good)*
> ~~*Ten and twenty-five cents*~~ *(not good)*

Review the *be* verb in its singular and plural forms. Create two columns on the board with the headings *They are* and *It is*. Ask students to help you put the items of clothing from the picture in the appropriate columns.

(A) Write the words from the box next to the clothing above.

Do this activity with students while asking how much the items are. Encourage students to begin their answers with *They are* or *It is.*

Pronunciation

Dollar

Work with students to pronounce *dollar* correctly. Some students might have difficulty with the *o*. This is because the name of the letter is not the sound. Also, work with students to pronounce the *ar* like they might pronounce *er* at the end of words.

Prepare students for the practice by going over the question-and-answer exchanges in Exercise B. Show students how to substitute information in the conversation.

Practice 1   15-20 mins.

(B) Work in pairs. Ask and answer questions about the pictures.

(C) What is the total cost of each person's clothing?

Evaluation 1   7-10 mins.

Ask volunteers to demonstrate the exchanges in front of the class.

STANDARDS CORRELATIONS

CASAS: 1.1.6, 1.2.1, 1.2.2, 1.2.4, 1.3.9 (See CASAS Competency List on pages 169-175.)
SCANS: Resources Allocate money
Information Acquire and evaluate information
Basic Skills Reading, writing, listening, speaking
Personal Qualities Self-management
EFF: Communication Read with understanding, speak so others can understand, listen actively

Presentation 2
7–10 mins.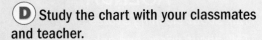

D Study the chart with your classmates and teacher.

Go over this chart with students and prepare them for the focused listening. This listening is part of the presentation, so go slowly and take it one section at a time.

E Listen to the conversations. Write the clothing on a piece of paper. Then, put the clothing in order from the cheapest to the most expensive in the chart below.

 Listening Script   CD 1, Tracks 23–25

Salesperson: *May I help you, miss?*
Lien: *Yes, I want to buy these pants. Can you tell me how much they cost?*
Salesperson: *Of course. They are on sale and I think the price is … yes, they are $22.00 plus tax.*
Lien: *Thanks. I will get two pairs, please.*

Steve: *Excuse me. I want to buy these sneakers, gloves, and these socks. How much are they?*
Salesperson: *Well, let's see. The sneakers are $15.00, the gloves are $10, and I think the socks are cheap. Let me look—yes, they are $3.00 a pair. Good deal!*

Mario: *I need a scarf right away, but these are so expensive.*
Salesperson: *Well, they are not cheaper anywhere else. I think you will find that $25.00 for a scarf is a good deal.*
Mario: *OK, and I also need a cap.*
Salesperson: *We do have hats on sale for $18.00.*
Mario: *That's the sale price?*
Salesperson: *I'm afraid so.*

Prepare students for the practice. Exercises F and G are information-gap activities. Model the activity carefully with students to show how it should be done.

Teaching Tip

Facilitating information-gap activities

Information-gap activities are activities that allow one student to give new information to another. In the *Stand Out* approach, there are many opportunities you can do these types of activities.

Sometimes the procedure of this activity is difficult for students to understand. There are several things you can do to help students understand.

1. Model the activity several times with several different students.
2. Make sure students know who is Student A and who is Student B. To do this, ask all Student As to stand up.
3. Monitor the practice. If a pair of students is having trouble, do the exercise with them.
4. Do the activity in groups of four with at least one student who can direct the others. In groups of four, one pair goes first and the other listens. Then, the other pair performs.

Practice 2
10–15 mins.

F Student A: Ask your partner about the prices of clothing for winter—a coat, gloves, scarf, boots, and a sweater. Write the prices in the chart from the cheapest to the most expensive.

G Student B: Ask your partner about the prices of clothing for summer—sunglasses, shorts, sandals, a t-shirt, and a baseball cap. Write the prices in the chart from the cheapest to the most expensive.

Evaluation 2
5–7 mins.

Ask partners to team up with other partners to compare answers. Then ask questions, such as: *What's cheaper—shorts or sandals?*

GOAL ➤ **Ask about prices**

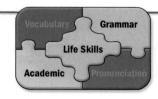

D Study the chart with your classmates and teacher.

Comparative and Superlative Adjectives		
Adjective	**Comparative adjective**	**Superlative adjective**
cheap	cheaper	the cheapest
expensive	more expensive	the most expensive

CD 1
TR 23–25

E Listen to the conversations. Write the clothing on a piece of paper. Then, put the clothing in order from the cheapest to the most expensive in the chart below.

	Clothing	Price
the cheapest	socks	$3
	gloves	$10
	sneakers	$15
	hat	$18
	pants	$22
the most expensive	scarf	$25

F **Student A:** Ask your partner about the prices of clothing for winter—a coat, gloves, scarf, boots, and a sweater. Write the prices in the chart from the cheapest to the most expensive.

EXAMPLE: *Student A:* How much is the coat?
　　　　　Student B: (Look on page 24.) It's $150.00.

scarf ($9)	sweater ($19)	gloves ($22)	boots ($50)	coat ($150)

the cheapest　　　　　　　　　　　　　　　　　　　　　　　　　　　the most expensive

G **Student B:** Ask your partner about the prices of clothing for summer—sunglasses, shorts, sandals, a t-shirt, and a baseball cap. Write the prices in the chart from the cheapest to the most expensive.

EXAMPLE: *Student B:* How much are the sunglasses?
　　　　　Student A: (Look on page 24.) They're $8.00.

sunglasses ($8)	t-shirt ($10)	cap ($12)	shorts ($18)	sandals ($28)

the cheapest　　　　　　　　　　　　　　　　　　　　　　　　　　　the most expensive

GOAL ➤ Ask about prices

RECEIPT
Dress..............$88.89
Tax....................$7.11

TOTAL..........$96.00
CUSTOMER COPY

RECEIPT
Suit...............$299.99
Tax..................$23.92

TOTAL.........$323.91
CUSTOMER COPY

RECEIPT
Shoes............$34.99
Tax...................$2.80

TOTAL..........$37.79
CUSTOMER COPY

H **Answer the questions about the receipts.**

1. How much is the dress? $88.89

2. How much is the suit? $299.99

3. How much are the shoes? $34.99

4. How much is the tax for the dress? $7.11

5. How much is the tax for the suit? $23.92

6. How much is the tax for the shoes? $2.80

7. How much is the total for the dress? $96.00

8. How much is the total for the suit? $323.91

9. How much is the total for the shoes? $37.79

How much is this shirt?

How much are these shoes?

I **Read the conversation between the customer and the salesperson. Make similar conversations.**

Customer: Excuse me. How much is this shirt?
Salesperson: It's $24.99.
Customer: How much is that with tax?
Salesperson: That's $26.25 with tax.
Customer: Great! / No, thanks. That's too expensive.

J **What clothing do you need right now? You have $300. Make a list and share it with the class.**

Presentation 3   10–15 mins. ▪▪▪

Read the receipts together as a class. Ask students to find the tax in each receipt and circle it. Then, ask the students to underline the totals.

(H) Answer the questions about the receipts.

Do this activity as a class to make sure students understand how to read the receipts. Show them how to form the questions and when to use the singular and plural forms of the verbs.

Prepare students to do the practice. Show them how to substitute information.

For shorter classes, have students do Exercise I for homework.

Practice 3   7–10 mins. ▪

(I) Read the conversation between the customer and the salesperson. Make similar conversations.

Make sure students change roles so each of them has the opportunity to play both parts.

Evaluation 3   3–5 mins. ▪

Ask volunteers to demonstrate their conversations in front of the class.

Application   10–15 mins. ▪▪▪

(J) What clothing do you need right now? You have $300. Make a list and share it with the class.

📖 Refer students to *Stand Out 2 Grammar Challenge*, Unit 2, Challenge 2 for more practice with comparative and superlative adjectives.

Activity Bank 💿

Unit 2, Lesson 2, Worksheet 1: Prices
Unit 2, Lesson 2, Worksheet 2: Ask about Prices

Instructor's Notes

_____
_____
_____
_____
_____
_____
_____
_____
_____
_____
_____
_____
_____
_____
_____
_____
_____
_____
_____
_____
_____
_____
_____
_____
_____
_____
_____
_____
_____
_____

AT-A-GLANCE PREP

Objective: Describe clothing
Grammar: Present continuous
Pronunciation: /ing/
Academic Strategy: Focused listening, peer-editing
Vocabulary: Clothing, colors, sizes, *striped, short-sleeved, flowered*

RESOURCES

Activity Bank: Unit 2, Lesson 3, Worksheets 1–3
Reading and Writing Challenge: Unit 2
Grammar Challenge: Unit 2, Challenge 3

■ 1.5 hour ■ 2.5 hour ■ 3⁺ hour

AGENDA

Describe people.
Read about size, color, pattern, and style.
Listen to identify people.
Use the present continuous tense.
Practice a conversation.
Write sentences.

Audio: CD 1, Track 26
Heinle Picture Dictionary: Clothing, pages 104–117

Warm-up and Review   10-15 mins.

Ask students to turn back to page 7 and describe two individuals in the picture to a partner. Review descriptive words for hair, eyes, and height.

Introduction   5-7 mins.

Ask students to describe what you are wearing. Write any adjectives plus the clothing items on the board. Underline the colors. Go over the agenda and state the objective: *Today we will describe clothing.*

Teaching Tip

Stating the goal

We always suggest that you state the objective and write it on the board for all students to see. Although we don't mention it, it is important to revisit the objective at the end of the class so students can see that they have learned something new. This process will give them confidence. Revisiting the objectives in the review and in the project is also important.

Presentation 1   15-20 mins.

(A) Look at the sizes, colors, patterns, and styles.

Go over the new vocabulary with students by modeling and drilling. Ask questions, such as:

Who is wearing an extra-large shirt? This lesson serves as an introduction to the present continuous. It will be taught in Practice 2.

Although adjective order is a very difficult concept for students to learn, this lesson gives an introduction to it by placing the items in order in the picture. Explain to students that when they have any two, three, or all of the adjectives together, they should be in this order. Give a few examples, such as:

> *the large, red shirt* (<u>Not:</u> *the red, large shirt*)
>
> *the blue and white, striped, short-sleeved shirt*

Practice 1   3-10 mins.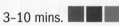

(B) Listen and write the name of one of the brothers above.

Play the recording three times. Ask students to listen but not write the first time. Then, have them write and compare answers with other students. Finally, ask them to listen again and confirm their answers.

Note: The listening script for Exercise B is on page 28a.

Evaluation 1   5 mins.

Review their answers and be prepared to play the recording again.

STANDARDS CORRELATIONS

CASAS: 1.1.9, 1.3.9 (See CASAS Competency List on pages 169–175.)
SCANS: **Information** Acquire and evaluate information
Basic Skills Reading, writing, listening, speaking

EFF: **Communication** Convey ideas in writing, speak so others can understand, listen actively, observe critically

---

What are they wearing?

GOAL ➤ Describe clothing

A Look at the sizes, colors, patterns, and styles.

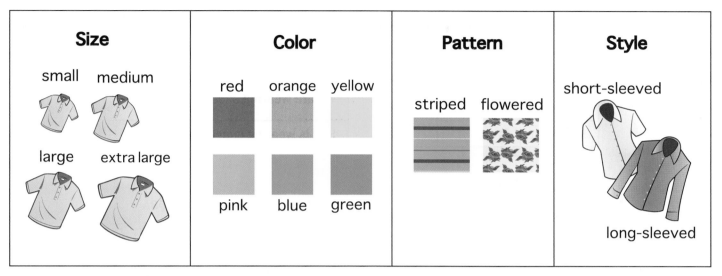

Size	Color	Pattern	Style
small medium	red orange yellow	striped flowered	short-sleeved
large extra large	pink blue green		long-sleeved

The Nguyen Brothers

So

Duong

Tan

Diem

B Listen and write the name of one of the brothers above.

CD 1
TR 26

1. _____Diem_____   3. _____Tan_____   5. _____Diem_____

2. _____So_____   4. _____Duong_____   6. _____So_____

GOAL ➤ Describe clothing

C Study the chart with your classmates and teacher.

Present Continuous			
Subject	*Be* verb	**Verb + -*ing***	**Example sentence**
I	am		I **am wearing** a sweater right now.
you, we, they	are	wearing	We **are wearing** shoes at this moment.
he, she, it	is		She **is wearing** sunglasses today.

D Complete the sentences with the present continuous form of *wear*.

1. He _____is wearing_____ a flowered shirt.

2. The woman _____is wearing_____ a beautiful dress.

3. They _____are wearing_____ new clothes.

4. Alan and I _____are wearing_____ sunglasses.

5. You _____are wearing_____ a flowered blouse.

6. I _____am wearing_____ a striped shirt.

E Write two sentences about each Nguyen brother from page 27.
(Answers will vary. Sample answers are given.)

1. So is wearing an extra-large, blue, striped shirt.

   He is wearing black pants and black shoes.

2. Duong is wearing a red sweater. He is also wearing work boots.

   _____

3. Tan is wearing a red and white striped. long-sleeved shirt. He is wearing

   black sandals.

4. Diem is wearing a flowered, short-sleeved shirt. He is wearing green pants

   and red shoes.

Listening Script CD 1, Track 26

1. *The Nguyen brothers live in Florida and are on their way to a party. One of the brothers is wearing a flowered shirt and red shoes. He is ready to go and looking good!*
2. *One of the brothers is bigger than the rest. He works out and exercises a lot. He is wearing an extra-large, blue, striped, short-sleeved shirt.*
3. *The most stylish of the brothers always wears long-sleeved shirts. He looks good in anything he wears.*
4. *The oldest of the brothers is worried that he doesn't have fancy clothes to wear. He is wearing a large red sweater and work boots. He is a good-looking guy though, so it shouldn't be a problem.*
5. *The youngest brother wears small shirts and often wears green pants. I think he thinks the color looks good on him.*
6. *One final word about the biggest guy. He usually wears black shoes and black pants.*

Presentation 2   10–15 mins.

With students' books closed, ask students what they are wearing. Have them respond in complete sentences. Write their responses on the board and make any corrections without drawing attention to the mistakes. Have students repeat the sentences you have written on the board.

C Study the chart with your classmates and teacher.

Go over the chart. Help students see the importance of both the *ing* ending and the *be* verb.

Pronunciation

ing

Sometimes pronunciation directly affects both spelling and grammar. Some students may write *wearin* or even *wear*, dropping the entire ending. Although it is logical to recognize these as most likely grammar errors, consider that it may also be reflecting the way students pronounce the words. Therefore, work diligently to encourage students to pronounce the *ing* ending clearly.

D Complete the sentences with the present continuous form of *wear*.

Since this is the presentation stage, do the exercise as a class. Then, have students repeat the sentences out loud.

One of the most difficult concepts at this level is to help students see that they must use an article (*a/an*) before singular nouns, but not before plural ones. Write two columns on the board label *singular* and *plural*. Then, ask students to help you put the items in Exercise D in the correct column and explain when to use *a* or *an*.

For shorter classes, have students do Exercise E for homework.

Practice 2   10–20 mins.

E Write two sentences about each Nguyen brother from page 27.

Allow students to do this activity on their own. Spend time with students who might be struggling with these concepts.

Evaluation 2   3–5 mins.

Ask students to peer-edit their work and make any corrections.

Presentation 3   7–10 mins.

F Look at the pictures and describe what the people are wearing.

Practice this activity by asking students questions about the pictures. Then, ask volunteers to describe the pictures. Review the present continuous once again, and correct students when they make an error.

For shorter classes, do Exercise G for homework.

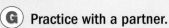

Overcorrection

As the instructor, it is very important to understand that students at this level will need repeated exposure to grammar and pronunciation, and to a lesser extent vocabulary, before they become adequate at using what you have taught on a daily basis. Be careful not to correct so much that students become timid about participating. Instead, wait until several students have made the same mistake and then go over the concept with the class. Also, when students do make errors, repeat their answers back to the class, but use the correct structure.

Practice 3   5–7 mins. ■

G Practice with a partner.

Evaluation 3   5 mins. ■

Observe students as they do this activity.

Application   5–7 mins. ■■■

H Write sentences about what you and your partner are wearing.

 Refer students to *Stand Out 2 Grammar Challenge*, Unit 2, Challenge 3 for more practice with the present continuous.

Activity Bank

Unit 2, Lesson 3, Worksheet 1: Describing Clothing

Unit 2, Lesson 3, Worksheet 2: Sizes, Colors, and Patterns

Unit 2, Lesson 3, Worksheet 3: Present Continuous / Simple Present

F Look at the pictures and describe what the people are wearing.

Come shop our 50 stores!

MOUNTAIN VIEW MALL

Men's and Women's Career Wear

School Clothing

Teen's Dress and Casual Clothing

Men's and Women's Work Clothing

G Practice with a partner.

EXAMPLE: *Student A:* What is the man wearing in this picture?
Student B: He is wearing a gray suit and a red tie.

H Write sentences about what you and your partner are wearing.
(Answers will vary.)

1. I _____.

2. I _____.

3. I _____.

4. I _____.

5. My partner _____.

6. My partner _____.

7. My partner _____.

8. My partner _____.

Advertisements

GOAL ➤ **Read advertisements and receipts**

CD 1
TR 27

A Read the advertisement. How much money can you save on each item?
Listen and fill in the missing information.

SALE COUPON
★ ★ ★
Valid Tuesday,
Wednesday, and
Thursday *only*

SALE

SAM'S
UNIFORM COMPANY

SAM'S
UNIFORM COMPANY

Men's Shirts, Regular Price: $26.00
Sale Price: _____$22_____ **You save:** _____$4_____

Women's Pants, Regular Price: $45.00
Sale Price: _____$36_____ **You save:** _____$9_____

Sneakers, Regular Price: $22.00
Sale Price: _____$15.40_____ **You save:** _____$6.60_____

Baseball Caps, Regular Price: $23.00
Sale Price: _____$20_____ **You save:** _____$3_____

SHOP NOW AND SAVE!

CD 1
TR 28

B Listen again and check the clothing that needs a coupon.

✔ 1. men's shirts   _____ 2. women's pants   _____ 3. sneakers   ✔ 4. baseball caps

C Practice the conversation with a partner. Then, use the information above to make new conversations.

Salesperson: Can I help you?
Customer: How much are the <u>shirts</u>?
Salesperson: The shirts are <u>$26.00</u>.
Customer: The ad says they are <u>$4.00</u> off.
Salesperson: Sorry. You're right. They are <u>$22.00</u>.

> The shirts are $4.00 off.
>
> They are $4.00 off with a coupon.
>
> They are $4.00 off the regular price.

AT-A-GLANCE PREP

Objective: Read advertisements and receipts
Grammar: *because* and comparative adjectives
Academic Strategies: Focused listening, reading charts and graphs
Vocabulary: *unit price, quantity, item, grand total, coupon, sale price, off*

RESOURCES

Activity Bank: Unit 2, Lesson 4, Worksheet 1
Reading and Writing Challenge: Unit 2
Grammar Challenge: Unit 2, Challenge 4

Audio: CD 1, Tracks 27–28
Heinle Picture Dictionary: Clothing, pages 104–117; Money and Shopping, pages 8–9

■ 1.5 hour ■ 2.5 hour ■ 3· hour

AGENDA
Describe what you are wearing.
Read advertisements.
Read receipts.
Make a graph.
Talk about prices.

Warm-up and Review   15-20 mins.

Have students write descriptive sentences about their clothing on 3-by-5 index cards. Students should not write their names on the cards. Then, collect the cards and randomly redistribute them. Ask students to find the person who the card belongs to based on the description.

Introduction   5-7 mins.

Elicit the names of clothing stores in the community from students again. Ask which ones are cheaper. Take a class poll or a vote. Go over the agenda with students. State the objective: *Today we will read advertisements and receipts.*

Presentation 1   10-12 mins.

(A) Read the advertisement. How much money can you save on each item? Listen and fill in the missing information.

Ask students to look at the advertisement. Write on the board: *On sale, $4.00 off, Regular, with a coupon,* and *without a coupon.* Help students understand the meaning of each of these words or expressions.

The listening activity is part of the presentation stage so spend time starting and stopping the recording.

(B) Listen again and check the clothing that needs a coupon.

STANDARDS CORRELATIONS

CASAS: 0.1.2, 0.1.3, 1.2.1, 1.2.2, 1.2.4, 1.3.9, 4.8.1
(See CASAS Competency List on pages 169-175.)
SCANS: **Resources** Allocate money
Information Organize and maintain information, interpret and communicate information
Interpersonal Participate as a member of a team

Listening Script   CD 1, Track 27

Come to Sam's Uniform Company this Tuesday, Wednesday, and Thursday! We're having an end-of-the-season blowout sale! Do you want to save money? Of course, you do! Listen carefully for special coupon savings on select clothing.

Shop Sam's Uniform Company for big savings on men's shirts. Men's shirts are now only $22 with a coupon from this week's newspaper. You save $4! What a deal!

Big savings this month at Sam's Uniform Company! Women's pants—regularly $45—are on sale for only $36! Come in now before this special offer ends. Today and tomorrow only—all Sam's sneakers are on sale for only $15.40. No coupon necessary! Bring the whole family!

We have baseball caps for every fan at Sam's. A special savings of $3 off all baseball caps for every purchase made with a Sam's coupon. Look for coupons in the mail or in your local newspaper.

Practice 1   10-20 mins.

(C) Practice the conversation with a partner. Then, use the information above to make new conversations.

Go over the conversation with students. Help them speak with proper intonation and rhythm. Show them how to substitute information.

Evaluation 1   7-10 mins.

Ask volunteers to demonstrate their new conversations in front of the class.

Basic Skills Reading, writing, listening, speaking
EFF: **Communication** Read with understanding, convey ideas in writing, speak so others can understand, listen actively
Decision Making Solve problems and make decisions
Interpersonal Cooperate with others, advocate and influence, resolve conflict and negotiate, guide others

Presentation 2   10-15 mins. ◼◻◼◼

D Read the receipt and answer the questions. Then, use the advertisement on page 30 to complete the receipt.

Go over the receipt with the class and introduce any vocabulary students might not know. Then, answer the questions together. Show students how to find the information on the previous page.

Ask students if they think that the prices are good at Sam's Uniform Company. Encourage students to share their opinions.

Show students how to do Exercise E and prepare them to do the math.

For shorter classes, ask students to do Exercise E for homework.

Practice 2   8-12 mins. ◼◼

E Complete the receipt.

Ask students to do this activity on their own and then to compare their answers with a partner.

Evaluation 2   5-7 mins. ◼◼

F In a group, discuss which store has better prices and why. Report to the class.

Before students complete this activity, write on the board: *cheap, cheaper, more expensive*, and *most expensive*. Observe students as they discuss in groups. In this activity, students probably won't notice that one store favors men's clothes with cheaper prices and the other favors women's. If they don't catch this, don't tell them right now because they will discover this in the next practice.

LESSON 4   **GOAL** ➤ **Read advertisements and receipts**

 Read the receipt and answer the questions. Then, use the advertisement on page 30 to complete the receipt.

1. How many shirts are on the receipt?

   _____3_____

2. What does *unit price* mean?
   a. how many
   b. how much for one
   c. total price

3. What does *item* mean?
   a. the price
   b. how many
   c. kind of clothing

4. What does *grand total* mean?
   a. price for all items
   b. coupon price
   c. number of clothes

SAM'S UNIFORM COMPANY
20 Row St., Chicago, IL 80000

Quantity	Item	Unit Price	Total
3	Men's shirts	$ 26	$ 78
2	Women's pants	$ 45	$ 90
1	Men's boots	$37	$ 37
2	Women's belts	$18	$ 36

Grand Total $ _____241_____

 Complete the receipt.

ADDY'S
• CLOTHING COMPANY •
25 First St., Chicago, IL 80000
• • • • • • • • • • • •

Quantity	Item	Unit Price	Total
2	Men's shirts	$32	$ 64
4	Women's pants	$34	$ 136
1	Men's boots	$48	$ 48
1	Women's belt	$16	$ 16

Grand Total $ 264

F In a group, discuss which store has better prices and why. Report to the class.

LESSON **4**   **GOAL** > **Read advertisements and receipts**

Why does Alexi shop at Addy's?

G Read the paragraph.

I shop at Addy's because it is close to my house on First Street. Addy's has good prices. Sam's is far away. The prices at Sam's are also good. I think they have boots on sale for $37. Addy's boots are more expensive, but I don't need boots right now. Maybe they will be on sale in the future.

H Complete the graph about Sam's Uniform Company and Addy's Clothing Company.

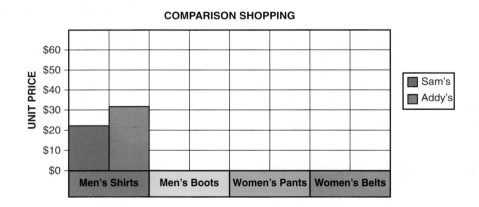

COMPARISON SHOPPING

I Talk again in a group. Which store has better prices?

 J **Active Task.** Visit two clothing stores near your home or on the Internet. Choose one item of clothing and compare the prices. Report to the class.

Presentation 3   7-10 mins.

As a class, make a list of reasons to shop at different stores. The list might include the following items:

> *location*
> *prices*
> *salespeople*
> *quality*
> *supply*

Ask students to open their books and look at the picture of Alexi. Ask the question in the box. Some students might read ahead in the paragraph and decisively answer the question. This is to be expected. Introduce the word *because* so students begin to use it in their answers.

G   Read the paragraph.

Ask the students to read the paragraph quickly to themselves. Ask them to underline any words they don't understand, but to read quickly. Then, discuss the paragraph and confirm that students have understood it all.

Ask questions about the graph in Exercise H. Make sure students understand how the graph works. Ask: *How much are shirts at Sam's? Are shirts cheaper at Addy's or at Sam's?*

For shorter classes, ask students to do Exercise H for homework.

Practice 3   8-10 mins. ▪

H   Complete the graph about Sam's Uniform Company and Addy's Clothing Company.

See that students recognize that the information is on the receipts on the previous page.

Evaluation 3   7-10 mins. ▪

Recreate the graph on the board and ask students to complete it.

Application   5-7 mins. ▪▪▪

I   Talk again in a group. Which store has better prices?

Ask students to debate this question. Make sure groups have both men and women in them.

J   Active Task. Visit two clothing stores near your home or on the Internet. Choose one item of clothing and compare the prices. Report to the class.

📖 Refer students to *Stand Out 2 Grammar Challenge*, Unit 2, Challenge 4 for more practice with *because*.

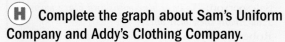

Activity Bank 💿

Unit 2, Lesson 4, Worksheet 1: Reading Ads

Instructor's Notes

_____
_____
_____
_____
_____
_____
_____
_____
_____
_____
_____
_____
_____
_____
_____
_____
_____
_____
_____
_____

Objective: Ask for assistance
Grammar: Demonstrative pronouns
Pronunciation: *this, these*
Academic Strategy: Focused listening
Vocabulary: Return phrases

RESOURCES

Activity Bank: Unit 2, Lesson 5, Worksheet 1
Reading and Writing Challenge: Unit 2

Grammar Challenge: Unit 2, Challenge 5
Audio: CD 1, Tracks 29–34
Heinle Picture Dictionary: Clothing, pages 104–117

■ 1.5 hour ■ 2.5 hour ■ 3⁺ hour

AGENDA
Write an advertisement.
Read about Roberto at a store.
Listen for information.
Learn about this, that, these, and those.
Learn return phrases.

Warm-up and Review   15–20 mins.

Write *blouses, dresses, shoes,* and *hats* on the board. Ask students in groups to design an advertisement with these items in it. Then, ask groups to share their advertisements.

Introduction   5–7 mins.

Write *exchange* on the board. Ask students if they have ever bought something and then returned or exchanged it. Go over the agenda with students and explain the objective: *Today we will learn about making returns.*

Presentation 1   15–20 mins.

Play the recording in Exercise A with books closed and see how much students understand. Play it again and ask comprehension questions. Have students open their books and look at the picture. Ask the questions in the question box.

(A) Listen to the conversation between Roberto and the salesperson.

> **Listening Script**   CD 1, Track 29
>
> *The listening script matches the conversation in Exercise A.*

Play the conversation again while students follow along in their books. Review colors. Ask students what Roberto prefers. Show them how he would prefer a black cap, but it is too expensive.

Practice 1   5–7 mins.

(B) Listen to the conversations. Circle the items Roberto wants.

 Listening Script   CD 1, Tracks 30–33

1. **Roberto:** *Excuse me. Can you help me?*
   Salesperson: *Sure. What can I do for you?*
   Roberto: *I want a cap among other things.*
   Salesman: *What color do you want? We have an assortment.*
   Roberto: *I want this black one, but it is too expensive.*
   Salesperson: *Oh, I'm sorry. Maybe a yellow one?*
   Roberto: *I prefer orange.*
2. **Roberto:** *My wife asked me to pick up an umbrella for her.*
   Salesperson: *We have plenty of umbrellas. What color does she want?*
   Roberto: *She said she doesn't want anything plain, but it has to go with her brown dress.*
   Salesperson: *How about this green one? It will look good with brown.*
   Roberto: *I'll take it!*
3. **Roberto:** *I really need some jeans.*
   Salesperson: *We have blue jeans and black jeans. How about these blue ones?*
   Roberto: *No, thank you. I want the black ones.*
   Salesperson: *OK, here you go. What size do you wear?*
4. **Salesperson:** *Do you need some socks?*
   Roberto: *Yes, I need socks for running.*
   Salesperson: *So, do you want some white athletic socks?*
   Roberto: *That would be great. Thanks.*

Evaluation 1   5–7 mins.

Go over the answers and show students how to do Exercise C.

(C) Practice the conversation in Exercise A with the information from Exercise B.

Which one do you want?

GOAL ➤ Ask for assistance

> Where is Roberto? Who is talking to Roberto?

 A Listen to the conversation between Roberto and the salesperson.

CD 1
TR 29

Roberto: Excuse me. Can you help me?
Salesperson: Sure. What can I do for you?
Roberto: I want a cap among other things.
Salesperson: What color do you want? We have an assortment.
Roberto: I want this black one, but it is too expensive.
Salesperson: Oh, I'm sorry. Maybe a yellow one?
Roberto: I prefer orange.

 B Listen to the conversations. Circle the items Roberto wants.

CD 1
TR 30-33

1. (orange cap)	red cap	blue cap	yellow cap
2. (green umbrella)	blue umbrella	black umbrella	red umbrella
3. gray jeans	brown jeans	blue jeans	(black jeans)
4. (white socks)	brown socks	black socks	yellow socks

 C Practice the conversation in Exercise A with the information from Exercise B.

D Study the chart with your classmates and teacher.

	Near	Far
Singular	this	that
Plural	these	those

E Look at the picture above. Fill in the blanks with *this, that, these,* or *those*.

1. _____*That*_____ cap is yellow and _____*this*_____ cap is orange.

2. _____*That*_____ umbrella is _____*red*_____ and _____*this*_____ umbrella is green.

3. _____*Those*_____ jeans are blue and _____*these*_____ jeans are _____*black*_____.

4. _____*These*_____ socks are _____*white*_____ and _____*those*_____ socks are yellow.

Pronunciation

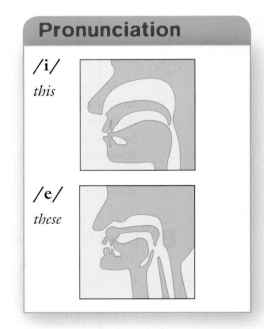

/i/
this

/e/
these

F Ask your partner five questions about clothes your classmates are wearing. Use *this, that, these,* or *those*.

EXAMPLES: *Student A:* What color is *that* shirt?   *Student B:* What color are *these* pants?
               Student B: It's blue.   *Student A:* They're black.

Presentation 2   15–20 mins. ■■■

Walk around the room and make statements about different items. Say, for example: *That is the door.* Use the four demonstrative pronouns: *this, that, these, those.*

D **Study the chart with your classmates and teacher.**

Go over the chart carefully as a class providing examples for each pronoun.

Pronunciation

this/these

Many languages don't have the /ɪ/ sound that English has in *this*. There are several ways to help students hear the difference between /ɪ/ and /i/ and to produce the new sound.

First, help students hear how /ɪ/ and /i/ are different. Produce both vowel sounds in *this* and *these*. There are other distinct features between the two words, for example, the /s/ versus the /z/ phoneme, but students will get a greater benefit if they deal with only one of these distinctions at a time.

You can help students hear the difference by putting *this* at the top left corner of the board and *these* in the opposite corner. Pronounce the two words first in isolation, then in sentences, and then in discourse as students point to the one you are saying.

Next, work from a sound most students are familiar with. Most students can pronounce the /i/ in *these*, so ask them all to pronounce it together for an extended period. Help students identify where their tongues are situated in their mouths (at the roof of the mouth).

Next, do the same for the /ɛ/ sound in *let*. Have students identify where their tongues are for this sound (at the bottom of the mouth). Then, ask students to slide from the /i/ to the /ɛ/. Have them do this several times and finally stop them halfway through the slide and identify this as the target sound (/ɪ/).

Teaching Tip

Overcorrection

As the instructor, it is very important to understand that students at this level will need repeated exposure to grammar and pronunciation, and to a lesser extent vocabulary, before they become adequate at using what you have taught on a daily basis. With pronunciation points, students should be able to recognize the target sound even if they can't produce it yet. They will have many opportunities to practice the sounds throughout the course. It is not productive to spend hours on refining students' pronunciation at this level. Think of these mini lessons on pronunciation as introductions to the target sounds.

E **Look at the picture above. Fill in the blanks with *this, that, these, or those.***

Complete this activity together as a class.

Practice 2   5–7 mins. ■■

F **Ask your partner five questions about clothes your classmates are wearing. Use *this, that, these, or those.***

Evaluation 2   5–7 mins. ■

Ask volunteers to demonstrate their exchanges in front of the class.

Presentation 3 15–20 mins.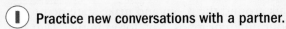

Ask students again if they have returned anything to a store before. Ask them if they were nervous and if it was easy or difficult. Ask them if they spoke in English or in their native language.

Direct students to the picture at the top of the page and ask them what Roberto is returning. Ask them to speculate as to why. Remind them to use the word *because* in their responses.

 Look at the reasons for returning clothing.

Go over the phrases in the box and practice them with students. Walk around the room and role-play quickly with several students, prompting them to reply with one of the phrases.

 Read and listen to the conversation.

> 🎧 **Listening Script** CD 1, Track 34
>
> *The listening script matches the conversation in Exercise H.*

Go over the conversation with students. Make sure students understand every word and also the concept of returns with receipts. Also, help them with rhythm and intonation.

Show students how to do Exercise I by substituting information.

Practice 3 8–12 mins. ■

I **Practice new conversations with a partner.**

Teaching Tip

Inside/Outside circles

At this level, students are asked to do short dialogs often in order to provide practice. This is necessary because they don't have an extensive vocabulary to discuss things yet. It is a good idea to provide different ways to approach pair practice. In the previous unit, students used conversation or substitution cards. This can work again here. Another approach is *inside/outside circles*. Students stand in two circles, one circle inside the other. Both circles contain the same number of students. The students in the outer circle face the students in the inner one. They do the dialog once, and then you ask one of the circles to rotate so each student has a new conversation with another student. This activity continues until you feel students have gotten enough practice.

Evaluation 3 5–7 mins.

Ask volunteers to demonstrate their new conversations in front of the class.

Application 10–15 mins. ■ ■ ■

J **Imagine that you need to return something. Write a new conversation with a partner and perform it for the class.**

📖 Refer students to *Stand Out 2 Grammar Challenge*, Unit 2, Challenge 5 for more practice with *this, that, these,* and *those*.

Activity Bank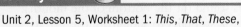

> Unit 2, Lesson 5, Worksheet 1: *This, That, These, and Those*

 LESSON 5 **GOAL** ➤ Ask for assistance

G Look at the reasons for returning clothing.

> I don't like the color.
>
> It is damaged.
>
> It doesn't fit.
>
> I don't like it.
>
> It is the wrong size.

  H Read and listen to the conversation.

CD 1
TR 34

Manager: May I help you?
Roberto: Yes, I want to return these jeans.
Manager: Yes, sir. Why do you want to return them?
Roberto: They don't fit.
Manager: OK. Do you have the receipt?
Roberto: Oh, no, I don't.
Manager: I'm sorry, you can't return them without a receipt, but you can exchange them.
Roberto: OK. Maybe I will get those brown ones over there.
Manager: That's fine, sir. Please make sure you get the right size this time.

Singular	Plural
return it	return them
exchange it	exchange them

 I Practice new conversations with a partner.

Return these items:

blouse / damaged   *Manager:* May I help you?
shoes / don't fit   *Customer:* Yes, I want to return _____.
shorts / don't like   *Manager:* Of course. Why do you want to return _____?
dress / wrong size   *Customer:* _____

 J Imagine that you need to return something. Write a new conversation with a partner and perform it for the class.

Review

Look at the advertisements. (Lessons 1 and 4)

1. Sale Price: $14 — Regular Price: $28 — Sizes M and L only

2. Sale Price: $15 WITH COUPON — Regular Price: $25 — All sizes and colors

3. Sale Price: $45 — Regular Price: $52 COUPON REQUIRED — Small sizes only

4. All sizes — Sale Price: $22 — Regular Price: $25 NO COUPON REQUIRED

5. All men's and women's sizes — Sale Price: $24 — Savings: $5 NO COUPON NECESSARY

6. Regular Price: $44 — All sizes of women's shoes — Sale Price: $34 WITH COUPON

B **Fill in the information from the advertisements above. (Lessons 1, 3, and 4)**

1.
Item: t-shirt
Need Coupon? no
Color: blue
Style: short-sleeved
Size: medium & large
Sale Price: $ 14
Regular Price: $ 28
Savings: $ 14

2.
Item: shirt
Need Coupon? yes
Color: all colors
Pattern: striped
Style: long-sleeved
Size: all sizes
Sale Price: $ 15
Regular Price: $ 25
Savings: $ 10

3.
Item: dress
Need Coupon? yes
Color: red/orange
Pattern: flowered
Size: small
Sale Price: $ 45
Regular Price: $ 52
Savings: $ 7

4.
Item: jeans
Need Coupon? no
Color: blue
Size: all sizes
Sale Price: $ 22
Regular Price: $ 25
Savings: $ 3

5.
Item: sneakers
Need Coupon? no
Color: red
Size: all sizes
Sale Price: $ 24
Regular Price: $ 29
Savings: $ 5

6.
Item: shoes
Need Coupon? yes
Color: black
Size: all sizes
Sale Price: $ 34
Regular Price: $ 44
Savings: $ 10

Objective: All unit objectives
Grammar: All unit grammar
Academic Strategies: Reviewing, evaluating, developing study skills
Vocabulary: All unit vocabulary

AGENDA

Discuss unit objectives.
Complete the review.
Do My Dictionary.
Evaluate and reflect on progress.

■ 1.5 hour   ■ 2.5 hour   ■ 3⁺ hour

Warm-up and Review   10–15 mins.

Ask additional students to perform their conversations from the previous lesson in front of the class.

Introduction   2–5 mins. ■■■

Write all the objectives on the board from Unit 2. Show students the first page of the unit and say the five objectives. Explain that today they will review the whole unit.

Note: Depending on the length of the term, you may decide to have students do Presentation 1 and Practice 1 for homework and then review student work as either the warm-up or another class activity.

Presentation 1   10–15 mins. ■■■

This presentation will cover the first three pages of the review. Quickly go to the first page of each lesson. Discuss the objective of each. Ask simple questions to remind students of what they have learned.

Practice 1   15–20 mins.

(A) Look at the advertisements. (Lessons 1 and 4)

(B) Fill in the information from the advertisements above. (Lessons 1, 3, and 4)

Teaching Tip

Recycling/Review

The review and the project that follows are part of the recycling/review process. Students at this level often need to be reintroduced to concepts to solidify what they have learned. Many concepts are learned and forgotten while learning other new concepts. This is because students learn but are not necessarily ready to acquire language concepts.

Therefore, it becomes very important to review and to show students how to review on their own. It is also important to recycle the new concepts in different contexts.

STANDARDS CORRELATIONS

CASAS: 0.1.2, 0.1.3, 1.1.6, 1.1.9, 1.2.1, 1.2.2, 1.2.4, 1.3.3, 1.3.9
(See CASAS Competency List on pages 169–175.)
SCANS: **Information** Acquire and evaluate information, organize and maintain information

Basic Skills Reading, writing, speaking
Personal Qualities Responsibility, self management
EFF: **Communication** Speak so others can understand
Lifelong Learning Take responsibility for learning, reflect and evaluate

Practice 1 *(continued)*

C Read the receipts and answer the questions. (Lessons 2 and 4)

D Complete the sentences with the present continuous form of *wear*. (Lesson 3)

C Read the receipts and answer the questions. (Lessons 2 and 4)

LANA'S
BOUTIQUE

Women's boots.......$32.55
Women's pants.......$24.50
Belt.........................$18.95
Blouse....................$32.50
TOTAL................$108.50

Clothing for Less

Women's boots......$28.55
Women's pants.......$30.00
Belt................$12.95
Blouse.............$28.50

TOTAL..........$100.00
CUSTOMER COPY

THE True SHOPPER

Women's boots........$40.00
Women's pants........$34.00
Belt................$24.50
Blouse..............$26.95
TOTAL.....$125.45
NO REFUNDS WITHOUT RECEIPT

1. Which store has the cheapest total? <u>Clothing for Less</u>

2. Where are blouses the cheapest? <u>The True Shopper</u>

3. Where are blouses the most expensive? <u>Lana's Boutique</u>

4. Which store has women's pants cheaper than *Clothing for Less*? <u>Lana's Boutique</u>

5. Which store has blouses more expensive than *Clothing for Less*? <u>Lana's Boutique</u>

6. Which do you think is the best store? <u>Clothing for Less</u>

D Complete the sentences with the present continuous form of *wear*. (Lesson 3)

1. Maria <u>is wearing</u> red pants and a pink blouse.

2. Alan <u>is wearing</u> new shoes and socks.

3. Marjorie and Paula <u>are wearing</u> beautiful dresses.

4. The children <u>are wearing</u> shorts.

5. I <u>am wearing</u> a suit and tie.

6. We <u>are wearing</u> coats.

7. She <u>is wearing</u> a new scarf.

Review

E Write three things you can say if you want to make a return. (Lesson 5)
(Answers will vary. Sample answers are given.)

1. Excuse me, I'd like to return this.

2. May I exchange this?

3. I would like to exchange these for a different size.

F Look at the picture. Complete the sentences below with *this, that, these,* or *those.* (Lesson 5)

1. _____This_____ white shirt is perfect. I don't want _____that_____ blue one.

2. _____Those_____ white shoes are great, but I think I want _____these_____ blue ones.

3. _____This_____ shirt is cheap. _____That_____ shirt is better, but it is too expensive.

4. _____That_____ table has a blue shirt and white shoes on it.

G Write what you and your partner are wearing right now. (Lesson 3)
(Answers will vary.)
You: I am wearing _____

_____

_____

Your partner: _____

_____

_____

Practice 1 (continued)

(E) Write three things you can say if you want to make a return. (Lesson 5)

(F) Look at the picture. Complete the sentences below with *this, that, these,* or *those. (Lesson 5)*

(G) Write what you and your partner are wearing right now. (Lesson 3)

Evaluation 1   15 mins. ■ ■ ■

Go around the room and check on students' progress. Help individuals when needed. If you see consistent errors among several students, interrupt the class and give a mini lesson or review to help students feel comfortable with the concept.

Activity Bank

Unit 2: Computer Worksheets
Unit 2: Internet Worksheets

Presentation 2   7-10 mins.

My Dictionary

Go over the steps of My Dictionary as a class.

Practice 2   5-7 mins.

Do the dictionary activity as a class before students work on their own for at least the first few units of the book to ensure that students understand what to do.

Evaluation 2   5 mins.

Ask students to share their cards.

Presentation 3   5 mins.

Learner Log

Review the concepts of the Learner Log. Make sure students understand the concepts and how to complete the log including circling the answers, finding page numbers where the concept is taught, and ranking favorite activities.

Teaching Tip

Learner Logs

Learner Logs function to help students in many different ways.

1. They serve as part of the review process.
2. They help students to gain confidence and to document what they have learned. Consequently, students see that they are progressing in their learning.
3. They provide students with a tool that they can use over and over to check and recheck their understanding of the target language. In this way, students become independent learners.

Practice 3   10-15 mins.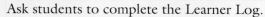

Ask students to complete the Learner Log.

Evaluation 3   2 mins.

Go over the Learner Log with students.

Application   5-7 mins.

Ask students to record their favorite lesson or page in the unit.

 Assessment

Use the Stand Out 2 Assessment CD-ROM with Exam*View*® to create a posttest for Unit 2.

Refer students to *Stand Out 2 Grammar Challenge*, **Unit 2, Extension Challenge 1 for more practice with** *yes/no* **questions and the simple present and Extension Challenge 2 for more practice with** *yes/no* **questions and the present continuous.**

Instructor's Notes

_____

_____

_____

_____

_____

_____

_____

_____

_____

_____

_____

_____

_____

_____

_____

_____

_____

My Dictionary

Make flash cards to improve your vocabulary.

1. Choose four new words from this unit.

2. Write each word on an index card or on a sheet of paper.

3. On the back of the card or paper, draw a picture, find and write a sentence from the book with the word, and write the page number.

4. Study the words.

$20.00 ($84.00)

a lot of money

That's too expensive!

page 26

Learner Log

Circle how well you learned each item and write the page number where you learned it.

1. I can identify clothing.
   Yes   Maybe   No   Page _____

2. I can read receipts.
   Yes   Maybe   No   Page _____

3. I can describe clothing (*yellow, striped, etc.*).
   Yes   Maybe   No   Page _____

4. I can read advertisements.
   Yes   Maybe   No   Page _____

5. I can make returns and ask for help.
   Yes   Maybe   No   Page _____

Rank what you like to do best from 1 to 6. 1 is your favorite activity. Your teacher will help you.

_____ Practice listening

_____ Practice speaking

_____ Practice reading

_____ Practice writing

_____ Learn new words

_____ Learn grammar

In the next unit, I want to practice more

_____.

Team Project

Design a clothing store.

In this project, you are going to design your own clothing store and create an advertisement for it.

1. Form a team with four or five students. In your team, you need:

POSITION	JOB	STUDENT NAME
Student 1: **Team Leader**	See that everyone speaks English. See that everyone participates.	
Student 2: **Artist**	Design an advertisement with help from the team.	
Student 3: **Sales Specialist**	Write a conversation and practice it with your team.	
Students 4/5: **Spokespeople**	Prepare a class presentation with help from the team.	

2. Choose a name for your store. What do you sell? Women's clothes? Men's clothes? Children's clothes?

3. Make a list of clothing you sell on a piece of paper. List at least eight items. Describe the clothing by size, color, pattern, and price. Are your clothes for work, sports, or school?

4. Draw or find and cut out pictures of the clothing items in your store. Make a newspaper advertisement for your store using the pictures of the items.

5. Practice asking for prices, selling clothing, and returning clothing with your teammates.

6. Present your advertisement to the class.

Introduction
5 mins.

Team Project

Design a clothing store.

In this project, students will work in teams to create a department store, make an advertisement for it, and present it to the class.

Stage 1
10-15 mins.

Form a team with four or five students.

Help students form groups and assign positions in their groups. On the spot, students will have to choose who will be the leader of their group. Review the responsibility of the leader and ask students to write the name of their leader in their books.

Do the same with the remaining positions: artist, sales specialist, and spokesperson. If there are five people in the group, double up on the spokesperson position. Every member of each group should have a responsibility.

Stage 2
10-15 mins.

Choose a name for your store. What do you sell?

Ask students to choose a name for their department store and write the names of the stores on the board.

Then, ask students to draw a floor plan of their store showing the type of items they sell, such as, women's and men's clothing.

Stage 3
10-15 mins.

Make a list of clothing you sell on a piece of paper. List at least eight items.

Ask students to make a list of items they will sell. Make sure that they choose at least eight

things from more than one department. There is a template available for planning a store on the Activity Bank CD-ROM (Unit 2, Project, Worksheet 1).

Stage 4
25-30 mins.

Draw or find and cut out pictures of the clothing items in your store.

Provide materials for students to find pictures of clothing in. They may use newspapers, magazines, or the Internet. If these materials are unavailable, students may draw the items in their advertisements. Make sure that students include prices in their advertisements. They may include sale prices and regular prices as well as coupons. There is a template available for creating advertisements on the Activity Bank CD-ROM (Unit 2, Project, Worksheet 2).

Stage 5
10-20 mins.

Practice asking for prices, selling clothing, and returning clothing with your teammates.

Help students understand how to make conversations. Show them different models from the unit that they can use if they choose.

Stage 6
10-30 mins.

Present your advertisement to the class.

Ask the spokespeople of each team to present their team's advertisement to the class. If there is time, have students also present their conversations from the previous stage to the class.

Activity Bank

Unit 2, Project, Worksheet 1: Clothing Store Data
Unit 2, Project, Worksheet 2: Advertisements
Unit 2, Extension, Worksheet 1: Paragraph Writing
Unit 2, Extension, Worksheet 2: Checks and Ledgers

STANDARDS CORRELATIONS

CASAS: 0.1.2, 0.1.3, 1.1.6, 1.1.9, 1.2.1, 1.2.4, 1.3.3, 1.3.9 (See CASAS Competency List on pages 169-175.)
SCANS: **Resources** Allocate time, allocate materials and facility resources, allocate human resources
Information Acquire and evaluate information, organize and maintain information, interpret and communicate information
Interpersonal Participate as a member of a team, teach others, exercise leadership, negotiate to arrive at a decision, work with cultural diversity
Systems Understand systems, monitor and correct performance
Basic Skills Reading, writing, listening, speaking

Thinking Skills Think creatively, make decisions, solve problems, see things in the mind's eye
Personal Qualities Responsibility, sociability, self management
EFF: **Communication** Read with understanding, convey ideas in writing, speak so others can understand, listen actively, observe critically
Decision Making Solve problems and make decisions, plan
Interpersonal Cooperate with others, advocate and influence, resolve conflict and negotiate, guide others
Lifelong Learning Take responsibility for learning, reflect and evaluate

AT-A-GLANCE PREP

Objective: Read a menu
Grammar: Questions with *can*
Academic Strategies: Focused listening, note taking, scanning
Vocabulary: Menus, sandwiches, vegetables, beverages, desserts ·

RESOURCES
Activity Bank: Unit 3, Lesson 1, Worksheets 1–2
Reading and Writing Challenge: Unit 3
Grammar Challenge: Unit 3, Challenge 1

☐ 1.5 hour classes   ■ 2.5 hour classes   ▨ 3⁺ hour classes

AGENDA
List foods.
Read a menu.
Give an order.
Take an order.
Make a menu.

Audio: CD 1, Tracks 35–38
Heinle Picture Dictionary: Food, pages 82–103

Stand Out 2 Assessment CD-ROM with Exam *View*®

📀 Preassessment (optional)

Use the Stand Out 2 Assessment CD-ROM with Exam *View*® to create a pretest for Unit 3.

Warm-up and Review   10-15 mins.

Write *needs* on the board. Ask students to list the things they need to live. Write a few ideas on the board to get them started, such as *sleep*, and *housing*. Elicit ideas and write them on the board. You may do this activity as a class or in groups.

Introduction   5 mins.

Circle *food* from your list on the board. Ask the class if food and drink are always good. They may respond *yes*. If they do, ask them if twenty cups of coffee is good. They will probably say *no*. Suggest that in this unit you will be learning about food and what is good and not good for you. State the objective: *Today, we will learn to read a menu.*

Teaching Tip

State the objective

We always suggest that you state the objective and write it on the board for all the students to see. Although we don't mention it, it is important to revisit the objective at the end of the class so students can see that they have learned something new. This process will give them confidence. Revisiting the objectives in the review and in the project is also important.

Presentation 1   10-15 mins.

With students' books closed, write two columns on the board with the headings *International Dishes* and *American Dishes*. Ask students to help you complete the columns by calling out items you might find on a menu. You may get them started by writing *hamburgers* in the column for American dishes and *tacos* in the other column.

Ask students to open their books and look at the picture of Gilberto. Ask them to cover the paragraph in Exercise A and try to answer the questions in the box under the picture.

Practice 1   5-7 mins.

(A) Close your book and listen to Gilberto's story. Then, open your book and read about Gilberto.

> 🎧 **Listening Script**   CD 1, Track 35
>
> *The listening script matches the paragraph in Exercise A.*

(B) Circle the correct answer.

Ask students to complete this activity on their own and then to compare answers with a partner.

Evaluation 1   10-12 mins.

Show students how to make the statements in Exercise B into questions by using *do* and *does*. Write the questions for each statement on the board and have students ask a partner each question.

STANDARDS CORRELATIONS

CASAS: 1.3.8, 2.6.4 (See CASAS Competency List on pages 169-175.)
SCANS: **Resources** Allocate money
Information Acquire and evaluate information
Interpersonal Participate as a member of a team, serve clients and customers

Basic Skills Reading, listening, speaking
Thinking Skills Think creatively
EFF: **Communication** Read with understanding, speak so others can understand, listen actively

---

UNIT 3

Food and Nutrition

GOALS

➤ Read a menu

➤ Make a shopping list

➤ Locate items in a supermarket

➤ Plan meals

➤ Read recipes

LESSON 1

Augustin's Restaurant

GOAL ➤ Read a menu

Where is Gilberto?
What is his job?
What is he cooking?

**CD 1
TR 35**

A Close your book and listen to Gilberto's story. Then, open your book and read about Gilberto.

    I am a cook in my father's restaurant. His name is Augustin. My name is Gilberto. My mother, sister, and brother work here, too. We have American food in our restaurant. I want to have some food from other countries, too. Maybe someday we can have an international restaurant.

B Circle the correct answer.

1. Gilberto works in a restaurant.   (True)   False

2. Gilberto only cooks American food   (True)   False
   for his father's restaurant.

3. His sister doesn't work in the restaurant.   True   (False)

4. He wants the restaurant to have food   (True)   False
   from many different countries.

Vocabulary   Grammar
Life Skills
Academic   Pronunciation

AUGUSTIN'S RESTAURANT

LUNCH MENU

Soups and Salads
Caesar salad $2.49
Dinner salad $1.85
Potato soup $1.49

Sandwiches
Big burger $2.98
Big cheeseburger $3.49
Super burger combo $5.99
Turkey sandwich $2.25

Main Courses
(All main courses come with a vegetable)
Sirloin steak and potatoes $8.50
Fried chicken and french fries $5.99

Side Orders
French fries $1.85
Potato chips $.85
Rice $1.25
Beans $1.25
Vegetable of the day $2.00

Beverages
Soda $1.19
Milk $1.29
Coffee $2.00
Tea $1.75

Desserts
Chocolate cake $2.75
Cheesecake $2.00
Vanilla or chocolate ice cream $1.75
Fresh fruit $2.00

C Look at the menu. What do you want for lunch? (Answers will vary. Sample answers are given.)

Guest Check

TABLE NO.	CHECK NO. 200345	SERVER NO.

Soup or Salad:	Potato soup	$ 1.49
Sandwich or Main Course:	Big burger	$ 2.98
Side Order:	Vegetable of the day	$ 2.00
Beverage:	Soda	$ 1.19
Dessert:	Fresh fruit	$ 2.00
	TOTAL: $	9.66

CD 1
TR 36–38

D Listen to the people ordering food in a restaurant. Write down the orders and total the cost.

1.
Guest Check

TABLE NO. 1	CHECK NO. 1001
1 Super burger combo	$5.99
1 Dinner salad	$1.85
	$
	$
	$
TOTAL: $	7.84

2.
Guest Check

TABLE NO. 2	CHECK NO. 1002
2 Steak & potatoes	$8.50
2 Vegetables of the day	$2.00
	$
	$
	$
TOTAL: $	21.00

3.
Guest Check

TABLE NO. 3	CHECK NO. 1003
1 Caesar salad	$2.49
1 Milk	$1.29
1 Fresh fruit	$2.00
	$
	$
TOTAL: $	5.78

Presentation 2   10–15 mins. ■■■□

Write *menu* on the board. Then, write *beverages*. Ask students what the second word means. Then, ask them for suggestions of beverages that might be included on a menu.

Ask students to open their books. Go over the categories of the menu, such as *sandwiches* and *side orders*. Then, drill students on the other vocabulary. Help students scan the menu by asking questions, such as: *How much is the rice?*

Walk around the room and ask individual students if you can take their orders based on the menu. Briefly role-play with the individuals, giving them as much support as necessary.

C Look at the menu. What do you want for lunch?

Encourage students to write their order. Then, ask them to share their orders with the class or with a group.

Prepare students for focused listening by asking them to listen to your order and write down what you would like from the menu. Ask them to also add up the total just as they did for their own orders in the book.

Teaching Tip

Listening as a worker

There are many purposes for listening activities. Students don't only need to understand what people are saying, but they also need to be able to take notes in the workplace. You will notice in the activity that follows that students are asked to *take* orders, not merely give them.

In *Stand Out*, we try to give students an opportunity to take on the role of a worker as well as of a customer. This process provides confidence when students apply for jobs.

Practice 2   15–20 mins. ■■□

D Listen to the people ordering food in a restaurant. Write down the orders and total the cost.

This activity will be a challenge for students because they are writing and listening.

Most students will need to listen several times before they get all the information. A good practice would be to have students listen to the recording and then discuss their answers in a group before listening again.

🎧 Listening Script   CD 1, Tracks 36–38

1. **Server:** *Good afternoon, sir. Are you ready to order?*
   Customer: *Yes, thanks. I'm very hungry.*
   Server: *We'll take care of that. What would you like?*
   Customer: *I'd like the Super Burger.*
   Server: *Great, the Super Burger Combo, right?*
   Customer: *Yes. Can I have a dinner salad, too?*
   Server: *Sure. Your food will be coming right up.*
   Customer: *Thanks.*

2. **Server:** *Hello. Can I take your order?*
   Customer: *Yes. We would like two sirloin steaks—rare—with potatoes and the vegetable of the day.*
   Server: *OK, two sirloin steak lunches. Do you want dinner salads with that?*
   Customer: *No, thank you, but could you please hurry? We have an appointment in an hour.*
   Server: *What would you like to drink?*
   Customer: *Water is fine. Thanks.*

3. **Server:** *Hi. Are you about ready?*
   Customer: *Yes. Can I have the Caesar salad, please?*
   Server: *Sure. Anything to drink?*
   Customer: *Yes, a glass of milk would be great.*
   Server: *OK, the Caesar and a milk.*
   Customer: *Oh, and how about some fruit on the side?*
   Server: *Sounds good. It will only be a few minutes.*
   Customer: *Thanks.*

Evaluation 2   7–15 mins. ■■□

First, as a class, check the totals of the orders. Then, check for certain items. There is a built-in discrepancy in the second listening. This will allow for discussion if your students catch it. Main courses come with vegetables and the second person orders a side of vegetables. You can accept either answer or discuss what the server could do for clarification. This is a great place to go over the listening script students have in the appendix of their books.

Presentation 3   10–15 mins. ■■■

E Study the chart with your classmates and teacher.

This chart allows students to learn the common phrases or questions used often in a customer service setting. Students have heard these expressions before. Walk through the questions with them and practice a few more role plays with individual students. Then, introduce them to Exercise F. Make sure students work on appropriate intonation as they practice the *yes/no* questions.

Practice 3   7–10 mins. ■

F Read the conversation. Then, practice placing new orders with a partner. Use the menu on page 42.

Evaluation 3   5–7 mins. ■

Ask volunteers to role-play their conversations in front of the class.

Application   15–20 mins. ■■■

G In a group, make a menu. Use food from your country.

Ask students to either display their menus or to report to the class.

Refer students to *Stand Out 2 Grammar Challenge*, Unit 3, Challenge 1 for more practice with using *can* to form questions.

Activity Bank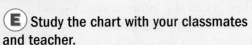

Unit 3, Lesson 1, Worksheet 1: Menus

Unit 3, Lesson 1, Worksheet 2: Taking Orders

Instructor's Notes

E Study the chart with your classmates and teacher.

Questions with *Can*			
Can	Pronoun	Base verb	Example question
can	I	take help	Can I take your order? Can I help you? Can you take my order? Can you take our order, please? Can you help me? Can you help us?
can	you		

F Read the conversation. Then, practice placing new orders with a partner. Use the menu on page 42.

EXAMPLE: *Server:* Can I take your order?
Customer: Yes, I want a Caesar salad, please.

G In a group, make a menu. Use food from your country.
(Answers will vary.)

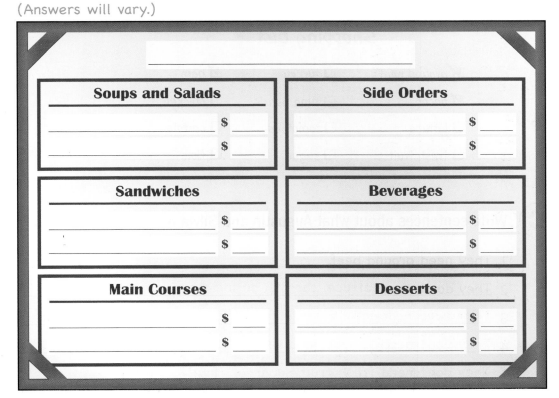

Do we need carrots?

GOAL ➤ **Make a shopping list**

Where are Augustin and Silvia?
What are they doing?
What are they saying?

A **Read the paragraph.**

Augustin and Silvia make a shopping list for the restaurant every Thursday morning. On Thursdays, they are not busy. They already have a lot of food this week. They don't need to buy very much.

  B **Listen to Augustin and Silvia make their shopping list. Put a check (✓) next to each item they need.**

CD 1
TR 39

Shopping List

☑ ground beef	☐ turkey	☑ ham
☑ bacon	☐ tuna fish	☐ chicken
☐ lettuce	☐ tomatoes	☐ carrots
☐ fresh fruit	☐ sugar	☐ flour

C **Write sentences about what Augustin and Silvia need and don't need.**

1. They need ground beef.

2. They don't need lettuce, carrots, or tomatoes.

3. They need ham and bacon.

4. They don't need turkey, tuna fish, or chicken.

5. They don't need fresh fruit, sugar, or flour.

AT-A-GLANCE PREP

Objective: Make a shopping list
Grammar: Count and noncount nouns, *some/any*
Pronunciation: /z/ and /ez/
Academic Strategies: Focused listening
Vocabulary: Containers and quantities

RESOURCES

Activity Bank: Unit 3, Lesson 2, Worksheets 1–2
Reading and Writing Challenge: Unit 3
Grammar Challenge: Unit 3, Challenge 2

Audio: CD 1, Track 39
Heinle Picture Dictionary: Food, pages 82–103

■ 1.5 hour classes   ■ 2.5 hour classes   ▨ 3⁺ hour classes

AGENDA

Place orders at a restaurant.
Listen for items on a shopping list.
Identify containers and quantities.
Practice making a list.
Use much *and* many *correctly.*
Make a shopping list.

Warm-up and Review   10-15 mins.

Ask students in groups to practice placing orders using the menus they made in the previous lesson.

Introduction   5 mins.

Discuss what *stuffed potatoes* are. (Or choose another dish.) Ask students if they were to make these potatoes for the class, what they would need at the store. Make a shopping list on the board. State the objective: *Today we will make shopping lists.*

Presentation 1   10-15 mins.

Prepare for the reading on this page by asking students to look at the picture and answer the questions in the box.

 Read the paragraph.

Read the short paragraph as a class and ask additional comprehension questions.

Together with students, find the word *not* in two places. They will have to find one of them within a contraction. Ask them to underline all the negatives in the paragraph. Remind students how to form the negative simple present with *don't.* It may help to refer them to page 23.

Prepare students for the focused-listening activity.

STANDARDS CORRELATIONS

CASAS: 1.1.7, 1.3.8 (See CASAS Competency List on pages 169-175.)
SCANS: **Resources** Allocate materials and facility resources
Interpersonal Participate as a member of a team
Basic Skills Reading, writing, listening, speaking
Thinking Skills Think creatively, make decisions, solve problems

Practice 1   10-15 mins.

 Listen to Augustin and Silvia make their shopping list. Put a check next to each item they need.

> #### 🎧 Listening Script   CD 1, Track 39
>
> On Thursdays, Augustin and Silvia are not busy at the restaurant. They make a shopping list every Thursday morning. Today, they don't have to buy a lot of food at the store. Augustin says they need ground beef. Silvia says they don't need turkey, and they don't need tuna fish or chicken. Augustin says they need ham and bacon. Silvia says they don't need lettuce, carrots, or tomatoes, and they don't need fresh fruit, sugar, or flour.
>
> Augustin doesn't like to shop for food, but he wants to help Silvia. Silvia doesn't shop for food because she works many hours at the restaurant. Silvia and Augustin try to help each other. Augustin doesn't like to shop, but he shops anyway to make his wife happy. They are not a rich couple, but they are a happy couple.

Evaluation 1   10-15 mins.

 Write sentences about what Augustin and Silvia need and don't need.

Ask volunteers to rewrite the sentences on the board and go over them as a class. Here is a good place to work on pronunciation. Students should emphasize *don't* as they read the sentences. The negative is prominent because there is a distinction made between the affirmative and the negative.

EFF: **Communication** Read with understanding, speak so others can understand, listen actively
Decision Making Solve problems and make decisions, plan
Interpersonal Cooperate with others

Presentation 2 — 10–15 mins.

Write the shopping list on the board that Augustin and Silvia would make if they only needed the items checked in the previous practice. Write *ground beef* and discuss the meaning. Then, write *2 lbs.* Ask: *How much ground beef do they need?* See how many students understand the abbreviation for *pounds* and write the word out. As a class, go over each item on the list and ask how much or how many Augustin and Silvia need. There will be a discussion about count and noncount nouns in Presentation 3 so only explain which phrase is appropriate if asked. The purpose of this presentation is to identify the container and quantity vocabulary. Expand the list to include *ice cream, soup, oil,* and *bread.* As a class, decide on a quantity of these items for the restaurant. As the containers or quantities come up, write them on the board. If they don't come up, you should bring up *carton, bag, bottle,* and *loaf.*

Teaching Tip

Eliciting information

Often in the presentation stage, it is important to first elicit information from students to determine what they know. Teachers that do this get more student involvement, and the class becomes more student-centered. It would be easier to merely open the book to the page where the pictures identify the vocabulary clearly, but it is much more productive to first attempt to elicit information from students. In this way, students participate and become part of the presentation. There are times when presenting the vocabulary first is necessary to save time, but when time permits, eliciting information can be more effective.

Ask students to open their books and go over the new vocabulary with them.

D **Complete Augustin's shopping list with the words from the pictures.**

Do this activity as a class to evaluate students' comprehension.

Briefly go over the grammar point (*some/any*) and prepare students to do Exercise E. Show students how to substitute information for the underlined words.

Pronunciation

Final /z/, /ez/

Final sounds in words are often difficult for students. Many languages de-emphasize final consonants, almost dropping the sound completely. Other languages, including some Asian languages, do not have a marker for the plural form of the verb. Also, some students may read an *s* and, because their language may have a direct sound/symbol correspondence, may try to always pronounce /s/ instead of /z/. Finally, in some languages, the final sound of phrases and sentences, or words when spoken in isolation, end with the articulation point fixed and not released. In English, the mouth is generally open as the articulation point is released. In other words, students may attempt to leave the mouth closed and there may be little, if any, aspiration on sounds like the final /z/. Help students to release the /z/ and /ez/ sounds by exaggerating the release of the /z/ or /ez/.

Practice 2 — 10–15 mins.

E **Practice the conversation with a partner. Use items from the shopping list.**

Teaching Tip

Dialog cards

Another way to do pair work when substitution is involved is to use dialog cards.

1. Pass out 3-by-5 index cards to each student.
2. List the vocabulary on the board.
3. Divide the number of words by the number of students. In other words, if there are 32 students and 8 vocabulary words, the answer would be 4.
4. Instruct every four students to write a designated vocabulary word. When you are finished, you will have four cards for each word.
5. Collect the cards and randomly distribute them again.
6. Now, students are to find other students with the same word. They discover this by doing the conversation. The student recites the information on his or her card.
7. When students find matches, they write the classmate's name on the card. They continue until they find all matches.

Evaluation 2 — 7–10 mins.

Observe the activity and ask volunteers to demonstrate in front of the class.

GOAL ➤ **Make a shopping list**

D Complete Augustin's shopping list with the words from the pictures.

carton(s)

pound(s)

jar(s)

bottle(s)

box(es)

loaf(loaves)

bag(s)

can(s)

Shopping List

milk 3 gallons	ground beef 2 pounds
flour 2 bags	sugar 3 bags
tomatoes 5 pounds	jam 1 jar
bread 3 loaves	oil 2 bottles
cake mix 2 boxes	oranges 3 pounds
ice cream 4 cartons	chicken soup 4 cans

gallon(s)

Pronunciation

/z/		/ez/
cartons	loaves	boxes
pounds	bags	
jars	cans	
bottles	gallons	

Some / any	
Question	Do we need **any** milk?
Statement	We need **some** milk.

E Practice the conversation with a partner. Use items from the shopping list.

EXAMPLE: *Augustin:* Do we need any <u>milk</u> at the store?
Silvia: Yes, we need some <u>milk</u>.
Augustin: How many <u>gallons</u> do we need?
Silvia: We need <u>three gallons</u>.

LESSON 2

GOAL ➤ **Make a shopping list**

F Study the chart with your classmates and teacher.

Count and Noncount Nouns	
Count nouns	**Noncount nouns**
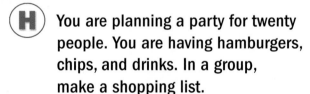	
Use *many* with nouns you can count.	Use *much* with nouns you cannot count.
Example sentences	
How **many** tomatoes do we need? How **many** pounds of tomatoes do we need?	How **much** flour do we need? How **much** rice do we need?

G Complete the sentences with *much* or *many*.

1. How _____many_____ bananas do we need?

2. How _____many_____ bottles of oil do we need?

3. How _____much_____ oil do we need?

4. How _____much_____ flour do we need?

5. How _____many_____ apples do we need?

6. How _____many_____ pounds of apples do we need?

H You are planning a party for twenty people. You are having hamburgers, chips, and drinks. In a group, make a shopping list.

(Answers will vary.)

Shopping List

I **Active Task.** Go to a local market or on the Internet to find the total cost of your food items.

Presentation 3   7–10 mins. ■ ■ ■

F Study the chart with your classmates and teacher.

Teach students that we can count some things, but there are other things we cannot count. A good way to do this is to bring in some salt. Take out two pencils and ask students: *How many pencils do I have?* After they respond, count them. Do the same with other items in the classroom. Then, write on the board: *How many salt do I have?* Pour a little salt on a piece of paper for all students to see. Ask someone to count the salt. Cross out *many* and write *much*.

For shorter classes, ask students to do Exercise G for homework.

Practice 3   7–10 mins. ■

G Complete the sentences with *much* or *many*.

With little explanation, ask students to complete the exercise individually.

Evaluation 3   7–10 mins. ■

Ask volunteers to write their sentences on the board and review the exercise.

Application   15–20 mins. ■ ■ ■

H You are planning a party for twenty people. You are having hamburgers, chips, and drinks. In a group, make a shopping list.

I Active Task. Go to a local market or on the Internet to find the total cost of your food items.

Refer students to *Stand Out 2 Grammar Challenge*, Unit 3, Challenge 2 for more practice with *how much* and *how many*.

Activity Bank

Templates: Two-Column Chart
Unit 3, Lesson 2, Worksheet 1: Shopping Lists
Unit 3, Lesson 2, Worksheet 2: Containers

Instructor's Notes

AGENDA
Take a class poll.
Talk about sections in a supermarket.
Read a store directory.
Ask for help.
Listen for sections in a supermarket.
Do a cluster activity.

Objective: Locate items in a supermarket
Grammar: Information questions with *be*
Pronunciation: Rhythm
Academic Strategies: Focused listening, predicting
Vocabulary: Sections in a supermarket, food vocabulary

RESOURCES

Activity Bank: Unit 3, Lesson 3, Worksheets 1–2
Reading and Writing Challenge: Unit 3
Grammar Challenge: Unit 3, Challenge 3

Audio: CD 1, Track 40
Heinle Picture Dictionary: Food, pages 82–103

■ 1.5 hour classes ■ 2.5 hour classes ■ 3⁺ hour classes

Warm-up and Review   10-15 mins. ■■■

Ask students what they buy at supermarkets. Tell them that you can never find the milk. Ask them where the milk is in a grocery store. See if they can come up with *the dairy section*. If they can't, give them the phrase. Now, ask students where they shop. Take a class poll and record the results by making a graph on the board. You may also supply students with a graph template from the Activity Bank CD-ROM templates folder.

Introduction   7-10 mins. ■■■

Continue talking about supermarkets. Design one on the board. Ask students where the parking lot might be and the checkout counters could be. State the objective: *Today we will learn to locate items in a supermarket.*

Presentation 1   30-40 mins. ■■■

Write *canned goods* on the board. Go over what this phrase means. Ask students to work in groups to create a list of all the different sections in a supermarket. Ask groups to report to the class and make a complete list on the board.

Ask students to open their books and go over the sections at the top of the page. Review the food vocabulary. Then, ask where different items are located in a supermarket.

 Look at the pictures and complete the chart below.

Since this is still the presentation stage, do this activity as a class. Drill students briefly to make sure they understand. Review the grammar box. You may decide to make two columns on the board and ask students to help you put the items under the headings *singular* and *plural*.

Prepare students to do Exercise B.

Practice 1   7-10 mins.

 Practice the conversation with a partner. Make new conversations with *milk, tomatoes, canned corn, chicken, pears, ice cream, butter, soup, sugar,* and *oranges*.

Evaluation 1   5-7 mins.

Observe students doing the practice and then ask questions to confirm that they understand.

STANDARDS CORRELATIONS

CASAS: 1.1.7, 1.3.7, 1.3.8, 2.5.4 (See CASAS Competency List on pages 169-175.)
***SCANS:* Information** Interpret and communicate information, use computers to process information
Interpersonal Participate as a member of a team

Systems Understand systems
Basic Skills Writing, listening, speaking
***EFF:* Communication** Speak so others can understand, listen actively
Interpersonal Cooperate with others

LESSON 3

At the supermarket

GOAL ➤ Locate items in a supermarket

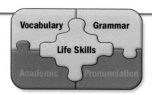

A Look at the pictures and complete the chart below.

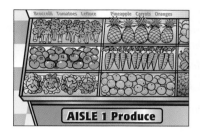

Item	Section	Aisle
flour	Baking Needs	4
milk	Dairy/Frozen Foods	5
tomatoes	Produce	1
meat	Meats	8

Be Verb	
Singular	Where **is** the flour? It **is** in Aisle 4.
Plural	Where **are** the cake mixes? They **are** in Aisle 4.

B Practice the conversation with a partner. Make new conversations with *milk, tomatoes, canned corn, chicken, pears, ice cream, butter, soup, sugar,* and *oranges.*

EXAMPLES:

Augustin: Excuse me. Where is the flour?
Store Clerk: It's in Aisle 4.

Augustin: Where are the cake mixes?
Store Clerk: They are also in Aisle 4.

GOAL ➤ **Locate items in a supermarket**

C **Read the store directory.**

Product	Section	Aisle	Product	Section	Aisle	Product	Section	Aisle
Apples	*Produce*	1	Cheese	*Dairy*	5	Ice cream	*Frozen Foods*	5
Bread	*Bakery*	2	Chicken	*Meats*	8			
Brown sugar	*Baking Needs*	4	Cookies	*Bakery*	2	Lettuce	*Produce*	1
			Cream	*Dairy*	5	Milk	*Dairy*	5
Butter	*Dairy*	5				Oranges	*Produce*	1
Cake	*Bakery*	2	Cucumbers	*Produce*	1	Pears	*Produce*	1
Cake mix	*Baking Needs*	4	Eggs	*Dairy*	5	Soup	*Canned Goods*	3
Canned corn	*Canned Goods*	3	Flour	*Baking Needs*	4			
						Sugar	*Baking Needs*	4
Canned peas	*Canned Goods*	3	Ground beef	*Meats*	8	Turkey	*Meats*	8
Cantaloupe	*Produce*	1	Ham	*Meats*	8	Yogurt	*Dairy*	5

D **Answer the questions with complete sentences.**

1. Where are the cookies? _____ They are in the bakery section in Aisle 2. _____

2. Where is the brown sugar? It is in the baking needs section in Aisle 4.

3. Where is the ground beef? It is in the meats section in Aisle 8.

4. Where are the eggs? They are in the dairy section in Aisle 5.

Pronunciation

Rhythm

_____ • • _____ •
Where are the cook ies?

E **Practice the conversation with a partner. Ask more questions with information from the directory.**

EXAMPLE: *Augustin:* Can you help me? I'm looking for the <u>canned corn</u>.
  Store Clerk: It's in the <u>canned goods</u> section.
  Augustin: Where is the <u>canned goods</u> section?
  Store Clerk: It's in <u>Aisle 3</u>.
  Augustin: Thanks!

Presentation 2   15–20 mins. ▪▪▫

C Read the store directory.

Ask students to cover the *Section* column in the directory. Ask students what section they think each product is in. Ask questions about the entire directory and go over any new vocabulary. Help students with the pronunciation of difficult words.

D Answer the questions with complete sentences.

Do this activity as a class and ask students to write sentences on the board. Refer back to the chart you created on the board with plural and singular items to remind students that sometimes they will use *they* and sometimes *it* to describe the locations.

Pronunciation

Rhythm

There is a rhythm to English that is similar to some languages and very distinct from others. Speakers vary in which words they emphasize to show rhythm in discourse. However, important words are regularly given emphasis and words that answer a specific question are given emphasis. Words with less emphasis are generally spoken quickly while words with more emphasis are lengthened.

For people who understand music notation, English is loosely based on an eighth note followed by a sixteenth note feel. In stressing rhythm, an instructor might have students clap along with this pattern several times before they attempt to produce it so they have a general feel for the speech pattern.

Next, ask students only to say the syllables that receive more emphasis. In this case they might say:

    Where-cook(ies)

The rest of the syllables are roughly ½ the length of the emphasized ones. Once students are comfortable with the rhythm, say the question and ask them to repeat.

Prepare students to do Exercise E.

Practice 2   7–10 mins. ▪▫

E Practice the conversation with a partner. Ask more questions with information from the directory.

Evaluation 2   7–10 mins. ▪▫

Observe the activity and ask volunteers to demonstrate in front of the class.

Instructor's Notes

_____

_____

_____

_____

_____

_____

_____

_____

_____

_____

_____

_____

_____

_____

_____

_____

_____

_____

_____

_____

_____

Presentation 3　　　　　7-10 mins.

F Read the shopping list. Predict what section each item is in. Then, listen to the conversation and complete the chart.

Go over the new vocabulary in the shopping list. Discuss possibilities with students and prepare them for the focused-listening activity.

Practice 3　　　　　　7-10 mins.

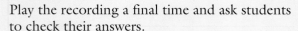
Listening Script　　　　CD 1, Track 40

Manager: *Can I help you?*
Shopper: *Yes, I can't find several items. Do you think you could help me?*
Manager: *That's why I'm here. What do you need?*
Shopper: *Well, I can't find the beets.*
Manager: *What kind do you want—canned, fresh, or frozen?*
Shopper: *Canned, please.*
Manager: *OK, let's go over to the canned goods section—Aisle 3—to find the beets.*
Shopper: *I also need muffins.*
Manager: *Those are in the bakery section—Aisle 2.*
Shopper: *And the orange juice . . . I need frozen, please.*
Manager: *The frozen foods section is right here in Aisle 7.*
Shopper: *Thanks so much. I suppose I can find the chicken breasts. They are with the other meats in the meat section—Aisle 8, right?*
Manager: *Right.*

You may need to play the recording two or three times for students to complete the chart.
Briefly go over the shopping list.

Evaluation 3　　　　　　3 mins.

Play the recording a final time and ask students to check their answers.

Application　　　　　10-15 mins.

G In a group, complete the cluster diagram with items from your local supermarket. Do not look at page 48.

✏ Refer students to *Stand Out 2 Grammar Challenge*, Unit 3, Challenge 3 for more practice with questions and answers with *be*.

Instructor's Notes

_____

_____

_____

_____

_____

_____

_____

_____

_____

_____

_____

_____

_____

_____

_____

_____

_____

_____

_____

_____

_____

_____

LESSON **3**   **GOAL** ➤ **Locate items in a supermarket**

CD 1
TR 40

 F Read the shopping list. Predict what section each item is in. Then, listen to the conversation and complete the chart.

Shopping list	Section	Aisle
beets	canned goods	3
muffins	bakery	2
orange juice	frozen foods	7
chicken breasts	meats	8

G In a group, complete the cluster diagram with items from your local supermarket. Do not look at page 48. (Answers will vary. Sample answers are given.)

A healthy diet

GOAL ➤ Plan meals

CD 1
TR 41

A Close your books and listen to the paragraph. Then, read about nutrition and discuss the paragraph with the class.

> Nutrition means the food we eat and how much we eat of each food group. Good nutrition is important. When we eat good food, our bodies are stronger and we stay healthy. The nutrition pyramid is a guide that helps us choose the best foods for a balanced diet. It is healthy to eat food from each of the main food groups.

B Look at the nutrition pyramids. How are they the same? How are they different?

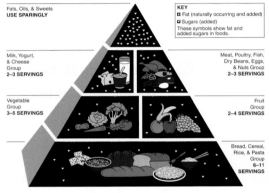

Food Guide Pyramid
A Guide to Daily Food Choices

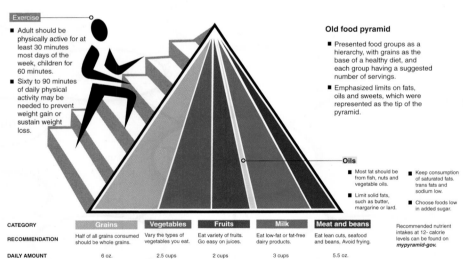

Old food pyramid

- Presented food groups as a hierarchy, with grains as the base of a healthy diet, and each group having a suggested number of servings.

- Emphasized limits on fats, oils and sweets, which were represented as the tip of the pyramid.

C Which food groups are healthier? Rank the food groups from 1 to 6. 1 is the healthiest.
(Answers will vary. Sample answers are given.)

_5_ Meat	_1_ Vegetables	_2_ Fruit
_4_ Dairy	_3_ Breads, Grains	_6_ Fats, Oils, and Sweets

AT-A-GLANCE PREP

Objective: Plan meals
Grammar: Simple present: *have*
Academic Strategies: Focused listening, Venn diagrams
Vocabulary: Food groups, *breakfast, lunch, dinner*

RESOURCES

Activity Bank: Unit 3, Lesson 4, Worksheets 1–4
Reading and Writing Challenge: Unit 3

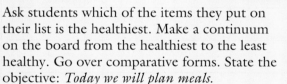

■ 1.5 hour classes ■ 2.5 hour classes ■ 3⁺ hour classes

Grammar Challenge: Unit 3, Challenge 4
Audio: CD 1, Track 41
Heinle Picture Dictionary: Food, pages 82–103

> ## AGENDA
> *Talk about food groups and nutrition.*
> *Evaluate nutrition.*
> *Rank diets for nutrition.*
> *Make a Venn diagram.*

Warm-up and Review   15-20 mins. ■■■

List all the food vocabulary used in this unit thus far on the board. Make sure students know what each word means. Make a four-column chart on the board with the following headings: *fruit, vegetables, meat,* and *drinks.* Ask students to work together in groups to quickly put all the items in the appropriate columns. You can make this a competition if you wish.

Teaching Tip

Group participation

There are many ways to encourage all students to participate in groups. It helps when students are working on a written task if they work on one chart for the entire group and not their own individual ones. One student is chosen as the writer and the others offer suggestions.

Ask group representatives to complete the chart on the board.

Introduction   5-7 mins. ■■■

Ask students which of the items they put on their list is the healthiest. Make a continuum on the board from the healthiest to the least healthy. Go over comparative forms. State the objective: *Today we will plan meals.*

Presentation 1   10-15 mins. ■■■

Write the word *nutrition* on the board and elicit the meaning. Tell them that they will listen to a short paragraph about nutrition. Write the following terms on the board: *diet, stronger, stay, balanced, bodies,* and *food groups,* and go over their meanings. Then, ask students to listen to the paragraph with their books closed and raise their hands and put them down again every time they hear one of them.

(A) **Close your books and listen to the paragraph. Then, read about nutrition and discuss the paragraph with the class.**

> 🎧 **Listening Script**   CD 1, Track 41
>
> *The listening script matches the paragraph in Exercise A.*

(B) **Look at the nutrition pyramids. How are they the same? How are they different?**

Go over the pyramids. Discuss how opinions change about what is healthy and that the second pyramid reflects the fact that "one size doesn't fit all." Talk about the food groups and prepare students to do Exercise C.

Practice 1   7-10 mins. ■■■

(C) **Which food groups are healthier? Rank the food groups from 1–6. 1 is the healthiest.**

Ask students to do this in groups.

Evaluation 1   5-7 mins. ■■■

Ask groups to report to the class.

> ### STANDARDS CORRELATIONS
>
> **CASAS:** 1.3.8, 3.5.2, 3.5.9 (See CASAS Competency List on pages 169-175.)
> **SCANS: Resources** Allocate materials and facility resources
> **Information** Acquire and evaluate information, organize and maintain information, interpret and communicate information
> **Interpersonal** Participate as a member of a team, teach others
> **Basic Skills** Reading, writing, listening, speaking
> **Thinking Skills** See things in the mind's eye
> **Personal Qualities** Self management
> **EFF: Communication** Read with understanding, speak so others can understand, listen actively, observe critically
> **Decision Making** Solve problems and make decisions, plan
> **Interpersonal** Cooperate with others, advocate and influence, resolve conflict and negotiate

Presentation 2   15–20 mins. ■■■

Draw three large connected circles (a Venn diagram) on the board. Venn diagrams are also available on the Activity Bank CD-ROM. Label the circles *Breakfast, Lunch,* and *Dinner.* Ask students to list any foods they eat for each meal in the circles. Complete the diagram as a class on the board.

(D) **Augustin and his family don't eat together because they are very busy. Read what they eat.**

Go over the meals each family member eats and ask questions, such as: *What does Gilberto have for lunch?* Remind students of the simple present forms. This would be a good time to show students the grammar charts in the appendix of their books. Show them *have* and the regular simple present charts. Write the following on the board: *I think that _____ has a better diet because _____.* Show students how to use comparative forms here and prepare them for Exercise E.

Practice 2   10–15 mins. ■■

(E) **Who has the best diet? In a group, rank the family members in order from the best diet to the worst. 1 is the best.**

Evaluation 2   5–10 mins. ■■

Ask groups to report.

Instructor's Notes

GOAL ➤ **Plan meals**

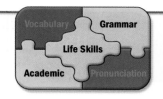

D Augustin and his family don't eat together because they are very busy. Read what they eat.

Silvia

Breakfast: cereal and milk
Lunch: green salad and fruit juice
Dinner: spaghetti with meatballs and ice cream

Augustin

Breakfast: coffee
Lunch: sausage, beans, rice, and water
Dinner: cheese, bread, green salad, and fruit

Fernando

Breakfast: fruit, cereal, milk, and toast
Lunch: pepperoni pizza and milk
Dinner: fried chicken and a baked potato

Rosa

Breakfast: toast and coffee
Lunch: soup, bread, fruit, and yogurt
Dinner: turkey, potatoes, green salad, and water

Gilberto

Breakfast: doughnut and coffee
Lunch: hamburger, fries, and soda
Dinner: pepperoni pizza and beer

Simple Present: *Have*
I **have** . . .
You **have** . . .
He/She **has** . . .

E Who has the best diet? In a group, rank the family members in order from the best diet to the worst. 1 is the best. (Answers will vary. Sample answers are given.)

<u> 3 </u> Silvia

<u> 2 </u> Augustin

<u> 4 </u> Fernando

<u> 1 </u> Rosa

<u> 5 </u> Gilberto

F Complete the diagram. Write the foods Rosa and Augustin eat for breakfast, lunch, and dinner.

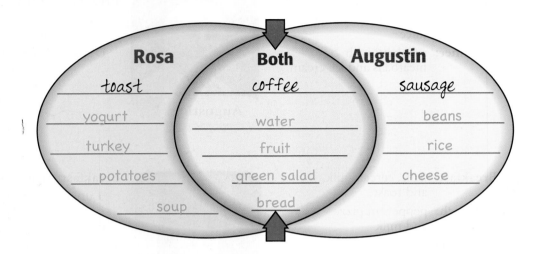

Rosa

| toast |
| yogurt |
| turkey |
| potatoes |
| soup |

Both

| coffee |
| water |
| fruit |
| green salad |
| bread |

Augustin

| sausage |
| beans |
| rice |
| cheese |

G What do you and your family eat for breakfast, lunch, and dinner? Complete the chart. (Answers will vary.)

Breakfast	Lunch	Dinner

H Ask a partner. (Answers will vary.)

1. What do you eat for breakfast? _____

2. What do you eat for lunch? _____

3. What do you eat for dinner? _____

Presentation 3   10–15 mins. ■■■

Refer back to your Venn diagram on the board and discuss the information once again. Then, create a new Venn diagram with circles referring to you and a volunteer. Complete the diagram similar to the way students are expected to in Exercise F.

Practice 3   7–10 mins. ■

(F) **Complete the diagram. Write the foods Rosa and Augustin eat for breakfast, lunch, and dinner.**

Evaluation 3   5–10 mins. ■■

Make a new Venn diagram on the board and ask volunteers to fill it in with the information they have already written in the practice.

Application   20–30 mins. ■■■

(G) **What do you and your family eat for breakfast, lunch, and dinner? Complete the chart.**

Have students complete this activity individually. Help them with vocabulary as needed.

(H) **Ask a partner.**

Ask students to do this activity and then to make a Venn diagram of the information from Exercises G and H. You may choose to use a Venn diagram template from the Activity Bank CD-ROM template folder.

📖 **Refer students to *Stand Out 2 Grammar Challenge*, Unit 3, Challenge 4 for more practice with *have*.**

Activity Bank

Templates: Four-Column Chart

Templates: Three-Circle Venn Diagram

Templates: Two-Circle Venn Diagram

Unit 3, Lesson 4, Worksheet 1: Food Groups

Unit 3, Lesson 4, Worksheet 2: Nutrition

Unit 3, Lesson 4, Worksheet 3: Meals

Unit 3, Lesson 4, Worksheet 4: A Balanced Diet

Instructor's Notes

AGENDA

Make Venn diagrams.
Read and talk about recipes.
Learn new verbs.
Listen to recipes.
Write recipes.

Objective: Read recipes
Grammar: Imperatives and negative imperatives
Pronunciation: Clarification
Academic Strategies: Focused listening, clarification, predicting
Vocabulary: Recipe verbs and instructions

RESOURCES

Activity Bank: Unit 3, Lesson 5, Worksheets 1–2
Reading and Writing Challenge: Unit 3
Grammar Challenge: Unit 3, Challenge 5

Audio: CD 1, Track 42
Heinle Picture Dictionary: Food, pages 82–103

■ 1.5 hour classes ■ 2.5 hour classes ■ 3⁺ hour classes

Warm-up and Review   10-12 mins.

Ask students to work with a different partner from the one in the previous lesson. Have pairs make Venn diagrams of their eating habits similar to the application in Lesson 4. Ask the pairs to team up with another pair and report what they have created.

Introduction   5-7 mins.

Write the word *ingredients* on the board. Then, under the word, list all the ingredients of a dish students might be familiar with. For example, if you have Mexican students, you could list *corn tortillas, beef, cheese, lettuce,* and *jalapenos.* Ask students to guess what the dish is. State the objective: *Today we will read recipes.*

Presentation 1   15-20 mins.

With students' books closed, try to make a recipe based on the ingredients and the dish from the introduction. Ask students to help you write out the instructions.

(A) Read the recipe.

Go over the recipe step by step with students. Remind them of containers and count and noncount nouns. Refer them to the grammar box to review the use of *how much* and *how many.* Ask students to underline the verb in each of the sentences in the instructions. They

will notice that many of the verbs start a new sentence. The imperative verb form will be discussed in more detail in Presentation 3.

Ask comprehension questions about the recipe to ensure that students understand.

Prepare students for the practice in Exercise B. Go over the stress given to the number in clarification information.

Practice 1   5-7 mins.

(B) Ask a partner questions about the recipe.

Teaching Tip

Time management

Always give time parameters on activities. It is helpful to tell students that they should work on the activity for five minutes or, in this case, until you stop them. Tell students that they shouldn't stop until you stop them. Sometimes students will feel like they have understood the activity and don't need to practice anymore. They should be encouraged to continue the activity for additional practice. This will allow students to not only practice, but to also help one another and to ask the instructor questions.

Evaluation 1   5 mins.

Observe the activity and check for understanding.

STANDARDS CORRELATIONS

CASAS: 1.1.1, 1.1.7, 1.3.8 (See CASAS Competency List on pages 169-175.)
SCANS: Resources Allocate materials and facility resources
Information Acquire and evaluate information, organize and maintain information, interpret and communicate information
Interpersonal Participate as a member of a team, teach others

Basic Skills Reading, writing, listening, speaking
Thinking Skills Think creatively
EFF: Communication Read with understanding, convey ideas in writing, speak so others can understand, listen
Decision Making Solve problems and make decisions, plan
Interpersonal Cooperate with others

Following instructions

GOAL ➤ **Read recipes**

(A) Read the recipe.

Spaghetti and Meatballs

Serves 6 people

Ingredients:	2 jars of tomato sauce		2 pounds of ground beef
	2 eggs		salt
	1 onion		pepper
	1 package spaghetti		

| Instructions: | Cook the pasta according to package directions. Combine the eggs, chopped onions, salt, and pepper in a large bowl. Add the beef and mix well. Shape the mixture into approximately 48 balls and fry until cooked.

Heat the tomato sauce for 10 minutes on medium heat. Add the meatballs and simmer for 15 minutes. Then add to pasta and serve. |
| --- | --- |

How much? / How many?

How many eggs do we need?

How much sauce do we need?

Pronunciation

Clarification
Put stress on the clarification word.

TWO jars

(B) Ask a partner questions about the recipe.

EXAMPLE: *Student A:* How much tomato sauce do we need?
Student B: We need two jars.
Student A: How many?
Student B: two jars

GOAL ➤ **Read recipes**

C Read the recipe for mashed potatoes. Underline the new words.

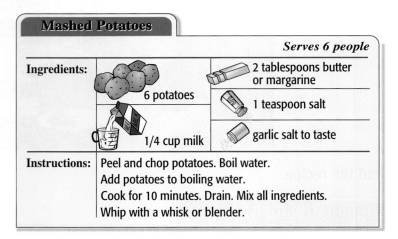

Mashed Potatoes

Serves 6 people

Ingredients:	6 potatoes	2 tablespoons butter or margarine
		1 teaspoon salt
	1/4 cup milk	garlic salt to taste
Instructions:	Peel and chop potatoes. Boil water. Add potatoes to boiling water. Cook for 10 minutes. Drain. Mix all ingredients. Whip with a whisk or blender.	

D Match the pictures with the words by drawing a line. Then, order the steps by writing numbers under the pictures.

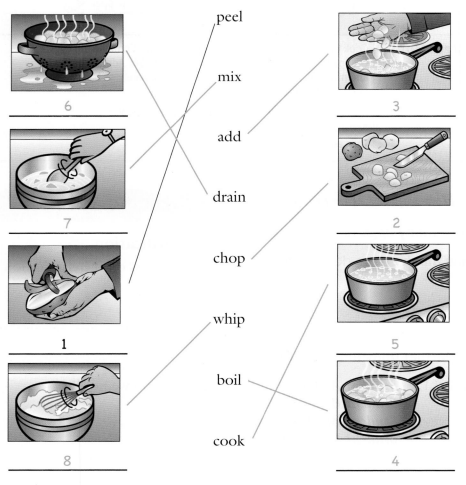

peel

mix

add

drain

chop

whip

boil

cook

6

7

1

8

3

2

5

4

Presentation 2   10-15 mins.

Ask students to close their books. Pantomime the process of making mashed potatoes as described on the recipe card on the page. Ask students if they can identify the verbs of some or all of the actions. Write the verbs they suggest on the board as they give them. Write *mashed potatoes* on the board. See if students know how to make mashed potatoes. Elicit instructions. Ask them what the ingredients might be.

C **Read the recipe for mashed potatoes. Underline the new words.**

Go over the recipe and compare it to the ideas you and the class came up with earlier.

Practice 2   10-15 mins. ■■

D **Match the pictures with the words by drawing a line. Then, order the steps by writing numbers under the pictures.**

Have students complete this activity individually.

Evaluation 2   10-15 mins. ■■

Ask students to check their answers to Exercise D by comparing them with their partner's.

Write all the verbs from the exercise on the board. As a class go over other words that can go with the verbs. For example:

boil: water, eggs, rice
add: potatoes, water, soup
peel: potatoes, apples, oranges
cook: potatoes, fish, noodles
chop: potatoes, celery, carrots
whip: potatoes, cream, eggs

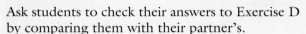

Presentation 3   8-10 mins. ▪▪▪

 E **Study the charts with your classmates and teacher.**

Teach students that an imperative is like a command. It can be used to give instructions that you might see or hear on the street, on medicine bottles, and in recipes. Show them how the subject is implied and generally that a new verb indicates a new sentence unless there is a conjunction such as *and*. Return to the two previous pages in the lesson and identify the imperatives. Students should understand that the imperative is the only time the subject is omitted in English when expressing complete sentences.

Pantomime each verb and test students. As you pantomime, they say one of the example sentences. Have them do this with their books open and then closed.

Practice 3   10-15 mins. ▪▪▪

F **Listen to the instructions. Number them in the correct order.**

Before students listen, ask them in groups of three or four to predict the correct answers.

> 🎧 **Listening Script**   CD 1, Track 42
>
> 1. *Heat oven to 350°. Combine cake mix, water, oil, and eggs in a large bowl. Pour mixture into a pan. Bake for 35 minutes.*
>
> 2. *Fry ground beef. Drain excess grease. Cut tomatoes, onions, cheese, and lettuce. Fry corn tortillas until crisp. Add ground beef, cheese, tomatoes, and lettuce to the fried tortillas.*

Evaluation 3   5-7 mins. ▪▪▪

Go over the answers to Exercise F. Help students understand all the vocabulary and imperative verbs. Try pantomiming again and check for students' understanding of the new vocabulary.

Application   10-15 mins. ▪▪▪

G **In a group, write a recipe.**

 Refer students to *Stand Out 2 Grammar Challenge*, Unit 3, Challenge 5 for more practice with imperatives.

Activity Bank
Unit 3, Lesson 5, Worksheet 1: Recipes
Unit 3, Lesson 5, Worksheet 2: Candy and Meatloaf

Instructor's Notes

_____

_____

_____

_____

_____

_____

_____

_____

_____

_____

_____

_____

_____

_____

_____

_____

_____

_____

_____

_____

_____

_____

LESSON 5   **GOAL** ➤ **Read recipes**

 E   Study the charts with your classmates and teacher.

Imperatives		
	Base verb	**Example sentence**
	drain	**Drain** the water.
~~you~~	chop	**Chop** the potatoes.
	peel	**Peel** the potatoes.

Negative Imperatives			
	Negative	**Base verb**	**Example sentence**
		boil	**Do not boil** the water. (**Don't boil** the water.)
~~you~~	do not don't	use	**Do not use** salt. (**Don't use** salt.)
		cook	**Do not cook** in the microwave. (**Don't cook** in the microwave.)

  F   Listen to the instructions. Number them in the correct order.

CD 1
TR 42

1. **Recipe: Cake**

   ___4___ Bake for 35 minutes.

   ___2___ Combine cake mix, water, oil, and eggs in a large bowl.

   ___1___ Heat oven to 350°.

   ___3___ Pour mixture into a pan.

2. **Recipe: Tacos**

   ___5___ Add ground beef, cheese, tomatoes, and lettuce to the fried tortillas.

   ___3___ Cut tomatoes, onions, cheese, and lettuce.

   ___2___ Drain grease.

   ___4___ Fry corn tortillas.

   ___1___ Fry ground beef.

 G   In a group, write a recipe. (Answers will vary. Sample answer is given.)

Chocolate Chip Cookies	
Ingredients:	milk, eggs, flour, sugar, vanilla, baking powder, chocolate cookies
Instructions:	Mix all ingredients in a large mixing bowl. Put in small portions on a baking pan and bake for 20 min. at 365°.

Review

A Look at the menu. Fill in the name of each section. (Lesson 1)

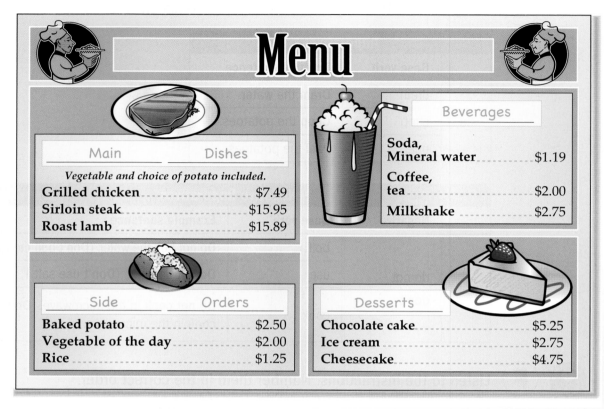

Menu

Main Dishes
Vegetable and choice of potato included.
Grilled chicken $7.49
Sirloin steak $15.95
Roast lamb $15.89

Side Orders
Baked potato $2.50
Vegetable of the day $2.00
Rice $1.25

Beverages
Soda,
Mineral water $1.19
Coffee,
tea $2.00
Milkshake $2.75

Desserts
Chocolate cake $5.25
Ice cream $2.75
Cheesecake $4.75

B Number the conversation in the correct order. (Lesson 1)

__3__ *Server:* What do you want to drink?

__6__ *Customer:* That's all, thank you.

__2__ *Customer:* Yes, I'll have the steak and a baked potato, please.

__4__ *Customer:* Mineral water, please.

__1__ *Server:* Can I take your order?

__5__ *Server:* Anything else?

C Practice more conversations with food from the menu in Exercise A. (Lesson 1)

Objective: All unit objectives
Grammar: All unit grammar
Academic Strategies: Reviewing, evaluating, developing study skills
Vocabulary: All unit vocabulary

■ 1.5 hour classes ■ 2.5 hour classes ■ 3⁺ hour classes

AGENDA
Discuss unit objectives.
Complete the review.
Do My Dictionary.
Evaluate and reflect on progress.

Warm-up and Review 7-10 mins. ■■■

Ask individuals what they like to eat. Make a list on the board of all the vocabulary students can come up with from the unit.

Introduction 5 mins. ■■■

Write all the objectives on the board from Unit 3. Show students the first page of the unit and say the five objectives. Explain that today they will review the whole unit.

Note: Depending on the length of the term, you may decide to have students do Presentation 1 and Practice 1 for homework and then review student work as either the warm-up or another class activity.

Presentation 1 10-15 mins. ■■■

This presentation will cover the first three pages of the review. Quickly go to the first page of each lesson. Discuss the objective of each. Ask simple questions to remind students of what they have learned.

Practice 1 15-20 mins. ■■

Ⓐ Look at the menu. Fill in the name of each section. (Lesson 1)

Ⓑ Number the conversation in the correct order. (Lesson 1)

Ⓒ Practice more conversations with food from the menu in Exercise A. (Lesson 1)

Teaching Tip

Recycling/Review

The review and the project that follows are part of the recycling/review process. Students at this level often need to be reintroduced to concepts to solidify what they have learned. Many concepts are learned and forgotten while learning other new concepts. This is because students learn but are not necessarily ready to acquire language concepts.

Therefore, it becomes very important to review and to show students how to review on their own. It is also important to recycle the new concepts in different contexts.

STANDARDS CORRELATIONS

CASAS: 1.1.1, 1.1.7, 1.3.7, 1.3.8, 2.5.4, 2.6.4, 3.5.2, 3.5.9 (See CASAS Competency List on pages 169-175.)
SCANS: Information Acquire and evaluate information, organize and maintain information

Basic Skills Reading, writing, speaking
EFF: Communication Speak so others can understand
Lifelong Learning Take responsibility for learning, reflect and evaluate
Personal Qualities Responsibility, self management

Practice 1 *(continued)*

D Write *How much* or *How many.* (Lesson 2)

E Draw a line from the picture to the correct word. Write the name of the food under the picture. (Lesson 2)

D Write *How much* or *How many*. (Lesson 2)

1. _____How many_____ oranges do we need?

2. _____How many_____ tomatoes do we need?

3. _____How much_____ milk do we need?

4. _____How many_____ gallons of milk do we need?

5. _____How much_____ bread do we need?

6. _____How much_____ ice cream do we need?

 E Draw a line from the picture to the correct word. Write the name of the food under the picture. (Lesson 2)

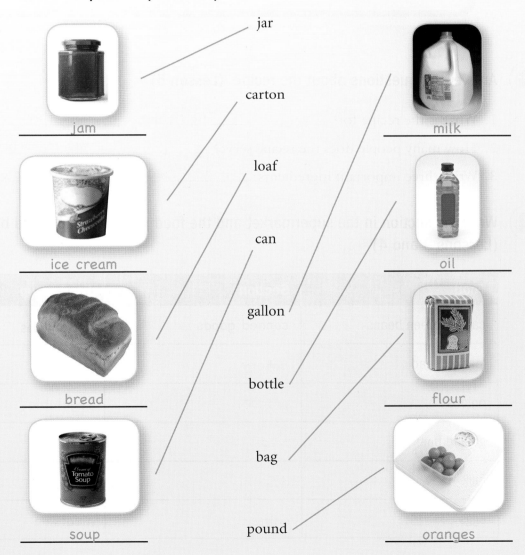

jar

carton

loaf

can

gallon

bottle

bag

pound

jam

ice cream

bread

soup

milk

oil

flour

oranges

Review

 F Read the recipe. Underline the verbs in the instructions. (Lesson 5)

Beef Stew

Serves 10 people

Ingredients:

3 lbs beef	1-1/2 onion	1 cup chili sauce
4 carrots	2 potatoes	1 cup brown sugar

Instructions:
Chop carrots, potatoes, and onions. Boil water. Add potatoes, carrots, and onions to water. Boil for 15 minutes. Cook beef until brown in separate pan. Add chili sauce. Mix in brown sugar. Add all ingredients to vegetables and cook over low heat for two hours.

 G Answer the questions about the recipe. (Lesson 5)

1. What is the recipe for? _____ The recipe is for beef stew.

2. How many people does the recipe serve? _____ It serves ten people.

3. Write three important ingredients. _____ beef, carrots, and potatoes

H Write the section in the supermarket and the food group for each food below. (Lessons 3 and 4)

Food	Section	Food group
canned green beans	canned goods	vegetables
loaf of bread	bakery	grains
onions	produce	vegetables
ground beef	meats	meats
milk	dairy	dairy
eggs	dairy	meats

Practice 1 (continued)

F Read the recipe. Underline the verbs in the instructions. (Lesson 5)

G Answer the questions about the recipe. (Lesson 5)

H Write the section in the supermarket and the food group for each food below. (Lessons 3 and 4)

Evaluation 1   15 mins.

Go around the room and check on students' progress. Help individuals when needed. If you see consistent errors among several students, interrupt the class and give a mini lesson or review to help students feel comfortable with the concept.

Activity Bank

Unit 3: Computer Worksheets

Unit 3: Internet Worksheets

Presentation 2 7-10 mins.

My Dictionary

Go over the steps of My Dictionary as a class.

Practice 2 5-7 mins.

Do the dictionary activity as a class before students work on their own for at least the first few units of the book to ensure that students understand what to do.

Evaluation 2 5 mins.

Ask students to share their cards.

Presentation 3 5 mins.

Learner Log

Review the concepts of the Learner Log. Make sure students understand the concepts and how to complete the log including circling the answers, finding page numbers where the concept is taught, and ranking favorite activities.

Teaching Tip

Learner Logs

Learner Logs function to help students in many different ways.

1. They serve as part of the review process.

2. They help students to gain confidence and to document what they have learned. Consequently, students see that they are progressing in their learning.

3. They provide students with a tool that they can use over and over to check and recheck their understanding of the target language. In this way, students become independent learners.

Practice 3 10-15 mins.

Ask students to complete the Learner Log.

Evaluation 3 2 mins.

Go over the Learner Log with students.

Application 5-7 mins.

Ask students to record their favorite lesson or page in the unit.

TB Assessment

Use the Stand Out 2 Assessment CD-ROM with Exam*View*® to create a posttest for Unit 3.

Refer students to *Stand Out 2 Grammar Challenge*, Unit 3, Extension Challenge 1 for more practice with *some / any* and Extension Challenge 2 for more practice with *There is / There are.*

Instructor's Notes

_____

_____

_____

_____

_____

_____

_____

_____

_____

_____

_____

_____

_____

_____

_____

_____

_____

_____

_____

_____

_____

_____

_____

My Dictionary

Make flash cards to improve your vocabulary.

1. Choose four new words from this unit.

2. Write each word on an index card or on a sheet of paper.

3. On the back of the index card or paper, draw a picture, find and write a sentence from the book with the word, and write the page number.

4. Study the words.

<u>Peel</u> the potatoes.
page 55

Learner Log

Circle how well you learned each item and write the page number where you learned it.

1. I can read a menu.

   Yes   Maybe   No   Page _____

2. I can make a shopping list.

   Yes   Maybe   No   Page _____

3. I can find things in a supermarket.

   Yes   Maybe   No   Page _____

4. I can plan healthy meals.

   Yes   Maybe   No   Page _____

5. I can read recipes.

   Yes   Maybe   No   Page _____

Rank what you like to do best from 1 to 6. 1 is your favorite activity. Your teacher will help you.

_____ Practice listening

_____ Practice speaking

_____ Practice reading

_____ Practice writing

_____ Learn new words

_____ Learn grammar

In the next unit, I want to practice more

_____.

Team Project

Plan a menu.

In this project, you will plan a family menu. You are a family of four or five people. You have $150 for food for the next week. What can you make for breakfast, lunch, and dinner? Make a menu and go shopping.

1. Form a team of four or five students. In your team, you need:

POSITION	JOB	STUDENT NAME
Student 1: **Team Leader**	See that everyone speaks English. See that everyone participates.	
Student 2: **Chef**	Plan meals for the family with help from the team.	
Student 3: **Shopper**	Write a shopping list for the family with help from the team.	
Students 4/5: **Spokespeople**	Prepare a class presentation with help from the team.	

2. Choose a name for your family.

3. Fill in a calendar with your meal plans for breakfast, lunch, and dinner for one week.

4. Make a shopping list. How much of each item do you need? Estimate the prices of the items on your list. Make sure the total is under $150.

5. Write a recipe for one of your meals.

6. Make a family presentation to the class. Tell the class about the meals on your menu. How much money will you spend? How much money will be left? What can you do with the money that will be left over?

Introduction   5 mins.

Plan a menu.

In this project, students will plan a week's worth of meals for a family. There is a worksheet that can serve as a template for this activity on the Activity Bank CD-ROM (Unit 3, Project, Worksheet 1).

Stage 1   5-10 mins.
Form a team of four or five students.

Set the scene by showing students an example of the project if you have one. Use the sample from the Activity Bank CD-ROM if you don't (Unit 3, Project, Worksheet 1).

Help students form groups and assign positions in their groups. On the spot, students will have to choose who will be the leader of their group. Review the responsibility of the leader and ask students to write the name of their leader in their books. Do the same with the remaining positions: chef, shopper, and spokespeople.

Stage 2   10-15 mins.
Choose a name for your family.

Tell students that their group is a family. Ask them to talk about what types of foods they might all like to eat after they have decided on a family name.

Stage 3   20-30 mins.
Fill in a calendar with your meal plans for breakfast, lunch, and dinner for one week.

The team should work together to plan meals for one week. Have them fill in a calendar with three meals a day.

Stage 4   10-30 mins.
Make a shopping list.

Ask teams to make a shopping list for all of the ingredients they will need to make their meals for the whole week. They may look at the advertisements in the unit to estimate prices of each item, or you may choose to provide real supermarket flyers for them to reference. Make sure that the cost of their total shopping list will not exceed $150. There are worksheets for prices and shopping lists that you may want to provide to teams here available on the Activity Bank CD-ROM (Unit 3, Project, Worksheets 2–3).

Stage 5   20-25 mins.
Write a recipe for one of your meals.

Have students use the various recipe cards in the unit as models for their recipe. Make sure they include ingredients and instructions. The recipe should be for one of their meals in their calendar.

Stage 6   30-40 mins.
Make a family presentation to the class.

Ask teams to present their meal plans, shopping lists, and recipes to the class.

Activity Bank

Unit 3, Project, Worksheet 1: Family Menu

Unit 3, Project, Worksheet 2: Prices

Unit 3, Project, Worksheet 3: Shopping List

Unit 3, Project, Worksheet 4: Recipes

Unit 3, Extension, Worksheet 1: Negative Simple Present

STANDARDS CORRELATIONS

CASAS: 1.1.1, 1.1.7, 1.3.7, 1.3.8, 2.5.4, 2.6.4, 3.5.2, 3.5.9 (See CASAS Competency List on pages 169–175.)
SCANS: **Resources** Allocate time, allocate materials and facility resources, allocate human resources
Information Acquire and evaluate information, organize and maintain information, interpret and communicate information
Interpersonal Participate as a member of a team, teach others, exercise leadership, negotiate to arrive at a decision, work with cultural diversity
Systems Understand systems, monitor and correct performance
Basic Skills Reading, writing, listening, speaking

Thinking Skills Think creatively, make decisions, solve problems, see things in the mind's eye
Personal Qualities Responsibility, sociability, self management
EFF: **Communication** Read with understanding, convey ideas in writing, speak so others can understand, listen actively, observe critically
Decision Making Solve problems and make decisions, plan
Interpersonal Cooperate with others, advocate and influence, resolve conflict and negotiate, guide others
Lifelong Learning Take responsibility for learning, reflect and evaluate

Objective: Describe housing
Grammar: Information questions
Pronunciation: Rhythm
Academic Strategies: Focused listening, predicting, designing pie charts
Vocabulary: Housing vocabulary

RESOURCES

Activity Bank: Unit 4, Lesson 1, Worksheet 1
Reading and Writing Challenge: Unit 4
Grammar Challenge: Unit 4, Challenge 1

Audio: CD 1, Track 43
Heinle Picture Dictionary: Housing, pages 62–67

■ 1.5 hour classes   ■ 2.5 hour classes   ■ 3⁺ hour classes

Stand Out 2 Assessment CD-ROM with Exam*View*®

AGENDA

Do a corners activity.
Listen about Kyung's family.
Read advertisements and ask questions.
Take a survey and make a pie chart.

Preassessment *(optional)*

Use the Stand Out 2 Assessment CD-ROM with Exam*View*® to create a pretest for Unit 4.

Warm-up and Review   10-15 mins.

Ask students where they live. They will answer with the name of a city. Ask: *Who lives in an apartment? In a house? In a mobile home? In a condominium?* Do a corners activity. Designate one corner as a one-bedroom home, a second corner as a two-bedroom home, and so on. Ask students to get in the corner that represents where they live. Then, have them ask one another the following questions: *Where do you live? Do you live in a house, a mobile home, a condominium, or an apartment?*

Introduction   5 mins.

Ask students to think about the place where they live. Ask: *How did you find it? What are some different ways to find housing?* State the objective: *Today we will describe different types of housing.*

Presentation 1   30-45 mins.

(A) Work in groups. Read the questions and predict possible answers.

Have students open their books and look at the picture of the Kyung family. Ask them questions about what they see in the picture. Encourage them to guess.

Practice 1   5-7 mins.

(B) Listen and answer the questions in Exercise A.

You may need to play the recording more than once. Ask the students to discuss the answers between each listening.

Evaluation 1   5-20 mins.

Direct students to the listening script in the back of their books to check their answers. You may extend the activity by giving a dictation of the story.

 Listening Script   CD 1, Track 43

My name is Kyung. My family and I moved from Korea to Arcadia, Florida, last month. I have a good job here in Arcadia, but we need to find a place to live. We are living with friends right now in a small house. We need to find a house, apartment, condominium, or mobile home. We need to buy furniture and open a bank account. We have a lot to do.

Teaching Tip

Dictation

It is very difficult for students at this level to listen and write at the same time. Teach students the dictation strategy of listening to a sentence or phrase once completely before attempting to write anything. They should repeat it in their minds. The second time they hear the sentence or phrase they write, and the third time, they check their work.

STANDARDS CORRELATIONS

CASAS: 1.1.3, 1.4.1, 1.4.2, 6.7.2 (See CASAS Competency List on pages 169–175.)
SCANS: **Information** Acquire and evaluate information
Basic Skills Reading, writing, listening, speaking
EFF: **Communication** Read with understanding, convey ideas in writing, speak so others can understand, listen actively

---

UNIT 4 Housing

GOALS
➤ Describe housing
➤ Interpret classified ads
➤ Complete a rental application
➤ Identify rooms and furniture
➤ Make a family budget

LESSON 1

Looking for a place to live

GOAL ➤ Describe housing

Vocabulary | Grammar
Life Skills
Academic | Pronunciation

What are Kyung and his family doing?
What are they reading?

A Work in groups. Read the questions and predict possible answers.

1. Where is Kyung from?

   Kyung is from Korea.

2. Where does he work?

   He works in Arcadia, Florida.

3. Where is he living now?

   He is living with friends now.

4. What does he need to do?

   He needs to find a place to live, buy furniture, and open a bank account.

B Listen and answer the questions in Exercise A.

CD 1
TR 43

Unit 4   Lesson 1

61

LESSON **1**   **GOAL** ➤ **Describe housing**

C Read Kyung's story.

My name is Kyung. My family and I moved from Korea to Arcadia, Florida last month. I have a good job here in Arcadia, but we need to find a place to live. We are living with friends right now in a small house. We need to find a house, apartment, condominium, or mobile home. We need to buy furniture and open a bank account. We have a lot to do.

D Scan the advertisements for homes. Match the advertisement to the picture. Draw a line.

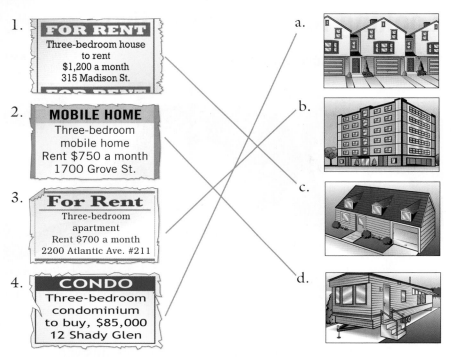

1.
FOR RENT
Three-bedroom house
to rent
$1,200 a month
315 Madison St.

2.
MOBILE HOME
Three-bedroom
mobile home
Rent $750 a month
1700 Grove St.

3.
For Rent
Three-bedroom
apartment
Rent $700 a month
2200 Atlantic Ave. #211

4.
CONDO
Three-bedroom
condominium
to buy, $85,000
12 Shady Glen

a.

b.

c.

d.

E Study the chart with your classmates and teacher.

Information Question	Answer
How **much** is the **house**?	It's $1,200 a month.
What **kind** of **hous**ing is **Num**ber **2**?	It's a mobile home.
Where is the condo**min**ium?	It's on Shady Glen.
How many **bed**rooms does the a**part**ment **have**?	It has three bedrooms.

Pronunciation

Rhythm

Emphasize the bold syllables in the chart and say the others quickly.

F Ask a partner information questions about the advertisements in Exercise D.

Presentation 2 15–20 mins.

C Read Kyung's story.

If you chose to do a dictation in the evaluation stage, ask students to check their work and further discuss the paragraph. If not, read the paragraph with students and discuss it again.

D Scan the advertisements for homes. Match the advertisement to the picture. Draw a line.

Review the vocabulary on this page with students by doing this activity as a class. Specifically review the types of housing. Introduce them to the verbs *buy* and *rent*.

Give a little information about the different homes listed under the picture and ask students to identify the picture by type of housing. For example, say: *This home is for rent for $750 a month. Which home is it?*

E Study the chart with your classmates and teacher.

Prepare students for the practice by asking about each home. For example, ask: *How much is the home on Grove Street?* Write the question on the board and underline *How much*. Explain to students that this phrase refers to the amount of money something costs. Go over the questions in the grammar box. Help students understand the information words. Write each one on the board and ask several questions.

Pronunciation

Rhythm

Practice the rhythm and intonation of the questions by showing students how to emphasize different words. For example, ask them to emphasize *How much* or *house* in the first question in the chart. Show them how emphasizing *house* shows the speaker wants to differentiate between houses and other type of housing. Also show how the other words are rarely emphasized.

Practice 2 15–20 mins.

F Ask a partner information questions about the advertisements in Exercise D.

Walk around the room and help students with their pronunciation. Have students line up and talk to a partner. Students face each other in two lines. Then, after a certain amount of time, ask one line to move or shift so each student is talking to another student. The student at the end of the line moves to the beginning of the line.

Evaluation 2 5–7 mins.

Observe the activity and ask students to create additional questions based on the models.

Instructor's Notes

Presentation 3   10-15 mins.

With students' books closed, ask students to listen to you describe your own home. Use the statements in Exercise G as models. See if students can repeat back what you say. You may choose to give the sentences as a dictation as well.

Ask students to open their books and help you create questions for each of the statements in Exercise G. Write the questions on the board.

Practice 3   7-10 mins. ■

(G) Read about Rosa and Gilberto. Then, ask and answer questions with a partner.

Ask students to ask one another questions about Rosa and Gilberto.

Evaluation 3   5-7 mins. ■

Observe students doing the activity. Then, ask a few volunteers to report to the class.

Application   10-15 mins.

Prepare students for this activity by showing them how a pie chart works.

(H) Do a housing survey in your class. Ask every classmate.

Here you might ask students to do their own informal survey. Have them walk around the room gathering information.

(I) Make a pie chart of your survey.

Ask students to complete the pie chart individually with the information they have gathered. The whole class should create the same pie chart. Ask for volunteers to recreate the chart on the board.

 Refer students to *Stand Out 2 Grammar Challenge*, Unit 4, Challenge 1 for more practice with information questions.

Activity Bank

Unit 4, Lesson 1, Worksheet 1: Housing

Instructor's Notes

_____
_____
_____
_____
_____
_____
_____
_____
_____
_____
_____
_____
_____
_____
_____
_____
_____
_____
_____
_____
_____
_____
_____
_____
_____

GOAL ➤ **Describe housing**

G Read about Rosa and Gilberto. Then, ask and answer questions with a partner.

Rosa

Gilberto

I live in a condominium.
It has three bedrooms.
It's on Adam's Street.
I like my home.

I live in an apartment.
It has one bedroom.
It's on Butcher Street.
I don't like my home. I want to move.

H Do a housing survey in your class. Ask every classmate.
(Answers will vary.)

What kind of home do you live in?	Number of classmates
House	
Condominium	
Apartment	
Mobile home	
Other	

I Make a pie chart of your survey. (Answers will vary.)

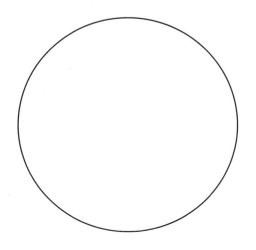

Finding a home

GOAL ➤ Interpret classified ads

  A Talk in groups about your home.

1. What kind of home do you live in?

2. How many bedrooms does it have?

3. Is your home large or small?

4. Is your home one-story or two?

5. Do you have a yard or a balcony?

6. Is your home old or new?

B Listen to the descriptions and point to the correct house.

CD 1
TR 44–47

a.

c.

b.

d.

 C Match the letter of the picture with the correct description below.

_c_ 1. This large four-bedroom, three-bathroom house is the perfect rental for a big family. The house is old but is in very good condition. The neighborhood is quiet and comfortable. There is a beautiful view from the balcony. This two-story house rents for $2,000 a month and utilities are included.

_a_ 2. Come and see this new, small, one-story dream house. It is in a small and friendly neighborhood. This house rents for $900 a month. It has one bedroom, one bathroom, and a large kitchen. You will love it when you see it!

_d_ 3. Sometimes older is better. This small two-bedroom, one-bathroom house has an interesting history. The same person has owned it for 50 years. Rent it for an amazing $700 a month.

_b_ 4. If you want to rent a big home and money is not important, rent this very large five-bedroom, three-bathroom house with a swimming pool. It is a great value for $3,000 a month.

Objective: Interpret classified ads
Grammar: Questions with *which*
Academic Strategies: Focused listening,
   scanning, note taking
Vocabulary: Housing amenities

RESOURCES

Activity Bank: Unit 4, Lesson 2, Worksheets 1–2

Reading and Writing Challenge: Unit 4

Grammar Challenge: Unit 4, Challenge 2

Audio: CD 1, Tracks 44–47
Heinle Picture Dictionary: Housing, Pages 68–75

■ 1.5 hour classes   ■ 2.5 hour classes   ■ 3+ hour classes

AGENDA

Discuss housing.
Read about housing.
Read classified ads.
Write classified ads.

Warm-up and Review   10-15 mins. ■ ■ ■

 Talk in groups about your home.

First, briefly go over the questions. Help students to
"feel" the intonation and rhythm of the questions
so they can ask them effectively. In each group, ask
the person answering the questions to stand so you
can readily see that the group is on task.

Another approach to help students stay on task is to
present them with a grid that they can duplicate for
recording the information. It might look like this:

Name	Questions					
	1	2	3	4	5	6

Introduction   10-15 mins. ■ ■ ■

Ask students where they live and how many of
them would like to move. Ask questions about
moving, such as: *Is it expensive to move?* Ask if
they would need to rent a truck. Ask who would
help them move. State the objective: *Today we
will interpret classified ads.*

Presentation 1   12-15 mins. ■ ■ ■

Ask students to look at the four houses on the
page and discuss any new vocabulary including
balcony, pool, and *chimney.*

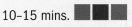 **Listen to the descriptions and point
to the correct house.**

This activity is especially helpful to prepare
students to use the new vocabulary. Since this
is the presentation stage, spend as much time as
needed to ensure that students understand.

Ask students to cover Exercise C while they are
doing Exercise B so they aren't able to read along.

 Listening Script   *CD 1, Tracks 44–47*

*The listening script matches the descriptions in
Exercise C.*

Practice 1   10-15 mins. ■ ■ ■

 **Match the letter of the picture with the
correct description below.**

Allow students to work in groups. As they are
working, take note of any new words they may
need help with and write the words on the
board. As students are working, don't answer
questions about vocabulary. Encourage them to
make educated guesses about meaning.

Evaluation 1   5-7 mins. ■ ■ ■

Go over the words on the board and any others
students may have had problems with. Ask
students for the key words they used to identify
which picture each paragraph describes.

STANDARDS CORRELATIONS

CASAS: 1.4.2 (See CASAS Competency List on pages 169-175.)
SCANS: **Information** Acquire and evaluate information, organize and
maintain information, interpret and communicate information
Interpersonal Participate as a member of a team, teach others
Basic Skills Reading, writing, listening, speaking
Thinking Skills Think creatively, make decisions, solve problems
EFF: **Communication** Read with understanding, convey ideas in
writing, speak so others can understand, listen actively
Decision Making Solve problems and make decisions
Interpersonal Cooperate with others, advocate and influence, resolve
conflict and negotiate, guide others

Presentation 2   10–15 mins.

D Summarize the information from Exercise C. Then, ask a partner about the houses.

Introduce the word *which* to students. If you have time, you may decide to review all of the *wh-* questions. Do this activity as a class for additional practice with the new vocabulary.

Teaching Tip

Academic skills

In the lower levels of *Stand Out*, many of the activities that we claim are academic skills may be preparatory activities that will help students when they get to higher levels.

For example, in this activity, we ask students to summarize. Ideally, they would take notes and record important information. For now, we give them a structure to take notes so they can better determine what is important to record. As students progress, they are expected to summarize without the structure given to them, which is an important academic skill.

For shorter classes, have students do Exercise E for homework.

Practice 2   7–10 mins.

E Scan the classified ads about the houses from Exercise C. Which ad is for which house? Write the number of the house.

Students have not been introduced to the abbreviations yet, and it isn't necessary to explain them at this time. They will get additional practice in Presentation 3. Instead, allow students to guess at their meanings.

Evaluation 2   5–7 mins.

Show students some scanning strategies that will help them in the future. Ask them to identify a few important words or give them specific numbers to scan for. Go over the answers and confirm that students have understood the activity.

Teaching Tip

Scanning

Scanning is another important academic skill. At this stage, students are not expected to scan large amounts of text. They begin by scanning basic life-skill readings to prepare them for the more difficult scanning skills they will need at higher levels.

To encourage students to scan instead of reading the classified ads in this exercise, make it a competition so students have to do it quickly.

Instructor's Notes

_____

_____

_____

_____

_____

_____

_____

_____

_____

_____

_____

_____

_____

GOAL ➤ Interpret classified ads

D Summarize the information from Exercise C. Then, ask a partner about the houses.

EXAMPLES: Which house has a pool?
Which house is 50 years old?

	House #1	House #2	House #3	House #4
Bedrooms	4	1	2	5
Bathrooms	3	1	1	3
Monthly rent	$2,000	$900	$700	$3,000
Other	balcony	large kitchen	one previous owner	swimming pool
Other	quiet neighborhood	friendly neighborhood	interesting history	very large
Other	utilities included		50 years old	

E Scan the classified ads about the houses from Exercise C. Which ad is for which house? Write the number of the house.

★ **House for Rent** ★
Old w/ character, 2 bdrm,
1 bath hse, frpl, nr schools
and shopping ctr.
a/c, $700.
2234 Rolling Hills.
Call Henry 555-3467.

1. House #___3___

FOR RENT
4 bed, 3 bath hse, quiet
community, 2-story, a/c,
utils pd, $2,000 mo.
Call 555-1425.

2. House #___1___

AVAILABLE
Lrg hse, 5 bdrms, 3 baths,
pool, nr park, 3 frpl,
a/c, 3-car garage,
lrg yard.
Call Francine 555-3323.

3. House #___4___

House for Rent
New construction,
1 bdrm, 1 bath house,
lrg kitchen and dining rm,
utils pd. Come and see.
2200 W. Alton Ave.

4. House #___2___

HOUSING FOR RENT

1. **FOR RENT**

2 bdrm, 2 bath condo, utils pd, a/c incl, nr park and schools, Daily City, $750. Call 555-7677.

2. **FOR RENT**

4 bdrm, 3 bath hse, pool, frpl, balcony, $1,050, lease only. 5253 Bountiful St., Luxury Heights. Come and see!

3. **FOR RENT**

3 bdrm apt, cln, a/c, new refr incl, no pets, $900. Tustin, 555-3722.

4. **FOR RENT**

1 bdrm, 1 bath apt, new carpet. Sycamore St., Costa Mesa, $725.

5. **FOR RENT**

3 bdrm, 1 bath condo, a/c, water pd, good community, nr shopping, Bridgemont, 555-3232.

6. **FOR RENT**

2 bdrm mobile home, utils pd, like new, $800. Seawall Estates, Newton. Call 555-3511.

F **Look at the ads and answer the questions.**

1. Which homes are under $800 a month?
2. Which homes have air-conditioning?
3. Which home has a new refrigerator?
4. Which home has three bathrooms?

G **Review the vocabulary below with your classmates and teacher. Can you find the abbreviations in the ads above?**

Vocabulary	Abbreviations
bedroom	bdrm
condominium	condo
utilities	utils
near	nr
bathroom	bath
apartment	apt

Vocabulary	Abbreviations
air-conditioning	a/c
house	hse
paid	pd
included	incl
refrigerator	refr
fireplace	frpl

H **In a group, write a classified ad. Answer these questions in your ad.**

1. How much is the rent?
2. How many bedrooms are there?
3. How many bathrooms are there?
4. What extras are there?
5. Who do you call?
6. What's the phone number?

  Active Task. Look in the newspaper or on the Internet to find classified ads for your area. Find a home for yourself. Report to the class.

Presentation 3

10-12 mins. ■■■

Explain to students that abbreviations in classified ads are not necessarily standard ones. Since every letter in an ad costs money, abbreviations are often used to save money. To explain this, write the following abbreviations on the board: *bedroom, bdroom, bdrms, bedrm.* Ask students which one they think is the best abbreviation. Ask them which one is the cheapest.

Go over the classified ads and ask questions other than those in Exercise F.

F Look at the ads and answer the questions.

Now, allow students to work in pairs or groups to answer the questions. Since this is part of the presentation stage, you might also choose to do this as a class.

For shorter classes, have students do Exercise G for homework.

Practice 3

10-15 mins. ■

G Review the vocabulary below with your classmates and teacher. Can you find the abbreviations in the ads above?

Students may work in groups to complete the chart. Students may still have problems with some of the vocabulary. Continue to go over new vocabulary.

Teaching Tip

Vocabulary

Vocabulary is one of the most essential things students need to learn. Presenting the vocabulary in context is very important. *Stand Out* always presents vocabulary in this way. Students can sometimes be overwhelmed with too much vocabulary at this level. Make sure you identify which words are essential for them to learn so students are not frustrated with the number of new items they are exposed to.

Evaluation 3

7-10 mins. ■

Go over each vocabulary word and confirm that students understand its meaning.

Application

10-15 mins. ■■■

H In a group, write a classified ad. Answer these questions in your ad.

An effective way to present these classified ads is to ask a representative of each group to write their ad on the board. Count the number of characters. Arbitrarily say each character costs $1.00 to put in the newspaper and see how much each ad would cost.

I Active Task. Look in the newspaper or on the Internet to find classified ads for your area. Find a home for yourself. Report to the class.

 Refer students to *Stand Out 2 Grammar Challenge*, Unit 4, Challenge 2 for more practice with information questions and *which.*

Activity Bank

Unit 4, Lesson 2, Worksheet 1: Reading Classified Ads

Unit 4, Lesson 2, Worksheet 2: Classified Ads

Objective: Complete a rental application
Grammar: Information questions
Academic Strategy: Focused listening
Vocabulary: Rental application vocabulary

RESOURCES

Activity Bank: Unit 4, Lesson 3, Worksheets 1–2
Reading and Writing Challenge: Unit 4
Grammar Challenge: Unit 4, Challenge 3

■ 1.5 hour classes   ■ 2.5 hour classes   ■ 3⁺ hour classes

AGENDA

Talk about needs and wants.
Discuss rental agencies and ads.
Read and discuss a rental application.
Ask questions.
Complete a rental application
   for your partner.

Audio: CD 1, Track 48
Heinle Picture Dictionary: Housing, pages 62–75

Warm-up and Review   10–15 mins. ■■■

Write *needs* and *wants* on the board. Say: *I need sleep. I need food.* Under *needs* on the board, write *sleep* and *food.* Say: *I want a million dollars.* Ask students to make their own lists and then share them with the class.

Introduction   5 mins. ■■■

Ask students what is needed to rent a house. Ask them what information is found on a rental application. State the objective: *Today we will complete a rental application.*

Presentation 1   15–20 mins. ■■■

Look at the picture with students and ask questions about Kyung and what he is doing. They will find clues in the sentences next to the picture. Help students understand the responsibilities of a rental agent.

 Listen to the conversation. What does Kyung need? What does he want? Complete the chart.

This listening activity is part of the presentation stage so spend sufficient time with students replaying the recording.

 Listening Script   CD 1, Track 48

Kyung: *Excuse me. I need some help.*
Agent: *What can I do for you?*
Kyung: *I need a three-bedroom house immediately.*
Agent: *How much can you spend?*
Kyung: *I need to find a house for $900 or less.*
Agent: *OK. I think we can help you. Do you want to be near schools and stores?*
Kyung: *Yes. I want to be near a school, but it isn't necessary.*

Agent: *All right. And do you have any pets?*
Kyung: *No, I don't. But maybe I could get a dog. . .*
Agent: *I see. Do you **want** a house with a big yard, or do you **need** one?*
Kyung: *I guess I want one. I don't have a dog right now.*
Agent: *Do you want a two-story house or a one-story house?*
Kyung: *I want a one-story because I don't like stairs.*
Agent: *I have one house, but it doesn't have a garage.*
Kyung: *I need a garage. That won't do.*
Agent: *Well, I'm sorry. That's all we have right now. I will call you when other homes are available.*
Kyung: *OK. Thank you for your help.*

Quickly review the information in the classified ads in Exercise B. Make sure students understand the information before you move on to Practice 1.

Practice 1   5–7 mins. ■■■

 In groups, choose which home is best for Kyung.

Note that there might be more than one answer here. Allow students to negotiate in their groups. Teach students vocabulary for negotiating such as *I think, because, I don't think so, maybe,* and so on.

Evaluation 1   7–10 mins. ■■■

Ask a representative from each group to report to the class.

 ### STANDARDS CORRELATIONS

CASAS: 1.4.2, 1.4.3 (See CASAS Competency List on pages 169–175.)
SCANS: Information Acquire and evaluate information, organize and maintain information, interpret and communicate information
Basic Skills Reading, writing, listening, speaking
EFF: Communication Read with understanding, convey ideas in writing, speak so others can understand, listen actively

---

LESSON **3** | **At the rental agency**
GOAL ➤ Complete a rental application

Where is Kyung? What is he doing?

CD 1
TR 48

A Listen to the conversation. What does Kyung need? What does he want? Complete the chart.

Needs	Wants
three-bedroom house	near a school
garage	big yard
$900 or less	one story

B In groups, choose which home is best for Kyung.

1. **FOR RENT**
2 bdrm, 2 bath hse, utils pd, big yd, nr schools, **$1,050**. Call Janet at **555-2438**.

2. **FOR RENT**
3 bdrm, 2 bath apt, utils pd, no deposit, big living rm, nr schools, small yard, separate garage, **$750 a month**, lease or rent. Call 555-6565.

3. **FOR RENT**
3 bdrm, 2 story hse, garage, a/c, near schools and shopping, **$1,500.** Call 555-3534.

4. **FOR RENT**
4 bdrm, 3 bath condo, nr schools, big yard, no pets, 1 story, **$925**. Call Rick at 555-6781.

GOAL ➤ **Complete a rental application**

Vocabulary | Grammar
Life Skills
Academic | Pronunciation

C Discuss the rental application with your classmates and teacher.

RENTAL APPLICATION FORM

Applicant: *Kyung Kim*   Interviewed by: *Paula Wharton*

Present Address: *33457 Akron St. Arcadia, FL 34265*

Phone: *555-5059*

Prior Address: *134-2 Chongun-Dong, Chongno-Ku, Seoul, Korea*

Landlord: *Fred Wharton*   Prior Landlord: *N/A*

Employer: *Sift Manufacturing*   Position: *Computer Technician*

Personal References: *James Baker; Manuel Acevedo*   Relationship: *Boss; Supervisor*

Co-Applicant or Spouse: *Anh Kim*

Employer: *Rosco Metals*   Position: *Assembly Worker*

Personal Reference: *George Pratt*   Relationship: *Supervisor*

BANK INFORMATION

Name of Bank: *Family Bank of Florida*

Checking Account No.: *011000111 001 0000*

Savings Account No.: *0XX000XXX00X 0000*

D Answer the questions about the application.

1. What's Kyung's address?

   Kyung's address is 33457 Akron St, Arcadia, FL 34265.

2. What was his address before he came to Florida?

   His address was 134-2 Chongun-Dong, Chongno-Ku, Seoul, Korea.

3. What is the name of the company where he works?

   He works for Sift Manufacturing.

4. What is the name of the company where Anh works?

   Anh works for Rosco Metals.

5. What is the name of their bank?

   The bank's name is Family Bank of Florida.

Presentation 2   15-20 mins.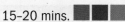

C Discuss the rental application with your classmates and teacher.

Ask students to close their books and briefly discuss again some of the information asked for on a rental application. Prompt them when needed. Accept all answers and write their ideas on the board.

Ask students to open their books and discuss the rental application. Make sure students don't do the practice in advance. You may consider asking them to cover the lower half of the page.

Go over the new vocabulary, particularly *landlord, spouse, relationship, prior,* and *references*.

There is a lot to teach students on this page. Make sure they understand that a reference is generally not a family member or close friend. Go over the different kinds of bank accounts. Explain to students that they can write *N/A* when the information required does not apply to them. Also, explain that neatness is important on applications whether they be work applications or rental applications.

For shorter classes, have students do Exercise D for homework.

Practice 2   10-12 mins.

D Answer the questions about the application.

Students should work alone to give them confidence that they understand the information. They need to understand this application so that they will be ready to complete an application form by themselves on the next page.

Teaching Tip

Working ahead

Some students will be tempted to work ahead. When they do this, they will miss important information in the presentation stage. At this level, students find it difficult to write and to listen at the same time.

Try to encourage students to stay on task and to avoid working ahead. If they work ahead, they will often be finished before the other students and become bored. It is suggested that you regularly ask students to avoid working ahead in the book and explain why it isn't a good idea.

Evaluation 2   5-7 mins.

Ask volunteers to write their answers on the board. Both complete sentences and single words are acceptable.

Instructor's Notes

_____
_____
_____
_____
_____
_____
_____
_____
_____
_____
_____
_____
_____
_____
_____
_____
_____
_____
_____
_____
_____
_____

Presentation 3   10–15 mins.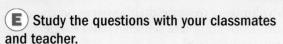

E Study the questions with your classmates and teacher.

Go over each question word (*who, what, where, when,* etc.) and create some different questions to ask students. Ask them to refer back to the application form on page 68. Ask the questions they will be expected to answer in order to prepare them for the practice. Work with pronunciation here. Ask students to underline the words they consider most important. For example: *What is your name?* Then, have them say only the important words with a short space between utterances. Then, ask them again to repeat the whole question using the same rhythm.

Practice 3   5–7 mins. ■

F Look at the rental application on page 68. Practice asking a partner questions. Your partner is Kyung.

You may want to divide the practice into two parts. Ask Student A to ask questions. Then, after five minutes, ask students to reverse roles.

Evaluation 3   5 mins. ■

Observe students as they do the activity.

Application   10–15 mins. ■■■

G Interview your partner. Complete the application about your partner.

You may wish to encourage students to write in their partner's book so the personal information remains with the person it is about.

H Active Task. Find a rental application form. Look at a real estate office or on the Internet. Share it with the class.

Refer students to *Stand Out 2 Grammar Challenge*, Unit 4, Challenge 3 for more practice with information questions.

Activity Bank

Unit 4, Lesson 3, Worksheet 1: Rental Application
Unit 4, Lesson 3, Worksheet 2: Asking Questions

LESSON **3** **GOAL** ➤ **Complete a rental application**

E Study the questions with your classmates and teacher.

Information Questions		
What is your name?	**Where** did you live before?	**Who** is your employer?
Where do you live now?	**How** long did you live there?	**What** is your position?

F Look at the rental application on page 68. Practice asking a partner questions. Your partner is Kyung.

G Interview your partner. Complete the application about your partner.
(Answers will vary.)

RENTAL APPLICATION FORM

Applicant: _____   Interviewed by: _____

Present Address: _____

Phone: _____

Prior Address: _____

Landlord: _____   Prior Landlord: _____

Employer: _____   Position: _____

Personal References: _____   Relationship: _____

Co-Applicant or Spouse: _____

Employer: _____   Position: _____

Personal Reference: _____   Relationship: _____

BANK INFORMATION

Name of Bank: _____

Checking Account No.: _____

Savings Account No.: _____

  H **Active Task.** Find a rental application form. Look at a real estate office or on the Internet. Share it with the class.

LESSON 4

We need furniture

GOAL ➤ Identify rooms and furniture

 A Kyung is ready to rent a home. Read about the home he rents.

For Rent

3 bdrm, 2 bath hse, utils pd, no deposit, big living rm, nr schools, small yard, separate garage, new remodeled kitchen, new washer/dryer, dishwasher, stove and oven, $750 a month. Rent or lease. Call 555-6295.

How many bedrooms and bathrooms does it have? How much is the rent? What is nearby?

  B Listen to the descriptions. Circle the description of Kyung's new home.

CD 1
TR 49-52

Home 1   (Home 2)   Home 3   Home 4

C Look at the home plans. Which one is Kyung's new home?

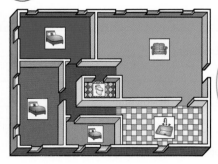 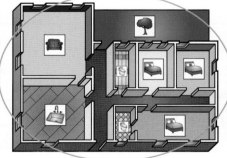 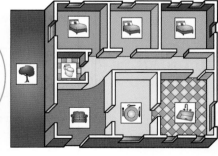

D Complete the floor plan key with words from the box.

| bathroom |
| bedroom |
| kitchen |
| yard |
| living room |
| dining room |

K E Y

 bedroom

dining room

 yard

 living room

 kitchen

 bathroom

AT-A-GLANCE PREP

Objective: Identify rooms and furniture
Grammar: Prepositions of location
Pronunciation: /ch/, /sh/, /s/
Academic Strategy: Focused listening
Vocabulary: Furniture vocabulary

RESOURCES

Activity Bank: Unit 4, Lesson 4, Worksheets 1–3
Reading and Writing Challenge: Unit 4
Grammar Challenge: Unit 4, Challenge 4

■ 1.5 hour classes ■ 2.5 hour classes ■ 3+ hour classes

AGENDA

Make a classified ad.
Read about Kyung's new home.
Learn new furniture vocabulary.
Practice describing rooms in a house.
Complete an invoice.

Audio: CD 1, Tracks 49–52
Heinle Picture Dictionary: Housing, pages 68–75

Warm-up and Review   10-15 mins. ■■■

Ask students in groups to make a classified ad about one of their group member's homes. They will need to find out how many bedrooms it has and what other amenities it has. You may refer students to Exercise A on page 64 to help them form questions. Then, ask students to share their ads with the class.

Introduction   5 mins. ■■■

Ask students how many bedrooms are in their home. Ask if they are large or small, and if they can fit a lot of furniture in the rooms. State the objective: *Today we will identify rooms and furniture.*

Presentation 1   10-15 mins. ■■■

(A) Kyung is ready to rent a home. Read about the home he rents.

Ask the questions to the right of the classified ad. Ask additional questions to check understanding.

(B) Listen to the descriptions. Circle the description of Kyung's new home.

 Listening Script   *CD 1, Tracks 49–52*

Home 1: *This house is in a beautiful area near schools and a park. It has three very large bedrooms and is ideal for a growing family. Please come and see the new appliances, including a dishwasher and a washer and dryer. Don't miss this chance!*

Home 2: *There are nice homes and then there are amazing ones. This apartment has a new kitchen and is near schools. You can entertain with the large living room and beautiful view. It is on the second floor, so we also have a very nice balcony that looks over the city.*

Home 3: *This three-bedroom, two-bathroom apartment is in the perfect location—near schools, businesses, and shopping. The kitchen is not new, but it is spacious and inviting. The three bedrooms are furnished. There is even a big yard.*

Home 4: *This apartment overlooks a school, and it also has a small yard of its own. It is great for families just starting out. It is inexpensive and, with its two bedrooms and two bathrooms, you will have a perfect room for the new baby! Come and see this terrific choice.*

Practice 1   5-7 mins. ■■■

(C) Look at the home plans. Which one is Kyung's new home?

(D) Complete the floor plan key with words from the box.

Ask students to do this practice in groups.

Evaluation 1   3-5 mins. ■■■

Review the names of rooms in a home and ask students questions about their own homes.

STANDARDS CORRELATIONS

CASAS: 4.1.1, 6.1.1, 6.1.3 (See CASAS Competency List on pages 169–175.)
SCANS: Resources Allocate money, allocate materials and facility resources
Information Acquire and evaluate information, organize and maintain information, interpret and communicate information
Interpersonal Participate as a member of a team, teach others
Basic Skills Listening, speaking
Thinking Skills Think creatively, make decisions, solve problems
EFF: Communication Speak so others can understand, listen actively
Decision Making Solve problems and make decisions, plan
Interpersonal Cooperate with others

Presentation 2   15–20 mins.

Ask students to close their books. Put students into groups of four or five. Give each group one of the following rooms: *living room*, *bedroom*, *kitchen*, or *dining room*. Ask each group to make a list of all the furniture they can think of for that room. Ask students to refrain from using picture dictionaries at this stage of the lesson. Also, to encourage group work, ask students to make only one list per group. Have them assign a recorder or writer. When they finish their lists, ask a member of each group to put the information on the board.

Teaching Tip

Picture dictionaries

One of the purposes of the presentation stage of a good lesson plan should be to see what students already know. Picture dictionaries are great tools, but sometimes it is better to see what students know before opening them.

Also, picture dictionaries have more vocabulary than a student can process at one time. It is important for the instructor to decide what vocabulary he or she is going to focus on. Usually the list should include vocabulary students need outside of class and words students are most interested in knowing.

E Study the new words with your classmates and teacher.

Go over each word carefully and practice correct pronunciation.

Pronunciation

/ch/ and /sh/

Students often have trouble making a distinction between the sounds /ch/ in *chair* and /sh/ in *washer*. The difference in the production of the two sounds is in the tongue placement. In /sh/ the tongue is near the top of the mouth but doesn't obstruct the airflow. The tongue does stop the airflow in /ch/. Other words you may include in the discussion are *chimney* and *shower*. Asian students may also have trouble with /s/ as in *dresser*. They may try to make it sound like /sh/. With /s/ the tongue is lowered slightly from the /sh/ and the airflow is even less obstructed.

Use a simple diagram to show students the difference between the three sounds, or use the back of your hand (as your tongue) propped up against the palm of the other hand (as the roof of the mouth) to demonstrate. Start with the /ch/. Put your knuckles up into the palm with the hand curved in a semi-shut position and say /ch/. Open the hand slightly and pull away from the palm for /sh/, and finally flatten the hand for /s/. Ask students to mimic your actions and then try to do the same with their tongue.

For shorter classes, have students do Exercise F for homework.

Practice 2   10–15 mins.

F Where can Kyung put his furniture? Draw on the floor plan.

Ask students in groups to add furniture to the floor plan.

Evaluation 2   10 mins.

Observe students as they do the activity. There will be a review of prepositions in the next presentation.

Vocabulary | Grammar
Life Skills
Academic | Pronunciation

E Study the new words with your classmates and teacher.

a couch
$850.89

a table lamp
$34.49

a dresser
$369.89

a washer
$1,200.00

an armchair
$449.99

a rocking chair
$79.50

a dining room set
$875.00

a bookcase
$225.89

a coffee table
$275.99

a refrigerator
$1,050.89

Pronunciation

/ch/	/sh/	/s/
chair	washer	dresser
couch		bookcase

F Where can Kyung put his furniture?
Draw on the floor plan. (Answers will vary.)

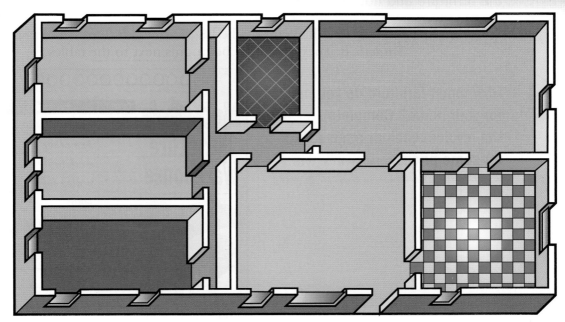

GOAL ➤ **Identify rooms and furniture**

G Study the chart with your classmates and teacher.

Prepositions of Location	
	The dresser is **in** the bedroom.
	The pillows are **on** the bed.
	The picture is **over** the sofa.
	The soap is **under** the sink.
	The microwave is **between** the toaster and the refrigerator.
	The lamp is **in the corner**.
	The nightstand is **next to** the bed.
	The chair is **in front of** the window.
	The yard is **in back of** the house.

H Practice the conversation with a partner. Make similar conversations using the furniture and floor plan on page 71.

EXAMPLE: *Student A:* Where are the beds?
Student B: They are in the bedrooms next to the tables.

I How much furniture do you need for your home? Complete the invoice. Look at page 71 for some prices. (Answers will vary. Sample answers are given.)

McCarthy's Furniture Warehouse

Quantity	Merchandise	Unit Price	Total
1	sofa	$850.89	$850.89
1	armchair	$449.99	$449.99
2	end table	$115.00	$230.00
1	coffee table	$275.99	$275.99
3	lamp	$34.49	$103.47
1	dining room set	$875.00	$875.00
1	bed	$425.75	$425.75
		Subtotal	$3,211.09
		Total	

Presentation 3   10-15 mins.

Review prepositions of location with students by first talking about furniture in the classroom.

(G) Study the chart with your classmates and teacher.

Continue reviewing prepositions by asking students about the floor plan they filled in with furniture in Exercise F on the previous page.

Prepare students for doing Exercise H by modeling the conversation with a few students. Make sure students mention the room and then the location relative to other things in the room. Substitute school and classroom furniture into the conversation.

Practice 3   5-7 mins.

(H) Practice the conversation with a partner. Make similar conversations using the furniture and floor plan on page 71.

Evaluation 3   7-10 mins. ■

Ask students to describe their floor plans to a group. Then, ask a few volunteers to describe their floor plans to the class.

Application   10-15 mins. ■■■

(I) How much furniture do you need for your home? Complete the invoice. Look at page 71 for some prices.

Refer students to *Stand Out 2 Grammar Challenge*, Unit 4, Challenge 4 for more practice with prepositions of location.

Activity Bank

Unit 4, Lesson 4, Worksheet 1: Furniture and Appliances

Unit 4, Lesson 4, Worksheet 2: Floor Plans

Unit 4, Lesson 4, Worksheet 3: Prepositions of Location

Instructor's Notes

Objective: Make a family budget
Grammar: Modals: *may* and *might*
Academic: Focused listening, academic reading
Vocabulary: Household expenses, *income, withdrawal, monthly, deposit, bills, savings, checking*

AGENDA

Make a floor plan.
Learn about budgets.
Read a budget.
Make a budget.

RESOURCES

Activity Bank: Unit 4, Lesson 5, Worksheets 1–2
Reading and Writing Challenge: Unit 4
Grammar Challenge: Unit 4, Challenge 5

Audio: CD 1, Track 53
Heinle Picture Dictionary: Housing, pages 62–67

■ 1.5 hour classes   ■ 2.5 hour classes   ■ 3⁺ hour classes

Warm-up and Review   15-20 mins.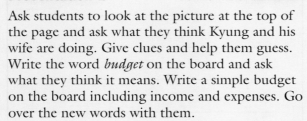

Ask students in groups to make a floor plan of one of their group member's homes. Ask them to add furniture. They will have to ask the group member about the location of each piece of furniture in each room. Ask the groups to briefly report to the class.

Introduction   7-10 mins.

Ask students how much money they spend on gas and water for their homes. Ask how much they spend on food. The word *spend* may be a new word. Try to see how many students catch on without explaining its meaning. State the objective: *Today we will make family budgets.*

Presentation 1   15-20 mins.

Ask students to look at the picture at the top of the page and ask what they think Kyung and his wife are doing. Give clues and help them guess. Write the word *budget* on the board and ask what they think it means. Write a simple budget on the board including income and expenses. Go over the new words with them.

Explain to students that sometimes reading information is like focused listening and that they don't have to understand every word to be able to get the gist. Tell students that they will read Exercise A on their own and that they should not stop to look up words. Tell them that they will not understand every word, but they should try to understand the overall meaning of the text.

Before students read, explain what the reading is about. The purpose of the article is to help them learn to use their money wisely. You may have to explain the word *wisely*. Write the two headings on the board: *Manage your money well.* and *Plan your budget.* Make sure students understand the topics before reading.

Practice 1   7-12 mins.

(A) **Read about managing money and budgets. Underline the new words.**

Give the students only one minute and thirty seconds to read on their own. A native speaker reading at an average pace may read the passage in 35–40 seconds. Tell students how much time they will have before they begin so that they know to read fast enough to finish in the allotted time.

Ask students to read the text again. Point out how the parentheses in this case show examples. Finally, read the article as a class and go over words students may not know.

Evaluation 1   5-7 mins.

(B) **Match the word with the definition. Write the correct letter.**

Check students' answers.

STANDARDS CORRELATIONS

CASAS: 1.5.1, 1.8.1, 6.1.1 (See CASAS Competency List on pages 169–175.)
SCANS: **Allocate** money, allocate materials and facility resources, allocate human resources
Information Acquire and evaluate information, organize and maintain information, interpret and communicate information
Interpersonal Participate as a member of a team, teach others, exercise leadership
Systems Understand systems
Basic Skills Reading, listening, speaking
Thinking Skills Make decisions, solve problems
Personal Qualities Self management
EFF: **Communication** Read with understanding, speak so others can understand, listen actively
Decision Making Solve problems and make decisions, plan
Interpersonal Cooperate with others, advocate and influence, resolve conflict and negotiate, guide others
Lifelong Learning Reflect and evaluate

LESSON 5 — Family budget

GOAL ➤ Make a family budget

Where are Kyung and his wife? What are they doing?

 A Read about managing money and budgets. Underline the new words.

Manage your money well. Follow these steps:
- Deposit your salary in checking and savings accounts.
- Keep cash on hand for emergencies.
- Only withdraw money when it is on your budget.
- Don't use credit cards a lot. Use an ATM card when you need cash.

Plan your budget. Follow these steps:
- Estimate how much you need for housing and regular bills (gas, water, electric, etc.).
- Estimate how much you need for other things for the year (clothing, car repair, etc.).
- Estimate entertainment costs and plan entertainment.
- Budget money for emergencies.
- Plan how much you can put in a savings account every month.

 B Match the word with the definition. Write the correct letter.

___c__ 1. ATM   a. put money in the bank

___a__ 2. deposit   b. paper money and coins

___d__ 3. withdraw   c. automated teller machine

___b__ 4. cash   d. take money out of the bank

GOAL ➤ **Make a family budget**

C Study Kyung and Anh's family budget with your classmates and teacher.

D Listen and complete the budget.

CD 1
TR 53

MONTHLY INCOME	
Kyung's wages	$3,000
Anh's wages	$2,500
Total Income	$5,500

MONTHLY EXPENSES	
Rent	$1,200
Gas	$50
Electric	$125
Water	$32
Food	$1,100
Life insurance	$91
Auto insurance	$125
Gasoline	$150
Phone	$250
Credit cards	$300
Entertainment	$300
Clothing	$200
Household repairs	$100
Savings	$100
Taxes	$900
Other	
Total Expenses	$5,023

E Study the chart with your classmates and teacher.

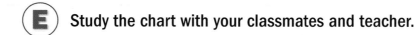

Modals: *May* and *Might*			
Subject	**Modal**	**Base verb**	**Example sentence**
I, you, he, she, we, they	may might	spend earn	I **may** spend $50 on gasoline this month. They **might** spend $300 a month on food. We **may** earn $3,500 a month.

Presentation 2   10–15 mins.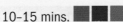

C **Study Kyung and Anh's family budget with your classmates and teacher.**

Go over all new vocabulary. Ask questions to check comprehension. Remember to give students plenty of time to respond. In this case, they may need to scan the budget to find the information. Show them how the next exercise will be a focused-listening activity where they have to listen for specific budget items and their amounts.

Ask students to predict how much the items will be and to write the amount to the right of each. In the listening, they will write the exact amount in the correct column.

Practice 2   10–15 mins.

D **Listen and complete the budget.**

> **Listening Script**   CD 1, Track 53
>
> *Kyung and Anh both work. They have to make a budget, so they don't spend too much money every week. It is important that they keep track of everything they spend. Kyung works for a company in Florida. He makes $3,000 a month. That is enough money for some things but not for everything his family needs.*
>
> *Kyung and Anh look over their bills for the past year. They make a budget based on the amount they spent each month last year. They decide that they will spend $50 on gas and $32 on water. One of their big expenses is food. They shop every week and since their children are older, they have a lot to buy. They budgeted $1,100 a month on food.*
>
> *They both drive a long distance to work, so they need money for gasoline and gasoline prices are going up. They budgeted $150 for gas. They speak to friends in Korea every month, so they also have to budget a lot for the phone bill. They decide on $250 a month for the phone.*
>
> *Kyung and his wife believe they should have a special night every week to go out to a restaurant or a show. They also want to go out as a family occasionally. Kyung says they probably should budget a lot for entertainment, maybe $300 a month. Then they need to plan for things they need to repair around their apartment. Most of the time the landlord will pay for repairs, so they only budget $100 a month for household repairs.*

Play the recording three times. Allow students to compare answers between listenings.

Evaluation 2   5–7 mins.

Go over the answers as a class. Be prepared to play the recording one more time for confirmation if needed.

Presentation 3   7–10 mins.

E **Study the chart with your classmates and teacher.**

Teach students that the two modals are almost the same. *Might* means with a little less certainty.

Drill students and ask them questions about the budget they completed in the listening activity.

Instructor's Notes

_____

_____

_____

_____

_____

_____

_____

_____

_____

_____

_____

_____

_____

_____

_____

Practice 3   10–15 mins.

F Practice the conversation with a partner.
Make new conversations.

Ask students to imagine that they are Kyung and
Anh. Have them ask one another more questions
about their budget.

Evaluation 3   10 mins.

Observe students as they practice the activity.

Application   15–20 mins.

G Work with a group. Imagine that you are a
family. Make a budget. Write the information below.

Make sure students understand that this is a new
budget based on what they think things might
cost and that they should use an income they
think is reasonable.

Ask groups to report to class.

**Refer students to *Stand Out 2 Grammar
Challenge*, Unit 4, Challenge 5 for more
practice with the modals *may* and *might*.**

Activity Bank

Unit 4, Lesson 5, Worksheet 1: Reading Budgets

Unit 4, Lesson 5, Worksheet 2: Family Budget

Instructor's Notes

LESSON 5

GOAL ➤ **Make a family budget**

F Practice the conversation with a partner. Make new conversations.

EXAMPLE: *Student A* (**Anh**): How much do we spend on water every month?
Student B (**Kyung**): We may spend about $32.

G Work with a group. Imagine that you are a family. Make a budget.
Write the information below. (Answers will vary.)

EXAMPLE: *Student A:* How much do we spend on clothing each month?
Student B: We might spend $200.

MONTHLY INCOME	
_____	_____
_____	_____
Total Income	_____
MONTHLY EXPENSES	
_____	_____
_____	_____
_____	_____
_____	_____
_____	_____
_____	_____
_____	_____
_____	_____
_____	_____
_____	_____
_____	_____
_____	_____
_____	_____
Total Expenses	_____

Review

 A Complete the questions. (Lesson 1)

1. _____What type_____ of housing do you want?

2. _____How much_____ is the rent?

3. _____Which_____ house do you want, the three- or four-bedroom?

4. _____Which_____ is the condominium? Is it on Main Street?

5. _____How many_____ bedrooms does the apartment have?

 B Scan the classified ads and answer the questions below. (Lesson 2)

Community Valley News

FOR RENT

❶ 3 bdrm, 2 bath condo, near schools and park, frpl, a/c, utils pd, **$1,200.** Call Margaret: 555-3444.

❸ 2 bdrm, 2 bath fireplace, a/c, lrg garage, balcony, nr park, **$900.** 555-9992

❷ lrg 5 bdrm hse, 3 bath, pool, nr schools, low move-in cost, **$2,900.** 333 W. Maple Dr. See Tony.

❹ 2 bdrm, 1 bath mobile home on spacious lot. Utilities pd. **$700.** Come and see for yourself. 555-5657

1. Which homes have a fireplace? Homes 1 and 3

2. Which homes have utilities included? Homes 1 and 4

3. Which home is less than $900? Home 4

4. Which homes have air-conditioning? Homes 1 and 3

5. Which homes are near schools? Homes 1 and 2

AT-A-GLANCE PREP

Objective: All unit objectives
Grammar: All unit grammar
Academic Strategies: Reviewing, evaluating, developing study skills
Vocabulary: All unit vocabulary

■ 1.5 hour classes   ■ 2.5 hour classes   ■ 3⁺ hour classes

AGENDA

Discuss unit objectives.
Complete the review.
Do My Dictionary.
Evaluate and reflect on progress.

Warm-up and Review   7–10 mins.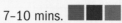

Ask students about their homes. Make a list on the board of all the vocabulary students can come up with from the unit.

Introduction   5 mins.

Write all the objectives on the board from Unit 4. Show students the first page of the unit and say the five objectives. Explain that today they will review the whole unit.

Note: Depending on the length of the term, you may decide to have students do Presentation 1 and Practice 1 for homework and then review student work as either the warm-up or another class activity.

Presentation 1   10–15 mins.

This presentation will cover the first three pages of the review. Quickly go to the first page of each lesson. Discuss the objective of each. Ask simple questions to remind students of what they have learned.

Practice 1   15–20 mins.

A Complete the questions. (Lesson 1)

B Scan the classified ads and answer the questions below. (Lesson 2)

Teaching Tip

Recycling/Review

The review and the project that follows are part of the recycling/review process. Students at this level often need to be reintroduced to concepts to solidify what they have learned. Many concepts are learned and forgotten while learning other new concepts. This is because students learn but are not necessarily ready to acquire language concepts.

Therefore, it becomes very important to review and to show students how to review on their own. It is also important to recycle the new concepts in different contexts.

STANDARDS CORRELATIONS

CASAS: 1.4.1, 1.4.2, 1.4.3, 1.5.1, 6.1.1, 6.1.3 (See CASAS Competency List on pages 169–175.)
SCANS: **Information** Acquire and evaluate information, organize and maintain information

Basic Skills Reading, writing, speaking
Personal Qualities Responsibility, self management
EFF: **Communication** Speak so others can understand
Lifelong Learning Take responsibility for learning, reflect and evaluate

Practice 1 *(continued)*

C Answer the questions. (Lesson 3)

D Write sentences about the location of furniture in the picture. Use prepositions. (Lesson 4)

E Talk in a group about the pictures. Use the words from the box. (Lesson 5)

Answer the questions. (Lesson 3) (Answers will vary.)

1. What is your present address? _____

2. What is your prior address? _____

3. What is your employer's name? _____

4. How many children live in your house? _____

5. Give one reference. _____

 Write sentences about the location of furniture in the picture. Use prepositions. (Lesson 4)

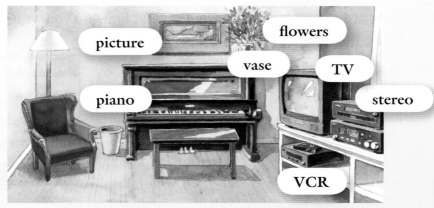

(Answers will vary. Sample answers are given.)

EXAMPLE: The piano is under the picture. _____

1. The TV is next to the stereo. _____

2. The vase is on the piano. _____

3. The lamp is in the corner. _____

4. The picture is over the piano. _____

 Talk in a group about the pictures. Use the words from the box. (Lesson 5)

> withdrawal
>
> deposit
>
> ATM
>
> debit card
>
> cash

Review

RENTAL APPLICATION

Date: **1.** _____   Name: **2.** _____

Present Address: **3.** _____

Prior Address: **4.** _____

Employer: **5.** _____

Position: **6.** _____

How many adults in unit: **7.** _____

How many children in unit: **8.** _____

F Look at the application above. On what lines do you write the following information? Circle the answer. (Lesson 3)

1. June 3, 2008
   (a. 1)   b. 2   c. 5   d. 6

2. 8237 Henderson Park Rd.
   a. 2   b. 3   (c. 4)   d. 5

3. Sift Company
   a. 1   b. 3   (c. 5)   d. 6

G Choose the correct answer.

1. What is Kyung's income?
   _____$3,000_____

2. How much is the apartment?
   _____$1,200_____

3. How much are the utilities?
   _____$207_____

MONTHLY INCOME	
Kyung's wages	$3,000
Anh's wages	$2,500
Total Income	

MONTHLY EXPENSES	
Rent	$1,200
Gas	$50
Electric	$125
Water	$32
Food	$1,100
Life insurance	$91
Auto insurance	$125
Gasoline	$150
Phone	$250
Credit cards	$300
Entertainment	$300
Clothing	$200
Household repairs	$100
Savings	$100
Taxes	$900
Other	
Total Expenses	

Practice 1 *(continued)*

(F) Look at the application above. On what lines do you write the following information? Circle the answer. (Lesson 3)

(G) Choose the correct answer.

Evaluation 1   15 mins. ■■■■

Go around the room and check on students' progress. Help individuals when needed. If you see consistent errors among several students, interrupt the class and give a mini lesson or review to help students feel comfortable with the concept.

Lesson Planner: Unit 4, Review   **78a**

Presentation 2
7-10 mins.

My Dictionary
Go over the steps of My Dictionary as a class.

Practice 2
5-7 mins.

Do the dictionary activity as a class before students work on their own for at least the first few units of the book to ensure that students understand what to do.

Evaluation 2
5 mins.

Ask students to share their cards.

Presentation 3
5 mins.

Learner Log
Review the concepts of the Learner Log. Make sure students understand the concepts and how to complete the log including circling the answers, finding page numbers where the concept is taught, and ranking favorite activities.

Teaching Tip

Learner Logs

Learner Logs function to help students in many different ways.

1. They serve as part of the review process.

2. They help students to gain confidence and to document what they have learned. Consequently, students see that they are progressing in their learning.

3. They provide students with a tool that they can use over and over to check and recheck their understanding of the target language. In this way, students become independent learners.

Practice 3
10-15 mins.

Ask students to complete the Learner Log.

Evaluation 3
2 mins.

Go over the Learner Log with students.

Application
5-7 mins.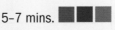

Ask students to record their favorite lesson or page in the unit.

TB Assessment

Use the Stand Out 2 Assessment CD-ROM with Exam *View*® to create a posttest for Unit 4.

Refer students to *Stand Out 2 Grammar Challenge*, Unit 4, Extension Challenge 1 for more practice with *Have to / Must* and Extension Challenge 2 for more practice with adjectives and noun modifiers.

Instructor's Notes

_____

_____

_____

_____

_____

_____

_____

_____

_____

_____

_____

_____

_____

_____

_____

_____

_____

_____

_____

_____

_____

_____

My Dictionary

Make flash cards to improve your vocabulary.

1. Choose four new words from this unit.

2. Write each word on an index card or sheet of paper.

3. On the back of the card or paper, draw a picture of the word, write a definition if you can, find a sentence in the book with the word, and write the page number.

4. Study the words.

Definition: paper money
Keep <u>cash</u> on hand for emergencies.
page 73

Learner Log

Circle how well you learned each item and write the page number where you learned it.

1. I can describe housing.
   Yes   Maybe   No   Page _____

2. I can understand classified ads.
   Yes   Maybe   No   Page _____

3. I can complete a rental application.
   Yes   Maybe   No   Page _____

4. I can identify rooms and furniture.
   Yes   Maybe   No   Page _____

5. I can make a family budget.
   Yes   Maybe   No   Page _____

Rank what you like to do best from 1 to 6. 1 is your favorite activity. Your teacher will help you.

_____ Practice listening

_____ Practice speaking

_____ Practice reading

_____ Practice writing

_____ Learn new words

_____ Learn grammar

In the next unit, I want to practice more

_____ .

Team Project

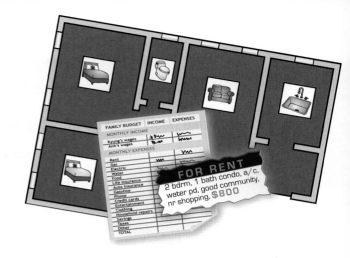

Plan a move.

Your team is a family who is going to move
to a new home. Work together to plan
the move.

1. Form a team with four or five students. In your team, you need:

POSITION	JOB	STUDENT NAME
Student 1: **Team Leader**	See that everyone speaks English. See that everyone participates.	
Student 2: **Finance Planner**	Make a family budget with help from the team. Plan to pay rent and buy furniture.	
Student 3: **Writer**	Write a classified ad and fill out a rental application with help from the team.	
Students 4/5: **Decorators**	Buy and arrange furniture in the home with help from the team.	

2. Describe your family and the home you want. Write a classified ad for the home
   you want.
   • How many bedrooms do you need?
   • What kind of home do you need (house, condo, apartment)?
   • How much money can you pay for rent?

3. Fill out a rental application.

4. Make a family budget.

5. Make a list of the furniture you need and fill out an invoice for furniture.

6. Make a floor plan of the home and add the furniture.

7. Report to the class. Show the floor plan and classified ad.

Introduction   5 mins.

Team Project

Plan a move.

In this project, teams will work as a family who is planning a move. The family will create a budget, write a classified ad, fill out a rental application, and buy and arrange furniture for the new home.

Stage 1   5–10 mins.

Form a team with four or five students.

Help students form groups and assign positions. Students will have to choose who will be the leader of their group. Review the responsibility of the leader and ask students to write the name of their leader in their books. Do the same with the remaining positions: finance planner, writer, and decorators.

Make sure students understand that all team members should work on every task. No team member should move to the next stage until the previous one is complete.

Stage 2   20–30 mins.

Describe your family and the home you want. Write a classified ad for the home you want.

Teams should describe their family and their family's wants and needs in a home. They then create a classified ad based on their wants and needs. Make sure they answer the three questions in their classified ad. They may include any other amenities and features they like. There is a classified ad template available on the Activity Bank CD-ROM (Unit 4, Project, Worksheet 1).

Stage 3   20–30 mins.

Fill out a rental application.

There is a rental application form on the Activity Bank CD-ROM (Unit 4, Project, Worksheet 3) that you may provide to teams.

Stage 4   10–15 mins.

Make a family budget.

There is a budget template available on the Activity Bank CD-ROM (Unit 4, Project, Worksheet 4).

Stage 5   15–20 mins.

Make a list of the furniture you need and fill out an invoice for furniture.

The decorators should lead the discussion of what furniture is needed in each room of the home. The finance planner and writer should fill out the invoice for the new furniture, including prices. Make sure that the amount of money spent on furniture fits into the family budget.

Stage 6   15–20 mins.

Make a floor plan of the home and add furniture.

There is a template for organizing furniture available on the Activity Bank CD-ROM (Unit 4, Project, Worksheet 2). The decorators should lead the discussion, but all team members should help.

Stage 7   30–40 mins.

Report to the class. Show the floor plan and classified ad.

Consider videotaping the presentations. Students will prepare better for formal presentations if they know they will be videotaped. Another approach is to have the teams videotape themselves in order to polish their presentations before giving them to the class.

Activity Bank

Unit 4, Project, Worksheet 1: Daily News Classifieds

Unit 4, Project, Worksheet 2: Furniture List

Unit 4, Project, Worksheet 3: Rental Application

Unit 4, Project, Worksheet 4: Family Budget

Unit 4, Extension, Worksheet 1: Write a Paragraph

Unit 4, Extension, Worksheet 2: Rooms in a House

STANDARDS CORRELATIONS

CASAS: 1.4.1, 1.4.2, 1.4.3, 1.5.1, 4.8.1 6.1.1, 6.1.3, (See CASAS Competency List on pages 169–175.)
SCANS: **Resources** Allocate time, allocate materials and facility resources, allocate human resources
Information Acquire and evaluate information, organize and maintain information, interpret and communicate information
Interpersonal Participate as a member of a team, teach others, exercise leadership, negotiate to arrive at a decision, work with cultural diversity
Systems Understand systems, monitor and correct performance
Basic Skills Reading, writing, listening, speaking

Thinking Skills Think creatively, make decisions, solve problems, see things in the mind's eye
Personal Qualities Responsibility, sociability, self management
EFF: **Communication** Read with understanding, convey ideas in writing, speak so others can understand, listen actively, observe critically
Decision Making Solve problems and make decisions, plan
Interpersonal Cooperate with others, advocate and influence, resolve conflict and negotiate, guide others
Lifelong Learning Take responsibility for learning, reflect and evaluate

Objective: Describe your community
Grammar: Questions with *where* and *when*
Academic Strategies: Focused listening, brainstorming, classifying
Vocabulary: Community vocabulary, directions, *northeast, northwest, southeast, southwest*

RESOURCES

Activity Bank: Unit 5, Lesson 1, Worksheets 1–3
Reading and Writing Challenge: Unit 5
Grammar Challenge: Unit 5, Challenge 1

■ 1.5 hour classes   ■ 2.5 hour classes   ■ 3+ hour classes

Audio: CD 2, Track 1
Heinle Picture Dictionary: Places Around Town, pages 46–47; Public Transportation, pages 128–129; Recreation, pages 210–227
Stand Out 1 Assessment CD-ROM with Exam*View*®

AGENDA

Do a corners activity.
Read about Palm City.
Read a bus schedule and ask questions.
Talk about places in the community.

 Preassessment *(optional)* ■■■

Use the Stand Out 2 Assessment CD-ROM with Exam*View*® to create a pretest for Unit 5.

Warm-up and Review   10-15 mins. ■■■

Ask students where they live. Help them use the preposition *in* before the name of their city. Ask students what they like to do in their city. Tell them what you like to do. Write *entertainment* on the board and list various activities you do for entertainment. Elicit student ideas to add to the list. Choose four types of entertainment and do a corners activity where each corner represents a different activity. Ask students to go to the corner that represents the activity they prefer. The corners might include *movies, restaurants, sports,* and *shopping.* When students reach their corners, have them ask one another what they like about the activity they have chosen.

Introduction   7-10 mins. ■■■

With the class, brainstorm different places to obtain services in your community. Start them off with a few ideas such as *the post office* and *hospital.* State the objective: *Today we will describe our community.*

Presentation 1   20-30 mins. ■■■

Write *north, south, east,* and *west* on the board and use each wall of the classroom as a compass point to demonstrate the concept. Go over the primary compass points until students are comfortable with them. Then, add *northeast, northwest, southeast,* and *southwest.*

A Read the paragraph.

Read the paragraph with students and ask them to underline any words they don't know. Write *places* on the board and, as a class, make a list of places mentioned in the reading. Go over the vocabulary with them. Leave the words on the board and ask students to close their books. Give students a dictation of the paragraph.

Ask students questions, such as: *Where are the schools?* Write the questions and correct responses on the board: *They're in the northwest.* Review the verb *be,* in both its singular and plural forms.

Practice 1   7-10 mins. ■■■

B Fill in the chart about Palm City.

Evaluation 1   5-7 mins. ■■■

When students have finished completing the chart, go over their answers as a class.

Our Community

GOALS
➤ **Describe your community**
➤ **Scan a directory index**
➤ **Give and follow directions**

➤ **Read a message or letter**
➤ **Write and send a letter**

LESSON **1**

Getting around town

GOAL ➤ **Describe your community**

A Read the paragraph.

Palm City is a small community. The homes and schools are all in the northwest. There is a mall with 100 stores in the northeast. In the southeast, there is a big entertainment center with a bowling alley, movie theaters, a miniature golf course, and many other kinds of entertainment. There are factories and companies in the southwest part of town. The bus circles the city in exactly an hour.

B Fill in the chart about Palm City.

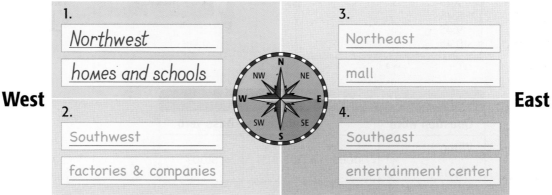

North

1.
Northwest
homes and schools

3.
Northeast
mall

West

2.
Southwest
factories & companies

4.
Southeast
entertainment center

East

South

LESSON 1

GOAL ➤ Describe your community

C Look at the bus schedule. Write the names of the streets on the map.

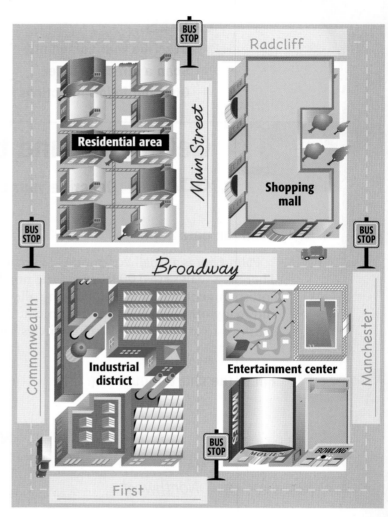

PALM CITY Bus Schedule Morning Service

Residential area
Radcliff and Main St.
7:00
8:00
9:00
10:00

Shopping mall
Broadway and Manchester
7:15
8:15
9:15
10:15

Entertainment center
First and Main St.
7:30
8:30
9:30
10:30

Industrial district
Broadway and Commonwealth
7:45
8:45
9:45
10:45

Information Questions			
Question word		**Subject**	**Base verb**
When	does	the bus	stop?
Where			

 D Ask a partner questions about the schedule.

EXAMPLES: *Student A:* When does the bus stop in the residential area?
Student B: at 7:00 A.M.

Student B: Where does the bus stop at 8:45?
Student A: in the industrial district

Presentation 2   10-15 mins.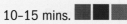

C **Look at the bus schedule. Write the names of the streets on the map.**

Teach students about the bus schedule. The map is like a puzzle. Students will need to understand the bus schedule to write the missing street names on the map.

Ask questions about the schedule and about the map, such as what time the bus arrives. Be careful to allow students plenty of time to respond. As stated in an earlier teaching tip, research shows that instructors, on average, answer their own questions before students have a chance to respond. However, if students are given enough time to process the information, they will come up with the correct answer.

Prepare students to do Exercise D. Go over the grammar box. Even at this level, students may still be struggling with the difference between *where* and *when*. Help them hear and pronounce the difference in the two words. Drill them on when you use *where* for several examples and suddenly throw in *when*. This will keep students thinking about what you are asking.

For shorter classes, ask students to do Exercise D for homework.

Practice 2   7-10 mins.

D **Ask a partner questions about the schedule.**

Evaluation 2   5-7 mins.

Monitor students' practice and then ask volunteers to demonstrate their exchanges in front of the class.

Instructor's Notes

_____
_____
_____
_____
_____
_____
_____
_____
_____
_____
_____
_____
_____
_____
_____
_____
_____
_____
_____
_____
_____
_____
_____
_____
_____
_____
_____
_____

Presentation 3   15–20 mins.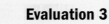

Make a cluster diagram on the board or make copies of a cluster diagram from the template folder on the Activity Bank CD-ROM. Label the center circle *Community* and the secondary circles *Residential, Shopping, Companies,* and *Entertainment.* As a class, brainstorm and classify places in the community and list three items off of each secondary circle.

(E) Study these words with your classmates and teacher.

Go over each word and its correct pronunciation. Ask students to make an educated guess as to which column each item should go in. Some items could go in more than one column. Accept all answers and ask students to write the answers in pencil in their books but to be prepared to erase the answers while listening.

Practice 3   7–10 mins. ■

(F) Write the words from the box in the correct category below. Then, listen and check your answers.

Prepare students for the listening activity by explaining that they will not write the words that they hear, but rather they check them off on their lists or make arrows to the correct locations if there are errors.

🎧 Listening Script   CD 2, Track 1

In Palm City, there are public services where you can take care of any type of business that you have. For example, in the center of town, we have City Hall and the courthouse. Other public services include banks, fire stations, police stations, libraries, a post office, and a large hospital.

We also have many shops, including clothes stores and supermarkets. You can buy hammers and nails at the hardware store and go across the street and get something to eat at several fast-food restaurants. You don't have to drive far to find gas stations, a pharmacy, shoe stores, and, of course, a very large department store.

Palm City is a great place to live. Here we have apartments, condominiums, houses, and even mobile homes.

Evaluation 3   5–7 mins. ■

Check the answers as a class and be prepared to play the listening again for confirmation.

Application   10–15 mins. ■■■

(G) List places in your community that are less than one mile from your home.

Refer students to *Stand Out 2 Grammar Challenge,* Unit 5, Challenge 1 for more practice with forming questions with *when, where* and prepositions.

Activity Bank 💿

Templates: Cluster diagram

Unit 5, Lesson 1, Worksheet 1: Parts of a Community

Unit 5, Lesson 1, Worksheet 2: Read a Bus Schedule

Unit 5, Lesson 1, Worksheet 3: Places in the Community

 LESSON **1**   **GOAL** ➤ **Describe your community**

E Study these words with your classmates and teacher.

apartment	courthouse	hardware store	pharmacy
bank	department store	hospital	police station
City Hall	fast-food restaurant	house	post office
clothes store	fire station	library	shoe store
condominium	gas station	mobile home	supermarket

CD 2
TR 1

F Write the words from the box in the correct category below. Then, listen and check your answers.

Residential	Public and Service	Retail
house	bank	clothes store
apartment	city hall	department store
condominium	courthouse	fast-food restaurant
mobile home	fire station	gas station
	hospital	hardware store
	library	pharmacy
	police station	shoe store
	post office	supermarket

G List places in your community that are less than one mile from your home.

_____ _____ _____

_____ _____ _____

_____ _____ _____

_____ _____ _____

LESSON 2 What's the number?

GOAL ➤ Scan a directory index

What is Marie doing?
What does Marie need?

 Read the paragraph about Marie.

Marie lives in Palm City. She is a nurse at the hospital. She has a friend in Brazil. She wants to send a package to her friend. She has questions and needs to find the number and address for the nearest post office. Does she send the package with insurance? Does she send it first class? When will the package arrive in Brazil? Her phone book has White Pages and Yellow Pages.

B Circle the correct answer.

1. Why does Marie want to call the post office?

   a. She wants to send a letter.

   b. She needs information.

   c. She has a friend in Brazil.

2. What does Marie want to do?

   a. She wants to get insurance.

   b. She wants to travel to Brazil.

   c. She wants to send a package.

 Circle the places you can find in the Yellow Pages.

museums   the post office   supermarkets

churches   a friend   city agencies

Objective: Scan a directory index
Grammar: Simple present
Pronunciation: Clarification
Academic Strategies: Focused listening, scanning, clarification strategies
Vocabulary: Community places, *lawyers, attorneys, playgrounds, grocers, home improvement, physicians*

RESOURCES

Activity Bank: Unit 5, Lesson 2, Worksheet 1
Reading and Writing Challenge: Unit 5
Grammar Challenge: Unit 5, Challenge 2

Audio: CD 2, Tracks 2–7
Heinle Picture Dictionary: Community, pages 46–55

AGENDA

List places in the community.
Talk about the post office.
Read an index.
Read a directory.
Listen for information.

■ 1.5 hour classes   ■ 2.5 hour classes   ■ 3⁺ hour classes

Warm-up and Review   10-12 mins.

Ask students in groups to make a list of community places within one mile of the school. Ask them next to identify what street each place is on. Write on the board: *Where is the post office?* Make sure students know how to answer the question with *on* and the name of the street. Ask them to ask the question about all the places on their list.

Introduction   5-7 mins. ■■■

Ask students for the phone number of the local post office. They most likely will not be able to respond. Ask them how you might find the information. Hopefully, they will say to look in the phone book. They may also say to look on the Internet. Write *Yellow Pages* and *White Pages* on the board. See if students know how they are different. State the objective: *Today we will scan directories like the Yellow Pages and White Pages for important information and phone numbers.*

Presentation 1   30-40 mins. ■■■

Ask students to open their books and cover the paragraph in Exercise A. Ask the questions in the box and any others that might be helpful. Make a list on the board of new vocabulary, including words that relate to the post office. Include items such as *package, send, phone book,* and *scan.* Check for student understanding and tap into their background knowledge by asking questions about sending a package. For example, ask them

what they think is in the package in the picture and if they think Marie should insure it.

(A) Read the paragraph about Marie.

Ask the class to read the paragraph silently and then go over it as a class. Briefly discuss different mailing options that you know about. Ask what the benefits are of shipping something first class. You might choose to use the U.S. Postal Service Web site (www.usps.com) if you have access to a computer in your classroom, or you can study the options Marie has ahead of time and present them to the class.

(B) Circle the correct answer.

Since this is still the presentation stage, ask and answer these questions as a class.

Practice 1   5-7 mins.

(C) Circle the places you can find in the Yellow Pages.

Allow students in groups to discuss the locations. They may not all agree on which ones are in the Yellow Pages. This is to be expected. City agencies are generally not in the Yellow Pages but rather in the front section of the White Pages. Allow students to discuss these ideas.

Evaluation 1   3-7 mins.

Discuss the places and people as a class. Classify the items on the board by making a chart with two columns representing the Yellow Pages and the White Pages.

STANDARDS CORRELATIONS

CASAS: 2.1.1, 2.4.2 (See CASAS Competency List on pages 169-175.)
SCANS: **Information** Acquire and evaluate information
Basic Skills Reading, writing, listening, speaking

EFF: **Communication** Read with understanding, convey ideas in writing, speak so others can understand, listen actively

Presentation 2

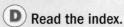

15–20 mins.

(D) Read the index.

As a class, go over the index carefully with students. Remind students of alphabetical order. Ask them questions, such as: *What pages are the lawyers on?* Go over any new vocabulary including *lawyers, attorneys, playgrounds, grocers, home improvement,* and *physicians.*

Have a competition in the class to see who can find certain information the fastest. Give students a situation and ask them to quickly find help for you. For example, you might say that you have a problem: You have a job interview and nothing to wear. Encourage students to find the clothing stores and the shoe stores.

Teaching Tip

Scanning

At lower levels, students may not be accustomed to scanning for information in English. They may feel they need to read and understand everything on a page to get the information. Do activities that encourage them to look over the information quickly so that they are forced to scan rather than read. Competitions like the one suggested in Exercise D above serve this purpose.

The skill of scanning is closely related to focused listening. When people focus their listening, they are filtering out all extraneous information and listening for specific information. The same skill is necessary for scanning.

To prepare students for the practice activity, remind them about the simple present tense as indicated in the small grammar chart. If you would prefer to use a more complete chart of the grammar, direct students to the grammar reference charts in the back of the book.

Teaching Tip

Grammar review

As we have mentioned previously, students may be exposed to grammar structures in various lessons throughout *Stand Out*, but acquiring the language and grammar concepts comes at a different rate for each student. This is why it becomes very important to regularly review grammar points, especially ones where students make common errors while speaking and not thinking about form. The chart below may make this concept clearer.

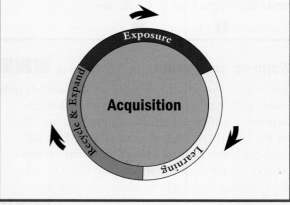

Practice 2

7–10 mins.

(E) Marie needs things at different locations in the community. Work in a group to write what she needs.

Make sure students understand how to do this activity. They must look in the directory for the page numbers that are listed in the chart and find the corresponding locations. Then, they write a sentence about what Marie might need at the location.

Evaluation 2

7–10 mins.

Ask volunteers to write their sentences on the board. Sentences may vary so accept most answers. Allow other students to help edit errors in the sentences on the board.

LESSON 2

GOAL ➤ **Scan a directory index**

D Read the index.

PALM CITY
Local Phone Directory Index

Art Galleries	8
Attorneys	9-12
Banks	12-13
Churches	13-17
Clothes–Retail	17-21
Community Services–See White Pages	iv
Libraries	
Playgrounds and Parks	
Dentists	21
Department Stores	22-23
Doctors–See Physicians, Optometrists, Dentists	
Fast Food–See Restaurants	
Furniture–Retail	24
Government–See White Pages	
Grocers and Markets	24-25
Home Improvement	25-26
Hospital	27
Lawyers–See Attorneys	

PALM CITY
Local Phone Directory Index

Museums	27
Optometrists	27-28
Physicians	28
Real Estate Agencies	29
Rental cars	29-30
Restaurants	30-32
Schools (private)	32
Schools (public)	32
Shoes–Retail	32-33
Supermarkets–See Grocers	
Transportation	33-35
Bus Lines	
Car Rental	
Shuttle Service	
Train	
Taxis	
Travel Agencies	35

E Marie needs things at different locations in the community. Work in a group to write what she needs.

Simple Present	
Subject	**Verb**
I, you, we, they	need, want
he, she	needs, wants

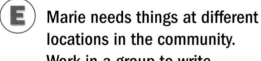

Page	
24–25	Marie needs to go to the market.
17–21	Marie needs some new clothes.
29–30	Marie needs to rent a car.
30–32	Marie needs to find a restaurant.
25–26	Marie needs to work on her home.

 LESSON 2

GOAL ➤ Scan a directory index

F Study the directory with your classmates and teacher.

Palm City Government Agencies and Services

City Hall 555-3300 160 W. Broadway	**Angel Park** 137 Monroe St. 555-3224
Courthouse 555-5245 150 W. Broadway	**Lilly Community Park** 275 Carpenter 555-2211
DMV (Department of Motor Vehicles) Information 555-2227 Appointments 555-2778 375 Western Ave.	**Police Department** 555-4867 **Emergencies call 911** 140 W. Broadway
Fire Department 555-3473 **Emergencies call 911** 145 W. Broadway	**Schools (Public)** **Jefferson Middle** 555-2665 122 Jefferson St.
Library (Public) 555-7323 125 E. Broadway	**Lincoln High** 555-8336 278 Lincoln Ave.
Playgrounds and Parks	**Washington Elementary** 555-5437 210 Washington St.
Department of Parks and Recreation 160 W. Broadway, Suite 15 555-7275	**U.S. Post Office** 555-6245 151 E. Broadway

CD 2
TR 2

G Listen and practice the conversation. Then, ask a partner for information about the *post office, courthouse, DMV, fire department, City Hall,* and *Jefferson Middle School.*

Student A: Where's the post office?
Student B: The post . . . ?
Student A: The post office.
Student B: Oh, it's at 151 East Broadway.
Student A: What's the phone number?
Student B: It's 555-6245.

Pronunciation

Clarification

Use stress to clarify information.

the post OFFICE

CD 2
TR 3–7

H Cover the directory and listen to the conversations. Write the places, addresses, and phone numbers you hear in the chart.

Place	Address	Phone
1. post office	151 E. Broadway	555–6245
2. library	125 E. Broadway	555–7323
3. City Hall	160 W. Broadway	555–3300
4. DMV	375 Western Ave.	555–2778
5. police dept.	140 W. Broadway	555–4867

I What are the most important phone numbers to have? Make a list with a group.

Presentation 3 30-40 mins.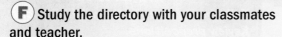

F **Study the directory with your classmates and teacher.**

Look at the listening script for Exercise H. As you go over the directory with the students, ask them questions related to what they will have to do in the later exercise.

G **Listen and practice the conversation. Then, ask a partner for information about the *post office, courthouse, DMV, fire department, City Hall*, and *Jefferson Middle School*.**

Talk about clarification strategies. Point out the clarification strategies on the recording. Do a chain drill where students ask the student next to him or her a question. That student answers and asks the next student a different question.

Practice 3 10-12 mins. ■

 Listening Script CD 2, Track 2

The listening script matches the conversation in Exercise G.

H **Cover the directory and listen to the conversations. Write the places, addresses, and phone numbers you hear in the chart.**

Play the recording three times and ask students to collaborate on the answers.

 Listening Script CD 2, Tracks 3–7

1. **Post Office:** *Hello. Jefferson Street Post Office.*
   Raquel: *I need to send some letters to my family in Brazil tonight. Can I buy stamps there in the evening?*
   Post Office: *No. This post office closes at 5 P.M., but the post office on East Broadway is open tonight.*
   Raquel: *That's great. What is the address again?*
   Post Office: *It is at 151 East Broadway.*
   Raquel: *OK. Do you have the phone number there?*
   Post Office: *Yes. It's 555-6245.*
   Raquel: *Thanks for your help. Goodbye.*
2. **Raquel:** *Hello. I want to get a new library card and borrow some books to read. Can you give me the address of the library?*
   Librarian: *Sure. We are at 125 East Broadway.*
   Raquel: *Thanks. And could you tell me your phone number? I got your number from the operator and forgot to write it down.*
   Librarian: *No problem. I'm happy to help. It's 555-7323.*

3. **Raquel:** *Hello. I just arrived here from Brazil, and I need some help understanding my visa. Who can I talk to about that?*
   Operator: *Hmm. You need to talk to Immigration and Naturalization right here in City Hall. Please hold and I will transfer you.*
   Immigration: *Immigration and Naturalization Agency. How can I be of assistance?*
   Raquel: *I'd like to make an appointment to discuss my visa.*
   Immigration: *How's next Monday at 9 A.M.?*
   Raquel: *Excellent. Thanks. Could you tell me where you're located?*
   Immigration: *We're at City Hall at 160 West Broadway. Our phone number is 555-3300.*
4. **DMV:** *Hello, DMV.*
   Raquel: *I need to find out about getting a driver's license. Can you give me some information?*
   DMV: *Yes, of course. You have to make an appointment. I'll give you the number. Do you have a pen?*
   Raquel: *Yes. Go ahead.*
   DMV: *The number is 555-2778.*
   Raquel: *OK, great. Where is the office located?*
   DMV: *It's at 375 Western Avenue. Our hours are 8:30 A.M. to 4:00 P.M.*
   Raquel: *OK. Thanks!*
5. **Police:** *Police Department.*
   Raquel: *Hi. I lost my purse on the bus yesterday. Do you think someone turned it in?*
   Police: *Hold on. I'll transfer your call to Lost and Found.*
   Raquel: *Thanks.*
   Police: *Lost and Found.*
   Raquel: *Hi. I lost my purse on the bus yesterday. Do you think someone turned it in?*
   Police: *You'll have to come in to our office to identify it.*
   Raquel: *OK. What's your address?*
   Police: *It's 140 West Broadway.*
   Raquel: *And what's your number?*
   Police: *It's 555-4867.*
   Raquel: *Thank you. Goodbye.*

Evaluation 3 5-7 mins. ■

Go over the answers to the listening activity and play the recording a final time for confirmation.

Application 5-7 mins. ■■■

I **What are the most important phone numbers to have? Make a list with a group.**

Refer students to *Stand Out 2 Grammar Challenge*, Unit 5, Challenge 2 for more practice with the simple present tense.

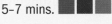 **Activity Bank**

Unit 5, Lesson 2, Worksheet 1: Phone Directory

Objective: Give and follow directions
Grammar: Prepositions, imperatives
Academic Strategy: Focused listening
Vocabulary: *blocks, miles, turn, left, right, intersection, north, south, east, west*

RESOURCES

Activity Bank: Unit 5, Lesson 3, Worksheets 1–2
Reading and Writing Challenge: Unit 5
Grammar Challenge: Unit 5, Challenge 3

Audio: CD 2, Tracks 8–9
Heinle Picture Dictionary: Community, pages 46–55

■ 1.5 hour classes   ■ 2.5 hour classes   ■ 3⁺ hour classes

AGENDA

Talk about places in the neighborhood.
Review prepositions.
Listen and follow directions.
Write directions.
Write about the community.

Warm-up and Review   10-15 mins. ■■■

Ask students in groups to list their favorite stores and businesses in the neighborhood. Ask them to classify the list by eating places, businesses that provide services, clothing stores, and so on. After each group finishes its list, have a representative share it with the class.

Introduction   5-7 mins. ■■■

Give directions to a place in the community not too far from the school without disclosing the place itself. Ask students to follow the directions in their minds and see if they can identify the place. Do this a few times with different locations. State the objective: *Today we will give and follow directions.*

Presentation 1   15-20 mins. ■■■

Ask students to look at the map on the student book page. Ask them questions about the locations.

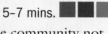 **A** Look at the map.

 B Study the prepositions with your classmates and teacher.

Go over the prepositions. Students may have trouble distinguishing between *in* and *on*. Show them how *in the corner* is used to described things inside. Demonstrate by asking where items in the corner of the classroom are. Use the map to show them that *on the corner* is used to identify things outside on the corner of a street. They may also have trouble with *across from*. Explain how *across from* is different from *in front of* because it generally means on the other side of the street or other obstacle. Teach students additional vocabulary including *intersection* and *block*. Although students may already be familiar with prepositions of locations, spend enough time to make sure students are comfortable with them.

Practice 1   7-10 mins. ■■■

 C Look at the map in Exercise A. Complete the sentences with prepositions.

Ask students to do this activity on their own, not in pairs or groups. They will peer-edit in the evaluation stage.

Evaluation 1   7-10 mins. ■■■

Ask volunteers to write the complete sentences on the board from Exercise C. Ask the other students to check their work.

STANDARDS CORRELATIONS

CASAS: 1.1.3, 1.9.4, 2.2.1, 2.2.5 (See CASAS Competency List on pages 169-175.)
SCANS: **Information** Acquire and evaluate information
Basic Skills Reading, writing, listening, speaking

Thinking Skills Think creatively
EFF: **Communication** Read with understanding, convey ideas in writing, speak so others can understand, listen actively, observe critically

Finding your way

GOAL ➤ Give and follow directions

A Look at the map.

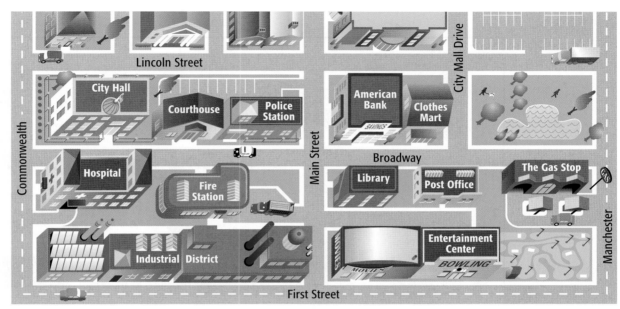

B Study the prepositions with your classmates and teacher.

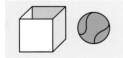      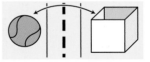

next to   on the corner   between   across from

C Look at the map in Exercise A. Complete the sentences with prepositions.

1. The gas station is _____on the corner_____ of Broadway and Manchester.

2. The courthouse is _____between_____ City Hall and the police station.

3. The post office is _____next to_____ the library.

4. The police station is _____across from_____ the fire station.

5. City Hall is _____across from_____ the hospital.

6. The post office is _____between_____ the public library and the gas station.

CD 2
TR 8

D Marie's friend is lost and needs directions. Listen to the conversation. Find Marie's apartment on the map.

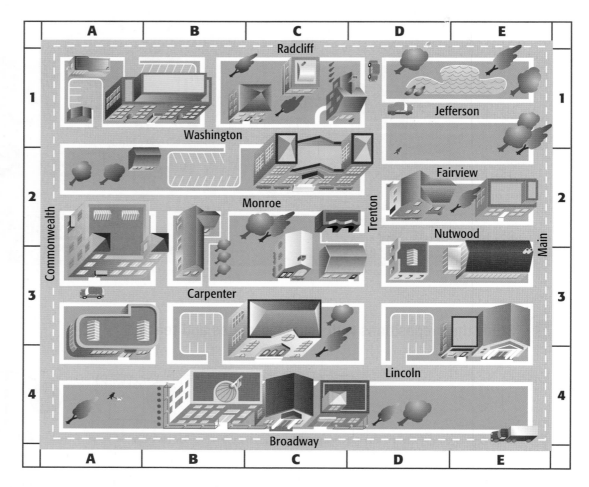

CD 2
TR 9

E Listen to the directions. Find the locations on the map.

F Write the letter and number for each location below.

1. the museum	A3
2. the real estate office	E3
3. the computer store	A1
4. the coffee shop	E2

Presentation 2   20-30 mins. ▪▪▪

Go over the map and discuss the locations of different places. Practice giving students directions similar to the ones on the upcoming listening activity. Ask volunteers to give directions from one location to another.

Talk about places in your own community. Give directions from one place to another and ask students for the name of the place. Also, go over the map quadrants. You might ask what is in C5 for example.

Teaching Tip

Using the classroom

We try to give suggestions in *Stand Out* that we feel most teachers would be comfortable with. It is important to note that each teacher has a unique teaching style and students have different learning styles. It is important to find what your strengths are and what the needs of your students are. We encourage teachers to try new things beyond our suggestions.

One way to be creative is to try to use the learning environment in interesting ways. For example, in this lesson you might consider putting the chairs in rows that represent streets and having the desks represent buildings. This gives a nice visual.

Another idea would be to introduce the word *steps* and ask students to guess how many steps it is from one place in the room to another. After students are comfortable using the vocabulary, show them how to transfer this experience to the real world by substituting *blocks* and/or *miles* for *steps*.

D Marie's friend is lost and needs directions. Listen to the conversation. Find Marie's apartment on the map.

Do this listening activity as a class in preparation for the practice in Exercise E.

 Listening Script   CD 2, Track 8

Marie: *Hello.*
Ana: *Hi, Marie. I'm here!*
Marie: *Where?*
Ana: *Here in Palm City.*
Marie: *Really? Where are you right now?*
Ana: *I'm at the intersection of Main and Lincoln.*
Marie: *Wow, that's great! You can walk here. Go north on Main. Walk straight ahead for three blocks and turn left on Fairview. Go one block and turn right. Turn left on Washington. My apartment is on the right at 133 Washington, Number 15.*

Practice 2   7-10 mins. ▪▪

E Listen to the directions. Find the locations on the map.

 Listening Script   CD 2, Track 9

1. *You are at the intersection of Broadway and Main. Find the museum. Go north on Main one block and turn left. Go three blocks and it's on the right.*

2. *You are at the intersection of Carpenter and Commonwealth. Find the real estate office. Go east on Carpenter two blocks and turn right. Go one block and turn left. It's on the left.*

3. *You are at the intersection of Fairview and Trenton. Find the computer store. Go north on Trenton and turn left on Washington. Walk straight ahead one block and turn right. Then turn left and it's on the left.*

4. *You are at the intersection of Commonwealth and Radcliff. Find the coffee shop. Go straight on Radcliff three blocks. Turn right on Main. Walk two blocks. It is across the street, on your right.*

Evaluation 2   3-5 mins. ▪▪

Go over the answers as a class. Be prepared to play the recording again for a final check.

F Write the letter and number for each location below.

Ask students to complete this activity individually. Then, go over the answers as a class.

Presentation 3   10–15 mins.   ■■□

Show students where to find the listening scripts in the back of their books. Ask them to find the previous listening script and review the vocabulary. Ask them to identify the verbs in the four sets of directions.

Show students how in English there is almost always a subject or a word that indicates who or what is operating the verb. (You might want to refer them to the grammar reference charts in the appendix.) Next, tell them that there is one occasion where the subject is implied. Show them what you mean by going over the chart in Exercise G.

G Study the chart with your classmates and teacher.

Briefly drill students on the imperative sentences. Explain that when people give instructions like street directions or recipes, they usually use the imperative. Remind them that they studied the imperative on page 55 when they wrote recipes. Make sure they understand that usually each verb indicates a new sentence, and it should be capitalized. Also, it is always a good idea to remind students that a period is needed at the end of sentences.

H Study the map with your classmates and teacher.

Go over locations briefly and give a few directions. Ask students to also give directions.

For shorter classes, have students do Exercise I for homework.

Practice 3   15–20 mins.   ■

I Look at the map above. Write directions to the locations below.

Evaluation 3   3–7 mins.   ■

Ask volunteers to write their directions on the board. Have the other students check that the volunteers have capitalized the first word of each sentence and street names, and that they have used periods at the end of the sentences.

Application   10–15 mins.   ■■□

J On a sheet of paper, write directions from the school to your home.

Some students may not want to share the location of their home. If so, ask those students to write directions to a different location in the community.

Another approach would be to pass out 3-by-5 index cards to each student in a group of four or five. Ask students in the group to come up with, but not to disclose to the class, a place in the community. Ask them to write directions from the school to that place. Then, have each student in the group copy the directions. Collect the cards from one group at a time and pass out one of the cards to each of the other groups. Ask each group to read the card they just received and guess the place in the community it is referring to.

📖 **Refer students to *Stand Out 2 Grammar Challenge*, Unit 5, Challenge 3 for more practice with imperatives.**

Activity Bank 💿

Unit 5, Lesson 3, Worksheet 1: Prepositions of Location

Unit 5, Lesson 3, Worksheet 2: Give and Follow Directions

Instructor's Notes

_____

_____

_____

_____

_____

_____

_____

_____

_____

_____

LESSON 3

GOAL ➤ Give and follow directions

G Study the chart with your classmates and teacher.

Imperatives			
	Base verb		**Example sentence**
~~you~~	**go**	straight straight ahead	**Go** straight three blocks. **Go** straight ahead.
	turn	left right around	**Turn** left on Nutwood. **Turn** right on Nutwood. **Turn** around.
	stop	on the left on the right	**Stop** on the left. **Stop** on the right.

H Study the map with your classmates and teacher.

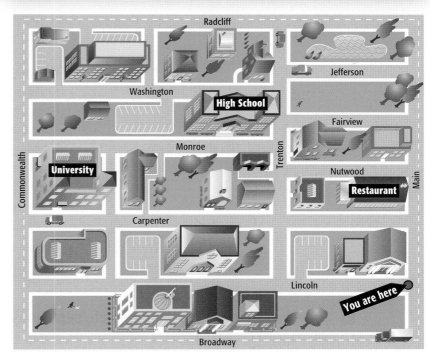

I Look at the map above. Write directions to the locations below.

1. The high school: Go straight ahead on Main for three blocks. Then, turn left on Fairview.
2. The restaurant: Go straight ahead on Main for two blocks. Then, turn left on Nutwood.
3. The university: Go straight one block on Main. Then, turn left on Carpenter and go three blocks.

J On a sheet of paper, write directions from the school to your home.

LESSON 4

Dear Raquel

GOAL ➤ Read a message or letter

 A Read Marie's letter to her friend Raquel in Brazil.

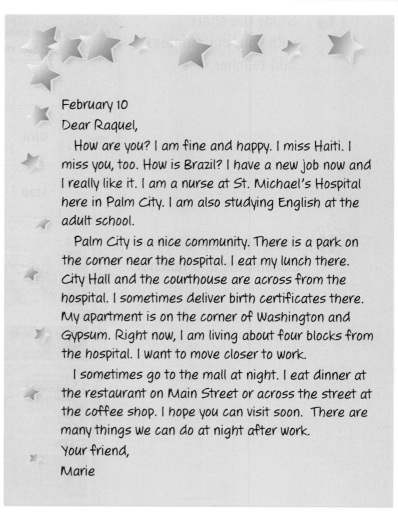

February 10
Dear Raquel,

How are you? I am fine and happy. I miss Haiti. I miss you, too. How is Brazil? I have a new job now and I really like it. I am a nurse at St. Michael's Hospital here in Palm City. I am also studying English at the adult school.

Palm City is a nice community. There is a park on the corner near the hospital. I eat my lunch there. City Hall and the courthouse are across from the hospital. I sometimes deliver birth certificates there. My apartment is on the corner of Washington and Gypsum. Right now, I am living about four blocks from the hospital. I want to move closer to work.

I sometimes go to the mall at night. I eat dinner at the restaurant on Main Street or across the street at the coffee shop. I hope you can visit soon. There are many things we can do at night after work.

Your friend,
Marie

 B Answer the questions in complete sentences. Use prepositions.

1. Where does Marie eat lunch? Where is it?

   She eats lunch in the park. It's on the corner near the hospital.

2. Where does Marie work? Where is the building?

   She works at St. Michael's Hospital, which is near a park.

3. Where does Marie deliver birth certificates? Where is the building?

   She delivers them at City Hall, which is across from the hospital.

4. Where does Marie eat dinner? Where is the building?

   She eats at the restaurant on Main Street or across the street at the coffee shop.

90   Unit 5   Lesson 4

Objective: Read a message or letter
Grammar: Simple present, present continuous
Academic Strategies: Focused listening, scanning, predicting
Vocabulary: Prepositions, *certificates, miss, closer, soon*

RESOURCES

Activity Bank: Unit 5, Lesson 4, Worksheet 1
Reading and Writing Challenge: Unit 5
Grammar Challenge: Unit 5, Challenge 4

■ 1.5 hour classes   ■ 2.5 hour classes   ■ 3⁺ hour classes

AGENDA

Write directions.
Read a letter.
Read a postcard.
Listen to a letter.
Answer questions.

Audio: CD 2, Track 10
Heinle Picture Dictionary: Community, pages 46–55

Warm-up and Review   15-20 mins.

Ask students to write directions to a place in the community. Then, have them pair up with another student and read the directions. Students try to determine the location based on their partners' directions.

Introduction   3-5 mins.

On the board, write: *Dear Raquel,*. Ask students what you have started. Ask if they have written a letter recently. State the objective: *Today we will read messages and letters.*

Presentation 1   15-20 mins.

With books closed, read the letter from Marie to Raquel out loud. Ask students to identify the purpose of the letter. Answers might include *an invitation to visit, a description of the city,* and *a description of what Marie does every day.* Refer students back to the map on page 88. Review prepositions like *across from* by asking questions about the map.

Prepare students for the reading by writing on the board: *miss you, too; birth certificates; I want to move closer to work;* and *I hope you can visit soon.* Discuss the meaning of each item.

Teaching Tip

Reading strategies

Like focused listening, students should understand that they will comprehend more of the letter if they don't get bogged down with all the vocabulary. Encourage them to read without stopping. If there are words they don't understand, they can underline them but they shouldn't stop reading.

Practice 1   7-10 mins.

 **(A) Read Marie's letter to her friend Raquel in Brazil.**

To encourage students to avoid stopping when they come across unfamiliar vocabulary, limit the reading time. Give two minutes. Ask students when they finish reading to close their books and look up.

After students have finished reading, ask a few comprehension questions not included in Exercise B, such as: *Where is Raquel from? What is Marie's job?*

Finally, ask students to open their books again. Ask questions and allow them to scan for information. Make it a competition so students will be prompted to scan and not read the entire letter again. Questions might include: *What does Marie deliver? What does Marie do at night? What is new with Marie?*

Evaluation 1   3-5 mins.

(B) Answer the questions in complete sentences. Use prepositions.

Ask students to do the activity and check their work. You may ask volunteers to write their complete sentences on the board.

STANDARDS CORRELATIONS

CASAS: 0.2.3 (See CASAS Competency List on pages 169-175.)
SCANS: Information Acquire and evaluate information
Basic Skills Reading, writing
EFF: Communication Read with understanding, convey ideas in writing

Presentation 2   10-15 mins.

Write *postcard* on the board and ask students if they know the meaning of the word. Tell students that they will read a postcard. Tell them that they will also practice identifying the simple present and present continuous tenses in the postcard.

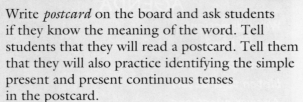

Teaching Tip

Multiple structures

Often, students will learn a structure and understand it well. Other times, when a new structure is introduced, students tend to confuse the form with previously learned forms. Sometimes this confusion causes students to write a unique form that doesn't exist in English, such as: *John is eat dinner*. Some students use the *be* verb as an auxiliary when there is no need for an auxiliary verb.

Another observation is that in real life there are very few occasions when one tense is used exclusively. Rather, two or more tenses are used within the same context.

For these reasons, we occasionally combine the simple present and the present continuous in the same activity in order to help students learn to differentiate between the two structures.

C Study the charts with your classmates and teacher.

Go over the charts with the class. You may wish to refer students to the grammar charts in the appendix to further emphasize different usages so that a more effective transfer can take place from a previous context.

For shorter classes, have students do Exercises D and E for homework.

Practice 2   7-10 mins. ■■■

D Read the postcard from Raquel to her husband. Circle the simple present verbs. Underline the present continuous verbs.

Ask students to do this activity on their own first and then ask them to check their work or peer-edit a partner's work. Allow students to come to conclusions about their work before you step in.

You may wish to extend the activity by either using portions of the postcard as a dictation or asking students to use the postcard as a model to write their own postcard message.

Evaluation 2   7-10 mins. ■■

E On a piece of paper, answer the questions in complete sentences.

Allow students to do this activity individually and then to report to the class or ask volunteers to write their answers on the board.

Instructor's Notes

_____
_____
_____
_____
_____
_____
_____
_____
_____
_____
_____
_____
_____
_____
_____
_____
_____
_____
_____
_____
_____
_____

GOAL ➤ **Read a message or letter**

C Study the charts with your classmates and teacher.

Simple Present	
Subject	**Verb**
I, you, we, they	eat
he, she	eats

Simple Present: *Be*		
Subject	***Be* verb**	
I	am	happy
you, we, they	are	sad
he, she, it	is	tired

Present Continuous			
Subject	***Be***	**Base verb + *ing***	**Example sentence**
I	am	writing	I **am writing** this letter in English.
you, we, they	are	going	We **are going** to the mall.
he, she	is	eating	He **is eating** at the coffee shop.

D Read the postcard from Raquel to her husband. Circle the simple present verbs. Underline the present continuous verbs.

March 12

Dear Antonio,

   I am writing to you from Palm City in California. I am staying for a few days with my friend, Marie. I am having a wonderful time. Palm City is beautiful. People are very friendly. Sometimes we go to Claudia's Restaurant to eat Mexican food. It's great.

   Marie works in the hospital here as a nurse. She goes to work early every day and she works very hard. She loves her new job, but she is a little sad because her family and friends aren't here.

   Right now I am doing my English homework and listening to music at Marie's house. I am waiting for Marie to finish work. See you soon.

Love,

Raquel

USA 41

Antonio Jobim

3450 Av. São João

21525-060

Rio de Janeiro-RJ

BRAZIL

E On a piece of paper, answer the questions in complete sentences.

1. Is Raquel happy or sad?
   Raquel is happy.
2. What is Raquel doing right now?
   She is doing her homework and listening to music.
3. What does Marie do every day?
   She goes to work and works hard.
4. Is Marie happy or sad?
   She is a little sad.

 LESSON 4 GOAL ➤ Read a message or letter

CD 2
TR 10

 F Read the questions. Then, listen to the letter from Raquel to Antonio and circle the answers.

1. How is the weather in Palm City?

   a. cold

   b. warm

   c. hot

2. What are in the parks?

   a. palm trees and cactus plants

   b. children

   c. tables

3. Where does the bus stop?

   a. near the park

   b. near the shopping mall

   c. near Marie's house

 G Answer the questions in complete sentences.
(Answers will vary.)

1. What do you do every day?

   _____

2. What are you doing right now?

   _____

3. Is your city beautiful, crowded, old, new, small, or large?

   _____

Presentation 3   7-10 mins. ■■□□

Teach students a testing technique. Tell them that at times they will have a series of listening questions on a test and that the test will be much easier if they read the questions beforehand. This is a focused-listening principle as well.

Go over each question from the listening practice students will do next. Ask them to guess what they think the answers might be. It isn't important that they get the right answers to the questions. It is important that they spend time thinking about what is to come. Take a class poll and see what people think about each question.

Practice 3   7-10 mins. ■

F Read the questions. Then, listen to the letter from Raquel to Antonio and circle the answers.

You may need to play the listening two to three times.

 Listening Script   CD 2, Track 10

March 12

Dear Antonio,

   I am writing to tell you that I am staying with Marie in Palm City for one more week. I am having a lot of fun. Marie is very nice and kind. We went to the mall last night. Today we walked in the park on her lunch break.

   This city is wonderful. The weather is warm most of the time. There are many parks, stores, and restaurants. There is good bus service. The bus goes around the city in an hour and stops near the shopping mall. The shopping mall has over a hundred stores and I go there every day. The parks are very beautiful. There are a lot of palm trees and cactus plants.

I will call you tomorrow.

Raquel

Evaluation 3   3-5 mins. ■

Check the students' work and be prepared to replay the listening for confirmation.

Application   5-7 mins. ■■□

G Answer the questions in complete sentences.

Students answer the questions in preparation for the next lesson, where they are asked to write a letter.

📖 Refer students to *Stand Out 2 Grammar Challenge*, Unit 5, Challenge 4 for more practice with the simple present and the present continuous.

Activity Bank

Unit 5, Lesson 4, Worksheet 1: Simple Present and Present Continuous

Instructor's Notes

_____

_____

_____

_____

_____

_____

_____

_____

_____

_____

_____

_____

_____

_____

_____

_____

_____

_____

_____

_____

Objective: Write and send a letter
Grammar: Simple past tense—regular and irregular
Pronunciation: Stress, -ed endings
Academic Strategy: Focused listening
Vocabulary: Past tense verbs

RESOURCES

Activity Bank: Unit 5, Lesson 5, Worksheets 1–3
Reading and Writing Challenge: Unit 5
Grammar Challenge: Unit 5, Challenge 5

■ 1.5 hour classes ■ 2.5 hour classes ■ 3⁺ hour classes

AGENDA

Talk about writing letters.
Learn about completing envelopes.
Learn the parts of a letter.
Use the simple past tense.
Write a letter.

Audio: CD 2, Track 11
Heinle Picture Dictionary: Community, pages 46–55

Warm-up and Review   10-15 mins.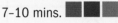

Ask students in groups to discuss who they would like to write a letter to and why. Remind them to use *because*. Ask students to tell about two things they are doing that they want to tell a relative or a friend in another country. You may suggest that the person reporting stands up so that you can monitor progress.

Introduction   5 mins.

Ask how many students have gone to a post office recently. Talk about packages and insurance. Ask how much it costs to send a letter to another country. State the objective: *Today we will write a letter.*

Presentation 1   10-15 mins.

Ask students to open their books and discuss the envelope. Ask questions to check for understanding. As a class, do Exercise A.

(A) Read the envelope. Complete the chart.

As a class, form questions for the information *What's your name? What's your address?* Go over the correct pronunciation and intonation for these questions.

Pronunciation

Stress

Intonation and stress are very difficult in English because they change depending on the circumstances. Therefore, it is important to take every opportunity once students have grasped basic communication to compare and contrast different ways to pronounce the same statement or question. Show students that while they are in a group and asking the same question several times to different people, *your* becomes the stressed word.

Make a grid on the board or use a grid from the template folder on the Activity Bank CD-ROM. Ask students to get the name and address of each group member. If students don't want to share personal information, they can say *I'm sorry, that's private* or make up the information.

Practice 1   7-10 mins.

(B) Complete the envelope from you to a partner's address.

Ask students to take the information from one member of the group and complete the envelope. You may bring real envelopes and have students address them so they can actually send correspondence to their group member, or you can use the envelopes that are available on the Activity Bank CD-ROM in Unit 5, Lesson 5.

Evaluation 1   5-7 mins.

Write some editing suggestions on the board:

1. *Capitalize all names.*
2. *Put a comma between the city and the state.*
3. *Use the two-letter postal code for states, such as* CA, *or* TX.

Ask students to peer-edit each other's envelopes.

STANDARDS CORRELATIONS

CASAS: 0.2.3 (See CASAS Competency List on pages 169–175.)
SCANS: **Information** Acquire and evaluate information
Basic Skills Reading, writing, listening, speaking
EFF: **Communication** Read with understanding, convey ideas in writing, speak so others can understand, listen actively, observe critically

The city is beautiful!

GOAL ➤ Write and send a letter

Raquel Jobim
133 Washington Street #15
Palm City, CA 92777

Antonio Jobim
3450 Av. São João
21525-060
Rio de Janeiro-RJ
BRAZIL

A Read the envelope. Complete the chart.

From:	Raquel Jobim	To:	Antonio Jobim
Street:	133 Washington St. #15	Street:	3450 Av. São João
City:	Palm City	City:	Rio de Janeiro
Zip code:	92777	Zip code:	21525-060
State:	CA	State:	RJ
Country:	USA	Country:	Brazil

B Complete the envelope from you to a partner's address.

_____
_____
_____

    _____
    _____
    _____
    _____

LESSON **5**   **GOAL** ➤ **Write and send a letter**

CD 2
TR 11

C Study the parts of a letter. Then, listen and number the parts.

Parts of a letter	Example
__4__ body	(most of the information)
__6__ closing	Sincerely, Love, Love always, *or* Your friend,
__5__ closing sentence	Call me! I hope to see you soon.
__1__ date	January 20, 2009
__3__ purpose or reason	I am writing because . . .
__2__ salutation	Dear Raquel,
__7__ your name	(first name or first and last name)

D Read the parts of the letter and put them in the correct order. Write the correct number next to each part.

a. __5__   I will call you tomorrow.

b. __1__   March 12

c. __4__   This city is wonderful. The weather is warm most of the time. There are many parks, stores, and restaurants. There is good bus service. The bus goes around the city in an hour and stops near the shopping mall. The shopping mall has over a hundred stores, and I go there every day. The parks are very beautiful. There are a lot of palm trees and cactus plants.

d. __2__   Dear Antonio,

e. __7__   Raquel

f. __3__   I am writing to tell you that I am staying with Marie in Palm City for one more week. I am having a lot of fun. Marie is very nice and kind. We went to the mall last night. Today we walked in the park on her lunch break.

g. __6__   Love,

94   Unit 5   Lesson 5

Presentation 2   20-30 mins.

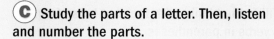 **C** **Study the parts of a letter. Then, listen and number the parts.**

Explain that letters to relatives do not have to be formal and they do not have to follow any specific structure. The suggestions here can be used in more formal letters, like business letters, and can help them be clear. This is the first opportunity for students to be exposed to an explanation that is similar to a lecture; however, they won't be taking notes. Give students a brief lecture on the different ideas and then have them listen to the recording, which is also a lecture, and allow them to put the information in order.

Teaching Tip

Developing academic skills

There is a temptation to help students be successful in every activity and never permit them to make mistakes. ESL teachers are often very nurturing, but remember that part of the mission statement of *Stand Out* is to help students become independent learners. They will undoubtedly face experiences where little context or interaction occurs in an academic setting. The purpose of this activity is to give students a taste of this type of instruction.

Listening Script   *CD 2, Track 11*

Students, please listen carefully to the steps to writing a well-formatted letter. If you write letters that have good organization, the people you are writing to will understand better what you want to say. Always start with the date. For our purposes, we will suggest you put the date on the left-hand side of the page near the top. Follow the date with your salutation. The salutation is a way to address the person you are writing to. You can use "dear" if it is a good friend, family member, or acquaintance.

Next, in the first paragraph, state briefly why you are writing. We call this the purpose. You might say, for example, "I am writing because," and then give the reason.

The fourth thing you want to do is write a paragraph or more about all the things you want to say. We call this the body.

The body can be followed by a closing sentence. This can be very short. For example, you might say, "I hope to see you soon," or you could say, "I will talk to you later."

The sixth thing you should do is to give a closing. You can use love, or sincerely, for example. Then add your name and you are done.

Any questions?

You may need to play the recording several times. Allow students to discuss the lecture in groups between listenings.

Practice 2   10-12 mins.

D **Read the parts of the letter and put them in the correct order. Write the correct number next to each part.**

Ask students to do this activity in pairs.

Evaluation 2   5-7 mins.

Ask volunteers to read the letter in the correct order and have students check their work.

Presentation 3   20–30 mins. ■■■

E Study the charts with your classmates and teacher.

Go over the charts with students carefully to make sure they understand.

Pronunciation

-ed

Students learning English often have trouble with the different pronunciations of the regular past tense *-ed* ending. In regular verbs with a base form that ends in a voiceless sound, the sound of *-ed* is /t/. However, when the verb ends in a voiced sound, the *-ed* is pronounced /d/. If the base verb ends in a /d/ or a /t/ sound, then the *-ed* is pronounced /ed/.

Given the complexity of this issue, students at this level may not be ready to tackle the distinctions of pronunciation. However, students may hear the differences and be confused; therefore, it is a good idea to expose them to this principle now.

A good way to do this is to make four columns on the board but don't immediately label them. Ask students to give you any verbs they can think of. (The final column is for irregular verbs. Tell them that you will include any irregular verbs they call out, but you are looking for regular verbs.) One column is for past tense forms that end with the voiceless /t/, one is for voiced /d/, and the third is for /ed/. As students give you verbs, put them in the correct columns. After a few verbs, have students guess at the column the next verbs they offer belong in. Then, explain the principle by asking students to put two fingers to their voice box and feel for vibration or lack of vibration when pronouncing the last sound of each of the verbs on the board.

Make sure you explain that this mini lesson is to give students an awareness of the three ways that the *-ed* ending can be pronounced, but they are not expected to use the correct pronunciation each time they say a regular past tense verb.

For shorter classes, have students do Exercise F for homework.

Practice 3   5–7 mins. ■

F Fill in the blanks with the past tense form of the verbs in parentheses.

Have students work on this activity on their own.

Evaluation 3   5–7 mins. ■

Ask volunteers to write the sentences on the board.

Application   20–30 mins. ■■■

G Complete the sentences.

Ask students to do this activity in preparation for writing a letter in the active task.

H Active Task. Write a letter, put it in an envelope, and send it to a classmate.

 Refer students to *Stand Out 2 Grammar Challenge*, Unit 5, Challenge 5 for more practice with the simple past tense.

Activity Bank

Templates: Two-Column Chart

Unit 5, Lesson 5, Worksheet 1: Letter Writing

Unit 5, Lesson 5, Worksheet 2: Addressing Envelopes

Unit 5, Lesson 5, Worksheet 3: Writing Letters

LESSON **5**   **GOAL** ➤ **Write and send a letter**

E Study the charts with your classmates and teacher.

Simple Past (Regular)		
Subject	**Verb (base + *ed*)**	**Example sentence**
I, you, he, she, it, we, they	talked	I **talked** with Marie.
	wanted	She **wanted** a sandwich.
	walked	We **walked** in the park.

Simple Past (Irregular)		
Subject	**Irregular verb**	**Example sentence**
I, you, he, she, it, we, they	went (go)	I **went** to the park.
	ate (eat)	She **ate** at the coffee shop.
	bought (buy)	We **bought** new dresses.
	send (sent)	They **sent** a letter.

F Fill in the blanks with the past tense form of the verbs in parentheses.

1. I ___walked___ (walk) to Marie's house.

2. You ___went___ (go) to school yesterday.

3. She ___sent___ (send) me a letter from Palm City.

4. I ___wanted___ (want) a new sweater.

5. Raquel and Marie ___bought___ (buy) new clothes at the store.

6. We ___ate___ (eat) at the restaurant on Main and Carpenter.

G Complete the sentences. (Answers will vary.)

1. My city is _____.

2. There is a _____.

3. Every day I _____.

4. Sometimes I _____.

5. Yesterday, I _____.

6. Yesterday, I _____.

H Active Task. Write a letter, put it in an envelope, and send it to a classmate.

Review

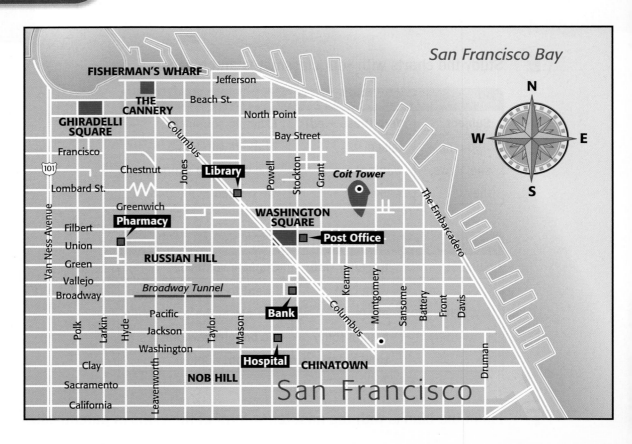

San Francisco Bay

FISHERMAN'S WHARF

THE CANNERY

GHIRADELLI SQUARE

Library

Coit Tower

WASHINGTON SQUARE

Pharmacy

Post Office

RUSSIAN HILL

Broadway Tunnel

Bank

Hospital

CHINATOWN

NOB HILL

San Francisco

(A) **Read the directions and follow the route on the map. Write the name of the place where you arrive. (Lesson 3)**

> post office   hospital   bank   library   pharmacy

1. You are at the intersection of Montgomery and Vallejo. Go west on Vallejo for three blocks and turn left. Go one block. It's on the right. _____bank_____

2. You are at the intersection of Chestnut and Powell. Go south on Powell for one block. Then go west on Lombard one block. It is across the street. _____library_____

3. You are at the intersection of Broadway and Powell. Go south on Powell. Go two blocks and turn left. It's on the right. _____hospital_____

4. You are at the intersection of Union and Mason. Go east on Union for two blocks. Then turn left. It's on the right. _____post office_____

5. You are at the intersection of Green and Mason. Go west on Green for four blocks. Then go north one block. It's on the corner. _____pharmacy_____

Objective: All unit objectives
Grammar: All unit grammar
Academic Strategies: Reviewing, evaluating, developing study skills
Vocabulary: All unit vocabulary

AGENDA

Discuss unit objectives.
Complete the review.
Do My Dictionary.
Evaluate and reflect on progress.

■ 1.5 hour classes   ■ 2.5 hour classes   ■ 3⁺ hour classes

Warm-up and Review   7-10 mins.

With their books closed, ask students to help you make a list on the board of all the vocabulary they can come up with from the unit. Then, have a competition where students in groups will write page numbers for each item on the list. The first group to have the correct page number for each item wins.

Introduction   5 mins.

Write all the objectives on the board from Unit 5. Show students the first page of the unit and say the five objectives. Explain that today they will review the whole unit.

Note: Depending on the length of the term, you may decide to have students do Presentation 1 and Practice 1 for homework and then review student work as either the warm-up or another class activity.

Presentation 1   10-15 mins.

This presentation will cover the first three pages of the review. Quickly go to the first page of each lesson. Discuss the objective of each. Ask simple questions to remind students of what they have learned.

Practice 1   15-20 mins.

(A) Read the directions and follow the route on the map. Write the name of the place where you arrive. (Lessons 3)

Teaching Tip

Recycling/Review

The review and the project that follows are part of the recycling/review process. Students at this level often need to be reintroduced to concepts to solidify what they have learned. Many concepts are learned and forgotten while learning other new concepts. This is because students learn but are not necessarily ready to acquire language concepts.

Therefore, it becomes very important to review and to show students how to review on their own. It is also important to recycle the new concepts in different contexts.

STANDARDS CORRELATIONS

CASAS: 0.2.3, 1.1.3, 1.9.4, 2.1.1, 2.2.1, 2.2.5 (See CASAS Competency List on pages 169–175.)
SCANS: Information Acquire and evaluate information, organize and maintain information
Basic Skills Reading, writing, speaking
Personal Qualities Responsibility, self management
EFF: Communications Speak so others can understand
Lifelong Learning Take responsibility for learning, reflect and evaluate

Practice 1 (continued)

B Answer the questions. (Lesson 1)

C Read the paragraph. Fill in the blanks with the correct form of the verb *be*. (Lessons 4 and 5)

D Read the letter. Circle the correct form of the verbs. (Lesson 4)

B) Answer the questions. (Lesson 1)

1. Where can you send a package? the post office
2. Where can you borrow a book? the library
3. Where can you buy gas for your car? a gas station
4. Where can you buy medicine? a pharmacy
5. Where can you eat a burger and french fries? a restaurant
6. Where can you find a doctor? a hospital
7. Where can you report a crime? the police station
8. Where can you register the birth of a new baby? City Hall

C) Read the paragraph. Fill in the blanks with the correct form of the verb *be*. (Lessons 4 and 5)

This city __is__ wonderful. The weather __is__ warm most of the time. There __are__ many parks, stores, and restaurants. There __is__ good bus service. The bus goes around the city in an hour and stops near the shopping mall. There __are__ over a hundred stores in the shopping mall and I go there every day. The parks __are__ very beautiful. There __are__ a lot of palm trees and beautiful flowers.

D) Read the letter. Circle the correct form of the verbs. (Lesson 4)

Dear Roberto,

    I (write / **am writing**) to you from California. I (sit / **am sitting**) on the beach. I (stay / **am staying**) here in Santa Barbara with my friend Suzanna. It's very warm and sunny. We (**walk** / are walking) on the beach every day. We often (**eat** / are eating) Mexican food in the evening. On weekends we (**visit** / are visiting) beautiful places along the coast.

    Is it warm in Texas? I hope you (have / **are having**) a nice holiday there.

Your friend,

Sara

Review

E Write down important locations. Look up their phone numbers and add them to your list. (Lesson 2) (Answers will vary. Sample answers are given.)

Important Numbers	
Hospital	(850) 555-9729
Police Station	(850) 555-1819
Fire Dept.	(850) 555-8580
Neighbors	(850) 555-7785

F Write a paragraph about what you did yesterday. (Lesson 5)
(Answers will vary.)

Practice 1 (continued)

E Write down important locations. Look up their phone numbers and add them to your list. (Lesson 2)

F Write a paragraph about what you did yesterday. (Lesson 5)

Evaluation 1   15 mins.

Go around the room and check on students' progress. Help individuals when needed. If you see consistent errors among several students, interrupt the class and give a mini lesson or review to help students feel comfortable with the concept.

Presentation 2   7–10 mins.

My Dictionary

Go over the steps of My Dictionary as a class.

Practice 2   5–7 mins.

Do the dictionary activity as a class before students work on their own for at least the first few units of the book to ensure that students understand what to do.

Evaluation 2   5 mins.

Ask students to share their cards.

Presentation 3   5 mins.

Learner Log

Review the concepts of the Learner Log. Make sure students understand the concepts and how to complete the log including circling the answers, finding page numbers where the concept is taught, and ranking favorite activities.

Teaching Tip

Learner Logs

Learner Logs function to help students in many different ways.

1. They serve as part of the review process.
2. They help students to gain confidence and to document what they have learned. Consequently, students see that they are progressing in their learning.
3. They provide students with a tool that they can use over and over to check and recheck their understanding of the target language. In this way, students become independent learners.

Practice 3   10–15 mins.

Ask students to complete the Learner Log.

Evaluation 3   2 mins.

Go over the Learner Log with students.

Application   5–7 mins.

Ask students to record their favorite lesson or page in the unit.

TB Assessment

Use the Stand Out 2 Assessment CD-ROM with ExamView® to create a posttest for Unit 5.

Refer students to *Stand Out 2 Grammar Challenge*, Unit 5, Extension Challenge 1 for more practice with prepositions to describe locations and Extension Challenge 2 for more practice with prepositions of time.

Activity Bank

Unit 5: Computer Worksheets

Unit 5: Internet Worksheets

Instructor's Notes

_____

_____

_____

_____

_____

_____

_____

_____

_____

_____

_____

_____

_____

_____

_____

_____

_____

_____

_____

My Dictionary

Make flash cards to improve your vocabulary

1. Choose four new words from this unit.

2. Write each word on an index card or on a sheet of paper.

3. On the back of the index card or paper, draw a picture, find and write a sentence from the book with the word, and write the page number.

4. Study the words.

Definition: a place to bowl
There is a big entertainment center
with a <u>bowling alley</u>.
page 81

Learner Log

Circle how well you learned each item and write the page number where you learned it.

1. I can name different places in my community.
   Yes   Maybe   No   Page _____

2. I can find information in a phone book.
   Yes   Maybe   No   Page _____

3. I can understand addresses and phone numbers.
   Yes   Maybe   No   Page _____

4. I can read a map.
   Yes   Maybe   No   Page _____

5. I can follow street directions.
   Yes   Maybe   No   Page _____

6. I can read a letter.
   Yes   Maybe   No   Page _____

7. I can write a letter.
   Yes   Maybe   No   Page _____

Rank what you like to do best from 1 to 6. 1 is your favorite activity. Your teacher will help you.

_____ Practice listening

_____ Practice speaking

_____ Practice reading

_____ Practice writing

_____ Learn new words

_____ Learn grammar

In the next unit, I want to practice more

_____.

Team Project

Describe your community.

In a group, you are going to describe your community and write a postcard to a friend.

1. Form a team with four or five students.
   In your team, you need:

POSITION	JOB	STUDENT NAME
Student 1: **Team Leader**	See that everyone speaks English. See that everyone participates.	
Student 2: **Writer**	Write a paragraph about your community with help from the team.	
Student 3: **Artist**	Make a map of your community with help from the team.	
Students 4/5: **Spokespeople**	Prepare a class presentation with help from the team.	

2. Draw a map of the community around your school. Think about these questions:
   • What buildings are there?
   • What are the names of the streets?
   • Is there a city bus? Where does it stop?

3. Write a paragraph about your community.

4. Write a postcard to a friend. Invite him or her to visit you.

5. Present your work to the class.

Introduction　　　　　　　　　　　　5 mins.

Team Project

Describe your community.

In this project, students will write a paragraph describing their community, create a map of their community, and write a postcard to a friend.

Stage 1　　　　　　　　　　　　15-20 mins.
Form a team with four or five students.

Help students form groups and assign positions in their groups. On the spot, students will have to choose who will be the leader of their group. Review the responsibility of the leader and ask students to write the name of their leader in their books. Do the same with the remaining positions: writer, artist, and spokespeople. Make sure that students understand that each team member will help with each stage. Team members should not be working on different stages at the same time.

Stage 2　　　　　　　　　　　　10-15 mins.
Draw a map of the community around your school.

Before students begin drawing the map, the artist should lead the team in discussing the questions. There is a worksheet with additional questions available on the Activity Bank CD-ROM (Unit 5, Project, Worksheet 1).

Stages 3 and 4　　　　　　　　　30-40 mins.
Write a paragraph about your community. Write a postcard to your friend. Invite him or her to visit you.

The writer should lead the production of a paragraph and a postcard. There is a template for writing a postcard on the Activity Bank CD-ROM (Unit 5, Project, Worksheet 2).

As an alternate activity, students could create a brochure about their city. Provide copies of the brochure template on the Activity Bank CD-ROM (Unit 5, Project, Worksheet 3).

Stage 5　　　　　　　　　　　　20-40 mins.
Present your work to the class.

Make sure that all group members are included in the presentation. Postcards, paragraphs, maps, and brochures should be posted and/or photocopied to share with the class after the presentation. Have students assist with the work of making the materials available.

Consider videotaping the presentations. Students will prepare better for formal presentations if they are videotaped. Another approach is for the students to videotape themselves and polish their presentations before giving them to the class.

Activity Bank

Unit 5, Project, Worksheet 1: Our City
Unit 5, Project, Worksheet 2: Postcard
Unit 5, Project, Worksheet 3: City Brochure
Unit 5, Extension, Worksheet 1: Prepositions of Location
Unit 5, Extension, Worksheet 2: Simple Present
Unit 5, Extension, Worksheet 3: Present Continuous

STANDARDS CORRELATIONS

CASAS: 0.2.3, 1.1.3, 1.9.4, 2.1.1, 2.2.1, 2.2.5, 4.8.1 (See CASAS Competency List on pages 169–175.)
SCANS: **Resources** Allocate time, allocate materials and facility resources, allocate human resources
Information Acquire and evaluate information, organize and maintain information, interpret and communicate information
Interpersonal Participate as a member of a team, teach others, exercise leadership, negotiate to arrive at a decision, work with cultural diversity
Systems Understand systems, monitor and correct performance
Basic Skills Reading, writing, listening, speaking

Thinking Skills Think creatively, make decisions, solve problems, see things in the mind's eye
Personal Qualities Responsibility, sociability, self management
EFF: **Communication** Read with understanding, convey ideas in writing, speak so others can understand, listen actively, observe critically
Decision Making Solve problems and make decisions, plan
Interpersonal Cooperate with others, advocate and influence, resolve conflict and negotiate, guide others
Lifelong Learning Take responsibility for learning, reflect and evaluate

AT-A-GLANCE PREP

Objective: Describe healthy practices
Grammar: Infinitives
Academic Strategies: Focused listening, predicting
Vocabulary: *stress, smoking, healthy, unhealthy, remedies, symptoms*

RESOURCES

Activity Bank: Unit 6, Lesson 1, Worksheets 1–2
Reading and Writing Challenge: Unit 6
Grammar Challenge: Unit 6, Challenge 1

Audio: CD 2, Track 12
Heinle Picture Dictionary: Health, pages 132–137

◼ 1.5 hour classes ◼ 2.5 hour classes ◼ 3+ hour classes

Stand Out 2 Assessment CD-ROM with *ExamView®*

AGENDA

Discuss exercise.
Discuss healthy and unhealthy
    practices.
Read about stress.
Listen for advice about healthy practices.
Make health goals.

 Preassessment *(optional)*

Use the Stand Out 2 Assessment CD-ROM with Exam*View®* to create a pretest for Unit 6.

Warm-up and Review   15–20 mins.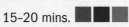

Ask students what they think about exercise. Pass out 3-by-5 index cards and ask students to write how many minutes they exercise every week. Make sure they don't write their names on the cards. Then, have them turn in their ballots to a pair of volunteers to tally. One volunteer will read out the minutes and the other will write on the board. They might use categories like *0, under 30 minutes, 30–60 minutes,* and so on.

Introduction   10–15 mins.

Write *healthy* on the board and see if students can tell you some healthy things to do. State the objective: *Today we will describe healthy practices.*

Presentation 1   7–10 mins.

Continue the list from the introduction and ask students to help you also list unhealthy practices.

STANDARDS CORRELATIONS

CASAS: 3.5.8, 3.5.9 (See CASAS Competency List on pages 169–175.)
SCANS: **Resources** Allocate time
Information Interpret and communicate information
Interpersonal Participate as a member of a team, teach others
Basic Skills Reading, writing, listening, speaking
Thinking Skills Think creatively, make decisions
Personal Qualities Self management
EFF: **Communication** Read with understanding, convey ideas in writing, speak so others can understand, listen actively
Decision Making Solve problems and make decisions, plan
Interpersonal Cooperate with others
Lifelong Learning Reflect and evaluate

A **Discuss the pictures with your classmates.**

Go over the pictures and ask questions. Make sure students understand the vocabulary.

Practice 1   12–15 mins.

B **Talk in a group. Answer the questions.**

Ask groups to choose a leader, a timekeeper, a recorder, and a spokesperson. The timekeeper should allot three minutes per task.

Teaching Tip

Group roles

Assigning roles in groups is very important for several reasons.

- The interaction more approximates real-world experiences.
- With chosen roles, each person has a responsibility and is more likely to participate.
- Community building in the classroom is essential to success.
- Student-centered activities provide students an opportunity to think critically.

The timekeeper's role in higher levels is to make sure the group talks no more than the time allotted. The timekeeper's role at this level is to insist that students talk the full time. Students at this level will be challenged by the requirement to talk three minutes per question. Insist that they challenge themselves to do it.

Evaluation 1   7–10 mins.

Discuss the questions in Exercise B. Avoid too much discussion about stress at this point.

101a   Lesson Planner: Unit 6, Lesson 1

Health

GOALS
➤ **Describe healthy practices**
➤ **Identify ailments**
➤ **Make a doctor's appointment**

➤ **Read medicine labels**
➤ **Identify and describe emergencies**

LESSON **1**

A healthy life

GOAL ➤ **Describe healthy practices**

Vocabulary · Grammar
Life Skills
Academic · Pronunciation

A Discuss the pictures with your classmates.

1.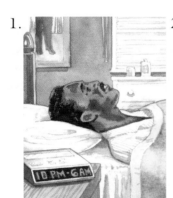
2.
3.
4.

B Talk in a group. Answer the questions.

1. How many hours of sleep do adults and children need?

2. Is smoking healthy or unhealthy? Why?

3. How much exercise do adults need a day? Make a list of different types of exercise.

4. What is stress? What can people do about stress?

GOAL ➤ **Describe healthy practices**

What is Chan's problem?
What can he do?

C Read the paragraph about health.

Many Americans have stress. Stress can make people tired. It can make them lose sleep and it can cause problems like high blood pressure and even heart problems. There is a cure! Doctors say that good exercise, a proper diet, meditation, and rest can help with stress. Exercise and a good diet help people to think more clearly and to have more energy. When people exercise, they sleep better and they have less stress.

D Complete the chart about stress.

Symptoms	Remedies (cures)
tired	good exercise
sleep loss	proper diet
high blood pressure	meditation
heart problems	rest

E Read the list below with a group. Check (✔) the healthy practices.

- ☑ eat three meals a day
- ☐ sleep twelve hours a day
- ☐ work twelve hours a day
- ☐ smoke
- ☑ exercise every day

- ☑ play sports
- ☐ eat a lot of candy
- ☐ drink alcohol regularly
- ☑ rest and take breaks

Presentation 2   15–20 mins. ■■□

Tell students that doctors say that a little stress is OK and may be helpful. It makes life interesting, but too much stress is not good. With students' books closed, ask students again about stress and what can be done to overcome it.

Write *Symptoms* and *Remedies* on the board as the headings for two columns. Discuss the meaning of these words and see how much students can add to a list of symptoms of stress and remedies for stress.

C Read the paragraph about health.

Read the paragraph as a class and discuss any unfamiliar words. Ask students if they agree with the text. As a class, try to come up with a one-sentence definition of *stress*.

D Complete the chart about stress.

Work on this chart with students. Compare it to what was written on the board earlier in this presentation. Students are at a point now where they can read some articles on the Internet and in the newspaper. You might consider identifying a short paragraph or article about stress for them to read and discuss as a class.

Practice 2   7–10 mins. ■■

E Read the list below with a group. Check the healthy practices.

This lesson has a lot of group discussion. Mix up the groups so that students are not discussing these issues with the same students as in Practice 1. Write on the board: *Smoking is not healthy because...* Ask students to use this sentence starter to begin their discussions.

Evaluation 2   10–12 mins. ■■

Ask representatives from each group to visit with the other groups in the class and compare notes. Then, go over each statement as a class. Make sure you prod students to give reasons for their answers.

Presentation 3   10-15 mins. ■■□

Take a class poll to find out how many meals a day students eat. Then ask students what they know about vitamins. Find out how many students take vitamins. Use a graph template from the Activity Bank CD-ROM and chart out how many times students go to the doctor in a year. Go over the meaning of *checkup* at this time.

Tell students that they will listen to a recording and that they are to complete the sentences in the book. Go over the sentences in Exercise F first. As a class, ask for predictions. Then, prepare students for focused listening.

Practice 3   7-10 mins. ■

(F) Predict the missing information in the sentences. Then, listen and check your answers.

 Listening Script   CD 2, Track 12

Good health habits are very important, and yet, many people don't follow basic health rules that will help them live longer and enjoy life more. For example, doctors say adults should exercise 30 minutes a day, but many people don't exercise that much in a week. They also suggest that we eat at least three balanced meals a day. Many doctors say we should eat even more times but consume less at each meal. Seeing the doctor is important, too. All adults should get a checkup at least once a year. Smoking is not healthy, so doctors agree that people should not smoke. Some doctors also believe we should take vitamins every day.

Evaluation 3   3-5 mins. ■

Check the answers to Exercise F as a class.

Application   7-10 mins. ■■□

(G) Answer the questions about yourself.

Ask students to quickly review the chart about the infinitive verb form.

(H) Write your health goals.

You may decide to have each student use a word-processing program to type a goal statement and create a typed class list. This will further enhance the class experience.

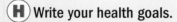 Refer students to *Stand Out 2 Grammar Challenge*, Unit 6, Challenge 1 for more practice with *need to*.

Instructor's Notes

_____

_____

_____

_____

_____

_____

_____

_____

_____

_____

_____

_____

_____

_____

_____

_____

_____

_____

_____

_____

_____

_____

_____

_____

_____

_____

GOAL ➤ **Describe healthy practices**

CD 2
TR 12

(F) Predict the missing information in the sentences. Then, listen and check your answers.

1. Doctors say most adults should exercise

   _____30_____ minutes a _____day_____.

2. Doctors say most adults should eat

   _____three_____ balanced meals a day.

3. Doctors say most adults should go in for a checkup

   _____one_____ time(s) a _____year_____.

4. Doctors say we should not _____smoke_____.

5. Many doctors say we should take _____vitamins_____.

(G) Answer the questions about yourself. (Answers will vary.)

1. Are you tired during the day?   Yes   No

2. Do you need more sleep?   Yes   No

3. Do you have a good diet?   Yes   No

4. Do you take vitamins?   Yes   No

5. How many checkups do you have a year?

   _____

Infinitives		
Subject	**Verb**	**to + Base verb**
I	need	to exercise

(H) Write your health goals. (Answers will vary.)

EXAMPLE: <u>I need to exercise 30 minutes every day.</u>

_____

_____

_____

What's the matter?

GOAL ➤ Identify ailments

A Look at the pictures and write the words.

shoulder(s)	heart	arm(s)	chest	eye(s)	hand(s)
head	mouth	neck	stomach	back	ear(s)
foot (feet)	tooth (teeth)	leg(s)	tongue	nose	lips

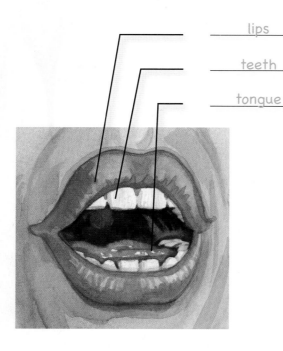

lips

teeth

tongue

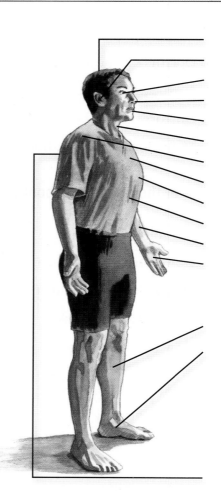

head
ear(s)
eye(s)
nose
mouth
neck
shoulder(s)
heart
chest
stomach
arm(s)
hand(s)

leg(s)
foot (feet)

back

B Practice the conversation with a partner. Use the words from Exercise A.

EXAMPLE: *Student A:* What's the matter?
Student B: My head hurts.

Simple Present		
Singular	it (head)	hurts
Plural	they (shoulders)	hurt

Objective: Identify ailments
Grammar: Simple past, comparatives and superlatives
Pronunciation: Final release of consonants
Academic Strategies: Focused listening, bar graph
Vocabulary: Parts of the body

RESOURCES

Activity Bank: Unit 6, Lesson 2, Worksheet 1
Reading and Writing Challenge: Unit 6

■ 1.5 hour classes   ■ 2.5 hour classes   ■ 3+ hour classes

Grammar Challenge: Unit 6, Challenge 2
Audio: CD 2, Tracks 13–17
Heinle Picture Dictionary: Health, pages 132–137

AGENDA

Rank exercises.
Talk about body parts.
Listen and read about symptoms.
Describe ailments.
Talk about how often you are sick.

Warm-up and Review   10-15 mins.

Write the following items on the board: *walking, riding a bicycle, swimming, running, playing soccer, going to the gym, cleaning the house,* and *working in the yard.* Ask students in groups to rank these activities from 1–7, with one being the most beneficial exercise. Then, ask the groups to report to the class.

Introduction   5-7 mins.

Ask students how often they have been sick in the past year and how often they go to the doctor. As a class, brainstorm different ailments and write them on the board. State the objective: *Today we will identify ailments.*

Presentation 1   15-20 mins.

Go over the list of ailments that you created on the board. Pantomime for each ailment and ask students to guess what you are pantomiming. Prepare 3-by-5 index cards with the names of ailments on them. Ask volunteers to pantomime while their classmates guess the ailment.

A Look at the pictures and write the words.

Go over the body parts. Have students quiz themselves by pointing to parts of the body and asking a partner to name the part.

Go over the grammar box of the simple present tense and discuss its pronunciation. Spend some time on the pronunciation of final consonants in a phrase and in isolation.

STANDARDS CORRELATIONS

CASAS: 3.1.1 (See CASAS Competency List on pages 169-175.)
SCANS: **Basic Skills** Reading, writing, listening, speaking
EFF: **Communication** Read with understanding, convey ideas in writing, speak so others can understand, listen actively, observe critically
Interpersonal Cooperate with others

Pronunciation

Final consonants

In many languages, the final consonants of words in isolation and/or phrases are "swallowed" or not given much emphasis. You might notice that some students will say the name of a body part and then immediately bring their lips together. Sometimes this habit is so pronounced that it sounds like they are saying an /m/ at the end of a word. Even /n/ may sound like an /m/.

The final consonant in English is important and pronouncing it is essential. Ask students to completely pronounce the last consonant of the words and to release it with their mouths open and not closed. For some students, this concept is so different from their native languages, that it will be difficult for them.

Students should be careful to pronounce the final consonants at the phrases as well. If students don't release the final /s/ in the sentence *My head hurts,* it will sound like they have forgotten the /s/ all together. Help students exaggerate this final-consonant sound so they realize the importance of it.

Practice 1   7-10 mins.

B Practice the conversation with a partner. Use the words from Exercise A.

Evaluation 1   3-5 mins.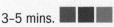

Observe and listen carefully to students' pronunciation. After the practice, ask various students: *What's the matter?* Ask for random answers or point to a body part and ask them to respond appropriately.

Presentation 2   20-25 mins.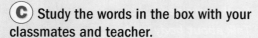

C Study the words in the box with your classmates and teacher.

If they are not already on the board, add the words in the box to your list of ailments. Circle them and circle any other things on the board that might be considered symptoms. Write the word *symptoms* on the board and ask students what they think it means. Continue to pantomime these words. Help students with pronunciation once again. Ask students to close their books and pantomime a few of the items. Then, ask them to write the word you are pantomiming and check their spelling.

D Write the words from the box under the pictures. Then, listen and write the number of the conversation above each picture.

Prepare students for the focused-listening activity. Stop the recording occasionally to help students understand what they are to do. You may prepare them for the listening if you have time by saying the words and asking them to point to the pictures, first in isolation and then in a paragraph.

 Listening Script   CD 2, Tracks 13–17

1. **Patient:** *Doctor, this cold is terrible. My nose is running, and I feel so tired.*
   Doctor: *You may have the flu. Let's check a few things.*
   Patient: *Is the flu dangerous?*
   Doctor: *Sometimes, but you may just have a cold.*
   Patient: *Should I stay home from work?*
   Doctor: *Maybe. Let's find out first if the runny nose is because of a cold or the flu.*

2. **Alexi:** *I am feeling really sick.*
   Franco: *What's the matter?*
   Alexi: *I'm not sure. I do know that I have a terrible headache.*
   Franco: *Maybe you should sit down and get some rest.*
   Alexi: *Maybe, but I have so much work to do. I think I will try to get something done first.*

3. **Don:** *Hello.*
   Supervisor: *Hello, Don. How are you feeling?*
   Don: *Oh, not too well. I have this high fever.*
   Supervisor: *When do you think you will be back to work?*
   Don: *Probably not for another week. I am having trouble shaking this thing.*
   Supervisor: *Well, just get a lot of rest. We are thinking of you.*
   Don: *Thanks.*

4. **John:** *You don't look very well.*
   Miriam: *Yes, I am a little under the weather.*
   John: *You are sick? What's the problem?*
   Miriam: *I have a cough that won't stop. I have been hacking all day.*
   John: *I have some cough syrup you might try. It has worked for me in the past.*

5. **Nelson:** *Marie, why do you have your hand to your throat?*
   Marie: *I have had this same sore throat for three days. It hurts to talk.*
   Nelson: *Maybe you shouldn't talk then.*
   Marie: *That's a good idea, but I have to answer phones for my job. You know I am a receptionist.*
   Nelson: *Maybe it is time to stay home.*
   Marie: *Maybe.*

For shorter classes, ask students to do Exercises E and F for homework.

Practice 2   10-15 mins.

The listening activity familiarized students with the vocabulary they will need when they read Exercise E.

E Read the paragraph.

F Bubble in the answers to the questions below.

Have students do Exercises E and F by themselves, not in pairs or groups. Ask them to read through the paragraph without stopping. If they run into any words they don't know, they should underline them but avoid looking them up.

Evaluation 2   5-7 mins.

Go over the answers to Exercise F with the class and review the paragraph. Then, quiz students on the differences between a cold and the flu.

GOAL ➤ **Identify ailments**

Vocabulary | Grammar
Life Skills
Academic | Pronunciation

C Study the words in the box with your classmates and teacher.

| cough | sore throat | fever | headache | runny nose |

CD 2
TR 13–17

D Write the words from the box under the pictures. Then, listen and write the number of the conversation above each picture.

2

4

1

3

5

headache — cough — runny nose — fever — sore throat

E Read the paragraph.

Colds and the Flu

Colds and the flu are similar illnesses and have some of the same symptoms. The symptoms of a cold are a low fever, a sore throat, a headache, and a runny nose. People usually have a cold for one or two weeks. People with the flu feel very tired and sick. They often have a high fever, a dry cough, a headache, and muscle aches. People can have the flu for two or three weeks. Many people get colds or the flu every year and hate them both!

F Bubble in the answers to the questions below.

1. People usually have the flu for _____.

   ○ 1 week   ○ 1–2 weeks   ● 2–3 weeks

2. A cold and the flu are types of _____.

   ○ symptoms   ● illnesses   ○ medicines

3. Headaches and fevers are types of _____.

   ● symptoms   ○ illnesses   ○ medicine

4. When you have the flu, you often _____.

   ○ have a low fever   ● feel very tired   ○ have a runny nose

LESSON 2 **GOAL** ➤ Identify ailments

G Study the chart with your classmates and teacher.

Adjective	Comparative Adjective	Superlative Adjective
serious	more serious	the most serious
	less serious	the least serious
common	more common	the most common
	less common	the least common

H Look at the problems. Which ones are the most serious? Which ones are the most common? Talk in a group and rank them from 1 to 8. Rank the most serious as 1.
(Answers will vary.)

_____ a backache

_____ a cold

_____ a headache

_____ a runny nose

_____ a sore throat

_____ a stomachache

_____ a toothache

_____ the flu

I How often do you get sick? Complete the bar graph about yourself.
(Answers will vary.)

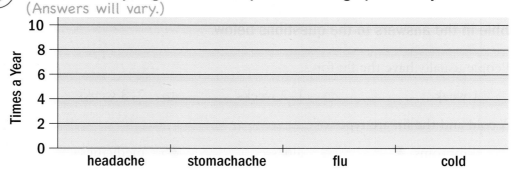

J Talk to a partner about your graph.

EXAMPLE: I get a headache about five times a year.

Presentation 3   10-15 mins.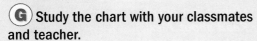

G Study the chart with your classmates and teacher.

Help students understand superlative forms. Show that they function as adjectives and not nouns by putting logical words after them. Students should understand that comparatives and superlatives work to modify nouns.

For shorter classes, ask students to do Exercise H for homework.

Practice 3   10-15 mins. ■

H Look at the problems. Which ones are the most serious? Which ones are the most common? Talk in a group and rank them from 1 to 8. Rank the most serious as 1.

Walk around the room and make sure that students are using comparative and superlative forms in their discussions.

Evaluation 3   7-10 mins. ■

Ask the groups to report to the class. Encourage them to use comparatives and superlatives in their reports.

Application   10-15 mins. ■■■

I How often do you get sick? Complete the bar graph about yourself.

Help students as they complete the graph about themselves.

J Talk to a partner about your graph.

Students may be unfamiliar with how to use the word *get*. Explain that it means *obtain* or *have*.

📖 Refer students to *Stand Out 2 Grammar Challenge*, Unit 6, Challenge 2 for more practice with comparatives and superlatives.

Activity Bank

Unit 6, Lesson 2, Worksheet 1: What hurts?

Objective: Make a doctor's appointment
Grammar: Simple past tense—regular, irregular, *be*
Academic Strategy: Focused listening, bar graphs
Vocabulary: *appointment, pay method, checks, credit card, insurance, heart attack*

RESOURCES

Activity Bank: Unit 6, Lesson 3, Worksheets 1–3
Reading and Writing Challenge: Unit 6
Grammar Challenge: Unit 6, Challenge 3

Audio: CD 2, Tracks 18–25
Heinle Picture Dictionary: Health, pages 132–137

■ 1.5 hour classes ■ 2.5 hour classes ■ 3⁺ hour classes

AGENDA
Make a bar graph.
Read about Alexi.
Listen about making an appointment.
Practice the simple past tense.
Make a conversation.

Warm-up and Review 15–20 mins. ■■■

Ask students to go over their bar graphs again with another partner from the previous lesson's application. Then, conduct a class discussion about how often people get sick. Make a bar graph about headaches for the whole class. You may choose to use the bar graph template in the Activity Bank CD-ROM template folder. Ask students how often they get headaches or any other ailment you would like. Label the *y* axis *Number of Students*. Label the *x* axis *Times a Year*, broken into four sections: 0–10 times, 11–20 times, 20–30 times, and more than 30 times.

Introduction 5–7 mins. ■■■

Pantomime illnesses as you did in the previous lesson. Encourage students to ask: *What's the matter?* Respond this time with the problem and ask what you should do. Answers will vary but some students will suggest going to the doctor. State the objective: *Today we will learn to make a doctor's appointment.*

Presentation 1 20–30 mins. ■■■

Go over the picture at the top of the page and ask students the questions along with others that you deem appropriate.

 **Read the story. What's the matter with Alexi? Why is he nervous?**

Read the paragraph with students and go over any new words. Encourage students to ask questions. Point out the spelling of difficult items. Then, ask students to close their books and do a quick dictation of the paragraph. Students can check their own work after you have finished dictating.

Practice 1 7–10 mins. ■■■

 First, draw a line from the questions to the answers. Then, listen to the conversation to check your answers.

Students should use their acquired linguistic knowledge to predict how to match the sentences. Go over this concept and then, prepare students for listening.

Note: The listening script for Exercise B is on page 108a.

Evaluation 1   5–7 mins. ■■■

Go over the answers as a class and then listen to the recording one more time as a final check.

Calling for an appointment

GOAL ➤ Make a doctor's appointment

What is Alexi doing? Who is he talking to?

A) Read the story. What's the matter with Alexi? Why is he nervous?

My name is Alexi. I'm from Russia. I like school and I want to learn English, but I don't come to school very much. I am tired a lot. I need to see a doctor, but I am very nervous. My teacher says I need to go right now. He says the doctor can help me.

B) First, draw a line from the questions to the answers. Then, listen to the conversation to check your answers.

CD 2
TR 18

_c_	1. What's your name?	a. 1427 Hamilton Street, New York City
_h_	2. What's your date of birth?	b. Yes.
_f_	3. Why do you want to see the doctor?	c. Alexi Tashkov
_e_	4. What's your phone number?	d. No, I don't.
_a_	5. Where do you live?	e. (212) 555-5755
_g_	6. When can you see the doctor?	f. I'm tired all the time.
_d_	7. Do you have insurance?	g. Anytime on Monday or Tuesday
_b_	8. Are you a new patient?	h. June 28, 1971

LESSON **3**   **GOAL** ➤ **Make a doctor's appointment**

C Study the charts with your classmates and teacher.

Simple Past (Regular)	
Subject	**Verb (base + *ed*)**
I, you, he, she, it, we, they	walked* (walk) talked* (talk) smoked* (smoke) played** (play)
Pronunciation:	* walk/t/, talk/t/, smoke/t/ ** play/d/

Simple Past (Irregular)	
Subject	**Verb**
I, you, he, she, it, we, they	had (have) went (go) say (said)

Simple Past: *Be*		
Subject	***Be***	**Example sentence**
I, he, she, it	was	I **was** sick.
you, we, they	were	You **were** at the hospital.

D Listen to Alexi. Write the letter to make sentences.

CD 2 TR 19

Before Alexi got sick, . . .

c	1. He walked	a. to a doctor once a year.
a	2. He talked	b. soccer on the weekends.
b	3. He played	c. a mile every day.
d	4. He smoked	d. a pack of cigarettes every day.

E Listen to Alexi. Write the letter to make sentences.

CD 2 TR 20

After Alexi got sick, . . .

e	1. He was	a. to smoke.
b	2. He went	b. to the doctor.
a	3. He continued	c. to stop smoking.
c	4. The doctor said	d. a heart attack.
d	5. He had	e. tired a lot.

108 Unit 6 Lesson 3

Listening Script *CD 2, Track 18*

Receptionist: *Good afternoon. Alliance Medical Offices. How can I help you?*
Alexi: *I need to make an appointment with Dr. Singh.*
Receptionist: *Very good. What's your name?*
Alexi: *Alexi Tashkov.*
Receptionist: *And, Alexi, are you a new patient?*
Alexi: *Yes.*
Receptionist: *Why do you want to see the doctor?*
Alexi: *I'm tired all the time.*
Receptionist: *What's your date of birth?*
Alexi: *June 28, 1971.*
Receptionist: *Where do you live?*
Alexi: *1427 Hamilton Street, New York City.*
Receptionist: *What's your phone number?*
Alexi: *It's (212) 555–5755.*
Receptionist: *When can you see the doctor?*
Alexi: *Anytime on Monday or Tuesday.*
Receptionist: *Dr. Singh can see you at 10 A.M. on Tuesday.*
Alexi: *Fine. Thank you.*
Receptionist: *How will you pay? Do you have insurance?*
Alexi: *No, I don't. I'll pay by check.*
Receptionist: *That's fine. We'll see you then.*
Alexi: *Thank you. Goodbye.*

Presentation 2 30–40 mins.

 Study the charts with your classmates and teacher.

Pronunciation of the past tense is sometimes problematic. Students learn this mostly by hearing and practicing over time, but it is still good to make them aware that there are different pronunciations for past tense verbs depending on each verb's last sound. You may choose to go over this pronunciation point by having students identify a voiced and a voiceless sound. Ask them to put two fingers on their voice box and ask them to pronounce different voiced and voiceless sounds. Voiced sounds are followed by /d/ and voiceless are followed by /t/ in regular past tense forms.

Go over Exercises D and E as a class and have students make predictions about what they will hear.

Practice 2 7–10 mins.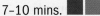

D **Listen to Alexi. Draw lines to make sentences.**

 Listening Script *CD 2, Track 19*

My name is Alexi Tashkov. I thought I was very healthy because I did many things to take care of my health. For example, I walked a mile every day. I saw a doctor once every year, and I played soccer on the weekends. I had a lot of energy for a while, but I had one very bad habit. I smoked a pack of cigarettes every day!

E **Listen to Alexi. Draw lines to make sentences.**

You may need to play the recording a few times.

 Listening Script *CD 2, Track 20*

After three years, my life changed. I was tired a lot. I went to the doctor and he said to stop smoking. I didn't know smoking was bad for my heart. He said it was very dangerous to smoke because I could get cancer or have a heart attack. I continued to smoke and three months later, I had a heart attack.

Evaluation 2 5–7 mins.

Go over the answers with students and play the recording a few more times to confirm answers.

Presentation 3   10–15 mins. ■■■

Go over what each heading of the chart represents. Discuss possible payment methods.

Practice 3   10–15 mins. ■

(F) Listen and complete the chart.

Listening Script   CD 2, Tracks 21–25

1. **Receptionist:** *Good afternoon. Alliance Medical Offices. How can I help you?*
   Alexi: *I need to make an appointment with Dr. Singh.*
   Receptionist: *Very good. What's your name?*
   Alexi: *Alexi Tashkov.*
   Receptionist: *And, Alexi, are you a new patient?*
   Alexi: *Yes.*
   Receptionist: *Why do you want to see the doctor?*
   Alexi: *I'm tired all the time.*
   Receptionist: *What's your date of birth?*
   Alexi: *June 28, 1971.*
   Receptionist: *Where do you live?*
   Alexi: *1427 Hamilton Street, New York City.*
   Receptionist: *What's your phone number?*
   Alexi: *It's (212) 555–5755.*
   Receptionist: *When can you see the doctor?*
   Alexi: *Anytime on Monday or Tuesday.*
   Receptionist: *Dr. Singh can see you at 10 A.M. on Tuesday.*
   Alexi: *Fine. Thank you.*
   Receptionist: *How will you pay? Do you have insurance?*
   Alexi: *No, I don't. I'll pay by check.*
   Receptionist: *That's fine. We'll see you then.*
   Alexi: *Thank you. Goodbye.*

2. **Receptionist:** *Hello. Can I help you?*
   Patient: *Yes. This is Ming Nguyen—M-I-N-G, N-G-U-Y-E-N. I need an appointment to see the doctor. I have terrible headaches every day.*
   Receptionist: *Every day?*
   Patient: *Yes. Every day for a week now.*
   Receptionist: *Can you come in at 3 P.M. today?*
   Patient: *That would be fine.*
   Receptionist: *Do you have insurance?*
   Patient: *No, I will pay cash.*
   Receptionist: *Sounds good. We will see you at 3:00.*
   Patient: *Thanks. Goodbye.*

3. **Receptionist:** *Hello. Dr. Angelo's office. What can I do for you?*
   Patient: *I need an appointment as soon as possible.*
   Receptionist: *Is this an emergency?*
   Patient: *No, not really. I need to see him about the stomachaches I have after I eat certain foods.*
   Receptionist: *OK. You can come in next Monday at 2:00 in the afternoon.*
   Patient: *That sounds fine, but isn't there anything sooner?*
   Receptionist: *I'm afraid not. What's your name?*
   Patient: *My name is Michael Chan—C-H-A-N. Do you take credit cards?*
   Receptionist: *Yes, we do. We take all major credit cards.*
   Patient: *Thanks. I'll see you then. Goodbye.*

4. **Receptionist:** *Hello. Can you hold, please?*
   Patient: *No. This is very important. My brother, Antonio Marco, is a regular patient with you and he has a very bad toothache. He also has a fever.*
   Receptionist: *Come right in.*
   Patient: *Right now?*
   Receptionist: *Yes, right now.*
   Patient: *Thanks! We have dental insurance.*
   Receptionist: *Excellent. We will be waiting for you.*

5. **Receptionist:** *Hello. Dr. Albert's office. Can I help you?*
   Patient: *Yes, my throat hurts a lot.*
   Receptionist: *Do you want an appointment?*
   Patient: *Yes, I do.*
   Receptionist: *Are you a new patient?*
   Patient: *No. My name is Sam Hosker —H-O-S-K-E-R. I was there last week for a physical.*
   Receptionist: *Oh, yes, Mr. Hosker. When can you come in?*
   Patient: *I can come in at 6:00 today.*
   Receptionist: *That's a little late, but I think the doctor can see you then.*
   Patient: *Can I pay by check?*
   Receptionist: *Yes, of course.*
   Patient: *Thanks very much.*

Evaluation 3   7–15 mins. ■

Go over the listening activity and be prepared to play the recording again.

Application   15–20 mins. ■■■

(G) Now fill in the chart with your information. Choose an illness from Lesson 2 or any other illness you can think of.

(H) Use the information from Exercise G to make a conversation with your partner. Make an appointment to see the doctor.

(I) Perform your conversation for the class.

Refer students to *Stand Out 2 Grammar Challenge*, Unit 6, Challenge 3 for more practice with the regular and irregular simple past.

Activity Bank

Templates: Bar Graph

Unit 6, Lesson 3, Worksheet 1: Making Appointments

Unit 6, Lesson 3, Worksheet 2: Confirming Appointments

Unit 6, Lesson 3, Worksheet 3: Past Tense

CD 2
TR 21–25

F Listen and complete the chart.

Name	Problem	Time and day	Method of payment
1. Alexi Tashkov	tired all the time	Monday or Tuesday	check
2. Ming Nguyen	headaches	3 PM today	cash
3. Michael Chan	stomachaches	2 PM Monday	credit
4. Antonio Marco	toothache and fever	now	insurance
5. Sam Hosker	sore throat	6 PM today	check

G Now fill in the chart with your information. Choose an illness from Lesson 2 or any other illness you can think of. (Answers will vary.)

Name (What's your name?)	Problem (What's the matter?)	Time (When can you see the doctor?)	Method of payment (How will you pay?)

H Use the information from Exercise G to make a conversation with your partner. Make an appointment to see the doctor. (Answers will vary.)

Receptionist: Hello, Alliance Medical Offices. Can I help you?

Sick Student: Hello, I want to make an appointment to see Dr. Singh.

Receptionist: OK. What's your name?

Sick Student: _____

Receptionist: _____

Sick Student: _____

Receptionist: _____

Sick Student: _____

Receptionist: _____

Sick Student: _____

I Perform your conversation for the class.

Take two tablets

GOAL ➤ **Read medicine labels**

A Find the words from the box on the medicine label and underline them.

directions	symptoms	uses	exceed	aches and pains
tablets	warning	reduce	persist	teenagers

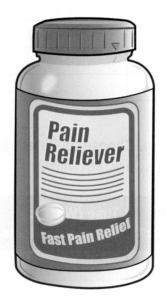

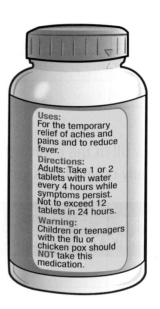

Pain Reliever

Fast Pain Relief

Uses:
For the temporary relief of aches and pains and to reduce fever.
Directions:
Adults: Take 1 or 2 tablets with water every 4 hours while symptoms persist. Not to exceed 12 tablets in 24 hours.
Warning:
Children or teenagers with the flu or chicken pox should NOT take this medication.

B Match the words on the left with the examples on the right. Draw lines.

1. Directions   a. for relief of headaches

2. Uses   b. Don't drive.

3. Warning   c. Take two tablets.

C Match the words on the left with the definitions or examples on the right. Draw lines.

1. teenager   a. aches, pains, and fever

2. symptoms   b. continues

3. not to exceed   c. someone between the ages of 13 and 19

4. persists   d. no more than

Objective: Read medicine labels
Grammar: Modal: *should*
Academic Strategy: Focused listening
Vocabulary: *tablets, pills, teaspoon, syrup, chew, chicken pox, warnings, directions, uses, acid indigestion*

RESOURCES

Activity Bank: Unit 6, Lesson 4, Worksheets 1–3
Reading and Writing Challenge: Unit 6
Grammar Challenge: Unit 6, Challenge 4

Audio: CD 2, Track 26
Heinle Picture Dictionary: Pharmacy, pages 142–143

■ 1.5 hour classes ■ 2.5 hour classes ■ 3⁺ hour classes

AGENDA

Practice making an appointment.
Read medicine labels.
Match labels to medicines.
Learn more about modals.
Listen for doctor's advice.
Use should in sentences.

Warm-up and Review   10-15 mins. ■■■

Ask students to present their conversations they created in the previous lesson to the class. Give them about five minutes to prepare in pairs first. Then, ask for volunteers to perform.

Teaching Tip

In front of the class

Sometimes students are shy about performing or presenting in front of the class. Help them understand that it is expected that they will be a little nervous the first few times that they do it. Having students perform or present in front of the class is an excellent way to prepare them to use the language in the real world when they may also be nervous and feel under pressure.

Introduction   15-20 mins. ■■■

Pantomime a few illnesses and encourage students to ask: *What's the matter?* Then, ask students: *What should I do?* Encourage them to tell you to take some medicine, go to the doctor, or call 911. State the objective: *Today we will read medicine labels.*

Presentation 1   30-40 mins. ■■■

Draw the following chart on the board and ask students to help you complete it.

Name:	
Illness	**Medicine**
Headache	
Stomachache	
Backache	
Cold	
Sore throat	
Fever	

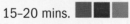 **Find the words from the box on the medicine label and underline them.**

Briefly go over the vocabulary. Make sure students are not working ahead in the book and trying to do the practice before you finish the presentation. Ask students why they would take this medication, how often they would take it, and if there is anything to be careful about when taking it.

Practice 1   8-10 mins. ■■■

 Match the words on the left with the examples on the right. Draw lines.

 Match the words on the left with the definitions or examples on the right. Draw lines.

Ask students to complete Exercises B and C individually.

Evaluation 1   5-8 mins. ■■■

Check the answers with students. Go over the new vocabulary again briefly.

STANDARDS CORRELATIONS

CASAS: 3.3.1, 3.3.2, 3.3.3, 3.4.1 (See CASAS Competency List on pages 169-175.)
SCANS: Resources Allocate materials and facility resources
Information Acquire and evaluate information
Systems Understand systems
Basic Skills Reading, writing, listening, speaking
EFF: Communication Read with understanding, convey ideas in writing, speak so others can understand, listen actively

Presentation 2

15-20 mins.

Go over the list again of medications and illnesses you created on the board. Introduce *brand names*. Ask students to help you identify brand names of medicines. Talk to students about brand names and other medicines. Also, write *over-the-counter medications* and *prescription medications* on the board. Have a discussion about the difference between the two.

Write three columns on the board with the following headings: *Uses, Directions,* and *Warnings*. Discuss the headings and put a possible sentence you might see on a medicine label in each column. This is a great time to bring in sample bottles with directions on them. If you do this, pass them around and ask students to read the authentic labels.

Next, write the following items on the board:

> *Take three tablets two times a day.*
> *Don't take this medicine and drive.*
> *For temporary relief of sore throat pain.*

Ask students to identify which of the three columns these sentences and phrases fall into.

Prepare students for the practice by listing a few other words on the board: *syrup, chew, muscle, irritation, acid indigestion,* and *acute*. See how many of these words students already know and then help them to understand the others by pantomiming. Tell students that as they do the practice, the meaning of the words will become clearer.

D Look at the medicines with your classmates and teacher.

Go over any new vocabulary. Pantomime an illness. Ask students what you need to do. Encourage them to ask: *What's the matter?*

For example:

> **Students:** *What's the matter?*
> **Teacher:** *I have a stomachache (or acid indigestion). What medicine do I need?*
> **Students:** *You need antacid.*

For shorter classes, have students do Exercise E for homework.

Practice 2

10-12 mins.

E Write the letter of the correct medicine above.

Evaluation 2

7-10 mins.

Go over the answers to Exercise E with students.

Instructor's Notes

_____
_____
_____
_____
_____
_____
_____
_____
_____
_____
_____
_____
_____
_____
_____
_____
_____
_____
_____
_____
_____
_____

D Look at the medicines with your classmates and teacher.

teaspoon

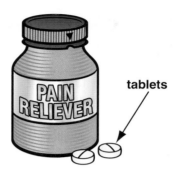

tablets

a. Cough syrup   b. Pain reliever   c. Antacid

E Write the letter of the correct medicine above.

___b___ **Uses:** For temporary relief of headache or muscle aches and fever.

___a___ **Uses:** For temporary relief of cough and throat irritation
          due to infections.

___c___ **Uses:** For fast relief of acid indigestion and stomach pain.

___c___ **Directions:** Chew 2–4 tablets as needed.

___b___ **Directions:** Adults take one or two tablets with water every 4 hours
          while symptoms persist. Not to exceed 12 tablets in 24 hours.

___a___ **Directions:** Take two teaspoons every four hours for cough.

___b___ **Warning:** Children or teenagers with the flu or chicken pox should NOT
          take this medicine.

___c___ **Warning:** Do not chew more than 12 tablets in 24 hours.

___a___ **Warning:** If sore throat pain persists or coughing is acute, contact your doctor.

LESSON 4   **GOAL** ➤ **Read medicine labels**

 F Study the chart with your classmates and teacher.

Modal: *Should*			
Subject	***Should***	**Base verb**	**Example sentence**
I, you, he, she, it, we, they	should shouldn't	take drink chew swallow	I **should take** two tablets. He **shouldn't drink** alcohol with this medicine. You **should take** this medicine for a headache. She **shouldn't chew** this tablet. They **should swallow** this tablet with water.

CD 2
TR 26

G Listen to Alexi's doctor's instructions. Check (✔) what he should do.

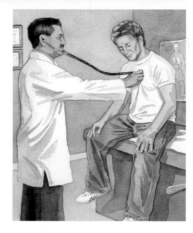

- ☐ Alexi should take medicine and drive.
- ☐ He should take two pills three times a day.
- ☑ He should take the pills with water.
- ☑ He should take three pills two times a day.
- ☐ He should drink a little alcohol with the medicine.
- ☑ He should take aspirin and medicine as directed by a doctor.

H Read your answers to Exercise E on page 111. Write statements to describe what you should do with cough syrup.

EXAMPLE: **Pain reliever:** <u>You should take this pain reliever for temporary relief</u>

<u>of headaches.</u>

Pain reliever: <u>Teenagers with chicken pox shouldn't take this pain reliever.</u>

Pain reliever: <u>You should take 1–2 tablets every 4 hours.</u>

1. **Cough syrup:** <u>For temporary relief of cough and throat irritations due to infection.</u>

2. **Cough syrup:** <u>Take two teaspoons every four hours for cough.</u>

3. **Cough syrup:** <u>If sore throat pain persists or coughing is acute, contact your doctor.</u>

  I **Active Task.** Find a medicine label at home or on the Internet. Share its uses, directions, and warnings with the class.

Presentation 3   10–15 mins. ■■■□

Write on the board the sentences students used in the previous presentation: *You need antacid.* Quickly review the simple present tense. Remind students to use the third-person singular *s: He needs antacid.*

Introduce modals. Have students look back at page 74. Remind them of *might* and *may.* Explain that these are modals and show them how the base form of the verb always follows them.

Note: In Spanish, words like *should* and *can* are verbs and not modals. In English, modals don't function like verbs because they don't change form with different subjects.

(F) Study the chart with your classmates and teacher.

As you go over the chart, make examples and ask students questions, such as: *Should I take an antacid?* Then, expand to ask: *What should I do?*

Practice 3   7–10 mins. ■

(G) Listen to Alexi's doctor's instructions. Check what he should do.

 Listening Script   CD 2, Track 26

Alexi: *Doctor, I am not sure I understand your instructions.*
Doctor: *OK, let's go over them again. It is very important that you understand.*
Alexi: *Yes, I know. I just forget easily.*
Doctor: *That's OK. You can read all about it here on the back of the medicine. It says, "Take three pills two times a day with water."*
Alexi: *Water?*
Doctor: *Water is best, but you can take it with juice if you like.*
Alexi: *Thanks. Is it OK to drive?*
Doctor: *No, you shouldn't drive. It says that here, under "Precautions." Oh, and take aspirin every day, too.*
Alexi: *OK. I will take the aspirin and the other medicine as you have directed me. Thank you!*

Evaluation 3   5–7 mins. ■

Go over the answers and be prepared to play the recording again.

Application   10–15 mins. ■■■□

(H) Read your answers to Exercise E on page 111. Write statements to describe what you should do with cough syrup.

(I) **Active Task.** Find a medicine label at home or on the Internet. Share its uses, directions, and warnings with the class.

Refer students to *Stand Out 2 Grammar Challenge*, Unit 6, Challenge 4 for more practice with *should*.

Activity Bank

Unit 6, Lesson 4, Worksheet 1: Over-the-Counter
                     Medications
Unit 6, Lesson 4, Worksheet 2: Home Remedies
Unit 6, Lesson 4, Worksheet 3: Reading Medicine
                     Labels

AT-A-GLANCE PREP

Objective: Identify and describe emergencies
Grammar: Irregular past tense verbs
Pronunciation: Intonation and rhythm
Academic Strategies: Focused listening, pie charts, percentages
Vocabulary: *robbery, heart attack, poison, choking, chest pains*

RESOURCES

Activity Bank: Unit 6, Lesson 5, Worksheets 1–2
Reading and Writing Challenge: Unit 6
Grammar Challenge: Unit 6, Challenge 5

Audio: CD 2, Tracks 27–31
Heinle Picture Dictionary: Health, pages 132–137

 1.5 hour classes　■ 2.5 hour classes　■ 3⁺ hour classes

AGENDA

Review Lesson 1.
Read a pie chart and read
  for information.
Identify 911 problems and make a call.
Listen for 911 information.
Make decisions about 911 calls

Warm-up and Review　　10–15 mins.

Ask students in groups to look back at Lesson 1. Ask them to identify what people *should* and *shouldn't* do based on what doctors say and their own ideas. They may use Exercise F as a model.

Introduction　　7–10 mins.

Ask students if they have ever called 911 and what the circumstances were. Ask when they should call 911. Give examples and have them respond with a thumbs up or down. For example, say: *You are having a heart attack.* (thumbs up) *You want to know about the weather.* (thumbs down) State the objective: *Today we will identify and describe emergencies.*

Presentation 1　　10–15 mins.

Write *medical, police,* and *fire* on the board. Ask students to think of emergencies for each.

(A) Look at the emergencies. Label them *a medical emergency, a police emergency,* and *a fire emergency.*

Since this is the presentation stage, do this as a class. Discuss the implications and some details of the pictures. Ask students to cover the paragraph and look at the pie chart. Discuss how to read the chart and ask questions about the percentages. You may want to show students how to interpret percentages.

Teaching Tip

Charts and graphs and multilevel instruction

The information in charts and graphs can be complicated and intense or it can be simple; however, for the most part it isn't text heavy. This means that low-level students can get as much out of a chart or graph as high-level students. Once students are able to interpret charts and graphs, they can understand a lot of information with very little English experience.

Practice 1　　8–12 mins.

(B) Read the paragraph and pie chart about emergencies in Westmont Village.

(C) Answer the questions about the paragraph and pie chart.

This is another opportunity for students to read and answer questions independently to check their understanding. Don't have students working in pairs at this point. This is good practice for a standardized reading test such as CASAS.

Evaluation 1　　8–10 mins.

Ask students to go over the answers to Exercise C in pairs and peer-edit if necessary.

STANDARDS CORRELATIONS

CASAS: 2.1.1, 2.1.8, 2.5.1, 3.1.1, 6.7.4 (See CASAS Competency List on pages 169–175.)
SCANS: **Resources** Allocate human resources
Information Acquire and evaluate information
Interpersonal Participate as a member of a team, negotiate to arrive at a decision
Basic Skills Reading, writing, listening, speaking
Thinking Skills Make decisions, solve problems

Personal Qualities Responsibility
EFF: **Communication** Read with understanding, convey ideas in writing, speak so others can understand, listen actively, observe critically
Decision Making Solve problems and make decisions
Interpersonal Cooperate with others, advocate and influence, resolve conflict and negotiate
Lifelong Learning Take responsibility for learning, reflect and evaluate

LESSON 5 **It's an emergency!**

GOAL ➤ Identify and describe emergencies

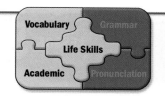

A Look at the emergencies. Label them *a medical emergency, a police emergency,* and *a fire emergency.*

1.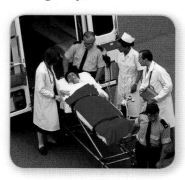

   a medical emergency

2.

   a fire emergency

3.

   a police emergency

B Read the paragraph and pie chart about emergencies in Westmont Village.

Westmont Village is a beautiful town in New Mexico. It is very small, and there are not many emergencies. There is a very small hospital in Westmont Village. I think there are only 20 beds. The paramedics are also fire fighters. They take care of all the medical emergencies and fires. We probably have three small fires, seven or eight medical emergencies, and nine or ten robberies a year. We live in a very quiet town.

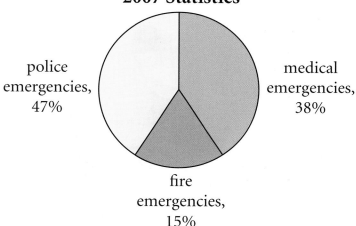

Emergencies in Westmont 2007 Statistics

police emergencies, 47%

medical emergencies, 38%

fire emergencies, 15%

C Answer the questions about the paragraph and pie chart.

1. How many emergencies does Westmont Village have every year?

   a. About 20.   b. 3.   c. 7 or 8.

2. How large is the hospital?

   a. It's very large.   b. It's very small.   c. It's average size.

3. What percentage of emergencies are police emergencies?

   a. About 15%.   b. About 10%.   c. About 50%.

GOAL ▸ Identify and describe emergencies

  D Listen and practice the conversation.

CD 2
TR 27

Operator: 911. What is your emergency?
A friend: It's a medical emergency.
Operator: What's the problem?
A friend: My friend is having chest pains.
Operator: I will send an ambulance immediately.
A friend: Thank you.
Operator: What's your name and phone number? Where is your friend?
A friend: My name is Teresa and my cell number is 555-4334. The address is 9976 West Burma Street. Please hurry!

Base Verb	Past
break	broke
take	took

E Practice the conversation again with the emergencies below. Use your address.

1. is unconscious   2. is choking   3. broke her nose   4. accidentally took poison

  F Listen to the conversations and circle the emergency in each.

CD 2
TR 28–31

1. robbery   car accident   (fire)
2. (heart attack)   fire   robbery
3. car accident   fire   (robbery)
4. fire   robbery   (heart attack)

Presentation 2   10-15 mins. ■■□

Review again the differences between a medical, police, and fire emergency. Make a cluster diagram on the board and brainstorm examples of each. Be sure to include *robbery* and *car accidents*. There is a cluster diagram you can duplicate for students in the template folder on the Activity Bank CD-ROM.

D Listen and practice the conversation.

 Listening Script   CD 2, Track 27

The listening script matches the conversation in Exercise D.

Pronunciation

Intonation

Go over the intonation and rhythm in the conversation. A good way to do this is to ask students to identify the words that are most important for the meaning. Have students underline them in the conversation and then say only these words. Do this several times and have them discern which words should have more emphasis than the rest. Finally, add the other words, but deemphasize them.

For example, they should underline the following words in the first three lines:

Operator: <u>What</u> . . . <u>emergency.</u>
A Friend: <u>It's</u> . . . <u>MEDICAL emergency.</u>
Operator: <u>What's</u> . . . <u>problem.</u>

Go over the pictures in Exercise E carefully to prepare students for the practice.

Practice 2   10-15 mins. ■■□

E Practice the conversation again with the emergencies below. Use your address.

Evaluation 2   5-7 mins. ■■□

Ask volunteers to demonstrate in front of the class. Then, ask for volunteers to improvise with you.

Presentation 3   5-7 mins. ■■■

Go over the new words from the lesson including the pictures from Practices 1 and 2. Have students show which picture from Exercise E you are describing by holding up the corresponding number of fingers. Do the same thing with the pictures from Exercise A.

Practice 3   7-10 mins. ■

F Listen to the conversations and circle the emergency in each.

 Listening Script   CD 2, Tracks 28–31

1. **Operator:** *911. Can I help you?*
   Rodrigo: *Yes, please help. My house is on fire and it is very serious.*
   Operator: *What is your address?*
   Rodrigo: *It's 3562 West Fallbrook Avenue.*
   Operator: *And your name, sir?*
   Rodrigo: *Rodrigo Martinez.*
   Operator: *I am calling the fire department now. Please do not go back into your house.*
   Rodrigo: *No, I won't. Thank you so much!*
2. **Operator:** *911. What is the emergency?*
   Anya: *I think my cousin is having a heart attack!*
   Operator: *Please try to stay calm. Is she conscious?*
   Anya: *Yes, but she is having sharp chest pains.*
   Operator: *I will send the paramedics. What is your name and address?*
3. **Operator:** *911. What is the emergency?*
   Felipe: *I lost my wallet, and I think someone stole it.*
   Operator: *You were robbed?*
   Felipe: *Yes, I guess so. I think a man bumped into me and took it right out of my pocket.*
   Operator: *Where are you?*
   Felipe: *I am on the corner of Walnut and Wall Street.*
   Operator: *I will send a police unit there immediately.*
4. **Operator:** *911. Can I help you?*
   Felipe: *I am sick and really can't move. Please send the paramedics.*
   Operator: *Are you in pain?*
   Felipe: *Yes, it is my chest.*
   Operator: *You have chest pains?*
   Felipe: *Yes, and I am dizzy and very uncomfortable.*
   Operator: *I will send the paramedics A-S-A-P. Try to call a friend to stay with you until they arrive. What is your name and address?*

Evaluation 3   7-10 mins.

Check students' work and play the recording again. Ask students other questions about the recording. For example, in Conversation 1, ask students to write the address. For Conversation 2, ask who is having the problem and who is called to help. For Conversation 3, ask what was lost and who is called. For Conversation 4, ask what Felipe should do if he is alone. You might have students review the listening scripts in the back of their books.

Application   10–15 mins. ■■■

G Read the chart with your classmates and teacher. Underline the words you don't know. Then in groups, complete the chart.

H Practice the conversation. Use the information from the chart in Exercise G.

✍ Refer students to *Stand Out 2 Grammar Challenge*, Unit 6, Challenge 5 for more practice with past tense irregular verbs.

Activity Bank 📀

Templates: Cluster Diagram
Unit 6, Lesson 5, Worksheet 1: Modal *Should*
Unit 6, Lesson 5, Worksheet 2: Emergencies

GOAL ➤ **Identify and describe emergencies**

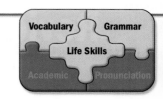

G Read the chart with your classmates and teacher. Underline the words you don't know. Then in groups, complete the chart. (Answers will vary. Sample answers are given.)

	Always call 911.	Sometimes call 911.	Never call 911.	Take medicine.	Brand name of medicine
She has a cold.			✓	✓	
A cat is in a tree.		✓			
She has terrible chest pains.	✓			✓	
They have the flu.		✓			
The man is not breathing.	✓				
There is no food in the house.			✓		
I am very tired.			✓		
He coughs every day.			✓	✓	
She has a sore throat.			✓	✓	
She has a stomachache.		✓			
She broke her arm.		✓			
He accidentally took poison.	✓				

H Practice the conversation. Use the information from the chart in Exercise G.

EXAMPLE: *Student A:* What's the matter?
Student B: I have chest pains.
Student A: You need to call a doctor or 911 right now.

Advice	
You should	take call
You need	to take to call

A Look at the picture and write the words. (Lesson 2)

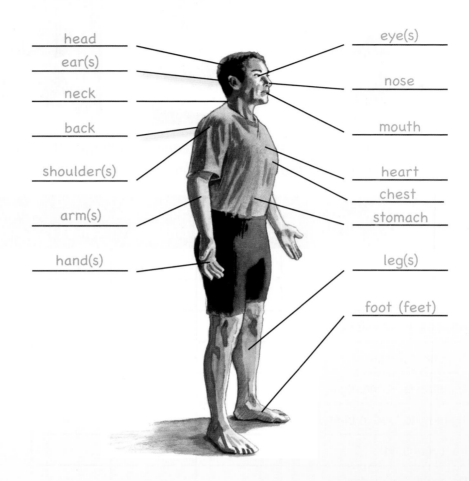

head

ear(s)

neck

back

shoulder(s)

arm(s)

hand(s)

eye(s)

nose

mouth

heart

chest

stomach

leg(s)

foot (feet)

B Draw a line from the illness to the advice. (Lessons 4 and 5)

1. I have a headache.

2. I have a bad toothache.

3. I have a stomachache.

4. I have chest pains.

a. You should go to the dentist.

b. You should call 911 right now.

c. You should take a pain reliever.

d. You should take some antacid tablets.

Objective: All unit objectives
Grammar: All unit grammar
Academic Strategies: Reviewing, evaluating, developing study skills
Vocabulary: All unit vocabulary

AGENDA

Discuss unit objectives.
Complete the review.
Do My Dictionary.
Evaluate and reflect on progress.

■ 1.5 hour classes   ■ 2.5 hour classes   ■ 3⁺ hour classes

Warm-up and Review   7-10 mins.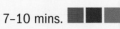

With their books closed, ask students to help you make a list on the board of all the vocabulary they can come up with from the unit. Then, have a competition where students in groups will write page numbers for each item on the list. The first group to have the correct page number for each item wins.

Introduction   5 mins.

Write all the objectives on the board from Unit 6. Show students the first page of the unit and say the five objectives. Explain that today they will review the whole unit.

Note: Depending on the length of the term, you may decide to have students do Presentation 1 and Practice 1 for homework and then review student work as either the warm-up or another class activity.

Presentation 1   10-15 mins.

This presentation will cover the first three pages of the review. Quickly go to the first page of each lesson. Discuss the objective of each. Ask simple questions to remind students of what they have learned.

Practice 1   15-20 mins.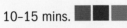

A Look at the picture and write the words. (Lesson 2)

B Draw a line from the illness to the advice. (Lessons 4 and 5)

Teaching Tip

Recycling/Review

The review and the project that follows are part of the recycling/review process. Students at this level often need to be reintroduced to concepts to solidify what they have learned. Many concepts are learned and forgotten while learning other new concepts. This is because students learn but are not necessarily ready to acquire language concepts.

Therefore, it becomes very important to review and to show students how to review on their own. It is also important to recycle the new concepts in different contexts.

STANDARDS CORRELATIONS

CASAS: 3.1.1, 3.1.2, 3.1.3, 3.3.1, 3.3.2, 3.4.1, 3.5.8, 3.5.9
(See CASAS Competency List on pages 169-175.)
SCANS: **Information** Acquire and evaluate information, organize and maintain information

Basic Skills Reading, writing, speaking
Personal Qualities Responsibility, self management
EFF: **Communication** Speak so others can understand
Lifelong Learning Take responsibility for learning, reflect and evaluate

Practice 1 *(continued)*

C Give someone advice on how to stay healthy. Choose a picture below. Write two things the person should do and two things he or she shouldn't do. (Lesson 1)

D Complete the sentences with the past tense form of the verbs in parentheses. (Lesson 3)

E Match the section of the medicine label to the information. Draw lines. (Lesson 4)

C Give someone advice on how to stay healthy. Choose a picture below. Write two things the person should do and two things he or she shouldn't do. (Lesson 1) (Answers will vary.)

1.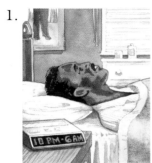
2.
3.
4.

1. _____

2. _____

3. _____

4. _____

D Complete the sentences with the past tense form of the verbs in parentheses. (Lesson 3)

1. Yesterday, I _____had_____ (have) a terrible headache.

2. Suzanne _____was_____ (be) sick last week.

3. Last summer, we _____talked_____ (talk) to the doctor.

4. I _____went_____ (go) to the hospital on Monday.

5. They _____called_____ (call) the doctor five minutes ago.

6. Last year, the children _____were_____ (be) sick a lot.

7. The doctor _____said_____ (say) I shouldn't smoke.

8. He _____went_____ (go) to the doctor's last week.

E Match the section of the medicine label to the information. Draw lines. (Lesson 4)

1. Uses   a. Take two tablets three times a day.

2. Directions   b. Do not take more than 12 tablets in 24 hours.

3. Warning   c. For the temporary relief of aches and pains.

F **Number the conversation in order. (Lesson 5)**

___6___ *Mario:* 66345 West Malvern Avenue.

___7___ *Operator:* Is anyone injured?

___2___ *Mario:* Yes, there is a fire.

___1___ *Operator:* 911. Can I help you?

___3___ *Operator:* A fire? What's your name?

___8___ *Mario:* I don't think so. Please hurry.

___10__ *Mario:* Thank you!

___9___ *Operator:* Yes, sir, they will be there very soon.

___5___ *Operator:* Yes, of course. What is the address?

___4___ *Mario:* Mario De la Vega. Please send the fire department.

G **Write the symptom under each picture and a possible medicine. (Lessons 2 and 4)**

1.

Symptom: _____ headache _____

Medicine: _____ pain reliever _____

2.

Symptom: _____ fever _____

Medicine: _____ pain reliever _____

3.

Symptom: _____ cough _____

Medicine: _____ cough syrup _____

4.

Symptom: _____ stomachache _____

Medicine: _____ antacid _____

Introduction   5 mins.

Team Project

Make a health pamphlet.

In this project, students will produce a health pamphlet. Explain that a pamphlet is the same as a brochure. You can use the worksheet on the Activity Bank CD-ROM (Unit 6, Project, Worksheet 1). This project may take two days.

Stage 1   5-10 mins.

Form a team with four or five students.

Help students form groups and assign positions in their groups. On the spot, students will have to choose who will be the leader of their group. Review the responsibility of the leader and ask students to write the name of their leader in their books. Do the same with the remaining positions: nurse, health expert, and artists.

Explain that all students should work on every task. Students shouldn't go on to the next stage until the previous one is complete.

Stage 2   15-20 mins.

Write three things people should do to be healthy. Write three things people should not do.

Have groups list three things people should and shouldn't do.

Stages 3 and 4   15-20 mins.

Think of three common illnesses to include in your pamphlet. Describe them. Write medicines people should take for these illnesses.

Have groups choose three illnesses and their treatments.

Stage 5   40-50 mins.

Design a pamphlet with pictures to present the information.

Help students find clip art if they are developing their projects on computers. You may also use the pamphlet worksheet on the Activity Bank CD-ROM (Unit 6, Project, Worksheet 1).

Stage 6   15-20 mins.

Prepare a presentation for the class.

Have groups give their presentations. Make sure that all group members participate. Consider videotaping the presentations. Students will prepare better for formal presentations if they are videotaped. Another approach is for students to videotape themselves and polish their presentations before giving them to the class.

Activity Bank

Unit 6, Project, Worksheet 1: Health Brochure

Unit 6, Extension, Worksheet 1: Body Parts

STANDARDS CORRELATIONS

CASAS: 3.1.1, 3.1.2, 3.1.3, 3.3.1, 3.3.2, 3.4.1, 3.5.8, 3.5.9 (See CASAS Competency List on pages 169–175.)

SCANS: **Resources** Allocate time, allocate materials and facility resources, allocate human resources

Information Acquire and evaluate information, organize and maintain information, interpret and communicate information

Interpersonal Participate as a member of a team, teach others, exercise leadership, negotiate to arrive at a decision, work with cultural diversity

Systems Understand systems, monitor and correct performance

Basic Skills Reading, writing, listening, speaking

Thinking Skills Think creatively, make decisions, solve problems, see things in the mind's eye

Personal Qualities Responsibility, sociability, self management

EFF: **Communication** Read with understanding, convey ideas in writing, speak so others can understand, listen actively, observe critically

Decision Making Solve problems and make decisions, plan

Interpersonal Cooperate with others, advocate and influence, resolve conflict and negotiate, guide others

Lifelong Learning Take responsibility for learning, reflect and evaluate

AT-A-GLANCE PREP

Objective: Evaluate learning and work skills
Grammar: Future: *will*—affirmative and negative
Academic Strategies: Focused listening, reading for main idea
Vocabulary: *several, teams, positive attitude, habits, skills, evaluation*

RESOURCES

Activity Bank: Unit 7, Lesson 1, Worksheets 1–2
Reading and Writing Challenge: Unit 7
Grammar Challenge: Unit 7, Challenge 1

Audio: CD 2, Track 32
Heinle Picture Dictionary: Jobs, pages 146–149

 1.5 hour classes ■ 2.5 hour classes ■ 3+ hour classes

Stand Out 2 Assessment CD-ROM with Exam*View*®

> ## AGENDA
> *Talk about skills and goals.*
> *Read about work habits.*
> *Read evaluation forms.*
> *Use the future tense.*
> *Set goals.*

Preassessment (optional)

Use the Stand Out 2 Assessment CD-ROM with Exam*View*® to create a pretest for Unit 7.

Warm-up and Review   15-20 mins.

Write the following words on the board: *Listening, Reading, Writing, Speaking.* Indicate one word for each corner of the room. Ask students to go to the corner that represents the most important skill they need to work on. Write *Goals* on the board. Ask students in the corners to identify a goal they would like to work on relative to the skill. Give some examples, such as: *I would like to read better so I can understand the newspaper.* Teach them how to use *so* and how it relates to *because.* Have students state their goals to their groups and then write their goals down. Ask a few volunteers to share their goals with the class.

Introduction   3-7 mins.

Ask students if they have work goals. For example: *I want to get a better job; I want to be a supervisor.* State the objective: *Today we will evaluate learning and work skills.*

Presentation 1   20-30 mins.

In groups, have students list the things that make a good student. Give an example, such as *come to school every day.* Ask groups to share their lists with the class.

(A) Read the paragraph about Dalva. Underline the new words.

Note: See the Teaching Tip at the top of page 122a about reading for understanding.

Give students 60 seconds to read the first paragraph, and then ask them to close their books. Then, ask students who the paragraph is about. Ask if Dalva has a job, needs a job, or needs to find a school to learn English. Finally, ask if Dalva has any skills. Discuss the meaning of *skills* and ask them to open their books and identify Dalva's skills. Go over the words students have underlined.

Now, read the second paragraph with students and ask them if they agree, disagree, or don't have an opinion.

Go over the skills and study habits in Exercise B. Make sure students understand their meanings.

Practice 1   7-10 mins.

(B) Are you a good student with good work habits? Circle the number that best describes you.

Ask students to do this activity in groups. Assign a group reporter who will report the results to the class. This activity will require negotiation to decide on ratings that the entire group is satisfied with.

Evaluation 1   3-5 mins.

Ask groups to report to the class.

STANDARDS CORRELATIONS

CASAS: 4.4.2, 4.7.3 (See CASAS Competency List on pages 169–175.)
SCANS: **Information** Acquire and evaluate information, organize and maintain information, interpret and communicate information
Interpersonal Participate as a member of a team, teach others, negotiate to arrive at a decision
Basic Skills Reading, writing, listening, speaking
Thinking Skills Make decisions, solve problems, see things in the mind's eye

Personal Qualities Self management
EFF: **Communication** Read with understanding, convey ideas in writing, speak so others can understand, listen actively, observe critically
Decision Making Solve problems and make decisions
Interpersonal Cooperate with others, advocate and influence, resolve conflict and negotiate, guide others
Lifelong Learning Take responsibility for learning, reflect and evaluate

UNIT 7

Work, Work, Work

GOALS

➤ Evaluate learning and work skills
➤ Identify jobs and job skills
➤ Apply for a job
➤ Interview for a job
➤ Follow instructions in an office

 **LESSON 1**

A good student and employee

GOAL ➤ Evaluate learning and work skills

 A Read the paragraph about Dalva. Underline the new words.

Dalva is an English student in Los Angeles, California. She needs a job. She had several jobs before she came to the United States, but it is more difficult now because she is learning English. She is a good worker and a good student. At school, she comes on time every day, participates, and has a positive attitude. She helps other students and they help her.

Good work habits are very important in the United States. Employees who come on time, work hard, and cooperate are more successful than other employees. Good work habits in the classroom are similar to good work habits in the workplace.

 B Are you a good student with good work habits? Circle the number that best describes you. (Answers will vary.)

	Always			Never
1. I come to class every day.	1	2	3	4
2. I come to class on time.	1	2	3	4
3. I participate in class and in groups.	1	2	3	4
4. I do my homework.	1	2	3	4
5. I listen carefully.	1	2	3	4
6. I help others.	1	2	3	4

LESSON

GOAL ➤ **Evaluate learning and work skills**

C Look at the evaluation with your classmates and teacher.

Fairview Hotel
Employee Evaluation Form

Employee Name: Dalva Mendes

Position: Administrative Assistant

Date: April 4

EVALUATION

1. Comes to work on time	S	(G)	NI
2. Follows instructions	(S)	G	NI
3. Helps others	(S)	G	NI
4. Works well with the team	(S)	G	NI
5. Understands the job	S	G	(NI)

New employee. She is still learning.

6. Has a positive attitude	(S)	G	NI

Enjoys her job and is always cheerful

Supervisor's signature: Patricia Macias

Employee's signature: Dalva Mendes

S = Superior   G = Good   NI = Needs improvement

CD 2
TR 32

D Listen to the conversation between Dalva and her boss about her evaluation. Circle the correct information on the form above.

E In a group, talk about which skills are the most important to have at work. Number the skills from 1 to 6. Number 1 is the most important skill. (Answers will vary.)

_____ Comes to work on time   _____ Works well with the team

_____ Follows instructions   _____ Understands the job

_____ Helps others   _____ Has a good attitude

122   Unit 7   Lesson 1

Reading for understanding

We have discussed scanning for specific information and suggested that this kind of reading is similar to focused listening. Now, we want students to find the main idea of a text. This skill is similar to scanning, but students should read more slowly. They should not get bogged down by words they don't understand, and they should avoid rereading every sentence before reading the entire passage all the way through. A good technique is to give students a minimal amount of time to read and then to have them close their books. Then, ask broad comprehension questions.

Presentation 2   10–15 mins. ■■□

C Look at the evaluation with your classmates and teacher.

Tell students that skills at school are similar to skills in the workplace. Ask them to open their books and to study the evaluation form. Ask comprehension questions about the evaluation form.

Teaching Tip

Asking questions about pictures and forms

It is important to get students to look at and study pictures and forms in *Stand Out*. Sometimes, as in this case, students may look at the form but not really understand what it is or how it applies to them. To help motivate them to look at the details of the form, ask questions, such as: *Who is the employee? What is an employee? Who is the supervisor? What is a positive attitude? Do you have a good attitude?*

D Listen to the conversation between Dalva and her boss about her evaluation. Circle the correct information on the form above.

Since this is still the presentation stage, go over the recording carefully. After students do the focused listening, you may also direct them to the script in the back of the book and read it as a class.

 Listening Script   *CD 2, Track 32*

Patricia: *Hello, Dalva. Please come in.*
Dalva: *Thank you.*
Patricia: *As you know, I evaluated you yesterday. I want you to know that we appreciate your work. I especially appreciate your attitude. You are always so happy and cheerful. I gave you an S for "superior" on your attitude.*
Dalva: *Thank you. I guess I am cheerful because I am so happy to work here.*
Patricia: *Well, it shows. Now, let's go down the list. I gave you a "good" for coming to work on time. You are doing fine, but you get here exactly on time. It would be nice to see you here a little early so if there is an emergency, you will not be late.*
Dalva: *I can do that. It is difficult because I have to take my daughter to school.*
Patricia: *I understand. I have given you superiors on following directions, helping others, and working well with the team. Good for you. You are becoming a great employee.*
Dalva: *What is this NI?*
Patricia: *That means "needs improvement." Don't worry about that one. You are new and need to learn more. So, for understands the job I had to give you an NI. Next time, I am sure it will be better.*
Dalva: *Thank you.*

Practice 2   7–10 mins. ■■

E In a group, talk about which skills are the most important to have at work. Number the skills from 1 to 6. Number 1 is the most important skill.

Some students may be tempted to do this activity on their own. Remind students what ranking means and ask them to choose a representative to list the ranking of the group on the board. This might help students to work in a group and not independently.

Evaluation 2   7–10 mins. ■■

Go over the lists on the board and compare the rankings.

Presentation 3 — 10-15 mins. ■■□

Revisit goals briefly and discuss what goals students might like to make based on what they have studied in this lesson.

(F) Study the charts with your classmates and teacher.

Show students that they can express their goals by using the future tense.

Practice 3 — 7-10 mins. ■

(G) Complete the sentences with the future. Use the affirmative for things that are good to do at school. Use the negative for things that are bad to do at school.

Have students complete these sentences individually.

Evaluation 3 — 5-7 mins. ■

Ask students to write the entire sentences on the board and allow everyone to check their work.

Application — 10-15 mins. ■■□

(H) Talk with a partner about goals you have. Write your goals.

Refer students to *Stand Out 2 Grammar Challenge*, Unit 7, Challenge 1 for more practice with the future *will*.

Activity Bank

Unit 7, Lesson 1, Worksheet 1: Work Evaluations
Unit 7, Lesson 1, Worksheet 2: Future—*Will*

Instructor's Notes

LESSON **1** **GOAL** ➤ **Evaluate learning and work skills**

Vocabulary | Grammar | Life Skills | Academic | Pronunciation

F Study the charts with your classmates and teacher.

Future: *Will* (Affirmative)			
Subject	***Will***	**Base verb**	**Example sentence**
I, you, he, she, it, we, they	will	come	I **will come** to class on time.
		listen	You **will listen** carefully and follow directions.
		help	He **will help** other students.
		work	She **will work** hard.
		have	We **will have** a positive attitude.
		do	They **will do** their homework.

Future: *Will* (Negative)			
Subject	***Will***	**Base verb**	**Example sentence**
I, you, he, she, it, we, they	will not (won't)	come	I **won't come** to class late.
		leave	He **won't leave** class early.
		forget	We **will not forget** our homework.

G Complete the sentences with the future. Use the affirmative for things that are good to do at school. Use the negative for things that are bad to do at school.

1. I __will come__ (come) to school on time every day.
2. Barry __won't smoke__ (smoke) in class.
3. The students __won't chew__ (chew) gum in class.
4. We __will participate__ (participate) in groups.
5. You __will have__ (have) a positive attitude.
6. They __won't forget__ (forget) their notebooks.
7. I __will listen__ (listen) carefully.

H Talk with a partner about goals you have. Write your goals. (Answers will vary.)

My goals

1. _____

2. _____

My partner's goals

1. _____

2. _____

What can you do?

GOAL ➤ Identify jobs and job skills

A Write the job titles under the correct picture.

carpenter	construction worker	delivery person	mechanic
custodian	computer programmer	homemaker	office worker

Kristina

1. computer programmer

Esteban

2. delivery person

Ivan

3. custodian

Salvador

4. construction worker

Dalva

5. office worker

Chang

6. mechanic

Natalia

7. carpenter

Phuong

8. homemaker

B Practice asking a partner about the jobs above.

EXAMPLE: *Student A:* What does Dalva do?
Student B: She's an office worker.

Objective: Identify job and job skills
Grammar: *can, can't*
Academic Strategies: Focused listening, brainstorming
Vocabulary: Occupation and tool vocabulary

RESOURCES

Activity Bank: Unit 7, Lesson 2, Worksheets 1–2
Reading and Writing Challenge: Unit 7
Grammar Challenge: Unit 7, Challenge 2

Audio: CD 2, Track 33
Heinle Picture Dictionary: Jobs, pages 146–151, 160–165

■ 1.5 hour classes   ■ 2.5 hour classes   ■ 3· hour classes

AGENDA
Talk about jobs and occupations.
Discuss tools and skills.
Read job history information.
Write about skills.
Write things you and a partner can do.

Warm-up and Review   10-15 mins. ■■■

Write on the board: *What do you do?* Ask various students this question. At first, students may describe what they are doing at the moment.

Then, ask a few other students to name their jobs or occupations. Explain that the question *What do you do?* often means *What is your job?*

Make a list on the board of students' jobs. Make sure they know that being a student or a homemaker is also a job. Help students with pronunciation as needed.

Introduction   3-5 mins. ■■■

Look at the list you have created with students' input on the board. Ask students if they can think of any other jobs and add them to the list. State the objective: *Today we will identify jobs and job skills.*

Presentation 1   15-20 mins. ■■■

 Write the job titles under the correct picture.

Ask students to look at the pictures in Exercise A. Go over the vocabulary and ask students to tell you where to write each word. Work on pronunciation.

Explain that many occupation words can be formed by identifying the verb that best describes the occupation. Hence, *worker* comes from *work*, *runner* comes from *run*, and so on.

Pronunciation

Schwa /ə/

In English, many unaccented vowels have a schwa sound. Now that students are using many more multisyllabic words, it is time to introduce the schwa. Say the word *delivery*. Help students see that when speaking at a normal pace, Americans will pronounce the schwa sound, or "uh," as opposed to what would be expected by nonnative speakers. Show them that it is pronounced: d "uh" liv "uh" ry.

Similarly, the final *r* in most words that identify jobs, such as *doctor* and *gardener*, can be preceded by an *o* or an *e* but they have the same final sound.

Prepare students for Exercise B by asking them what each person does. Quiz them on the vocabulary by describing a job and asking students to show which picture you are describing by the number of fingers they hold up.

Practice 1   7-10 mins. ■■■

 Practice asking a partner about the jobs above.

Evaluation 1   5-7 mins. ■■■

Ask volunteers to demonstrate their exchanges for the class. Then, improvise with a few students.

STANDARDS CORRELATIONS

CASAS: 4.1.2, 4.1.8, 4.5.1 (See CASAS Competency List on pages 169-175.)
SCANS: **Resources** Allocate materials and facility resources

Basic Skills Writing, listening, speaking
EFF: **Communication** Read with understanding, convey ideas in writing, speak so others can understand, listen actively, observe critically

Presentation 2   20-30 mins. ■■□

Draw a cluster diagram on the board. You might also duplicate the cluster template from the Activity Bank CD-ROM and distribute it to students. Label the center cluster *Jobs*. Next, label four secondary circles: *Store/Office*, *School*, *Private Service*, and *Public Service*. As a class, brainstorm more words for the cluster. Students can also use the occupations listed on the previous page.

Write the word *tools* on the board. Ask students what it means. Encourage students to give you examples instead of trying to make a formal definition. Pantomime a few tools such as *hammer* and *broom*.

C Talk about the tools.

Ask students which tools might go with the occupations depicted on the previous page.

D In a group, talk about the jobs below. Write one or two tools for each job.

After students have the jobs and tools in groups, go over the activity as a class.

For shorter classes, have students do Exercise E for homework.

Practice 2   10-15 mins. ■■□

E In your group, read the list of skills below. Then, write them in the chart above.

You may choose to do Exercise E as part of the presentation stage and have students practice a question-and-answer drill for the practice. The drill would go like this:

> **Question:** *What does a mechanic do?*
> **Answer:** *A mechanic fixes cars.*
> **Question:** *What tools does a mechanic use?*
> **Answer:** *A mechanic uses a wrench and sometimes a hammer.*

Evaluation 2   7-10 mins. ■■

Go over the chart in Exercise E as a class.

Instructor's Notes

_____

_____

_____

_____

_____

_____

_____

_____

_____

_____

_____

_____

_____

_____

_____

_____

_____

_____

_____

_____

_____

_____

_____

_____

_____

GOAL ➤ **Identify jobs and job skills**

Vocabulary · Grammar
Life Skills
Academic · Pronunciation

C Talk about the tools.

1. saw and hammer

2. wrench

3. broom and mop

4. copy machine

D In a group, talk about the jobs below. Write one or two tools for each job.
(Answer will vary.)

Job	Tool	Skill
carpenter		
computer programmer		
construction worker		
custodian		
delivery person		
driver		
mechanic		
office worker		
student		
teacher		

E In your group, read the list of skills below. Then, write them in the chart above.

drives a truck	builds houses	delivers packages	writes programs
makes furniture	helps students	types letters	cleans offices
fixes cars	listens carefully		

F Study the skills and job history sections of Dalva's job application.

SKILLS

Typing: _65 wpm_   Computer Skills: _Internet and word processing_

Languages: _Spanish, French, Portuguese (written and spoken), and English (learning)_

JOB HISTORY

POSITION	COMPANY	FROM	TO	DUTIES
Administrative Assistant	Fairview Hotel	12/2007	11/2008	Typed letters
Reason for leaving:				
Cashier	La Tostada Restaurant	6/2004	11/2007	Collected money, helped customers
Reason for leaving:				

  G Listen and write the dates and job duties on the application above.

CD 2
TR 33

Can	Can't
I **can** type.	I **can't** type.
He **can** type.	He **can't** type.

H What can Dalva do? Write sentences about her skills.

1. She _can type 65 words per minute._

2. _She can use the Internet and word processors._

3. _She can speak and write Spanish, French and Portuguese._

4. _She is learning English._

I Talk to a partner. What can you do? What can your partner do?
(Answers will vary.)

You   Your partner

_____   _____

_____   _____

Presentation 3　　　10–15 mins. ■■■□

F Study the skills and job history sections of Dalva's job application.

Explain that the job history is part of a larger employment application form and that they will be completing one in a later lesson.

G Listen and write the dates and job duties on the application above.

Go over the review grammar box in preparation for Practice 3.

For shorter classes, ask students to do Exercise H for homework.

Practice 3　　　8–10 mins. ■

H What can Dalva do? Write sentences about her skills.

Ask students to work on this activity individually.

Evaluation 3　　　5–7 mins. ■

Ask students to write their sentences on the board and allow them an opportunity to peer-edit if necessary.

Application　　　10–15 mins. ■■■

I Talk to a partner. What can you do? What can your partner do?

📖 Refer students to *Stand Out 2 Grammar Challenge*, Unit 7, Challenge 2 for more practice with the modal *can*.

Activity Bank 💿

Templates: Cluster Diagram
Unit 7, Lesson 2, Worksheet 1: Job Titles
Unit 7, Lesson 2, Worksheet 2: Using *Can*

Instructor's Notes

Objective: Apply for a job
Grammar: Questions with *may* and *can*
Pronunciation: Emphasis
Academic Strategy: Focused listening
Vocabulary: *BA, wpm,* classified ad vocabulary

RESOURCES

Activity Bank: Unit 7, Lesson 3, Worksheets 1–4
Reading and Writing Challenge: Unit 7
Grammar Challenge: Unit 7, Challenge 3

Audio: CD 2, Track 34
Heinle Picture Dictionary: Jobs, pages 146–151

■ 1.5 hour classes ■ 2.5 hour classes ■ 3· hour classes

AGENDA

Talk about employment status.
Read classified ads.
Request an application.
Complete an application.

Warm-up and Review   10-15 mins.

Do a corners activity where you send students to different corners of the room based on the following categories: *employed, unemployed but looking, unemployed and not looking,* and *retired.*

Note: If your school uses the demographic forms for CASAS, you can say *unemployed* and *not employed* for the two categories above.

Ask students to talk in their corners and interview each other. Write these questions on the board as a guide:

> **Employed:** *Where do you work? When do you start work?* **Unemployed:** *What job do you want? Where do you want to work?* **Not employed:** *What do you do? Where do you live?* **Retired:** *What do you do? Where do you live?*

Introduction   3-5 mins.

Tell students a little bit about your recent job history. Go over how you got your current job. State the objective: *Today we will apply for a job.*

Presentation 1   15-20 mins.

Ask students where they can find information on jobs that are available. They might mention help-wanted signs in store windows, the newspaper, and the Internet. Ask students what part of the newspaper has information about jobs. If they don't know, tell them that they can find information about jobs in the classified ads under *employment.*

Ask students to open their books and go over the classified ads with them. Ask them to

circle all the job titles. Help them to see that abbreviations are not necessarily standard in the newspaper. Teach them to scan the ad for important words similar to the way they have learned to do for focused listening.

Note: See the Teaching Tip box about "Scanning" on page 128a.

Practice 1   12-15 mins.

Ⓐ **Look at the classified ads. Write the correct jobs in the chart below.**

Ⓑ **What do these abbreviations mean?**

Review the new vocabulary. Review also what *benefits* and a *resume* are.

Evaluation 1   3-7 mins.

Check students' work and discuss the answers as a class.

STANDARDS CORRELATIONS

CASAS: 4.1.1, 4.1.2, 4.1.3, 4.1.6 (See CASAS Competency List on pages 169–175.)
SCANS: Information Acquire and evaluate information
Basic Skills Reading, writing, listening, speaking
EFF: Communication Read with understanding, convey ideas in writing, speak so others can understand, listen actively, observe critically

I'm looking for a job.

GOAL ➤ **Apply for a job**

A Look at the classified ads. Write the correct jobs in the chart below.

DAILY NEWS *Classified Ads*
EMPLOYMENT

Apartment Manager
FT, 2 yrs exp, free rent, speak Spanish and English, paint and minor maintenance. Available immediately.
Call Manor Apartments, 555-8976.

Full-Time Cook
No experience needed, training available, Martha's Kitchen, good hours, apply in person, 3456 W. Melrose, Hill City, 8am-5pm

Legal Assistant
45 wpm, filing, speak English, FT, great opportunity, Smith and Peterson Law Office. Call 555-9988.

Cashier
PT, $9/hr, no exp nec, Franklin's Cinema. Call for appl, 555-3344.

DRIVER
Alexander's Furniture Warehouse
Make deliveries to homes in Hill City, driver's license, driving experience necessary, FT, $10/hr, Monday-Friday, 6am-2:30pm. Call Alexander, 555-3300.

➤ **ESL TEACHER** ⬅
Casper Education Center
BA req, 1yr teaching exp, PT positions only, resume req, benefits. Call Nancy, 555-2000.

Information	Jobs
full-time	apartment manager, cook, legal assistant, driver
part-time	cashier, ESL teacher
paid hourly	cashier, driver
needs a BA degree	ESL teacher
needs a driver's license	driver
needs experience	apartment manager, driver, ESL teacher

B What do these abbreviations mean?

1. PT ___part time___
2. FT ___full time___
3. wpm ___words per minute___
4. BA ___Bachelor of Arts___

5. exp ___experience___
6. yrs ___years___
7. req ___required___
8. appl ___application___

Pronunciation

Emphasis

Emphasize and elongate words that are important in a sentence:

➤ *Who* is a hard worker?
SILvia is a hard worker.

➤ *What kind of* worker is Silvia?
Silvia is a HARD worker.

C Read the paragraphs below with your classmates and teacher. Practice pronunciation by emphasizing the words and syllables in bold. Then with a partner, decide which job from page 127 is best for each person.

1. **Sil**via is a **hard** worker. She can work **full** time or **part** time. She speaks **Eng**lish well. She can work in an **office** and knows how to **type**.

Job: _Legal assistant_

2. **Tanh** is always on time for **work**. He has a **driver**'s license and knows how to drive a **truck**.

Job: _Driver_

3. **Let**i has **three** children and wants to stay home with them. But she needs to **work**. She can **fix** things around the house and is **very** organized. Her **rent** is **very** expensive.

Job: _Apartment manager_

4. **Ri**go needs a **full**-time position. He **doesn't** have any experience. He wants to learn something **new**.

Job: _Cook_

CD 2
TR 34

D Listen to the people talking about the classified ads on page 127. Write the titles of the jobs they are talking about.

1. _Cashier_

2. _Cook_

3. _Driver_

Presentation 2   15–20 mins.

Go over the pronunciation box with students. Practice the pronunciation with students by choral drill of Exercise C.

C Read the paragraphs below with your classmates and teacher. Practice pronunciation by emphasizing the words and syllables in bold. Then, with a partner, decide which job from page 127 is best for each person.

Practice 2   8–10 mins.

D Listen to the people talking about the classified ads on page 127. Write the titles of the jobs they are talking about.

Play the recording three times. You may choose to play it and stop between listenings if students struggle with this activity.

 Listening Script   *CD 2, Track 34*

Esteban: *Gloria, I really need a job right away. I don't speak a lot of English and don't have much experience, but I know I can work really hard. What do you think I should do?*
Gloria: *Let's look in the newspaper and see what we can find.*
Esteban: *Good idea. I have the Daily News right here.*
Gloria: *Good. Let's find the classified ads and then find the employment section.*
Esteban: *Here it is.*

1. **Esteban:** *Here's one. It says "no experience necessary" and it pays $9 an hour. Maybe I should call them.*

2. **Gloria:** *That sounds great, but you should look at full-time jobs, too. For example, do you type? You could work in an office..*

3. **Esteban:** *No, I don't type. Here's one that says they will train me to cook. I love to eat, so maybe this is the best job for me. Only it doesn't say anything about the pay.*

4. **Gloria:** *Maybe you should be a driver. You can do that job with no problem. You have a driver's license and can follow directions. You work hard, too.*
   Esteban: *That's the job for me. I'm going to apply for the driver position.*

Evaluation 2   7–10 mins.

Be prepared to play the recording again and check students' answers.

Teaching Tip

Scanning

Scanning is a technique that students use to find important information without reading every word. It requires that the reader glance quickly over the reading. To help students practice this skill, make finding information a game in which students see how fast they can find the information you ask for. You might decide to divide the class into two teams and ask a question, such as: *Which position pays $10 an hour?* The first person on either team who raises his or her hand wins a point for the team, provided that the answer is correct.

Instructor's Notes

_____
_____
_____
_____
_____
_____
_____
_____
_____
_____
_____
_____
_____

Presentation 3   7–10 mins. ■■■

E Read the examples for asking
for an application.

Go over the examples in the box with students.
Practice with individuals and make sure students
are ready to go on to Exercise F.

Practice 3   10–15 mins. ■

F With a partner, write a conversation
and share it with the class. Use the phrases
in Exercise E.

Evaluation 3   7–10 mins. ■

Ask volunteers to perform their conversations
in front of the class.

Application   15–20 mins. ■■■

G Interview your partner and complete
the application.

Refer students to *Stand Out 2 Grammar
Challenge*, Unit 7, Challenge 3 for more
practice with using *can* and *may*
to form questions.

Activity Bank

Unit 7, Lesson 3, Worksheet 1: Classified Ads

Unit 7, Lesson 3, Worksheet 2: Application Questions

Unit 7, Lesson 3, Worksheet 3: Job Applications

Unit 7, Lesson 3, Worksheet 4: Job Application Practice

GOAL ➤ **Apply for a job**

E Read the examples for asking for an application.

> Excuse me. I'm interested in a job.   Do you have any openings?
>
> Do you have an application?   Can I have an application, please?
>
> May I have an application, please?

F With a partner, write a conversation and share it with the class. Use the phrases in Exercise E.

G Interview your partner and complete the application.
(Answers will vary.)

Pacific Hotel Application for Employment

PERSONAL INFORMATION

Name: _____   Date: _____

Address: _____

Social Security Number: __XXX-XX-XXXX__   Phone: _____

Postion Applied For: _____

SKILLS

Typing: _____   Computer Skills: _____

Languages: _____

JOB HISTORY

POSITION	COMPANY	FROM	TO	DUTIES
Reason for leaving:				
Reason for leaving:				

Job interviews

GOAL ➤ **Interview for a job**

A Read Dalva's job history.

Languages: _____

JOB HISTORY

POSITION	COMPANY	FROM	TO	DUTIES
Administrative Assistant	Fairview Hotel	December 2007	November 2008	

Reason for leaving: *want to use languages more*

Cashier	La Tostada Restaurant	June 2004	November 2007	

Reason for leaving: *moved*

What is Dalva doing?
Who is she talking to?

B Listen to the conversation and circle *true* or *false*.

CD 2
TR 35

1. Dalva was a cashier at La Tostada Restaurant.   (True)   False

2. Dalva was a desk clerk at the Fairview Hotel.   True   (False)

3. Dalva answered the phone at the Fairview Hotel.   True   (False)

4. Dalva talked to guests at the Fairview Hotel.   True   (False)

C Now read and listen to the conversation. Check your answers to Exercise B.

CD 2
TR 36

Ms. Cardoza: Good afternoon, Ms. Mendes. Please sit down. I have your application here. You were a desk clerk at the Fairview Hotel and before that you were a cashier. Is that right?

Dalva: I was an administrative assistant at the Fairview Hotel. I wasn't a desk clerk.

Ms. Cardoza: Oh, yes, that's right. What kind of work did you do?

Dalva: I checked reservations and typed letters.

Ms. Cardoza: So, you didn't answer the phone or talk to guests?

Dalva: No, I didn't talk to guests, but I learn quickly and speak many languages.

Ms. Cardoza: Did you work in the evenings?

Dalva: No, I didn't work in the evenings. I finished at 6:30 P.M.

Ms. Cardoza: Thank you, Ms. Mendes. We will call you.

AT-A-GLANCE PREP

Objective: Interview for a job
Grammar: Simple past tense
Pronunciation: Regular past tense verbs
Academic Strategies: Focused listening
Vocabulary: *along with, among other things, employee, employer, firm, interviewee, interviewer, prospective*

RESOURCES

Activity Bank: Unit 7, Lesson 4, Worksheets 1–2
Reading and Writing Challenge: Unit 7

Grammar Challenge: Unit 7, Challenge 4
Audio: CD 2, Tracks 35–36
Heinle Picture Dictionary: Documents, pages 42–43

 1.5 hour classes ■ 2.5 hour classes ■ 3⁺ hour classes

AGENDA

Complete an application.
Listen to a job interview.
Read about job interviews.
Review the simple past.
Practice a job interview.

Warm-up and Review   10-15 mins.

Provide students with copies of authentic job applications. You can print a complete application from the Internet or use the worksheet on the Activity Bank CD-ROM (Unit 7, Lesson 3, Worksheet 3). Go over some of the additional information such as references. Ask students to complete a draft. When they have finished or as they are doing the activity, you may choose to correct them and then give them a second application that they can complete in ink and have ready when applying for a job. They can then transfer the information over to the authentic form received from a company.

Introduction   15-20 mins. ■■■

Ask students where they worked before the job they have now, if they have one. Students will often respond with a city. Help them understand that you are asking what the name of the company or business was. As a second question, ask students what their job was, or what they did. Help them remember that when you ask this question, you want them to respond with a job title. Tell them that in a job interview, they may need to talk about past jobs. State the objective: *Today we will learn to interview for a job.*

Presentation 1   15-20 mins. ■■■

Ask students to open their books and to cover up Exercise C.

(A) Read Dalva's job history.

Go over the job history with students and check understanding. Go over the statements in Exercise B and ask them to predict the answers before listening.

Practice 1   10-15 mins. ■■■

(B) Listen to the conversation and circle *True* or *False*.

🎧 **Listening Script**   CD 2, Track 35

The listening script matches the conversation in Exercise C.

Make sure that students have Exercise C covered in their books. This activity will be difficult because students have been used to listening for one or two words that are familiar. This time, they may react early when they hear Mrs. Cardoza ask a question. Students may write the answer before hearing Dalva correct the statements. Play the recording several times and ask students to confirm their answers.

Evaluation 1   10-12 mins.

(C) Now read and listen to the conversation. Check your answers to Exercise B.

🎧 **Listening Script**   CD 2, Track 36

The listening script matches the conversation in Exercise C.

STANDARDS CORRELATIONS

CASAS: 4.1.5, 4.1.7 (See CASAS Competency List on pages 169-175.)
SCANS: **Information** Acquire and evaluate information, organize and maintain information
Basic Skills Reading, writing, listening, speaking
EFF: **Communication** Read with understanding, convey ideas in writing, speak so others can understand, listen actively, observe critically

Reviewing scripts

To reinforce focused listening, you can guide students to the listening scripts in the back of their books. In Exercise B and C, the script is included in the activity. When reviewing the scripts, students will see many words that they may not have understood during the listening. Go over each item. It is also helpful for students to work on intonation and rhythm. If students have access to the recordings, you might suggest that they practice these suprasegmental features outside of class.

Presentation 2   15-20 mins. ◼◼◼

Ask students what makes a good job interview. Draw two columns on the board, one labeled *What to do* and the other labeled *What not to do*. Ask students to help you come up with things for each column. You might ask them, for example, if it is OK to chew gum during a job interview.

D Read about job interviews. Underline the new words.

Ask students to read the paragraph first by themselves, but limit the time they can take to four minutes. Ask them to close their books when they finish so you can see who has finished. Ask some comprehension questions about the reading. This reading is slightly above the students' level. Let students know this, but explain that they will have to read passages like this one in higher levels, so it is a good opportunity to practice a more advanced text. Ask students to open their books and underline the words they are not sure of. Spend time in class discussing each one. Dissuade them from looking at the practice that will follow.

For shorter classes, ask students to do Exercise E for homework.

Practice 2   7-10 mins. ◼◼

 Match the new words with the definitions or examples. Draw lines.

Evaluation 2   5-10 mins. ◼◼

Go over each word and ask students to write the sentences in the paragraph where the word is used.

LESSON **4**   **GOAL** ➤ **Interview for a job**

D Read about job interviews. Underline the new words.

A Successful Job Interview

The job interview is an important step in getting a job. Yes, the application is important—a well-presented application can help you get an interview, but a bad interview means no job! There are many things that interviewers are looking for in an interview. Among other things, the employer wants an employee who has a positive attitude and is confident. The employer knows that a worker with a good attitude will probably work hard and stay on the job.

The prospective employee will show confidence in many ways in the interview. For example, he or she will look the employer in the eye and give a firm handshake. He will speak confidently and listen carefully to the questions. The interviewee will also dress nicely and be prepared for the interview. All of these things—along with no smoking, eating, or chewing gum—will ensure a good interview.

E Match the new words with the definitions or examples. Draw lines.

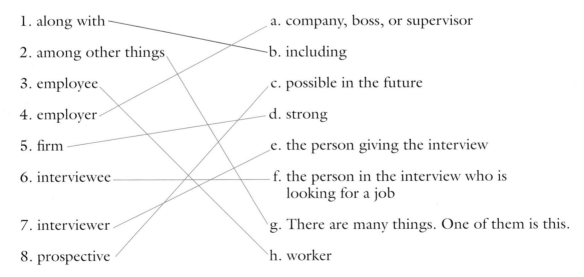

1. along with
2. among other things
3. employee
4. employer
5. firm
6. interviewee
7. interviewer
8. prospective

a. company, boss, or supervisor
b. including
c. possible in the future
d. strong
e. the person giving the interview
f. the person in the interview who is looking for a job
g. There are many things. One of them is this.
h. worker

GOAL ➤ **Interview for a job**

F Study the charts with your classmates and teacher.

Simple Past (Regular)	
Subject	**Past Verb (base + -ed)**
I, he, she, it we, you, they	checked worked cooked

Simple Past: *Be*	
Subject	**Be**
I, he, she, it,	was
we, you, they	were

Negative Simple Past (Regular)		
Subject	***Did + not***	**Base verb**
I, he, she, it, we, you, they	did not (didn't)	check work cook

Negative Simple Past: *Be*	
Subject	***Be + not***
I, he, she, it,	was not (wasn't)
we, you, they	were not (weren't)

G Answer the questions in the negative.

EXAMPLE: Was Dalva a student in 2001?
Dalva _____**wasn't**_____ a student in 2001. She was a student in 2004.

1. Did Dalva move in 2003?
   Dalva _____did not move_____ in 2003. She moved in 2005.

2. Did Dalva work at the Fairmont Hotel?
   Dalva _____did not work_____ at the Fairmont Hotel. She worked at the Fairview Hotel.

3. Did Dalva and Ms. Cardoza talk about the weather?
   Dalva and Ms. Cardoza _____did not talk_____ about the weather. They talked about Dalva's work experience.

4. Were Dalva and Ms. Cardoza at a restaurant?
   Dalva and Ms. Cardoza _____were not_____ at a restaurant. They were at the office.

5. Was Dalva late for the job interview?
   Dalva _____was not_____ late for the interview. She was on time.

H With a partner, write a conversation that is a job interview. Share it with the class.

Presentation 3   10-15 mins. ■■■

F Study the charts with your classmates and teacher.

Be sure to model the pronunciation of regular past tense verbs with students.

For shorter classes, ask students to do Exercise G for homework.

Practice 3   7-10 mins. ■

G Answer the questions in the negative.

Evaluation 3   5-7 mins. ■■■

Ask students to reproduce the sentences from Exercise G on the board and allow students to peer-edit.

Application   20-30 mins. ■■■

H With a partner, write a conversation that is a job interview. Share it with the class.

Refer students to *Stand Out 2 Grammar Challenge*, Unit 7, Challenge 4 for more practice with the simple past tense.

Activity Bank

Unit 7, Lesson 4, Worksheet 1: Simple Past

Unit 7, Lesson 4, Worksheet 2: Employment History

AT-A-GLANCE PREP

Objective: Follow instructions in an office
Grammar: Imperatives
Academic Strategies: Focused listening
Vocabulary: *connect, press, keep, enter, turn on, turn off, record, place*

RESOURCES

Activity Bank: Unit 7, Lesson 5, Worksheets 1–2
Reading and Writing Challenge: Unit 7
Grammar Challenge: Unit 7, Challenge 5

 1.5 hour classes   2.5 hour classes   3⁺ hour classes

Audio: CD 2, Track 37
Heinle Picture Dictionary: Office, pages 154–155

Warm-up and Review   10–15 mins.

Ask students who participated in the previous lesson to practice their new interviews from the application and present them to the class. Teach students appropriate etiquette when their classmates are performing in front of the class. Students should be paying attention and not doing other work or talking.

Introduction   7–10 mins.

Give directions to a few students. For example, ask a student to stand up, walk to the door, open the door, close the door, return to his or her seat, and to sit down. Ask the class to list all the verbs they just heard. Then, ask them to write out the directions. Help students see that, like other directions or instructions they have studied in *Stand Out* (medicine labels, recipes, etc.), the directions begin with an imperative verb. Check to see that every verb starts a new sentence. State the objective: *Today we will learn to follow instructions in an office*

Presentation 1   15–20 mins.

Write the names of several office machines on the board. Discuss what verbs might be included in instructions for these machines. Include words such as *put, open, close, turn on, choose, select*, etc. Don't worry about coming up with complete instructions at this time.

As a class, brainstorm instructions for a copy machine.

(A) Write the correct letter next to each machine in the picture.

Go over the vocabulary and talk in detail about the office picture. Ask questions about the picture to confirm understanding.

Go over the verbs in Exercise B. Ask students in groups to briefly predict the correct order of the statements in Exercise B.

Practice 1   10–15 mins.

(B) Listen to the instructions for the copier. Number the instructions in the correct order.

> 🎧 **Listening Script**   CD 2, Track 37
>
> It is important that you follow the instructions carefully while using this copier. Using the copier in any other way can cause paper jams and many other problems. First, turn on the machine. It will take a few minutes to warm up. Please be patient. Next, place the original on the glass. You will see arrows to direct you where you should place the original. Next, close the lid and then choose the number of copies. If you don't choose anything, it will automatically make one copy. If you choose too many copies, you can cancel and try again. Finally, press the start button and wait for your copies.

Evaluation 1   8–10 mins.

Ask a student to write the statements from Exercise B on the board. Allow students to peer-edit.

> ### STANDARDS CORRELATIONS
>
> *CASAS:* 1.7.3, 4.6.1 (See CASAS Competency List on pages 169–175.)
> *SCANS:* **Information** Acquire and evaluate information
> **Basic Skills** Reading, writing, listening, speaking
> *EFF:* **Communication** Read with understanding, convey ideas in writing, speak so others can understand, listen actively, observe critically

How does it work?

GOAL ➤ Follow instructions in an office

A Write the correct letter next to each machine in the picture.

a. fax machine   c. computer   e. printer

b. answering machine   d. shredder   f. copier

Where is Dalva? What is she doing?

CD 2
TR 37

B Listen to the instructions for the copier. Number the instructions in the correct order.

____4____ Choose the number of copies.

____2____ Place the original on the glass.

____1____ Turn on the machine.

____5____ Press the start button.

____3____ Close the lid.

LESSON **5** **GOAL** ➤ **Follow instructions in an office**

C Identify the machines.

1. _____fax machine_____ 2. _____shredder_____ 3. _____answering machine_____

D Use the words from the box to complete the directions below. Then, write the name of the machine from Exercise C.

Machine: _answering machine_

_____Connect_____ the machine to the phone.

_____Press_____ the button that says *message*.

_____Record_____ your message.

Machine: _____fax machine_____

_____Place_____ the paper in the machine.

_____Enter_____ the number.

_____Press_____ start.

Machine: _____shredder_____

_____Turn on_____ the machine.

_____Place_____ the paper carefully in the slot.

_____Keep_____ your fingers away from the machine.

_____Turn off_____ the machine after the paper is destroyed.

connect
press
keep
enter
turn on
turn off
record
place

Presentation 2   20–30 mins.

C **Identify the machines.**

Look at the pictures with students. As a class, label the machines.

Next, ask students to demonstrate what each word means in the vocabulary box in Exercise D. You might decide to do a charades game. Put each word on a 3-by-5 index card. Have students select a card and pantomime the action.

Practice 2   10–15 mins.

D **Use the words from the box to complete the directions below. Then, write the name of the machine from Exercise C.**

Evaluation 2   7–10 mins.

Go over the answers carefully with students.

Instructor's Notes

_____

_____

_____

_____

_____

_____

_____

_____

_____

_____

_____

_____

_____

_____

_____

_____

_____

_____

_____

_____

_____

_____

_____

_____

_____

_____

_____

_____

_____

_____

Presentation 3   10–12 mins. ■ ■ ■

E **Study the chart with your classmates and teacher.**

Ask students to find the grammar charts on imperatives in the grammar reference section in the back of their books. Also, review the imperative charts in other places in the book (pages 59 and 89).

Practice 3   10–15 mins. ■

F **We use imperatives to give instructions. Write out the directions from page 134. Start a new sentence with every verb.**

Students should write the sentences in paragraph form with periods and uppercase letters at the beginning of sentences.

Evaluation 3   10 mins. ■

Check each student's book as he or she completes the activity.

Application   10–15 mins. ■ ■ ■

G **Talk in a group. Think of another machine (microwave, washing machine, vending machine, etc.). Write instructions on a sheet of paper.**

Refer students to *Stand Out 2 Grammar Challenge*, Unit 7, Challenge 5 for more practice with imperatives.

Activity Bank

Unit 7, Lesson 5, Worksheet 1: Following Instructions
Unit 7, Lesson 5, Worksheet 2: Instruction Strips

E Study the chart with your classmates and teacher.

Imperatives		
	Base verb	**Example sentence**
~~you~~	place enter turn on	**Place** the paper in the machine. **Enter** the number. **Turn on** the computer.

F We use imperatives to give instructions. Write out the instructions from page 134. Start a new sentence with every verb.

EXAMPLE:

Copier Instructions

Turn on the machine. Place the original on the glass. Close
the lid. Choose the number of copies. Press the start button.

Shredder Instructions

Turn on the machine. Place paper carefully in the slot. Be careful
not to put your hands near the blades.

Fax Machine Instructions

Place paper in the tray. Enter the appropriate phone number.
Press "enter."

G Talk in a group. Think of another machine (microwave, washing machine, vending machine, etc.). Write instructions on a sheet of paper.

Review

JOB HISTORY

Position	Company	From	To
Computer Programmer	Datamix Computers	June 2006	Present
Assembly Worker	Datamix Computers	May 2004	June 2006

Youssouf Fosso

 A Read the information about Youssouf above. Complete the sentences with the correct negative or affirmative form of the verb in parentheses. (Lesson 4)

1. Youssouf _____ did not work _____ (work) at Datamix Computers in 2003.

2. Youssouf _____ was _____ (be) an assembly worker at Datamix Computers in 2005.

3. Youssouf _____ started _____ (start) his first job at Datamix in May 2004.

4. Youssouf _____ was not _____ (be) a programmer from May 2004 to June 2006.

5. Youssouf _____ did not change _____ (change) his job in May 2006.

SKILLS

Typing: 35 wpm

Computer Skills: Advanced programming, knowledge of many software programs

Languages: French – bilingual (fluent in reading, writing, listening, and speaking)

 B Write sentences about what Youssouf can and can't do. (Lesson 2)

1. speak French _____ Youssouf can speak French. _____

2. speak Spanish _____ Youssouf can't speak Spanish. _____

3. type 50 wpm _____ Youssouf can't type 50 wpm. _____

4. use the computer _____ Youssouf can use the computer. _____

Objective: All unit objectives
Grammar: All unit grammar
Academic Strategies: Focused listening, reviewing, evaluating, developing study skills
Vocabulary: All unit vocabulary

■ 1.5 hour classes ■ 2.5 hour classes ■ 3⁺ hour classes

AGENDA
Discuss unit objectives.
Complete the review.
Do My Dictionary.
Evaluate and reflect on progress.

Warm-up and Review   10–15 mins. ■■■

With their books closed, ask students to help you make a list on the board of all the vocabulary they can come up with from the unit. Then, have a competition where students in groups will write page numbers for each item on the list. The first group to have the correct page number for each item wins.

Introduction   5 mins. ■■■

Write all the objectives on the board from Unit 7. Show students the first page of the unit and say the five objectives. Explain that today they will review the whole unit.

Note: Depending on the length of the term, you may decide to have students do Presentation 1 and Practice 1 for homework and then review student work as either the warm-up or another class activity.

Presentation 1   10–15 mins. ■■■

This presentation will cover the first three pages of the review. Quickly go to the first page of each lesson. Discuss the objective of each. Ask simple questions to remind students of what they have learned.

Practice 1   15–20 mins. ■■■

 Read the information about Youssouf above. Complete the sentences with the correct negative or affirmative form of the verb in parentheses. (Lesson 4)

 Write sentences about what Youssouf can and can't do. (Lesson 2)

Teaching Tip

Recycling/Review

The review and the project that follows are part of the recycling/review process. Students at this level often need to be reintroduced to concepts to solidify what they have learned. Many concepts are learned and forgotten while learning other new concepts. This is because students learn but are not necessarily ready to acquire language concepts.

Therefore, it becomes very important to review and to show students how to review on their own. It is also important to recycle the new concepts in different contexts.

STANDARDS CORRELATIONS

CASAS: 1.7.3, 4.1.1, 4.1.2, 4.1.3, 4.1.5, 4.1.6, 4.1.7, 4.1.8, 4.4.2, 4.5.1, 4.6.1, 4.7.3 (See CASAS Competency List on pages 169–175.)
SCANS: **Information** Acquire and evaluate information, organize and maintain information

Basic Skills Reading, writing, speaking
Personal Qualities Responsibility, self management
EFF: **Communication** Speak so others can understand
Lifelong Learning Take responsibility for learning, reflect and evaluate

Practice 1 (*continued*)

C Identify the machines. (Lesson 5)

D Match the correct verb with the instruction. (Lesson 5)

E Complete the sentences with the future (*will*) affirmative and negative. (Lesson 1)

C Identify the machines. (Lesson 5)

1. ____fax machine____   2. _____shredder_____   3. _answering machine_

D Match the correct verb with the instruction. (Lesson 5)

__c__ 1. Press   a. the paper in the machine.

__a__ 2. Place   b. the number.

__b__ 3. Enter   c. start.

E Complete the sentences with the future (*will*) affirmative and negative. (Lesson 1)

1. I _____will come_____ (come) to work on time every day.

2. We _____will not eat_____ (eat) in class.

3. They _____will not play_____ (play) basketball in class.

4. I _____will work_____ (work) with a partner.

5. You _____will do_____ (do) the homework every day.

6. They _____will have_____ (have) a good attitude.

7. She _____will not sleep_____ (sleep) in class.

8. Dalva _____will like_____ (like) this class.

Review

F Write the name of the job under the picture. (Lesson 2)

1. _____mechanic_____

2. _____custodian_____

3. _____delivery person_____

4. _____carpenter_____

5. _____office worker_____

6. _____homemaker_____

G Read the classified ads. Complete the chart below. (Lesson 3)

1.
Help Wanted
Full-time custodian
John Adams School
$10 an hour
Benefits
No experience needed.

2.
Help Wanted
PT Mechanic,
$15.00 an hour,
1 yr. exp.
Apply at 2324 Johnson Street.

3.
Help Wanted
Nurse,
Mayfield Hospital.
FT, Tuesday thru Saturday.
AA degree and 1 year
experience req.

Position	Salary	Experience	Part-time/Full-time
1. custodian	$10/hr.	none	full-time
2. mechanic	$15/hr.	1 year	part-time
3. nurse	not given	1 year	full-time

Practice 1 (*continued*)

F Write the name of the job under the picture. (Lesson 2)

G Read the classified ads. Complete the chart below. (Lesson 3)

Evaluation 1

15 mins.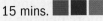

Go around the room and check on students' progress. Help individuals when needed. If you see consistent errors among several students, interrupt the class and give a mini lesson or review to help students feel comfortable with the concept.

Activity Bank

Unit 7: Computer Worksheets

Unit 7: Internet Worksheets

Presentation 2 7–10 mins.

My Dictionary

Go over the steps of My Dictionary as a class.

Practice 2 5–7 mins.

Do the dictionary activity as a class before students work on their own for at least the first few units of the book to ensure that students understand what to do.

Evaluation 2 5 mins.

Ask students to share their cards.

Presentation 3 5 mins.

Learner Log

Review the concepts of the Learner Log. Make sure students understand the concepts and how to complete the log including circling the answers, finding page numbers where the concept is taught, and ranking favorite activities.

Teaching Tip

Learner Logs

Learner Logs function to help students in many different ways.

1. They serve as part of the review process.
2. They help students to gain confidence and to document what they have learned. Consequently, students see that they are progressing in their learning.
3. They provide students with a tool that they can use over and over to check and recheck their understanding of the target language. In this way, students become independent learners.

Practice 3 10–15 mins.

Ask students to complete the Learner Log.

Evaluation 3 2 mins.

Go over the Learner Log with students.

Application 5–7 mins.

Ask students to record their favorite lesson or page in the unit.

Assessment

Use the Stand Out 2 Assessment CD-ROM with Exam*View*® to create a posttest for Unit 7.

Refer students to *Stand Out 2 Grammar Challenge*, Unit 7, Extension Challenge 1 for more practice with spelling and the regular past tense and Extension Challenge 2 for more practice with irregular verbs in the simple past.

Instructor's Notes

_____
_____
_____
_____
_____
_____
_____
_____
_____
_____
_____
_____
_____
_____
_____
_____
_____
_____
_____
_____

My Dictionary

Make flash cards to improve your vocabulary.

1. Choose four new words from this unit.

2. Write each word on an index card or on a sheet of paper.

3. On the back of the index card or paper, draw a picture, find and write a sentence from the book with the word, and write the page number.

4. Study the words.

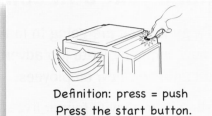

Definition: press = push
<u>Press</u> the start button.
page 133

Learner Log

Circle how well you learned each item and write the page number where you learned it.

1. I can identify good study skills.

   Yes   Maybe   No   Page _____

2. I can identify work skills.

   Yes   Maybe   No   Page _____

3. I can read classified ads and apply for a job.

   Yes   Maybe   No   Page _____

4. I can interview for a job.

   Yes   Maybe   No   Page _____

5. I can follow written instructions.

   Yes   Maybe   No   Page _____

Rank what you like to do best from 1 to 6. 1 is your favorite activity. Your teacher will help you.

_____ Practice listening

_____ Practice speaking

_____ Practice reading

_____ Practice writing

_____ Learn new words

_____ Learn grammar

In the next unit, I want to practice more

_____.

Team Project

Make your own company.

In a group, you are going to make a new company, write job advertisements, and interview new employees.

1. Form a team with four or five students. In your team, you need:

POSITION	JOB	STUDENT NAME
Student 1: **Team Leader**	See that everyone speaks English. See that everyone participates.	
Student 2: **Recruiter**	Write a classified ad with help from the team.	
Student 3: **Designer**	Prepare an application form with help from the team.	
Students 4/5: **Interviewers**	Prepare interview questions with help from the team.	

2. You are the owners of a new company. What is the name of your company? What kind of company is it?

3. What job are you going to advertise? What information will you put in the advertisement?

4. What questions will you have on the application form? What questions will you ask at the job interview?

5. Interview four students for your job.

6. Decide who you will hire and present your work to the class.

Introduction   5 mins.

Team Project

Make your own company.

In this project, teams will form a committee to hire an individual. Teams will create the company, write a classified ad for a job opening, prepare an application form, and prepare interview questions. Students perform the interviews by having individuals from other groups apply for jobs. At the end of the interviews, the group chooses whom they will hire. There is a template on the Activity Bank CD-ROM for a classified ad page (Lesson 7, Project, Worksheet 1). If you like, put the classified ads on a simulated newspaper page to pass out to students. This can be a two-day project.

Stage 1   10–15 mins.

Form a team of four or five students.

Help students form groups and assign positions in their groups. On the spot, students will have to choose who will be the leader of their group. Review the responsibility of the leader and ask students to write the name of their leader in their books. Do the same with the remaining positions: recruiter, designer, and interviewers.

Explain that all students should work on every task. Students shouldn't go to the next stage until the previous one is complete.

Stage 2   5–10 mins.

You are the owners of a new company. What is the name of your company? What kind of company is it?

Have students answer the two questions as they come up with ideas.

Stage 3   15–20 mins.

What job are you going to advertise? What information will you put in the advertisement?

Have students write a classified ad.

Stage 4   40–50 mins.

What questions will you have on the application form? What questions will you ask at the job interview?

Have students create an application form for the position and write interview questions. If there isn't enough time for students to create a job application, they can use the one available on the Activity Bank CD-ROM (Unit 7, Lesson 3, Worksheet 3).

Stages 5 and 6   15–20 mins.

Interview four students for your job. Decide who you will hire and present your work to the class.

Have students perform the interviews. After students have formed small groups, visit each one. Pretend you are looking for a job and have groups interview you. Be sure to follow good interviewing standards: don't sit until asked, shake hands, make eye contact, and so on.

Send one student from each group to another for an interview. Give them three minutes and then ask them to return to their group. Repeat this process until each student has had the opportunity to be interviewed.

Ask the groups to announce whom they will hire.

Activity Bank

Unit 7, Project, Worksheet 1: Daily News Classifieds

Unit 7, Project, Worksheet 2: Job Application

Unit 7, Extension, Worksheet 1: Negative Simple Past

STANDARDS CORRELATIONS

CASAS: 1.7.3, 4.1.1, 4.1.2, 4.1.3, 4.1.5, 4.1.6, 4.1.7, 4.1.8, 4.4.2, 4.5.1, 4.6.1, 4.7.3 (See CASAS Competency List on pages 169–175.)
SCANS: **Resources** Allocate time, allocate materials and facility resources, allocate human resources
Information Acquire and evaluate information, organize and maintain information, interpret and communicate information, use computers to process information
Interpersonal Participate as a member of a team, teach others, exercise leadership, negotiate to arrive at a decision, work with cultural diversity
Systems Understand systems, monitor and correct performance, improve and design systems

Basic Skills Reading, writing, listening, speaking
Thinking Skills Think creatively, make decisions, solve problems, see things in the mind's eye
Personal Qualities Responsibility, sociability, self management
EFF: **Communication** Read with understanding, convey ideas in writing, speak so others can understand, listen actively, observe critically
Decision Making: Solve problems and make decisions, plan
Interpersonal: Cooperate with others, advocate and influence, resolve conflict and negotiate, guide others
Lifelong Learning: Take responsibility for learning, reflect and evaluate

AT-A-GLANCE PREP

Objective: Identify goals
Grammar: Future plans with *want to, hope to, plan to,* and *be going to*
Academic Strategies: Focused listening, predicting
Vocabulary: *goals, success, graduate, to become*

RESOURCES

Activity Bank: Unit 8, Lesson 1, Worksheets 1–3
Reading and Writing Challenge: Unit 8
Grammar Challenge: Unit 8, Challenge 1

■ 1.5 hour classes ■ 2.5 hour classes ■ 3⁺ hour classes

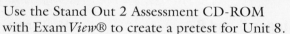

AGENDA

Rank what is important to you.
Read and answer questions.
Listen to identify goals.
Talk about the future.
Write about the future.

Audio: CD 2, Track 38
Heinle Picture Dictionary: Life Events, pages 30–31

Stand Out 2 Assessment CD-ROM with Exam*View*®

 Preassessment (optional) ■■■

Use the Stand Out 2 Assessment CD-ROM with Exam*View*® to create a pretest for Unit 8.

Warm-up and Review   10–15 mins. ■■■

Write *one million dollars* on the board and ask students if they would do things differently if they had a lot of money. Ask them to answer the following questions in groups:

1. Would you quit your job?
2. Would you buy a new house?
3. Would you put the money in the bank and live the same as you do now?
4. Would you spend all the money on things you need?

You may need to have a short discussion on the use of the conditional, but this is not the focus of the lesson and this structure is studied in another level. The purpose here is to get students talking about values so they can set reasonable goals for themselves based on things they believe in.

Introduction   3 mins. ■■■

Write the word *goal* on the board. Ask students what a goal is. See if any student has a goal he or she would like to share. State the objective: *Today we will identify goals.*

Presentation 1   10–15 mins. ■■■

Ask students to open their books and discuss the pictures on the page. Ask what they think the pictures mean.

 Rank what is most important to you. Number the items from 1 to 6. Number 1 is the most important to you.

This task may be difficult for some students because they may not have thought about their values in this way, or they may be concerned about what the "right" answer is. Help them understand that everyone is different. You might also suggest that their values can change over time. Ask them what they think the ranking for a teenage daughter or son might be.

Discuss students' rankings as a class. Don't place your own values above students' values. At this point, you may decide not to share your ranking so students are not influenced by your ideas.

Practice 1   10–15 mins. ■■■

 Read about what is important to Marie.

Have students read the paragraph on their own. Give them three minutes. Then, ask them to discuss the paragraph by doing Exercise C.

 In a group, rank what you think is important to Marie. Then, share your ideas with another group.

Evaluation 1   7–10 mins. ■■■

Ask comprehension questions about the reading. Ask students to share their ideas from Exercise C. Then, discuss how the answers compare with their personal answers in Exercise A.

STANDARDS CORRELATIONS

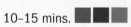

CASAS: 4.4.5, 7.1.1, 7.5.1 (See CASAS Competency List on pages 169–175.)
SCANS: **Information** Acquire and evaluate information, organize and maintain information, interpret and communicate information
Basic Skills Reading, writing, listening, speaking
Thinking Skills See things in the mind's eye

Personal Qualities Responsibility, self management
EFF: **Communication** Read with understanding, convey ideas in writing, speak so others can understand, listen actively, observe critically
Decision Making Solve problems and make decisions, plan
Lifelong Learning Take responsibility for learning, reflect and evaluate

UNIT 8

Goals and Lifelong Learning

GOALS

➤ Identify goals
➤ Set academic goals
➤ Set work goals

➤ Find ways to learn
➤ Record goals

LESSON **1**

What is success?

GOAL ➤ Identify goals

What is success? Some people think success is a good job and a lot of money. Others say it is love and family. What is success to you?

A Rank what is most important to you. Number the items from 1 to 6. Number 1 is the most important to you. (Answers will vary.)

_____ family   _____ employment   _____ money
_____ friends   _____ entertainment   _____ education

B Read about what is important to Marie.

My career is most important to me. I plan to study nursing and work part time as a home health-care aide. Then, I am going to get my degree in nursing and become a registered nurse— at least, this is my plan. I will save some money because I want to get married soon. My boyfriend's name is Jean. After we get married, we plan to have children. Maybe there will be money to go to the movies sometimes, too. I will work hard to make my plans happen.

C In a group, rank what you think is important to Marie. Then, share your ideas with another group. (Answers will vary.)

_____ family   _____ employment   _____ money
_____ friends   _____ entertainment   _____ education

GOAL ➤ **Identify goals**

Where is Lien?
What is she doing?

D Look at the goals below. Predict the goals you think are Lien's.

☑ buy a house	☑ get a job	☑ study English
☑ move	❏ keep a job	❏ participate in child's school
❏ get married	❏ learn new skills at work	☑ get a high school diploma
❏ have children	❏ get a promotion	☑ go to college
❏ become a citizen	☑ get a better job	☑ graduate from college

  E Listen to Lien's story. In the list above, check (✔) what Lien wants to do.

CD 2
TR 38

 F Look at Lien's goals. Write them in the correct box.

Personal and family

Lien wants to buy a house.
She wants to move to a safer place.

Vocational (Work)

Lien wants to become a counselor.
She wants to get a better job.

Academic (Educational)

She wants to study English.
Lien wants to get her high school diploma.

Presentation 2   10-15 mins. ■■ ■

Write *success* on the board. Ask students what success means to them. Does it mean a good family, a good job, a good education, or a combination of the three?

Ask students to look at the picture and answer the questions about Lien. Prepare students to do the listening by discussing the meaning of all the choices in Exercise D.

D **Look at the goals below. Predict the goals you think are Lien's.**

Do this activity as a class to make sure students understand the vocabulary and are ready for the listening.

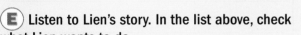

Teaching Tip

Predicting

Predicting is a strategy for reading, or in this case, listening. Students predict and, therefore, begin thinking of the vocabulary they are soon to hear or read. It allows them to focus their attention on the important parts of the story, discourse, or information that they will encounter.

Practice 2   10-15 mins. ■■

E **Listen to Lien's story. In the list above, check what Lien wants to do.**

Be prepared to play the recording three times. Play it once and ask students to discuss it together. Next, play it again and ask them to discuss it again. As they listen the third time, they will confirm their answers.

 Listening Script   *CD 2, Track 38*

My name is Lien Bui. I am from Vietnam. I came to the United States two years ago. I have many plans for my education, and I want to do many things in the future. My goal is to be a counselor for adults. Maybe I can work in an adult school or a college in the future. Right now, I want to speak English better. Also, I want a better job. Right now, I work at night and I am very tired all the time, so I don't like my job. I plan to get my high school diploma and then, I want to go to college to study counseling. I need to attend a university to be a counselor. When I graduate, I want to get a good job. I want to keep that job and maybe buy a house or condo with the money I earn because I don't like my neighborhood now. The streets are dirty and dangerous. I want to move to a safer place when I get a new job and enough money. I don't know if I'm going to get married or become a U.S. citizen, but I know I need a good education.

Evaluation 2   7-10 mins. ■ ■

 Look at Lien's goals. Write them in the correct box.

Do this activity as a class. Refer to the listening scripts in the back of the student book to verify the answers.

Presentation 3   10-15 mins. ■■■

Explain that there are various ways of expressing the future in English. Ask students what their hopes are for the future.

G Study the charts with your classmates and teacher.

This chart is a bit complicated for this level only because it is difficult to pinpoint exactly how definite someone is about his or her plans. Tell students that *hope, want,* and *plan* mean slightly different things to different people, but they all serve to express the future. *Will* will be discussed in subsequent lessons, so there is no need to introduce it here; however, it is likely that a student might ask about it. You can explain to them that *will* is more definite than *going to*.

For shorter classes, ask students to do Exercise H for homework.

Practice 3   7-10 mins. ■

H Complete the sentences with the correct forms of the verbs expressing future plans.

Evaluation 3   7-10 mins. ■

Ask students to write the completed sentences on the board and to peer-edit if necessary.

Application   10-15 mins. ■■■

I Write two future plans for you and a partner.

Students will have ample time to write goals. They may write some here, but it isn't necessary at this time.

 Refer students to *Stand Out 2 Grammar Challenge*, Unit 8, Challenge 1 for more practice with future infinitives and *going to*.

Activity Bank

Unit 8, Lesson 1, Worksheet 1: Setting Goals

Unit 8, Lesson 1, Worksheet 2: Infinitives

Unit 8, Lesson 1, Worksheet 3: *Going to*

Instructor's Notes

GOAL ➤ **Identify goals**

G Study the charts with your classmates and teacher.

Future Plans: *Want to, Hope to, Plan to*		
Subject	**Verb**	**Infinitive (*to* + base)**
I, you, we, they	hope, want, plan	to study in school for three years
he, she	hopes, wants, plans	to graduate from college to get married

Future Plans: *Be going to*		
Subject	***Be going to***	**Base verb**
I	am going to	get a high school diploma
you, we, they	are going to	participate in class
he, she	is going to	buy a house

want to	*hope to*	*plan to*	*be going to*
less definite ◄——————————————————————► more definite			

H Complete the sentences with the correct forms of the verbs expressing future plans.

1. Lien and Marie _____**want to speak**_____ (want / speak) English.

2. I _____**plan to come**_____ (plan / come) to class on time every day.

3. Marie _____**hopes to be**_____ (hope / be) a nurse some day.

4. Lien _____**is going to graduate**_____ (be going to / graduate) from a university very soon.

5. Marco and I _____**plan to visit**_____ (plan / visit) Mexico in the future.

6. They _____**want to move**_____ (want / move), but they have a three-year lease.

7. You _____**are going to get**_____ (be going to / get) married soon, right?

8. Lien _____**hopes to have**_____ (hope / have) children some day.

I Write two future plans for you and a partner. (Answers will vary.)

My future plans

_____

_____

My partner's future plans

_____

_____

LESSON 2 Education in the United States

GOAL ➤ Set academic goals

Vocabulary | **Grammar**
Life Skills
Academic | **Pronunciation**

A Discuss the pie chart with your classmates and teacher.

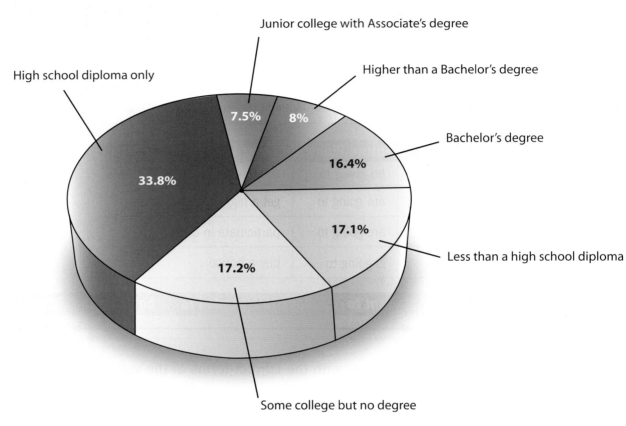

Junior college with Associate's degree

Higher than a Bachelor's degree

High school diploma only

7.5%   8%

Bachelor's degree

16.4%

33.8%

17.1%

Less than a high school diploma

17.2%

Some college but no degree

B Practice reading the pie chart and expressing decimals.

EXAMPLE: *Student A:* What percentage of people in the United States has less than a high school diploma?
Student B: Seventeen point one percent.

C Write one academic goal that you have. Use the ideas on page 142 and one of the ways to express future plans on page 143.

My academic goal

AT-A-GLANCE PREP

Objective: Set academic goals
Grammar: Use of *because*
Academic Strategies: Reading a pie chart, note taking, scanning
Vocabulary: *BA, MA, residence, GED,* academic vocabulary

RESOURCES

Activity Bank: Unit 8, Lesson 2, Worksheets 1–2
Reading and Writing Challenge: Unit 8
Grammar Challenge: Unit 8, Challenge 2

Audio: CD 2, Track 39
Heinle Picture Dictionary: Life Events, pages 30–31

■ 1.5 hour classes   ■ 2.5 hour classes   ■ 3+ hour classes

Warm-up and Review   15-20 mins. ■■■

Review page 142. Discuss all the possible goals in Exercise D again. Write *Personal and Family, Vocational,* and *Academic* as headings for three columns on the board. Ask students to work in groups to categorize all of the goals. You may use the three-column template in the template folder on the Activity Bank CD-ROM to facilitate this task. It is important to only have one handout for each group to encourage group work over individual work. Each group has a writer or recorder. Ask the groups when they finish to share with the class in a class discussion.

Introduction   5-7 mins. ■■■

Ask students if they plan on continuing school after they learn English. Write *BA, MA,* and *PhD* on the board. Ask students if they know what these abbreviations mean. State the objective: *Today we will learn about education in the United States and learn to set academic goals.*

Presentation 1   15-20 mins. ■■■

Draw a circle on the board and divide it into four equal parts. Write 25% in each piece of the pie. Show students how 25% is the same as 25/100 or 25 out of 100. Depending on the needs of the class, you may show them how to figure out a percentage when the total is not 100.

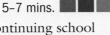 **A** Discuss the pie chart with your classmates and teacher.

Ask students to study the pie chart. Go over the new vocabulary. You can also diagram the higher education process on the board if you have time. Continue discussing the chart by asking questions. Alternate describing the numbers as percentages and with words. For example, sometimes say 8%, and sometimes say *8 out of 100.*

Practice 1   10-15 mins. ■■■

 B Practice reading the pie chart and expressing decimals.

Ask students to practice with a partner.

C Write one academic goal that you have. Use the ideas on page 142 and one of the ways to express future plans on page 143.

Briefly discuss the information on pages 142 and 143 as needed.

Evaluation 1   5-7 mins. ■■■

Observe students speaking. Ask them to share their academic goals with the class.

STANDARDS CORRELATIONS

CASAS: 4.4.5, 7.1.1, 7.5.1 (See CASAS Competency List on pages 169-175.)
SCANS: Information Acquire and evaluate information, organize and maintain information, interpret and communicate information
Systems Understand systems
Basic Skills Reading, writing, listening, speaking
Thinking Skills Make decisions, solve problems, see things in the mind's eye

Personal Qualities Responsibility, self management
EFF: Communication Read with understanding, convey ideas in writing, speak so others can understand, listen actively, observe critically
Decision Making Solve problems and make decisions, plan
Lifelong Learning Take responsibility for learning, reflect and evaluate

Presentation 2   15-20 mins.

Ask students to close their books and listen to information about degrees and opportunities in the United States

Ask students to listen for and list the different degrees and diplomas mentioned.

Teaching Tip

Note taking

Students will do more note taking in the next levels. This is a difficult skill because learners will need to separate what is important from what isn't. We have prepared students for note taking in Book 2 by giving them a framework. Here, we merely ask them to identify the broadest topic. If you think students are ready for more, play the recording three times and ask them for one piece of information about each opportunity.

Now, ask students to open their books and look over the information in print. Go over any new vocabulary.

(D) Listen and discuss the educational choices adults have in the United States.

 Listening Script   CD 2, Track 39

> In adult schools, you can learn English, but many students decide to go on and study more after they learn a little English. For example, some adult schools have high school classes and you can earn a high school diploma. Other adult schools have classes to help you prepare for a test. If you pass the test, you earn a GED, or General Equivalency Diploma. This diploma is similar to a high school diploma. Certificates for specific trades like nursing, computer programming, and mechanics can be earned from trade schools, some junior colleges, and some adult schools. This is called an Associate of Art or an Associate of Science Degree. Adults earn this degree from a two-year junior or community college. This is called a Bachelor of Arts or Bachelor of Science Degree. Adults earn this degree from a four-year college or university. After earning a Bachelor's Degree, adults can study more and receive additional degrees.

For shorter classes, ask students to do Exercise E for homework.

Practice 2   10-15 mins.

(E) Work with a partner. Circle *true* or *false* for each statement.

Evaluation 2   3-5 mins.

Go over Exercise E and discuss the implications of the statements.

LESSON 2   **GOAL** ➤ **Set academic goals**

CD 2
TR 39

D Listen and discuss the educational choices adults have in the United States.

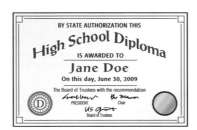

High School Diploma	**Certificates**	**BA/BS Degree**
Some adult schools have high school classes and you can earn a high school diploma.	Certificates for specific trades like nursing, computer programming, and mechanics can be earned from trade schools, some junior colleges, and some adult schools.	This is called a Bachelor of Arts or a Bachelor of Science degree. Adults earn this degree from a four-year college or university.
GED	**AA/AS Degree**	**Graduate Degree**
Some adult schools have classes to help you prepare for a test. If you pass the test, you earn a GED, or General Equivalency Diploma. This diploma is similar to a high school diploma.	This is called an Associate of Art or an Associate of Science degree. Adults earn this degree from a two-year junior or community college.	After earning a Bachelor's degree, adults can study more and receive additional degrees.

E Work with a partner. Circle *true* or *false* for each statement.

1. It is necessary to have a BA or a BS before you can get a graduate degree.   (True) False

2. You can receive a high school diploma from some adult schools.   (True) False

3. AA degrees are from four-year schools.   True (False)

4. You can earn a GED in high school.   True (False)

5. You can earn a certificate in trade schools.   (True) False

6. You can earn a Bachelor's Degree from any adult school or college.   True (False)

F Read about the different types of schools.

what you need to know...

Adult Schools

These schools are sometimes free. Students learn basic skills like reading and writing. They can learn about jobs and computers. These schools can help students get their GED.

Junior Colleges/Community Colleges

These schools are not expensive for residents. They offer two-year academic, technical, and vocational courses. They help students prepare for universities or jobs. Students can study part time in the evenings or on the weekends.

what you need to know...

Colleges/Universities

These schools prepare students for jobs and careers. They are often very expensive. They offer four-year academic courses.

Trade Schools

These schools are sometimes expensive. They help students learn job-related skills, such as computers or mechanics.

G Match the questions with the answers. Write the correct letter next to each question.

1. __b__ Why is it good to get a high school diploma?
2. __c__ Why do people go to a two-year college?
3. __d__ Why do people go to a university?
4. __a__ Why do people go to an adult school?

a. to learn to read and write English or to get a GED
b. to get a better job or prepare to go to a two-year college or university
c. to get an Associate's Degree, to get a better job, or to prepare to go to a university
d. to qualify for a career or to get a Bachelor's Degree

H Study the chart with your classmates and teacher.

Because			
Statement	**Reason**		
	Because	**Subject + verb**	**Information**
Marie plans to go to college	**because**	she wants	to be a nurse
Lien hopes to learn English better		she plans	to go to college

I Create two sentences from Exercise G. Write them on a sheet of paper.

J Write an academic goal. Use *because* and write why you want to reach this goal.

My academic goal

Presentation 3 20-30 mins. ■ ■ ■

Ask students to close their books and discuss again the school system for adults in the United States.

Ask students to list the types of schools.

F **Read about the different types of schools.**

Allow students to read the information first and then, ask comprehension questions about the different schools. Allow students to scan for information.

G **Match the questions with the answers. Write the correct letter next to each question.**

Do this activity as a class to help students understand the information in the reading.

H **Study the chart with your classmates and teacher.**

Go over the grammar box and prepare students for the practice. Make sure students understand that generally we don't use commas before *because*. Also, point out that *because* is usually followed by a subject and verb.

For shorter classes, ask students to do Exercise I for homework.

Practice 3 10-15 mins. ■

I **Create two sentences from Exercise G. Write them on a sheet of paper.**

Evaluation 3 10 mins. ■

Have volunteers write their sentences on the board. Go over the sentences as a class.

Application 10-15 mins. ■ ■ ■

J **Write an academic goal. Use *because* and write why you want to reach this goal.**

Teaching Tip

SMART goals

At this level, students need to start exploring why they make goals and how to make goals that are useful and achievable. Consider the SMART goal technique when discussing goals with students. It suggests that goals should be **s**pecific, **m**easurable, **a**ttainable, **r**easonable, and **t**imely.

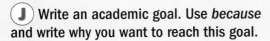Refer students to *Stand Out 2 Grammar Challenge*, Unit 8, Challenge 2 for more practice with *because* and adverbial clauses.

Activity Bank

Templates: Three-Column Chart

Unit 8, Lesson 2, Worksheet 1: U.S. Schools

Unit 8, Lesson 2, Worksheet 2: Sentence Strips—
Schools

Instructor's Notes

_____
_____
_____
_____
_____
_____
_____
_____
_____
_____
_____
_____
_____
_____
_____
_____
_____
_____
_____
_____
_____
_____

Objective: Set work goals
Grammar: Future with *will*
Pronunciation: Emphatic statements
Academic Strategies: Listening for the main idea, focused listening, Venn diagrams
Vocabulary: *time lines, counselor, career*

RESOURCES

Activity Bank: Unit 8, Lesson 3, Worksheet 1
Reading and Writing Challenge: Unit 8
Grammar Challenge: Unit 8, Challenge 3

Audio: CD 2, Tracks 40–41
Heinle Picture Dictionary: Life Events, pages 30–31

■ 1.5 hour classes ■ 2.5 hour classes ■ 3⁺ hour classes

AGENDA

Discuss the U.S. educational system.
Read about Lien.
Learn how to use will *for the future.*
Compare Lien's and Marie's goals.
Discuss Mario's goals.
Write personal work goals.

Warm-up and Review   10–15 mins. ■■■

Ask students to describe the educational systems in their countries and compare them to those in the United States. Have them refer to pages 145 and 146. Ask them to first discuss in groups and then to share their ideas with the class.

Introduction   5–7 mins. ■■■

Review Exercise J on page 146. Ask students to share some of their goals and the reasons for the goals. Note the ones that have work-related reasons. State the objective: *Today we will set work goals.*

Presentation 1   30–40 mins. ■■■

 Listen to and then read about Lien's work goals.

With books closed, ask students to listen to the paragraph about Lien and her goals. Ask students to identify the main idea and then ask comprehension questions. Ask students to open their books and look at the picture of Lien.

🎧 **Listening Script**   CD 2, Track 40

The listening script matches the paragraph in Exercise A.

Read the paragraph as a class. Ask students to underline any words they don't understand. Discuss the new vocabulary as a class. Ask additional comprehension questions and study the time line. Tell students that eventually they will make their own time lines.

Practice 1   5–7 mins. ■■■

 Study the chart and then talk about Lien's plans with a partner.

Evaluation 1   5–7 mins. ■■■

Ask individuals the same questions as in the practice.

STANDARDS CORRELATIONS

CASAS: 4.4.5 (See CASAS Competency List on pages 169–175.)
SCANS: **Resources** Allocate time
Information Acquire and evaluate information, organize and maintain information, interpret and communicate information
Basic Skills Reading, writing, listening, speaking
Thinking Skills See things in the mind's eye

Personal Qualities Responsibility, self management
EFF: **Communication** Read with understanding, convey ideas in writing, speak so others can understand, listen actively, observe critically
Decision Making Plan
Lifelong Learning Take responsibility for learning, reflect and evaluate

Workplace goals

GOAL ▶ Set work goals

CD 2
TR 40

A Listen to and then read about Lien's work goals.

Lien has many goals. She wants to have a career. She wants to be a counselor in an adult school or a college because she wants to help people. She needs to go to school for many years to study, but first she needs to learn English. She will go to Clear Mountain Adult School for two more years. She is going to learn English and get a GED. Lien also needs to work. She needs a part-time job now, and later she plans to work at a school for more experience.

What is Lien holding?
Why is she happy?

B Study the chart and then talk about Lien's plans with a partner.

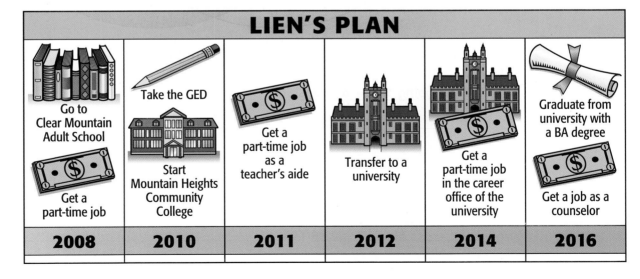

LIEN'S PLAN					
Go to Clear Mountain Adult School / Get a part-time job	Take the GED / Start Mountain Heights Community College	Get a part-time job as a teacher's aide	Transfer to a university	Get a part-time job in the career office of the university	Graduate from university with a BA degree / Get a job as a counselor
2008	**2010**	**2011**	**2012**	**2014**	**2016**

EXAMPLE: *Student A:* What does Lien want to do in 2008?
Student B: She plans to get a part-time job.

LESSON 3

GOAL ➤ **Set work goals**

 Study the chart with your classmates and teacher.

Future: *Will*			
Subject	***Will***	**Base verb**	**Information**
I, you, he, she, it, we, they	will	go	to school for two more years
		study	English this year

	want to	*hope to*	*plan to*	*be going to*	*will*	
less definite	←———————————————————————→					more definite

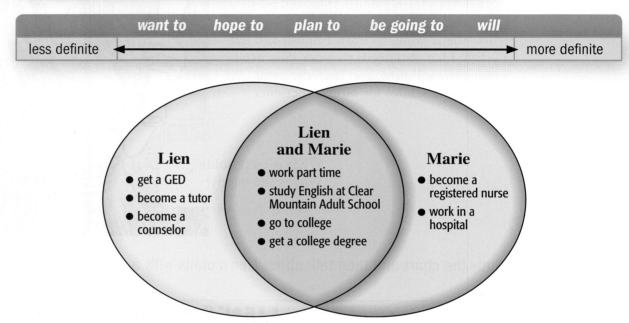

Lien
- get a GED
- become a tutor
- become a counselor

Lien and Marie
- work part time
- study English at Clear Mountain Adult School
- go to college
- get a college degree

Marie
- become a registered nurse
- work in a hospital

D Write sentences about Lien's and Marie's future plans.

(Answers will vary. Sample answers are given.)

1. Lien is going to be a counselor.

2. Lien will get her GED.

3. Lien plans to become a tutor.

4. Lien and Marie both hope to work part time.

5. They want to study English at Clear Mountain Adult School.

6. They both hope to go to college.

7. They both want to get a college degree.

8. Marie is going to become a registered nurse.

9. Marie will work in a hospital.

Presentation 2   15–20 mins.

Ask students to look back at page 143. Discuss the grammar chart and remind students that the continuum at the bottom is subjective.

C **Study the chart with your classmates and teacher.**

Drill students by going over the time line on the previous page. Ask them what Lien will do and by when.

Pronunciation

Emphatic expressions

Sometimes words are emphasized in English to express firmness or resolution. In this case, show students how giving more emphasis on *will* makes the speaker's declaration a commitment. You might do this by asking a student to ask you the same question three times. For example:

Student: *Will you teach tomorrow?*
Teacher: *Yes, I will.*
Student: *Will you teach tomorrow?*
Teacher: *Yes, I will teach tomorrow.*
Student: *Will you teach tomorrow?*
Teacher: *Yes, I WILL teach tomorrow.*

Ask students to close their books and make a Venn diagram on the board. One circle is for Lien and the other for Marie, as on the page in the book. Ask students to go back to pages 141, 142, and 147, and to avoid looking at page 148. See if students can fill in the Venn diagram about Lien and Marie from the information on those pages.

You may wish to supply students with the Venn diagram template with two circles from the Activity Bank CD-ROM template folder.

Once students have made an attempt to complete the diagram, make a similar Venn diagram on the board and go over it with students. Then, ask them to open to this page and check their work.

Practice 2   15–20 mins.

D **Write sentences about Lien's and Marie's future plans.**

Remind students to write uppercase letters where necessary and to complete each sentence with a period.

Evaluation 2   10–15 mins.

Ask students to trade papers and peer-edit for the proper use of grammar structures, uppercase letters, and periods. Then, have each student partner write the sentence he or she peer-edited on the board.

Instructor's Notes

_____
_____
_____
_____
_____
_____
_____
_____
_____
_____
_____
_____
_____
_____
_____
_____
_____
_____
_____
_____
_____
_____
_____

Presentation 3   7–10 mins. ▪▪▫▫

Ask students to close their books and take notes. Write four years across the board: *2008, 2009, 2010,* and *2011.* Next, ask students to listen as you describe Mario's time line from this page. They should write what Mario plans to accomplish in each of the years.

Now, ask students to open their books and look at the picture of Mario. Ask the questions in the question box.

(E) Read Mario's plans.

Go over the time line and have students check their notes.

Prepare them for listening by asking them to predict the answers to Exercise F.

Practice 3   10–15 mins. ▪

(F) Match the statements with the reasons below. Write the correct letter next to the statements. Then, listen and check your answers.

Evaluation 3   5 mins. ▪

Have students listen and check their predictions.

 Listening Script   *CD 2, Track 41*

Mario has many goals. He knows exactly what he wants to do with his life. First, he wants to go to school. He wants to go to school because he wants to learn English. He can get a better job if he speaks English. Mario is very good with his hands. He was a mechanic in Mexico. He wants to get a part-time job in an automobile shop because he wants experience in auto repair in the United States. Next, he plans to go to a community college. He wants to study auto repair and also accounting. This will help him prepare to start his own auto-repair business so he can be self-employed.

Application   10–15 mins. ▪▪▫▫

(G) Write a work goal. Use *because* and write why you want to reach this goal.

Refer students to *Stand Out 2 Grammar Challenge,* Unit 8, Challenge 3 for more practice with expressing future plans with *will.*

Instructor's Notes

_____

_____

_____

_____

_____

_____

_____

_____

_____

_____

_____

_____

_____

_____

_____

_____

_____

_____

_____

_____

_____

_____

_____

_____

_____

LESSON 3   **GOAL** ➤ Set work goals

What is Mario's job now?
What does he plan to do?
What do you think of his plan?

E Read Mario's plans.

MARIO'S PLAN			
Go to Clear Mountain Adult School	Get a part-time job in an automobile shop	Go to a community college and study auto mechanics and accounting	Start own auto repair business
2008	**2009**	**2010**	**2011**

F **Match the statements with the reasons below. Write the correct letter next to the statements. Then, listen and check your answers.**

CD 2
TR 41

_d_ 1. Mario wants to get a part-time job in an automobile shop

_a_ 2. Mario needs to start his auto-repair business

_c_ 3. Mario needs to go to Clear Mountain Adult School

_b_ 4. Mario plans to go to a community college

a. because he wants to be self-employed.

b. because he wants to study auto mechanics and accounting.

c. because he wants to learn English.

d. because he wants experience in auto repair.

G Write a work goal. Use *because* and write why you want to reach this goal.

My vocational (work) goal

Where is Ahmed?
Why isn't he sitting with the other students?
How does he feel?

 Read Ahmed's story.

Ahmed needs to make plans, but sometimes he has problems. His first day at Clear Mountain Adult School was difficult. He didn't speak English and many students only spoke Spanish or another language. He wanted to go home, but he didn't. He went to school every day. He worked hard and listened carefully. Now he can speak and understand English a little.

 Look at Ahmed's problems and find the solutions. Draw a line from the problem to the solution. There is more than one solution for every problem.

(Answers will vary. Sample answers are given.)

Problems	Solutions
1. didn't speak English	a. asked a friend for help
	b. looked in the newspaper
2. wanted a high school diploma	c. went to school every day
	d. worked hard and listened carefully
3. wanted to go to the library	e. called for the address
	f. looked on a map
4. didn't have a job	g. talked to a counselor

Objective: Find ways to learn
Grammar: Negative simple past tense with *so*
Academic Strategies: Focused listening, predicting
Vocabulary: Past tense verbs, *so*

RESOURCES

Activity Bank: Unit 8, Lesson 4, Worksheets 1–2
Reading and Writing Challenge: Unit 8
Grammar Challenge: Unit 8, Challenge 4

Audio: CD 2, Track 42
Heinle Picture Dictionary: Life Events, pages 30–31; Library, pages 54–55

■ 1.5 hour classes   ■ 2.5 hour classes   ■ 3⁺ hour classes

AGENDA

Talk about careers and education.
Discuss problems and solutions.
Use so.
Read about resources for learning.
Read about libraries.

Warm-up and Review   15-20 mins.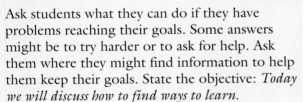

Ask students to share their work goals. Write the following professions on the board:

> *carpenter*
> *lawyer*
> *nurse*
> *compguter programmer*
> *nurse*
> *teacher*

Ask students in groups to decide what kind of education a person would need if he or she had a goal to have one of these professions or careers. Then, ask the groups to report and compare answers as a class.

Introduction   5-7 mins.

Ask students what they can do if they have problems reaching their goals. Some answers might be to try harder or to ask for help. Ask them where they might find information to help them keep their goals. State the objective: *Today we will discuss how to find ways to learn.*

Presentation 1   15-20 mins. ■■■

Ask students to open their books and look at Ahmed. Ask the questions in the question box.

(A) Read Ahmed's story.

Ask students to underline the verbs in the paragraph. List the verbs on the board. Analyze the paragraph with students and then ask them to close their books. Give a dictation of the paragraph with the cues still on the board.

Remind students of the dictation strategy of listening completely before attempting to write anything. They should listen, repeat the sentences in their minds, and then write.

Practice 1   10-15 mins.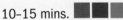

(B) Look at Ahmed's problems and find the solutions. Draw a line from the problem to the solution. There is more than one solution for every problem.

Ask students to complete this activity individually.

Evaluation 1   3-5 mins.

Go over students' answers as a class. Accept any reasonable answers.

Presentation 2

15-20 mins. ■■■

C Study the chart with your classmates and teacher.

Help students see the relationship between *because* and *so*. Go over the aspects of the simple present negative.

D Predict what Ahmed did to resolve his problems. Then, listen and check your answers.

 Listening Script   *CD 2, Track 42*

My name is Ahmed. School is difficult for me, but I want to learn English. I asked a friend for help and he told me to go to school. I also listen to tapes and use computers in the library.

I didn't have a job, but I needed money, so I looked for work in the newspaper. I found a great job.

I was very nervous in the United States because I didn't know what to do in an emergency. My friend told me to talk to a police officer if I ever have any emergency. That is great to know.

I am interested in becoming a citizen, too. I asked my teacher for advice, and he said I should talk to a counselor.

The teacher also showed me how to read a bus schedule so I could go to the courthouse and get more information on citizenship there.

When I arrived in the United States, I couldn't find a home. I tried to read the newspaper. It was hard at first, but I learned to read it enough to find a home for my family.

When my family arrived, my next task was to find a school for my children. When we moved in, I got a phone and it came with a phone book. I looked up schools in the phone book and found the school closest to our home.

Go over the listening and make sure students hear all the important information.

For shorter classes, ask students to do Exercise E for homework.

Practice 2

10-12 mins. ■■

E On a sheet of paper, write sentences about Ahmed. Use *so*.

Evaluation 2

7-10 mins. ■■

Check students' work.

Instructor's Notes

_____

_____

_____

_____

_____

_____

_____

_____

_____

_____

_____

_____

_____

_____

_____

_____

_____

_____

_____

_____

_____

_____

_____

_____

_____

C Study the chart with your classmates and teacher.

Past with *So*			
Base	**Affirmative**	**Negative** *didn't* + base verb	**Example sentence**
ask	asked *	didn't ask	He didn't speak English **so** he asked for help.
go	went	didn't go	She didn't speak English **so** she went to school.
Pronunciation: *ask/t/			

  D Predict what Ahmed did to resolve his problems. Then, listen and check your answers.

CD 2, TR 42

Problem	Ask a friend	Talk to the police	Go to school	Look in the phone book	Go to the library	Talk to a counselor	Ask the teacher	Look in a newspaper
1. He didn't speak English.	X		X		X			
2. He didn't have a job.								X
3. He didn't know what to do in an emergency.	X	X						
4. He didn't know where to find information about citizenship.				X		X	X	
5. He needed to find a home for his family.	X							X
6. He needed to find a school for his children.				X				

 E On a sheet of paper, write sentences about Ahmed. Use *so*.

EXAMPLE: Ahmed didn't speak English so he went to school.

 How can these places help us to learn? Draw a line from the place to the kind of learning you can do there. There can be more than one answer.

1. the public library
2. the Internet
3. hotline
4. an adult education center

a. get advice on health and legal problems
b. borrow books or videos
c. take classes in English, computer programming, or art
d. read the latest news and find jobs

 Read the flyer.

Come to the Mountain View Public Library

The Mountain View Public Library has books, videos, and CDs for adults and children of every age. Our staff will help you search our computer catalogs or access the Internet. Our collection includes books in more than forty languages.

Join one of our book discussion groups or try our creative writing workshop. Come to one of our lunchtime lectures to learn how to start your own business or to learn about countries around the world with one of our guest speakers.

For more information about our services, come to the information desk at the main entrance. Our services are free to all state residents.

**OPEN: Monday–Thursday 9–9,
Friday and Saturday 9–5, Sunday 1–5**

 List the things you can do at the Mountain View Public Library.

1. You can borrow books, videos, DVDs, and CDs.

2. You can search computer catalogs and access the Internet.

3. You can join a book discussion group or try a creative writing workshop.

4. You can attend a lunchtime lecture.

I Tell a group where you go for help when you have a problem. Look at Exercise D on page 151 for examples.

Presentation 3

10-15 mins. ■■□

Tell students that part of overcoming obstacles is to get good information. Ask them where they might find good information. Answers might include the library, friends, teachers, and the Internet.

(F) How can these places help us to learn? Draw a line from the place to the kind of learning you can do there. There can be more than one answer.

Do this activity as a class. Discuss the different possibilities and when each resource might be appropriate.

For shorter classes, ask students to do Exercises G and H for homework.

Practice 3

7-10 mins. ■

(G) Read the flyer.

Ask students to read the flyer on their own and to answer the questions the best they can.

(H) List the things you can do at the Mountain View Public Library.

Ask students to do this activity on their own and then to compare their answers with a partner.

Evaluation 3

5-7 mins. ■

Ask volunteers to write their answers on the board.

Application

10-15 mins. ■■□

(I) Tell a group where you go for help when you have a problem. Look at Exercise D on page 151 for examples.

📖 Refer students to *Stand Out 2 Grammar Challenge*, Unit 8, Challenge 4 for more practice with the simple past tense and *so*.

Activity Bank 💿

Unit 8, Lesson 4, Worksheet 1: Solutions
Unit 8, Lesson 4, Worksheet 2: Library

Instructor's Notes

AGENDA

Discuss where you will be in ten years.

Talk about goals.

Talk to a friend about goals.

Read about goals.

Write about goals.

Objective: Record goals

Grammar: Adverbs that show chronological order

Academic Strategies: Focused listening, paragraph writing

Vocabulary: Ordinal numbers

RESOURCES

Activity Bank: Unit 8, Lesson 5, Worksheet 1

Reading and Writing Challenge: Unit 8

Grammar Challenge: Unit 8, Challenge 5

Audio: CD 2, Track 43

Heinle Picture Dictionary: Life Events, pages 30–31

■ 1.5 hour classes ■ 2.5 hour classes ■ 3⁺ hour classes

Warm-up and Review   10–15 mins.

Ask students to imagine where they will be in ten years. Ask them to write down one or two sentences about where they think they will be. Then, ask them to form groups and to read their sentences to the group.

Introduction   10–15 mins. ■■■

Ask students what they think is the most important goal a person can have—*educational, personal/family,* or *work.* Students may come to the conclusion that the goals are interconnected and that one can't be said to be more important than another goal. State the objective: *Today we will record our goals and write a paragraph about them.*

Presentation 1   7–10 mins. ■■■

(A) Look at the pictures. What are Marie's plans in each picture?

Go over each picture as a class. Elicit ideas from students. Ask them to identify if each picture depicts a personal/family goal, a work goal, or an educational goal.

Remind students about ordinal numbers and prepare them for the listening. The listening script is the paragraph about Marie on page 141. Help students identify with the pictures by asking them if they want or have a high school

diploma, if they want to get married or are married, if they want or have children, and what job they might want in the future.

Practice 1   10–15 mins.

(B) Listen and write the sentences in order. Use *first, second, third,* and *fourth.*

Note that the recording doesn't use *first, second,* etc. The idea is to get students thinking about paragraph organization. Also, the answers are really in the pictures above that were already discussed, but students may choose to insert other things that are mentioned.

 Listening Script   CD 2, Track 43

My career is most important to me. I plan to study nursing and work part time as a home health-care aide. Then, I am going to get my degree in nursing and become a registered nurse—at least, this is my plan. I will save some money because I want to get married soon. My boyfriend's name is Jean. After we get married, we plan to have children. Maybe there will be money to go to the movies sometimes, too. I will work hard to make my plans come true.

Evaluation 1   3–5 mins.

Ask students to share their sentences.

STANDARDS CORRELATIONS

CASAS: 4.4.5 (See CASAS Competency List on pages 169–175.)

SCANS: Information Acquire and evaluate information, organize and maintain information, interpret and communicate information

Basic Skills Reading, writing, listening, speaking

Personal Qualities Responsibility, sociability, self management

EFF: Communication Read with understanding, convey ideas in writing, speak so others can understand, listen actively, observe critically

Decision Making Plan

Lifelong Learning Take responsibility for learning, reflect and evaluate

LESSON 5

My goals

GOAL ➤ Record goals

A Look at the pictures. What are Marie's plans in each picture?

Clear Mountain
Adult School

1. Marie plans to graduate from adult school.

2. Marie plans to become a nurse.

3. Marie plans to get married.

4. Marie plans to start a family.

CD 2, TR 43

B Listen and write the sentences in order. Use *first, second, third,* and *fourth.*

First, Marie plans to get a degree in nursing.

Second, she plans on becoming a nurse.

Third, she plans on getting married.

Fourth, she plans on starting a family.

GOAL ➤ **Record goals**

C Read the goals below. Check (✔) any goals you have. (Answers will vary.)

❐ buy a house   ❐ get a job   ❐ study English

❐ move   ❐ keep a job   ❐ participate in child's school

❐ get married   ❐ learn new skills at work   ❐ get a high school diploma

❐ have children   ❐ get a promotion   ❐ go to college

❐ become a citizen   ❐ get a better job   ❐ graduate from college

D Talk to a partner. Fill in the diagram about your goals. (Answers will vary.)

Presentation 2   15–20 mins.

With books closed, make a chart with three
columns as you did in the first lesson. Write
the headings: *personal/family, academic,* and
vocational. Ask students to brainstorm in groups
with their books closed and come up with four
items for each column. Then, ask people from
different groups to go to other groups and see if
they can add to their lists.

Ⓒ Read the goals below. Check any goals you have.

Ask students to work individually to complete
this activity about themselves. Then, have them
share their goals with the class. Ask them if there
are any goals that are not listed that they would
like to add based on their earlier discussion.

Practice 2   10–15 mins.

Ⓓ Talk to a partner. Fill in the diagram about your goals.

Pair students to ensure maximum effectiveness
in this activity. You may choose to put stronger
writers with weaker ones. After they have written
the information, ask the pairs to join another pair
to form a group of four. Have each pair report
to the group.

Evaluation 2   10 mins.

Observe students as they do the activity.

Presentation 3　　　　10-15 mins. ▪▪▪

The previous activities in this lesson are intentionally shorter to leave more time for this presentation and the following practice and application. You may choose to do this lesson over two days. Up to this point, students have been asked to write paragraphs, and they will write much more in the next level. This is a very good time to help them refine what they write. Of course, another way to do this is to use the *Stand Out Reading and Writing Challenge*.

E **Study the paragraph with your classmates and teacher.**

Go over the important points of the paragraph including indenting, margins, and the ordinal numbers.

Practice 3　　　　10-15 mins. ▪▪▪

F **Read the paragraph again. Look at the underlined words. What do they show?**

G **Write your plans for the next five years.**

Evaluation 3　　　　5-7 mins. ▪▪▪

Ask volunteers to write their sentences on the board in paragraph form and allow peer-editing if needed.

Application　　　　20-30 mins. ▪▪▪

H **Write a paragraph about your goals. Use the example paragraph on this page. When you are finished, share it with the class.**

Refer students to *Stand Out 2 Grammar Challenge*, Unit 8, Challenge 5 for more practice with transition words.

> **Activity Bank** 💿
>
> Unit 8, Lesson 5, Worksheet 1: Writing a Paragraph

E Study the paragraph with your classmates and teacher.

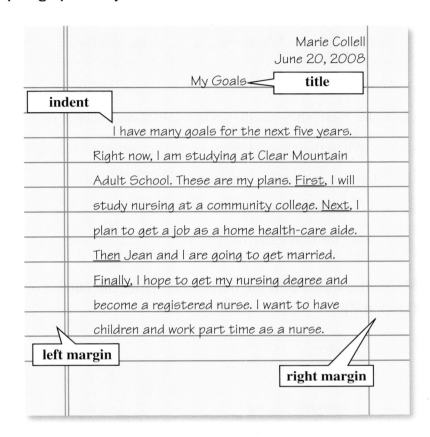

Marie Collell
June 20, 2008

My Goals — title

indent

I have many goals for the next five years.
Right now, I am studying at Clear Mountain
Adult School. These are my plans. First, I will
study nursing at a community college. Next, I
plan to get a job as a home health-care aide.
Then Jean and I are going to get married.
Finally, I hope to get my nursing degree and
become a registered nurse. I want to have
children and work part time as a nurse.

left margin

right margin

F Read the paragraph again. Look at the underlined words. What do they show?

G Write your plans for the next five years. (Answers will vary.)

First, I _____ .

Next, _____ .

Then, _____ .

Finally, _____ .

H Write a paragraph about your goals. Use the example paragraph on this page. When you are finished, share it with the class.

Review

A Complete the paragraph about the educational system in the United States. Use the words from the box.

> Bachelor's   Associate's   elementary   diploma   community

Children in the United States start _____elementary_____ school at five or six years old. Next, they usually go to a junior high school or middle school, and then to high school. When they finish high school, they receive a _____diploma_____. After that, they can get a job, or go to a junior college or a _____community_____ college for two years, where they get an _____Associate's_____ degree. They can also go to a university for four years and get a _____Bachelor's_____ degree.

B Match the words with the definitions. Write the correct letter next to each word. (Lesson 2)

_d_ 1. resident   a. finish school or college

_e_ 2. vocational   b. person who advises other people

_b_ 3. counselor   c. related to studying

_c_ 4. academic   d. person who lives in a country or state

_a_ 5. graduate   e. related to your job

C Ask three friends about their goals. Write sentences about them. (Lessons 1, 2, 3, and 5) (Answers will vary.)

1. _____

2. _____

3. _____

AT-A-GLANCE PREP

Objective: All unit objectives
Grammar: All unit grammar
Academic Strategies: Focused listening,
  reviewing, evaluating, developing study skills
Vocabulary: All unit vocabulary

■ 1.5 hour classes ■ 2.5 hour classes ■ 3⁺ hour classes

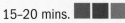

AGENDA

Discuss unit objectives.
Complete the review.
Do My Dictionary.
Evaluate and reflect on progress.

Warm-up and Review   7-10 mins. ■■■

With their books closed, ask students to help you
make a list on the board of all the vocabulary
they can come up with from the unit. Then,
have a competition where students in groups will
write page numbers for each item on the list.
The first group to have the correct page number
for each item wins. Explain that this review will
also include going through the entire book
for information.

Introduction   5 mins. ■■■

Write all the objectives on the board from Unit 8.
Show students the first page of the unit and say
the five objectives. Explain that today they will
review the whole unit.

Note: Depending on the length of the term, you
may decide to have students do Presentation 1
and Practice 1 for homework and then review
student work as either the warm-up or another
class activity.

Presentation 1   10-15 mins. ■■■

This presentation will cover the first three pages
of the review. Quickly go to the first page of
each lesson. Discuss the objective of each. Ask
simple questions to remind students of what they
have learned.

Practice 1   15-20 mins. ■■■

 Complete the paragraph about the
educational system in the United States.
Use the words from the box. (Lesson 2)

B Match the words with the definitions. Write
the correct letter next to each word. (Lesson 2)

C Ask three friends about their goals. Write
sentences about them. (Lessons 1, 2, 3, and 5)

Teaching Tip

Recycling/Review

The review and the project that follows are
part of the recycling/review process. Students
at this level often need to be reintroduced to
concepts to solidify what they have learned.
Many concepts are learned and forgotten while
learning other new concepts. This is because
students learn but are not necessarily ready to
acquire language concepts.

Therefore, it becomes very important to review
and to show students how to review on their
own. It is also important to recycle the new
concepts in different contexts.

STANDARDS CORRELATIONS

CASAS: 4.4.5, 7.1.1, 7.2.7, 7.5.1, 7.5.5 (See CASAS Competency List
on pages 169–175.)
SCANS: **Information** Acquire and evaluate information, organize
and maintain Information

Basic Skills Reading, writing, speaking
Personal Qualities Responsibility, self management
***EFF:* Communication** Speak so others can understand
Lifelong Learning Take responsibility for learning, reflect and evaluate

Practice 1 *(continued)*

D Read about Teresa. Use the words from the box to label the parts of the paragraph. (Lesson 5)

E Write a similar paragraph about yourself. Use *plan to, hope to, want to, going to,* and *will* to talk about your future plans. Choose one of the titles below. (Lesson 5)

D Read about Teresa. Use the words from the box to label the parts of the paragraph. (Lesson 5)

indent	left margin	title	right margin

indent

My Family ← title

My name is Teresa, I came to the United States two years ago. I don't want to get a job right now. My husband works very hard. He is an auto mechanic here in Chicago. He plans to start his own business soon. We have one daughter. Her name is Graciela. I am going to learn English so I can help her in school. I'm going to help the teacher in Graciela's school. My husband wants to work hard and help our family, too. We are going to be good parents.

left margin

right margin

E Write a similar paragraph about yourself. Use *plan to, hope to, want to, going to,* and *will* to talk about your future plans. Choose one of the titles below. (Lesson 5)

1. My Family   2. My Job   3. My Goals

(Answers will vary.)

Review

F Read the goals and write *P/F* for personal or family goals, *V* for vocational goals, and *A* for academic goals. (Lesson 1)

1. __A__ get a high school diploma

2. __P/F__ travel around the world

3. __V__ learn computers at a trade school

4. __P/F__ have two children

5. __V__ get a part-time job

6. __P/F__ buy a house

7. __P/F__ read a novel

8. __V__ work in a doctor's office

G List places where you can find information. (Lesson 4) (Answers will vary.)

library

City Hall

community centers

phone book

H Use the correct forms of the words in parentheses to express future plans. (Lesson 3)

1. Kimberly ___will___ (will) work in a doctor's office some day.

2. Paul and Kimberly ___are going to___ (be going to) have a baby.

3. She ___hopes to___ (hope to) finish school before the baby comes.

4. He ___wants to___ (want to) get a better job before the baby comes.

5. They ___plan to___ (plan to) build a new baby's room onto their home.

I Complete the sentences about yourself. (Lesson 3) (Answers will vary.)

1. I want to _____.

2. I hope to _____.

3. I plan to _____.

4. I am going to _____.

5. I will _____.

Practice 1 *(continued)*

 F Read the goals and write *P/F* for personal or family goals, *V* for vocational goals, and *A* for academic goals. (Lesson 1)

G List places where you can find information. (Lesson 4)

H Use the correct forms of the words in parentheses to express future plans. (Lesson 3)

I Complete the sentences about yourself. (Lesson 3)

Evaluation 1   10 mins. ■ ■ ■

Go around the room and check on students' progress. Help individuals when needed. If you see consistent errors among several students, interrupt the class and give a mini lesson or review to help students feel comfortable with the concept.

Activity Bank

Unit 8: Computer Worksheets
Unit 8: Internet Worksheets

Presentation 2 7-10 mins.

My Dictionary

Go over the steps of My Dictionary as a class.

Practice 2 5-7 mins.

Do the dictionary activity as a class before students work on their own for at least the first few units of the book to ensure that students understand what to do.

Evaluation 2 5 mins.

Ask students to share their cards.

Presentation 3 5 mins.

Learner Log

Review the concepts of the Learner Log. Make sure students understand the concepts and how to complete the log including circling the answers, finding page numbers where the concept is taught, and ranking favorite activities.

Teaching Tip

Learner Logs

Learner Logs function to help students in many different ways.

1. They serve as part of the review process.
2. They help students to gain confidence and to document what they have learned. Consequently, students see that they are progressing in their learning.
3. They provide students with a tool that they can use over and over to check and recheck their understanding of the target language. In this way, students become independent learners.

Practice 3 10-15 mins.

Ask students to complete the Learner Log.

Evaluation 3 2 mins.

Go over the Learner Log with students.

Application 5-7 mins.

Ask students to record their favorite lesson or page in the unit.

Assessment

Use the Stand Out 2 Assessment CD-ROM with Exam*View*® to create a posttest for Unit 8.

Refer students to *Stand Out 2 Grammar Challenge*, Unit 8, Extension Challenge 1 for more practice with *yes/no* questions and *will* and Extension Challenge 2 for more practice with information questions with *will* and *going to*.

Instructor's Notes

_____
_____
_____
_____
_____
_____
_____
_____
_____
_____
_____
_____
_____
_____
_____
_____
_____

My Dictionary

Make flash cards to improve your vocabulary.

1. Choose four new words from this unit.

2. Write each word on an index card or on a sheet of paper.

3. On the back of the index card or paper, draw a picture, find and write a sentence from the book with the word, and write the page number.

4. Study the words.

Definition: GED = General Equivalency Diploma (a test)

You earn a <u>General Equivalency Diploma</u>.

page 145

Learner Log

Circle how well you learned each item and write the page number where you learned it.

1. I can identify goals.
   Yes   Maybe   No   Page _____

2. I can make academic goals.
   Yes   Maybe   No   Page _____

3. I can make workplace goals.
   Yes   Maybe   No   Page _____

4. I can solve problems and find places for information.
   Yes   Maybe   No   Page _____

5. I can write my own goals.
   Yes   Maybe   No   Page _____

Rank what you like to do best from 1 to 6. 1 is your favorite activity. Your teacher will help you.

_____ Practice listening

_____ Practice speaking

_____ Practice reading

_____ Practice writing

_____ Learn new words

_____ Learn grammar

I think I improved most in

_____ .

Team Project

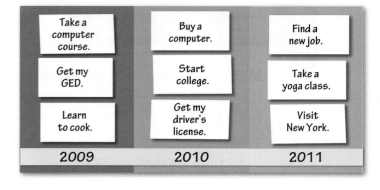

Make a timeline.

In a group, you are going to make
a time line of your goals.

1. Form a team with three or four students.

2. Draw a time line for your group for the next five years.

3. Each team member writes three goals on pieces of paper
   and puts them on the time line.

4. Show your time line to the other groups.

Portfolio

You are going to write a paragraph and make
a time line of your goals to include in your
personal portfolio.

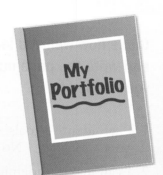

1. Make a time line on a large piece of paper. On your time line,
   write what you want to do for the next five years.

2. Write a paragraph about your family.

3. Write a paragraph about what you are doing now in your life.

4. Write a paragraph about your plans for the next five years.

5. Show your paragraphs to a friend and ask for comments. Use
   the comments to improve your writing.

6. Make a cover sheet for your time line and your paragraphs.

7. Present your portfolio to the class and read your paragraphs.

Introduction   5 mins.

Team Project

Make a timeline.

After forming teams, students will draw a five-year time line for their team. Each student will add three personal goals to the time line.

Stages 1–4   15–20 mins.

Have students form groups and make a group time line. There is a time line worksheet available on the Activity Bank CD-ROM (Unit 8, Project, Worksheet 1). Ask the groups to share with another group and then, with the class.

Team Project

Portfolio

This activity is a synthesis of the themes of *Stand Out*. Individuals will make a personal portfolio, including a time line and three paragraphs. They will present their portfolios to the class with a cover sheet. This can be a two- or three-day activity.

Stage 1   10–15 mins.

Make a time line on a large piece of paper.

Have students make a personal time line. Use the worksheet on the Activity Bank CD-ROM if you wish (Unit 8, Project, Worksheet 1).

Stages 2–4   40–50 mins.

Write a paragraph about your family. Write a paragraph about what you are doing now in your life. Write a paragraph about your plans for the next five years.

Use the worksheet provided on the Activity Bank CD-ROM if you wish (Unit 8, Project, Worksheet 2).

You may choose to have students type their paragraphs and add clip art or pictures.

Stage 5   15–20 mins.

Show your paragraphs to a friend and ask for comments.

Before you look at the students' work, have them show it to others to peer-edit. Give them the editing checklist on the Activity Bank CD-ROM (Unit 8, Project, Worksheet 3).

Stage 6   10–15 mins.

Make a cover sheet for your time line and your paragraphs.

Have students create their own cover sheet on a computer or provide them with the cover sheet worksheet from the Activity Bank CD-ROM (Unit 8, Project, Worksheet 4).

Stage 7   10–15 mins.

Present your portfolio to the class and read your paragraphs.

Have students read their edited and revised paragraphs to their team members. Then, have students give individual presentations of their portfolios. Consider videotaping the presentations. Students will prepare better for formal presentations if they are videotaped. Another approach is for the students to videotape themselves and polish their presentations before giving them to the class.

Activity Bank

Unit 8, Project, Worksheet 1: My Goals Time Line

Unit 8, Project, Worksheet 2: Paragraph Template

Unit 8, Project, Worksheet 3: Editing Checklist

Unit 8, Project, Worksheet 4: My Personal Portfolio

Unit 8, Extension, Worksheet 1: Advice

STANDARDS CORRELATIONS

CASAS: 4.4.5, 7.1.1, 7.2.7, 7.5.1, 7.5.5 (See CASAS Competency List on pages 169–175.)

SCANS: **Resources** Allocate time, allocate materials and facility resources, allocate human resources

Information Acquire and evaluate information, organize and maintain information, interpret and communicate information, use computers to process information

Interpersonal Participate as a member of a team, teach others, exercise leadership, negotiate to arrive at a decision, work with cultural diversity

Systems Understand systems, monitor and correct performance, improve and design systems

Basic Skills Reading, writing, listening, speaking

Thinking Skills Think creatively, make decisions, solve problems, see things in the mind's eye

Personal Qualities Responsibility, sociability, self management

EFF: **Communication** Read with understanding, convey ideas in writing, speak so others can understand, listen actively, observe critically

Decision Making Solve problems and make decisions, plan

Interpersonal Cooperate with others, advocate and influence, resolve conflict and negotiate, guide others

Lifelong Learning Take responsibility for learning, reflect and evaluate

Stand Out 2 Vocabulary List

Pre-Unit
Feelings
angry P2
happy P2
hungry P2
nervous P2
sad P2
tired P2
Numbers P5

Unit 1
Family
aunt 5
brother 5
daughter 5
father 5
granddaughter 5
grandfather 5
grandmother 5
husband 5
mother 5
nephew 5
niece 5
parents 5
sister 5
son 5
uncle 5
wife 5
Personal Information
eye color 7
hair color 7
heavy 9
height 7
old 9
short 9
tall 9
thin 9
weight 7
young 9
Weather
cloudy 13
foggy 13
rainy 13
snowy 13
sunny 13
windy 13

Unit 2
Clothing
baseball cap 24
blouse 22
boots 24
coat 22
dress 22
gloves 24

jacket 22
pants 22
sandals 24
scarf 24
shirt 22
shorts 24
skirt 22
sneakers 30
socks 22
sunglasses 24
sweater 22
tie 22
t-shirt 24
Colors
red 27
orange 27
yellow 27
pink 27
blue 27

Unit 3
Menus
beverage 42
dessert 42
main course 42
salad 42
sandwich 42
side order 42
soup 42
Containers and Units
bag 45
bottle 45
box 45
can 45
carton 45
gallon 45
jar 45
loaf 45
pound 45
Supermarket
baking needs 47
canned goods 47
checkout 47
dairy 47
frozen foods 47
meats 47
produce 47
Food Groups
breads, grains 50
dairy 50
fats, oils, sweets 50
fruit 50
meats 50
vegetables 50

Meals
breakfast 51
dinner 51
lunch 51
Cooking Verbs
add 54
boil 54
chop 54
cook 54
drain 54
mix 54
peel 54
whip 54

Unit 4
Housing and Rooms
apartment 62
balcony 64
bathroom 70
bedroom 70
condominium 62
dining room 70
kitchen 70
house 62
living room 70
mobile home 62
pool 64
yard 70
Furniture
armchair 71
bookcase 71
chair 71
coffee table 71
couch 71
dining room set 71
dresser 71
lamp 71
refrigerator 71
rocking chair 71
sofa 71
table 71
washer/dryer 71
Banking
ATM 73
cash 73
deposit 73
withdrawal 73

Unit 5
Public Services
bank 83
bowling alley 81
church 83
city hall 83

clothes store 83
courthouse 83
department store 83
fast-food restaurant 83
fire station 83
gas station 83
hardware store 83
hospital 83
library 83
movie theater 81
museum 84
pharmacy 83
police station 83
post office 83
shoe store 83
supermarket 83

Unit 6
Parts of the Body
arm 104
back 104
chest 104
ear 104
eye 104
foot (feet) 104
hand 104
head 104
heart 104
leg 104
lip 104
mouth 104
neck 104
nose 104
shoulder 104
stomach 104
tongue 104
tooth (teeth) 104
Symptoms
backache 106
cough 105
fever 105
headache 105
runny nose 105
sore throat 105
stomachache 106
toothache 106
Medicine Labels
aches and pains 110
directions 110
exceed 110
persist 110
reduce 110
symptoms 110
tablets 110
teenagers 110

Stand Out 2 Irregular Verb List

The verbs below are used in *Stand Out 2* and have irregular past tense forms.

Base Verb	Simple Past	Base Verb	Simple Past
be	was, were	have	had
break	broke	make	made
buy	bought	put	put
can	could	read	read
come	came	run	ran
cut	cut	say	said
do	did	sleep	slept
draw	drew	speak	spoke
drink	drank	swim	swam
eat	ate	take	took
find	found	wake	woke
get	got	wear	wore
go	went	write	wrote

Useful Words

Cardinal numbers

1	one
2	two
3	three
4	four
5	five
6	six
7	seven
8	eight
9	nine
10	ten
11	eleven
12	twelve
13	thirteen
14	fourteen
15	fifteen
16	sixteen
17	seventeen
18	eighteen
19	nineteen
20	twenty
21	twenty-one
30	thirty
40	forty
50	fifty
60	sixty
70	seventy
80	eighty
90	ninety
100	one hundred
1000	one thousand
10,000	ten thousand
100,000	one hundred thousand
1,000,00	one million

Ordinal numbers

first	1st
second	2nd
third	3rd
fourth	4th
fifth	5th
sixth	6th
seventh	7th
eighth	8th
ninth	9th
tenth	10th
eleventh	11th
twelfth	12th
thirteenth	13th
fourteenth	14th
fifteenth	15th
sixteenth	16th
seventeenth	17th
eighteenth	18th
nineteenth	19th
twentieth	20th
twenty-first	21st

Days of the week

Sunday
Monday
Tuesday
Wednesday
Thursday
Friday
Saturday

Seasons

winter
spring
summer
fall

Months of the year

January
February
March
April
May
June
July
August
September
October
November
December

Write the date

April 5, 2009 = 4/ 5/ 09

Temperature chart

Degrees Celcius (°C) and
Degrees Fahrenheit (°F)

100°C	212°F
30°C	86°F
25°C	77°F
20°C	68°F
15°C	59°F
10°C	50°F
5°C	41°F
0°C	32°F
–5°C	23°F

Weights and measures

Weights:
1 pound (lb.) = 453.6 grams (g)
16 ounces (oz.) = 1 pound (lb.)
1 pound (lb.) = .45 kilogram (kg)

Liquid of Volume
1 cup (c.) = .24 liter (l)
2 cups (c.) = 1 pint (pt.)
2 pints = 1 quart (qt.)
4 quarts = 1 gallon (gal.)
1 gallon (gal.) = 3.78 liters (l)

Length:
1 inch (in. or ″) = 2.54 centimeters (cm)
1 foot (ft. or ′) = .3048 meters (m)
12 inches (12″) = 1 foot (1′)
1 yard (yd.) = 3 feet (3′) or 0.9144 meters (m)
1 mile (mi.) = 1609.34 meters (m) or 1.609 kilometers (km)

Time:
60 seconds = 1 minute
60 minutes = 1 hour
24 hours = 1day
28-31 days = 1 month
12 months = 1 year

Be Verb to Express Feelings

Subject	*Be*	Feelings	Example sentence
I	am	fine	I **am** fine. (I**'m** fine.)
you, we, they	are	nervous sad tired happy angry hungry	You **are** tired. (You**'re** tired.) We **are** hungry. (We**'re** hungry) They **are** nervous. (They**'re** nervous.)
he, she, it	is		He **is** happy. (He**'s** happy.) She **is** angry. (She**'s** angry.)

Possessive Adjectives

Pronoun	Possessive adjective	Example sentence
I	my	**My** address is 3356 Archer Blvd.
you	your	**Your** phone number is 555-5678.
he	his	**His** last name is Jones.
she	her	**Her** first name is Lien.
we	our	**Our** teacher is Mr. Kelley.
they	their	**Their** home is in Sausalito.

Questions with *Can*

Can	Pronoun	Verb	Example sentence
Can	you	help answer repeat say speak spell	Can you help me? Can you answer the question? Can you repeat that, please? Can you say it again, please? Can you speak slower? Can you spell it, please?

Simple Present: *Be*

Subject	Verb	Information	Example sentence
I	am	from Mexico single divorced 23 years old	I **am** from Mexico.
we, you, they	are		We **are** single. You **are** 23 years old.
he, she	is		He **is** divorced. She **is** from Vietnam.

Simple Present: *Have*

Subject	Verb	Information
I, you, we, they	have	three brothers two sisters
he, she	has	no cousins three sons

Comparative and Superlative Adjectives

Adjective	Comparative adjective	Superlative adjective
tall	taller	the tallest
short	shorter	the shortest
heavy	heavier	the heaviest
thin	thinner	the thinnest
old	older	the oldest
young	younger	the youngest

Simple Present

Subject	Verb	Information	Example sentence
I, you, we, they	eat go help play	lunch to school with the children soccer	I **eat** lunch at 4:00 P.M. You **go** to school at 8:00 A.M. We sometimes **help** with the children. They **play** soccer on Saturday.
he, she	eat**s*** goe**s**** help**s*** play**s****	lunch to school with the children soccer	He **eats** lunch at 12:00 P.M. Nadia **goes** to school at 10:00 A.M. Gilberto **helps** with the children. She **plays** soccer on Friday.

Pronunciation: */s/　　**/z/

Negative Simple Present

Subject	Negative	Base verb	
I, you, we, they	don't	wear	sandals
he, she	doesn't		

Imperatives

	Base verb	Example sentence
~~you~~	drain	**Drain** the water.
	chop	**Chop** the potatoes.
	peel	**Peel** the potatoes.

Negative Imperatives

	Negative	Base verb	Example sentence
~~you~~	do not don't	boil	**Do not boil** the water. (**Don't boil** the water.)
		use	**Do not use** salt. (**Don't use** salt.)
		cook	**Do not cook** in the microwave. (**Don't cook** in the microwave.)

Imperatives

	Base verb		Example sentence
~~you~~	**go**	straight straight ahead	**Go** straight three blocks. **Go** straight ahead.
	turn	left right around	**Turn** left on Nutwood. **Turn** right on Nutwood. **Turn** around.
	stop	on the left on the right	**Stop** on the left. **Stop** on the right.

Information Question	Answer
How **much** is the **house**?	It's $1,200 a month.
What **kind** of **hous**ing is **Num**ber **2**?	It's a mobile home.
Where is the condo**min**ium?	It's on Shady Glen.
How many **bed**rooms does the a**part**ment **have**?	It has three bedrooms.

Information Questions	
What is your name?	**How** long did you live there?
Where do you live now?	**Who** is your employer?
Where did you live before?	**What** is your position?

Modals: *May* and *Might*

Subject	Modal	Base verb	Example sentence
I, you, he, she, we, they	may might	spend earn	I **may** spend $50 on gasoline this month. They **might** spend $300 a month on food. We **may** earn $3,500 a month.

Present Continuous

Subject	*Be*	Base verb + *ing*	Example sentence
I	am	writing	I **am writing** this letter in English.
you, we, they	are	going	We **are going** to the mall.
he, she	is	eating	He **is eating** at the coffee shop.

Simple Past (Regular)

Subject	Verb (base + *ed*)	Example sentence
I, you, he, she, it, we, they	talked wanted walked	I **talked** with Marie. She **wanted** a sandwich. We **walked** in the park.

Simple Past (Irregular)

Subject	Irregular verb	Example sentence
I, you, he, she, it, we, they	went (go) ate (eat) bought (buy) sent (send)	I **went** to the park. She **ate** at the coffee shop. We **bought** new dresses. They **sent** a letter.

Infinitives

Subject	Verb	*to* + base verb
I	need	to exercise

Modal: *Should*

Subject	*Should*	Base verb	Example sentence
I, you, he, she, it, we, they	should shouldn't	take drink chew swallow	I **should take** two tablets. He **shouldn't drink** alcohol with this medicine. You **should take** this medicine for a headache. She **shouldn't chew** this tablet. They **should swallow** this tablet with water.

Future Plans: *Want to, Hope to, Plan to*

Subject	Verb	Infinitive (*to* + base)
I, you, we, they	hope, want, plan	to study in school for three years
		to graduate from college
he, she	hopes, wants, plans	to get married

Future Plans: *Be going to*

Subject	*Be going to*	Base verb
I	am going to	get a high school diploma
you, we, they	are going to	participate in class
he, she	is going to	buy a house

Future: *Will* (Affirmative)

Subject	*Will*	Base verb	Example sentence
I, you, he, she, it, we, they	will	come listen help work have do	I **will come** to class on time. You **will listen** carefully and follow directions. He **will help** other students. She **will work** hard. We **will have** a positive attitude. They **will do** their homework.

Future: *Will* (Negative)

Subject	*Will*	Base verb	Example sentence
I, you, he, she, it, we, they	will not (won't)	come leave forget	I **won't come** to class late. He **won't leave** class early. We **will not forget** our homework.

Because

Statement	Reason		
	Because	Subject + verb	Information
Marie plans to go to college	because	she wants	to be a nurse
Lien hopes to learn English better		she plans	to go to college

Past with *So*

Base	Affirmative	Negative *didn't* + base verb	Example sentence
ask	asked *	didn't ask	He didn't speak English **so** he asked for help.
go	went	didn't go	She didn't speak English **so** she went to school.
Pronunciation: *ask/t/			

Simple Past (Regular)

Subject	Past Verb (base + -ed)
I, he, she, it we, you, they	checked worked cooked

Simple Past: *Be*

Subject	*Be*
I, he, she, it,	was
we, you, they	were

Negative Simple Past (Regular)

Subject	*Did + not*	Base verb
I, he, she, it, we, you, they	did not (didn't)	check work cook

Negative Simple Past: *Be*

Subject	*Be + not*
I, he, she, it,	was not (wasn't)
we, you, they	were not (weren't)

CASAS Competencies

0. Basic Communication

0.1 Communicate in interpersonal interactions
- 0.1.1 Identify or use appropriate non-verbal behavior in a variety of situations (e.g., handshaking)
- 0.1.2 Identify or use appropriate language for informational purposes (e.g., to identify, describe, ask for information, state needs, command, agree or disagree, ask permission)
- 0.1.3 Identify or use appropriate language to influence or persuade (e.g., to caution, request, advise, persuade, negotiate)
- 0.1.4 Identify or use appropriate language in general social situations (e.g., to greet, introduce, thank, apologize, compliment, express pleasure or regret)
- 0.1.5 Identify or use appropriate classroom behavior
- 0.1.6 Clarify or request clarification

0.2 Communicate regarding personal information
- 0.2.1 Respond appropriately to common personal information questions
- 0.2.2 Complete a personal information form
- 0.2.3 Interpret or write a personal note, invitation, or letter
- 0.2.4 Converse about daily and leisure activities and personal interests

1. Consumer Economics

1.1 Use weights, measures, measurement scales, and money
- 1.1.1 Interpret recipes
- 1.1.2 Use the metric system (see also 1.1.4, 6.6.1, 6.6.2, 6.6.3, 6.6.4)
- 1.1.3 Interpret maps and graphs (see also 1.9.4, 2.2.1, 2.2.5)
- 1.1.4 Select, compute, or interpret appropriate standard measurement for length, width, perimeter, area, volume, height, or weight (see also 1.1.2, 6.6.1, 6.6.2, 6.6.3, 6.6.4, 6.6.5)
- 1.1.5 Interpret temperatures (see also 6.6.4)
- 1.1.6 Count, convert, and use coins and currency, and recognize symbols such as ($) and (.) (see also 6.1.1, 6.1.2, 6.1.3, 6.1.4, 6.1.5)
- 1.1.7 Identify product containers and interpret weight and volume
- 1.1.8 Compute averages (see also 6.7.5)
- 1.1.9 Interpret clothing and pattern sizes and use height and weight tables

1.2 Apply principles of comparison-shopping in the selection of goods and services
- 1.2.1 Interpret advertisements, labels, charts, and price tags in selecting goods and services
- 1.2.2 Compare price or quality to determine the best buys for goods and services
- 1.2.3 Compute discounts (see also 6.4.1)
- 1.2.4 Compute unit pricing
- 1.2.5 Interpret letters, articles, and information about consumer-related topics

1.3 Understand methods and procedures used to purchase goods and services
- 1.3.1 Compare different methods used to purchase goods and services
- 1.3.2 Interpret credit applications and recognize how to use and maintain credit
- 1.3.3 Identify or use various methods to purchase goods and services, and make returns and exchanges
- 1.3.4 Use catalogs, order forms, and related information to purchase goods and services
- 1.3.5 Use coupons to purchase goods and services
- 1.3.6 Use coin-operated machines
- 1.3.7 Interpret information or directions to locate merchandise (see also 2.5.4)
- 1.3.8 Identify common food items
- 1.3.9 Identify common articles of clothing

1.4 Understand methods and procedures to obtain housing and related services
- 1.4.1 Identify different kinds of housing, areas of the home, and common household items
- 1.4.2 Select appropriate housing by interpreting classified ads, signs, and other information
- 1.4.3 Interpret lease and rental agreements
- 1.4.4 Interpret information to obtain, maintain, or cancel housing utilities
- 1.4.5 Interpret information about tenant and landlord rights
- 1.4.6 Interpret information about housing loans and home-related insurance
- 1.4.7 Interpret information about home maintenance, and communicate housing problems to a landlord (see also 1.7.4)
- 1.4.8 Recognize home theft and fire prevention measures

1.5 Apply principles of budgeting in the management of money
- 1.5.1 Interpret information about personal and family budgets
- 1.5.2 Plan for major purchases (see also 1.5.1)
- 1.5.3 Interpret bills (see also 2.1.4)

1.6 Understand consumer protection measures
- 1.6.1 Interpret food packaging labels (see also 1.2.1, 3.5.1)
- 1.6.2 Identify consumer protection resources available when confronted with fraudulent practices
- 1.6.3 Identify procedures the consumer can follow if merchandise or service is unsatisfactory
- 1.6.4 Check sales receipts

1.7 **Understand procedures for the care, maintenance, and use of personal possessions**

1.7.1 Interpret product guarantees and warranties
1.7.2 Interpret clothing care labels
1.7.3 Interpret operating instructions, directions, or labels for consumer products (see also 3.4.1)
1.7.4 Interpret maintenance procedures for household appliances and personal possessions
1.7.5 Interpret information to obtain repairs

1.8 **Use banking and financial services in the community**

1.8.1 Demonstrate the use of savings and checking accounts, including using an ATM
1.8.2 Interpret the procedures and forms associated with banking services, including writing checks
1.8.3 Interpret interest or interest-earning savings plans
1.8.4 Interpret information about the types of loans available through lending institutions
1.8.5 Interpret information on financial agencies and financial planning

1.9 **Understand methods and procedures for the purchase and maintenance of an automobile and interpret driving regulations**

1.9.1 Interpret highway and traffic signs (see also 2.2.2)
1.9.2 Identify driving regulations and procedures to obtain a driver's license (see also 2.5.7)
1.9.3 Compute mileage and gasoline consumption
1.9.4 Interpret maps related to driving (see also 1.1.3, 2.2.1, 2.2.5)
1.9.5 Interpret information related to the selection and purchase of a car
1.9.6 Interpret information related to automobile maintenance
1.9.7 Recognize what to do in case of automobile emergencies
1.9.8 Interpret information about automobile insurance

2. **Community Resources**

2.1 **Use the telephone and telephone book**

2.1.1 Use the telephone directory and related publications to locate information
2.1.2 Identify emergency numbers and place emergency calls (see also 2.5.1)
2.1.3 Interpret information about time zones (see also 2.3.1)
2.1.4 Interpret telephone billings
2.1.5 Interpret telegram rates and procedures
2.1.6 Interpret information about using a pay telephone
2.1.7 Take and interpret telephone messages, leave messages on answering machines, and interpret recorded messages (see also 4.5.4)
2.1.8 Use the telephone to make and receive routine personal and business calls

2.2 **Understand how to locate and use different types of transportation and interpret related travel information**

2.2.1 Ask for, give, follow, or clarify directions (see also 1.1.3, 1.9.4, 2.2.5)
2.2.2 Recognize and use signs related to transportation (see also 1.9.1)
2.2.3 Identify or use different types of transportation in the community, and interpret traffic information
2.2.4 Interpret transportation schedules and fares
2.2.5 Use maps relating to travel needs (see also 1.1.3, 1.9.4, 2.2.1)

2.3 **Understand concepts of time and weather**

2.3.1 Interpret clock time (see also 2.1.3, 6.6.6)
2.3.2 Identify the months of the year and the days of the week
2.3.3 Interpret information about weather conditions

2.4 **Use postal services**

2.4.1 Address letters and envelopes
2.4.2 Interpret postal rates and types of mailing services
2.4.3 Interpret postal service forms and instructions on returned mail
2.4.4 Purchase stamps and other postal items and services
2.4.5 Interpret procedures for tracing a lost letter or parcel
2.4.6 Interpret a postal money order form

2.5 **Use community agencies and services**

2.5.1 Locate and utilize services of agencies that provide emergency help
2.5.2 Identify how and when to obtain social and governmental services (e.g., low-income housing, Social Security, Medicare), and how to interact with service providers
2.5.3 Locate medical and health facilities in the community (see also 3.1.3)
2.5.4 Read, interpret, and follow directions found on public signs and building directories (see also 1.3.7)
2.5.5 Locate and use educational services in the community, including interpreting and writing school-related communications
2.5.6 Use library services
2.5.7 Interpret permit and license requirements (see also 1.9.2)
2.5.8 (unassigned)
2.5.9 Identify child care services in the community (see also 3.5.7)

2.6 **Use leisure time resources and facilities**

2.6.1 Interpret information about recreational and entertainment facilities and activities
2.6.2 Locate information in TV, movie, and other recreational listings

2.6.3 Interpret information in order to plan for outings and vacations

2.6.4 Interpret and order from restaurant and fast food menus, and compute related costs

2.7 Understand aspects of society and culture

2.7.1 Interpret information about holidays

2.7.2 Interpret information about ethnic groups, cultural groups, and language groups

2.7.3 Interpret information about social issues (see also 2.7.2)

2.7.4 Interpret information about religion

2.7.5 Interpret literary materials such as poetry and literature

2.7.6 Interpret materials related to the arts, such as fine art, music, drama, and film

3. Health

3.1 Understand how to access and utilize the health care system

3.1.1 Describe symptoms of illness, including identifying parts of the body; interpret doctor's directions

3.1.2 Identify information necessary to make or keep medical and dental appointments

3.1.3 Identify and utilize appropriate health care services and facilities, including interacting with providers (see also 2.5.3)

3.2 Understand medical and dental forms and related information

3.2.1 Fill out medical health history forms

3.2.2 Interpret immunization requirements

3.2.3 Interpret information associated with medical, dental, or life insurance

3.2.4 Ask for clarification about medical bills

3.3 Understand how to select and use medications

3.3.1 Identify and use necessary medications (see also 3.3.2, 3.3.3)

3.3.2 Interpret medicine labels (see also 3.3.1, 3.4.1)

3.3.3 Identify the difference between prescription, over-the-counter, and generic medications (see also 3.3.1)

3.4 Understand basic health and safety procedures

3.4.1 Interpret product label directions and safety warnings (see also 1.7.3, 3.3.2)

3.4.2 Identify safety measures that can prevent accidents and injuries

3.4.3 Interpret procedures for simple first-aid

3.4.4 Interpret information about AIDS and other sexually transmitted diseases (see also 3.1.1)

3.4.5 Recognize problems related to drugs, tobacco, and alcohol and identify where treatment may be obtained

3.5 Understand basic principles of health maintenance

3.5.1 Interpret nutritional and related information listed on food labels (see also 1.6.1)

3.5.2 Select a balanced diet

3.5.3 Interpret food storage information

3.5.4 Identify practices that promote dental health

3.5.5 Identify practices that promote cleanliness and hygiene

3.5.6 Interpret information and identify agencies that assist with family planning (see also 2.5.3, 3.1.3)

3.5.7 Identify child-rearing practices and community resources that assist in developing parenting skills (see also 2.5.9)

3.5.8 Identify practices that promote mental well being

3.5.9 Identify practices that promote physical well being

4. Employment

4.1 Understand basic principles of getting a job

4.1.1 Interpret governmental forms related to seeking work, such as applications for Social Security (see also 2.5.2)

4.1.2 Follow procedures for applying for a job, including interpreting and completing job applications, résumés, and letters of application

4.1.3 Identify and use sources of information about job opportunities such as job descriptions, job ads, and announcements, and about the workforce and job market

4.1.4 Identify and use information about training opportunities (see also 2.5.5)

4.1.5 Identify procedures involved in interviewing for a job, such as arranging for an interview, acting and dressing appropriately, and selecting appropriate questions and responses

4.1.6 Interpret general work-related vocabulary (e.g., experience, swing shift)

4.1.7 Identify appropriate behavior and attitudes for getting a job

4.1.8 Identify common occupations and the skills and education required for them

4.1.9 Identify procedures for career planning, including self-assessment

4.2 Understand wages, benefits, and concepts of employee organizations

4.2.1 Interpret wages, wage deductions, benefits, and timekeeping forms

4.2.2 Interpret information about employee organizations

4.2.3 Interpret employment contract and union agreements

4.2.4 Interpret employee handbooks, personnel policies, and job manuals

4.3 Understand work-related safety standards and procedures

4.3.1 Interpret safety signs found in the workplace (see also 3.4.1)

4.3.2 Interpret work safety manuals and related information

4.3.3 Identify safe work procedures and common safety equipment, including wearing safe work attire

4.3.4 Report unsafe working conditions work-related accidents, injuries, damages

4.4 Understand concepts and materials related to job performance and training

4.4.1 Identify appropriate behavior, attire, attitudes, and social interaction, factors that affect job retention advancement

4.4.2 Identify appropriate skills and education for keeping a job and getting a

4.4.3 Interpret job-related signs, charts, diagrams, forms, and procedures, record information on forms, charts, checklists, etc. (see also 4.2.1, 4.3.4)

4.4.4 Interpret job responsibilities and performance reviews (see also 4.4.2)

4.4.5 Identify job training needs and goals

4.4.6 Interpret work specifications and standards

4.4.7 Demonstrate the ability to apply skills learned in one job situation another

4.4.8 Interpret job-related technical information, such as from service manuals and classes

4.5 Effectively utilize common workplace technology and systems

4.5.1 Identify common tools, equipment, machines, and materials required one's job

4.5.2 Demonstrate simple keyboarding

4.5.3 Demonstrate ability to use a filing or other ordered system (e.g., coded numbered)

4.5.4 Demonstrate use of common business machines (see also 2.1.7, 2.1.8)

4.5.5 Demonstrate basic computer skills use of common software programs, including reading or interpreting computer generated printouts

4.5.6 Demonstrate ability to select, set use tools and machines in order accomplish a task, while operating a technological system

4.5.7 Demonstrate ability to identify resolve problems with machines follow proper maintenance procedures

4.6 Communicate effectively in the workplace

4.6.1 Follow, clarify, give, or provide feedback to instructions; give and respond appropriately to criticism

4.6.2 Interpret and write work-related correspondence, including notes, memos, letters, and e-mail (see also 4.4.3)

4.6.3 Interpret written workplace announcements and notices (see also 4.4.1, 4.4.3)

4.6.4 Report progress on activities, status of assigned tasks, and problems and other situations affecting job completion (see also 4.3.4)

4.6.5 Select and analyze work-related information for a given purpose and communicate it to others orally or in writing

4.7 Effectively manage workplace resources

4.7.1 Interpret or prepare a work-related budget, including projecting costs, keeping detailed records, and tracking status of expenditures and revenue

4.7.2 Identify or demonstrate effective management of material resources, including acquisition, storage, and distribution

4.7.3 Identify or demonstrate effective management of human resources, including assessing skills, making appropriate work assignments, and monitoring performance

4.7.4 Identify, secure, evaluate, process, and/or store information needed to perform tasks or keep records

4.8 Demonstrate effectiveness in working with other people

4.8.1 Demonstrate ability to work cooperatively with others as a member of a team, contributing to team efforts, maximizing the strengths of team members, promoting effective group interaction, and taking personal responsibility for accomplishing goals

4.8.2 Identify ways to learn from others and to help others learn job-related concepts and skills

4.8.3 Demonstrate effective communication skills in working with customers and clients

4.8.4 Demonstrate initiative and resourcefulness in meeting the needs and solving the problems of customers

4.8.5 Demonstrate leadership skills, including effectively communicating ideas or positions, motivating and respecting others, and responsibly challenging existing policies

4.8.6 Demonstrate negotiation skills in resolving differences, including presenting facts and arguments, recognizing differing points of view, offering options, and making compromises

4.8.7 Identify and use effective approaches to working within a multicultural workforce, including respecting cultural diversity, avoiding stereotypes, and recognizing concerns of members of other ethnic and gender groups

4.9 Understand how social, organizational, and technological systems work, and operate effectively within them

4.9.1 Identify the formal organizational structure of one's work environment

4.9.2 Demonstrate how a system's structures relate to its goals

4.9.3 Identify sources of information and assistance, and access resources within a system

4.9.4 Assess the operation of a system or organization and make recommendations for improvement, including development of new systems

5. Government and Law

5.1 Understand voting and the political process

5.1.1 Identify voter qualifications
5.1.2 Interpret a voter registration form
5.1.3 Interpret a ballot
5.1.4 Interpret information about electoral politics and candidates
5.1.5 Interpret information about special interest groups
5.1.6 Communicate one's opinions on a current issue

5.2 Understand historical and geographical information

5.2.1 Interpret information about U.S. history
5.2.2 Identify or interpret U.S. historical documents
5.2.3 Interpret information about world history
5.2.4 Interpret information about U.S. states, cities, geographical features, and points of interest
5.2.5 Interpret information about world geography

5.3 Understand an individual's legal rights and responsibilities and procedures for obtaining legal advice

5.3.1 Interpret common laws and ordinances, and legal forms and documents
5.3.2 Identify individual legal rights and procedures for obtaining legal advice (see also 5.3.1)
5.3.3 Interpret basic court procedures
5.3.4 Interpret laws affecting door-to-door sales (see also 1.6.2)
5.3.5 Interpret information about traffic tickets
5.3.6 Interpret information or identify requirements for establishing residency and/or obtaining citizenship
5.3.7 Identify common infractions and crimes, and legal consequences
5.3.8 Identify procedures for reporting a crime

5.4 Understand information about taxes

5.4.1 Interpret income tax forms
5.4.2 Compute or define sales tax
5.4.3 Interpret tax tables (see also 5.4.1, 5.4.2)
5.4.4 Interpret tax information from articles and publications

5.5 Understand governmental activities

5.5.1 Interpret information about international affairs
5.5.2 Interpret information about legislative activities
5.5.3 Interpret information about judicial activities
5.5.4 Interpret information about executive activities
5.5.5 Interpret information about military activities
5.5.6 Interpret information about law enforcement activities
5.5.7 Interpret information about local policymaking groups
5.5.8 Identify local, state and federal government leaders

5.6 Understand civic responsibilities and activities

5.6.1 Interpret information about neighborhood or community problems and their solutions
5.6.2 Interpret information about civic organizations and public service groups
5.6.3 Interpret civic responsibilities, such as voting, jury duty, taxes

5.7 Understand environmental and science-related issues

5.7.1 Interpret information about environmental issues
5.7.2 Interpret information related to physics, including energy
5.7.3 Interpret information about earth-related sciences
5.7.4 Interpret information about new technologies and scientific issues

5.8 Understand concepts of economics

5.8.1 Interpret economic information and statistics
5.8.2 Interpret information on economic issues and trends
5.8.3 Interpret information on world economic systems

6. Computation

6.0 Demonstrate pre-computation skills

6.0.1 Identify and classify numeric symbols
6.0.2 Count and associate numbers with quantities, including recognizing correct number sequencing
6.0.3 Identify information needed to solve a given problem
6.0.4 Determine appropriate operation to apply to a given problem
6.0.5 Demonstrate use of a calculator

6.1 Compute using whole numbers

6.1.1 Add whole numbers
6.1.2 Subtract whole numbers
6.1.3 Multiply whole numbers
6.1.4 Divide whole numbers
6.1.5 Perform multiple operations using whole numbers

6.2 Compute using decimal fractions

6.2.1 Add decimal fractions
6.2.2 Subtract decimal fractions
6.2.3 Multiply decimal fractions
6.2.4 Divide decimal fractions

6.2.5 Perform multiple operations using decimal fractions

6.2.6 Convert decimal fractions to common fractions or percents

6.3 Compute using fractions
6.3.1 Add common or mixed fractions
6.3.2 Subtract common or mixed fractions
6.3.3 Multiply common or mixed fractions
6.3.4 Divide common or mixed fractions
6.3.5 Perform multiple operations using common or mixed fractions
6.3.6 Convert common or mixed fractions to decimal fractions or percents
6.3.7 Identify or calculate equivalent fractions

6.4 Compute with percents, rate, ratio, and proportion
6.4.1 Apply a percent to determine amount of discount (see also 1.2.3)
6.4.2 Apply a percent in a context not involving money
6.4.3 Calculate percents
6.4.4 Convert percents to common, mixed, or decimal fractions
6.4.5 Use rate to compute increase or decrease
6.4.6 Compute using ratio or proportion (see also 6.4.5)

6.5 Use expressions, equations, and formulas
6.5.1 Recognize and evaluate simple consumer formulas
6.5.2 Recognize and apply simple geometric formulas
6.5.3 Recognize and apply simple algebraic formulas
6.5.4 Recognize and evaluate logical statements

6.6 Demonstrate measurement skills (see also 1.1)
6.6.1 Convert units of U.S. standard measurement and metric system (see also 1.1.2, 1.1.4)
6.6.2 Recognize, use, and measure linear dimensions, geometric shapes, or angles (see also 1.1.2, 1.1.4)
6.6.3 Measure area and volume of geometric shapes (see also 1.1.2, 1.1.4)
6.6.4 Use or interpret measurement instruments, such as rulers, scales, gauges, and dials (see also 1.1.2, 1.1.4, 1.1.5, 4.3.3, 4.4.3)
6.6.5 Interpret diagrams, illustrations, and scale drawings (see also 1.1.4, 4.4.3)
6.6.6 Calculate with units of time
6.6.7 Solve measurement problems in stipulated situations
6.6.8 Interpret mechanical concepts or spatial relationships
6.6.9 Use or interpret switches and controls

6.7 Interpret data from graphs and compute averages
6.7.1 Interpret data given in a line graph (see also 1.1.3)
6.7.2 Interpret data given in a bar graph (see also 1.1.3)
6.7.3 Interpret data given in a picture graph

6.7.4 Interpret data given in a circle graph (see also 1.1.3)
6.7.5 Compute averages, medians, or modes (see also 1.1.8)

6.8 Use statistics and probability
6.8.1 Interpret statistical information used in news reports and articles
6.8.2 Interpret statements of probability

6.9 Use estimation and mental arithmetic
6.9.1 Use computation short cuts
6.9.2 Estimate answers

7. Learning to Learn

7.1 Identify or practice effective organizational and time management skills in accomplishing goals
7.1.1 Identify and prioritize personal, educational, and workplace goals (see also 4.4.5)
7.1.2 Demonstrate an organized approach to achieving goals, including identifying and prioritizing tasks and setting and following an effective schedule
7.1.3 Demonstrate personal responsibility and motivation in accomplishing goals
7.1.4 Establish, maintain, and utilize a physical system of organization, such as notebooks, files, calendars, folders, and checklists (see also 4.5.3)

7.2 Demonstrate ability to use thinking skills
7.2.1 Identify and paraphrase pertinent information
7.2.2 Analyze a situation, statement, or process, identifying component elements and causal and part/whole relationships
7.2.3 Make comparisons, differentiating among, sorting, and classifying items, information, or ideas
7.2.4 Identify or make inferences through inductive and deductive reasoning to hypothesize, predict, conclude, and synthesize; distinguish fact from opinion, and determine what is mandatory and what is discretionary
7.2.5 Evaluate a situation, statement, or process, assembling information and providing evidence, making judgements, examining assumptions, and identifying contradictions
7.2.6 Generate ideas using divergent (brainstorming) and convergent (focus) approaches, and also through creative imagination
7.2.7 Identify factors involved in making decisions, including considering goals, constraints, and consequences, and weighing alternatives

7.3 Demonstrate ability to use problem-solving skills

7.3.1 Identify a problem and its possible causes

7.3.2 Devise and implement a solution to an identified problem

7.3.3 Evaluate the outcome of an implemented solution and suggest modifications to the solution as needed

7.3.4 Utilize problem-solving strategies, such as breaking down the problem into component parts and generating alternative or creative solutions

7.4 Demonstrate study skills

7.4.1 Identify or utilize effective study strategies

7.4.2 Take notes or write a summary or an outline

7.4.3 Identify, utilize, or create devices or processes for remembering information

7.4.4 Identify or utilize appropriate informational resources, including the Internet (see also 4.9.3)

7.4.5 Use reference materials, such as dictionaries and encyclopedias

7.4.6 Use indexes and tables of contents

7.4.7 Identify or utilize test-taking skills

7.4.8 Interpret visual representations, such as symbols, blueprints, flowcharts, and schematics (see also 6.6.5)

7.4.9 Identify personal learning style

7.5 Understand aspects of and approaches to effective personal management

7.5.1 Identify personal values, qualities, interests, abilities, and aptitudes

7.5.2 Identify or use strategies to develop a positive attitude and self-image, and self-esteem

7.5.3 Identify or use strategies to cope with negative feedback

7.5.4 Identify sources of stress, and resources for stress reduction

7.5.5 Identify personal, family, and work responsibilities, and ways to accommodate them and deal with related problems

7.5.6 Identify or use strategies for communicating more successfully

7.5.7 Identify constructive ways of dealing with change, including showing flexibility and adaptability, and updating skills

8. Independent Living

8.1 Perform self-care skills

8.1.1 Recognize and/or demonstrate hygiene and grooming skills (see also 3.5.5)

8.1.2 Recognize and/or demonstrate dressing skills

8.1.3 Recognize and/or demonstrate dining skills and manners

8.1.4 Recognize and/or demonstrate selection and care of clothing and personal property

8.2 Perform home-care skills

8.2.1 Recognize and/or demonstrate meal and snack preparation tasks and activities (see also 1.1.1, 3.5.2)

8.2.2 Recognize and/or demonstrate dishwashing and meal clean-up activities (see also 3.5.5)

8.2.3 Recognize and/or demonstrate housekeeping and house cleaning tasks

8.2.4 Recognize and/or demonstrate laundry skills and related clothing-care skills (see also 1.7.2, 1.7.3)

8.2.5 Recognize and/or demonstrate yard and garden tasks and activities

8.2.6 Recognize and/or demonstrate general household repair and maintenance (see also 1.4.7, 1.7.4)

8.3 Use support services to assist in maintaining independence and achieving community integration

8.3.1 Identify and interact with persons in the home environment who can provide support in achieving goals (e.g., family, friends, caregivers)

8.3.2 Identify and interact with persons in the community who can provide support in achieving goals (e.g., neighbors, contacts from human service agencies and recreation facilities)

Photo Credits

Frontmatter:
Page iv: © Courtney Sabbagh

Pre-Unit
Page P5: Top: © Michael Newman/ PhotoEdit; Center: © David Young-Wolff/ PhotoEdit; Bottom: © David Young-Wolff/ PhotoEdit
Page P7: Top Left: © STOCK4B-RF/Getty Images; Bottom Left: © Image State-Pictor/jupiterimages; Top Right: © Dennis Kitchen/PhotoEdit; Bottom Right: © George Doyle/Getty Images

Unit 1:
Page 1: Left: © Michael Newman/ PhotoEdit; Center: © John Lund/Sam Diephuis/jupiterimages; Right: © David Young-Wolff/PhotoEdit
Page 2: Left: © David Young-Wolff/ PhotoEdit; Left Center: © John Lund/Sam Diephuis/jupiterimages; Right Center: © Michael Newman/PhotoEdit; Right: © Michael Newman/PhotoEdit
Page 3: Top: © Michael Newman/ PhotoEdit; Bottom: © David Young-Wolff/ PhotoEdit
Page 4: Left: © Michael Newman/ PhotoEdit, © David Hanover/Getty Images, © Michael Newman/PhotoEdit; Center: © Paul Thomas/Getty Images, © Paul Thomas/Getty Images, © David Young-Wolff/PhotoEdit; Right: © Hans Neleman/Getty Images, © Bill Bachmann/PhotoEdit, © Peter Hendrie/Getty Images, © Mary Kate Denny/PhotoEdit, © Michael Newman/ PhotoEdit
Page 5: Top Left: © Paul Thomas/Getty Images, © Michael Newman/PhotoEdit; Top Center: © Paul Thomas/Getty Images, © Paul Thomas/Getty Images; Top Right: © David Hanover/Getty Images, © Michael Newman/PhotoEdit; Bottom Left: © Paul Thomas/Getty Images, © Mary Kate Denny/PhotoEdit; Bottom Center: © Peter Hendrie/Getty Images, © Michael Newman/PhotoEdit; Bottom Right: © Michael Newman/PhotoEdit, © Michael Newman/PhotoEdit
Page 13: Top Left: © Raimund Linke/ jupiterimages; Bottom Left: © Staffan Andersson/Getty Images; Top Center: © Photos.com/RF; Bottom Center: © Zara Art/jupiterimages; Top Right: © Photos. com/RF; Bottom Right: © Photos.com/ RF
Page 16: Left: © David Litschel/Alamy; Right: © John Lund/Sam Diephuis/ jupiterimages
Page 17: Top Left: © David Litschel/ Alamy; Top Right: © John Lund/Sam Diephuis/jupiterimages; Left: © Tony Freeman/PhotoEdit, © Myrleen Ferguson Cate/PhotoEdit, © Myrleen Ferguson Cate/PhotoEdit; Right: © Michael Newman/PhotoEdit, © Michael Newman/ PhotoEdit, © Tony Freeman/PhotoEdit, © Myrleen Ferguson Cate/PhotoEdit

Unit 3:
Page 45: Top Left: © The Advertising Archives; Top Center Left: © Chuha/ Dreamstime.com; Top Center Right: © Laborer/Dreamstime.com; Top Right: © Broker/Dreamstime.com; Bottom Left: ©Arnold Gold/New Haven Register/ The Image Works; Bottom Center Left: © Disorderly/Dreamstime.com; Bottom Center Right: © Andy Crawford/Getty Images; Bottom Right: © Robert Lawson/ photolibrary, © Sarah-Maria Vischer/The Image Works
Page 51: Top Left: © JFI/jupiterimages; Top Right: © Caterina Bernardi/Getty Images; Center Left: © Bananastock/ jupiterimages; Center Right: © Baoba Images/Getty Images; Bottom Left: © Tony Freeman/PhotoEdit
Page 57: Top Left: © Laborer/Dreamstime. com; Center Left: © The Advertising Archives, © Disorderly/Dreamstime.com; Bottom Left: © Robert Lawson/ photolibrary; Top Right: ©Sarah-Maria Vischer/The Image Works; Center Right: © Broker/Dreamstime.com, © Andy Crawford/Getty Images; Bottom Right: © Chuha/Dreamstime.com
Page 63: Left: © Baoba Images/Getty Images; Right: © Michael Newman/PhotoEdit

Unit 4:
Page 71: Top Left: © Fotogeek/ Dreamstime.com; Top Center Left: © Mandj98/Dreamstime.com; Top Center: © Fibobjects/Dreamstime.com; Top Center Right: © Fabinus08/Dreamstime.com; Top Right: © Gibsonff/Dreamstime.com; Bottom Left: © Kitsen/Dreamstime.com; Bottom Center Left: © Paha_l/ Dreamstime.com; Bottom Center: © Todd Harrison/iStockphoto; Bottom Center Right: © Tjurunga/Dreamstime.com; Bottom Right: © Chepe/ Dreamstime.com

Unit 6:
Page 103: © Brand X Pictures/photolibrary
Page 105: Left: © Bananastock/ jupiterimages; Center Left: © MIXA/Getty Images; Center: © Bananastock/ photolibrary; Center Right: © Stockbyte/ Getty Images; Right: © Custom Medical Stock Photo/Alamy
Page 113: Left: © Julian Calder/Getty Images; Center: © BHS Images/ jupiterimages; Right: © Ray Grover/Alamy
Page 114: © Peter Dazeley/Getty Images
Page 118: Top Left: © Peter Dazeley/Getty Images; Bottom Left: © Bananastock/ jupiterimages; Top Right: © Bananastock/ jupiterimages; Bottom Right: © axel leschinski/Alamy

Unit 7:
Page 125: Left: © Sumnersgraphicsinc/ Dreamstime.com; Center Left: © Icyimage/ Dreamstime.com; Center Right: © Alberto Tirado/iStockphoto; Right: © Albo/ Dreamstime.com
Page 128: © Stockbyte/Getty Images
Page 134: Left: © Kshevtsov/Dreamstime. com; Center: © Michaeldb/Dreamstime. com; Right: © QiLux/iStockphoto
Page 136: © LWA/Getty Images
Page 137: Left: © Kshevtsov/Dreamstime. com; Center: © Michaeldb/Dreamstime. com; Right: © QiLux/iStockphoto

Unit 8:
Page 152: © Photos.com/RF

Stand Out 2 Skills Index

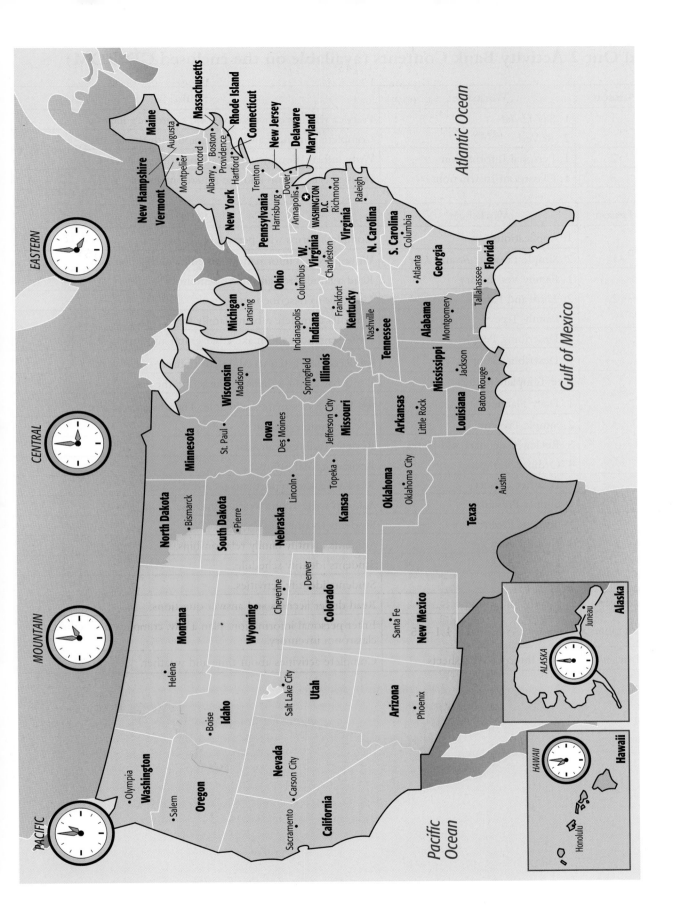

Stand Out 2 Activity Bank Contents (available on the enclosed CD-ROM)

Pre-Unit	Lesson	Worksheet	Skill
Welcome to Our Class	1	1. Say *Hello!*	Practice reading conversations and expressing feelings.
		2. *Be* Verb	Complete sentences and a paragraph with the *be* verb.
	2	1. Personal Information	Write information in a registration form.
	3	1. Classroom Instructions	Practice clarification and use classroom verbs.

Unit 1	Lesson	Worksheet	Skill
Everyday Life	1	1. Applications	Complete forms with personal information.
		2. Simple Present: *Be* and *Live*	Write personal information sentences and paragraphs
	2	1. Family Vocabulary	Read a family tree and make sentences.
		2. *Have* and Family	Use *have* to describe families.
		3. Family Tree	Students complete a blank family tree.
	3	1. Describing People	Write sentences and make a bar graph about people.
		2. Describing People	Read and listen to complete a chart.
	4	(See Template folder)	Use a bar graph template to describe the class.
		1. Daily Planner	Write a classmate's schedule. Then listen and write.
		2. Simple Present	Use the simple present.
		3. Review Calendars and Dates	Review reading a calendar.
		4. Ordinal Numbers	Review ordinal numbers.
	5	1. Weather Report	Read a weather report and record the weather.
		2. Simple Present	Ask and write about weather in other countries.
	Project	1. Student Profile	Students record data.
		2. Family Chart	Students identify family relationships.
		3. Daily Planner	Students identify schedule.
		4. Calendar	Students identify activities.
	Extension	1. Height and Weight	Read driver licenses and answer questions.
	Computer	Computer Worksheets 1.1–1.5	Enter personal information, plan a day, complete a schedule, take classroom inventory.
	Internet	Unit 1 Internet Worksheets	Complete activities about time and weather.

Unit 2	Lesson	Worksheet	Skill
Time to Go Shopping	1	1. Clothing	Identify clothing items.
		2. Simple Present	Complete and write sentences using the simple present.
	2	1. Prices	Use critical thinking to figure out prices.
		2. Ask about Prices	Practice asking for prices in a conversation.
	3	1. Describing Clothing	Study an inventory and do an information gap activity.
		2. Sizes, Colors, and Patterns	🎧 Read and listen to complete charts.
		3. Present Simple / Present Continuous	Complete sentences and a paragraph.
	4	1. Reading Ads	Read an ad and complete a chart and a graph.
	5	1. *This*, *That*, *These*, and *Those*	Practice writing in sentences and a paragraph.
	Project	1. Clothing Store Data	Template for clothing store details.
		2. Advertisements	Template to create an advertisement.
	Extension	1. Paragraph Writing	Learn to format a paragraph.
		2. Checks and Ledgers	Read and write checks.
	Computer	Computer Worksheets 2.1–2.2	Copy formatting and sort data.
	Internet	Unit 2 Internet Worksheets	Complete charts and conversations about clothing.

Unit 3	Lesson	Worksheet	Skill
Food and Nutrition	1	1. Menus	Read an international menu and take orders.
		2. Taking Orders	🎧 Read a conversation then listen and take orders.
	2	(See Template folder)	Use a 3-column chart to practice *how much, how many*.
		1. Shopping Lists	Read shopping lists and do an information gap activity.
		2. Containers	Identify containers on a chart with prices as clues.
	3	(See Template folder)	Use a bar graph to identify where students shop.
		1. Sections in a Supermarket	Brainstorm foods in different supermarket sections.
		2. Supermarket Vocabulary	Complete a chart and conversation about a supermarket.
	4	(See Template folder)	Use a 4-column chart to classify food and drinks.
		(See Template folder)	Use a 3-circle Venn Diagram to identify eating habits.
		(See Template folder)	Use a 2-circle Venn Diagram to compare eating habits.
		1. Food Groups	Identify food groups from a chart.
		2. Nutrition	Rank meals.
		3. Meals	Find out what others in the class eat.
		4. A Balanced Diet	Plan meals in a group.
	5	1. Recipes	Write two recipes in a group.
		2. Candy and Meatloaf	🎧 Read and listen to recipes.
	Project	1. Family Menu	Record food for a week.
		2. Prices	Find food prices.
		3. Shopping List	Make a shopping list.
		4. Recipes	Create two recipes.
	Extension	1. Negative Simple Present	Read a food inventory. Write sentences and a paragraph.
	Computer	Computer Worksheets 3.1–3.2	Copy formatting and write lists and sort.
	Internet	Unit 3 Internet Worksheets	Do activities on food groups and grocery shopping.

Unit 4	Lesson	Worksheet	Skill
Housing	1	1. Housing	🎧 Read and listen about housing. Complete activities.
	2	1. Reading Classified Ads	Identify parts and abbreviations in classified ads.
		2. Classified Ads	🎧 Read classified ads. Listen for information.
	3	1. Rental Application	Complete a rental application.
		2. Asking Questions	Write questions and then ask a partner.
	4	1. Furniture and Appliances	In groups, decide what is cheapest and most expensive.
		2. Floor Plans	Describe floor plans in an information gap.
		3. Prepositions of Location	Use prepositions of location to describe floor plans.
	5	1. Reading Budgets	Read a budget and add up income and expenses.
		2. Family Budget	Create a family budget in a group.
	Project	1. Daily News Classifieds	Template for teams to write classifieds.
		2. Furniture List	Template for teams to organize furniture.
		3. Rental Application	Rental application form.
		4. Family Budget	Family budget form.
	Extension	1. Write a Paragraph	Write a paragraph about a home from a model.
		2. Rooms in a House	Identify rooms in a house and write compound sentences.
	Computer	Computer Worksheet 4.1	Create a checklist about housing.
	Internet	Unit 4 Internet Worksheets	Complete charts about housing and furniture.

Unit 5	Lesson	Worksheet	Skill
Our Community	1	(See Template folder)	Use a cluster to brainstorm community places.
		1. Parts of a Community	Use a cluster to identify places in the community.
		2. Read a Bus Schedule	Read a schedule and do activities.
		3. Places in the Community	Identify places in your community and discuss.
	2	1. Phone Directory	🎧 Read a phone directory and answer questions.
	3	1. Prepositions of Location	Read instructions and label a map.
		2. Give and Follow Directions	🎧 Read and listen to street directions.
	4	1. Simple Present and Continuous	Write sentences about what people do and are doing.
	5	(See Template folder)	Use a 2-column template to list names and addresses.
		1. Letter Writing	Study a sample letter and its parts.
		2. Addressing Envelopes	Address envelopes to send to four classmates.
		3. Writing Letters	Write a letter and include important information.
	Project	1. Our City	Answer questions to identify new city.
		2. Postcard	Write a postcard from your city.
		3. City Brochure	Make a brochure of a city.
	Extension	1. Prepositions of Location	🎧 Identify locations in a mall using prepositions.
		2. Simple Present	Practice the simple present and adverbs of frequency.
		3. Present Continuous	Practice the present continuous.
	Computer	Computer Worksheets 5.1–5.2	Format and write a paragraph. Create directions.
	Internet	Unit 5 Internet Worksheets	Determine airfare, travel distance and travel time.

Unit 6	Lesson	Worksheet	Skill
Health and Fitness	1	1. Health Survey	Answer questions about personal health.
		2. Health Goals	Establish health goals.
	2	1. What hurts?	🎧 Read and listen for information.
	3	(See Template folder)	Use a bar graph to chart how often people are ill.
		1. Making Appointments	🎧 Read and listen to complete a ledger.
		2. Confirming Appointments	Practice confirming appointments using conversations.
		3. Past Tense	Complete sentences with past tense verbs.
	4	1. Over-the-Counter Medications	List medications with ailments.
		2. Home Remedies	Write a home remedy for common ailments.
		3. Reading Medicine Labels	Match label information with medication.
	5	(See Template folder)	Use a cluster to brainstorm types of emergencies.
		1. Modal *Should*	Write advice in sentences.
		2. Emergencies	Identify the type of an emergency.
	Project	1. Health Brochure	Make a health brochure.
	Extension	1. Body Parts	Match body parts to actions.
	Computer	Computer Worksheets 6.1–6.2	Format and write a paragraph. Create a bar graph.
	Internet	Unit 6 Internet Worksheets	Complete activities about medicine in a pharmacy.

Unit 7	Lesson	Worksheet	Skill
Work, Work, Work	1	1. Work Evaluations	🎧 Read and listen to a work evaluation.
		2. Future—*Will*	Write sentences in the future.
	2	(See Template folder)	Use a cluster diagram to brainstorm job types.
		1. Job Titles	Classify jobs by education and complete descriptions.
		2. Using *Can*	Answer questions about job histories.
	3	1. Classified Ads	Read and complete a chart.
		2. Application Questions	Ask a partner questions.
		3. Job Applications	Complete a job application.
		4. Job Application Practice	Read applications and answer questions.
	4	1. Simple Past	Complete sentences and a conversation.
		2. Employment History	Read and write about employment histories.
	5	1. Following Instructions	Write instructions and dictate to a partner.
		2. Instruction Strips	Put instructions in order.
	Project	1. Daily News Classified	Make a class classified ad section of a newspaper.
		2. Job Application	Complete a full and blank application form.
	Extension	1. Negative Simple Past	Read and write using the negative simple past.
	Computer	Computer Worksheets 7.1–7.2	Format a paragraph and make a pie graph.
	Internet	Unit 7 Internet Worksheets	Complete activities about a job search.

Unit 8	Lesson	Worksheet	Skill
Goals and Lifelong Learning	1	1. Setting Goals	List general goals.
		2. Infinitives	Practice describing needs and wants.
		3. *Going to*	Complete sentences and paragraphs using *going to*.
	2	(See Template folder)	Use a 3-column template to categorize goals.
		1. U.S. Schools	Listen and identify types of schools.
		2. Sentence Strips – Schools	Match descriptions with schools.
	3	(See Template folder)	Use a Venn diagram to compare Lien and Marie.
		1. Choices for the Future	Read timelines and make a personal timeline.
	4	1. Solutions	Identify solutions for common problems.
		2. Library	Read about a library. Use conversation cards.
	5	1. Writing a Paragraph	Interview a partner and write paragraphs about goals.
	Project	1. My Goals Time line	Write goals on a time line template.
		2. Paragraph Template	Write three paragraphs.
		3. Editing Checklist	Check a partner's work using a checklist.
		4. My Personal Portfolio	Complete a coversheet for a goal packet.
	Extension	1. Advice	Write a paragraph to give advice.
	Computer	Computer Worksheets 8.1–8.2	Make a table and formulate a total in a chart.
	Internet	Unit 8 Internet Worksheets	Complete a chart and write directions to a college.